Lecture Notes in Computer Science

Commenced Publication in 1973
Founding and Former Series Editors:
Gerhard Goos, Juris Hartmanis, and Jan van Leeuwen

Marco Bernardo   Flavio Corradini (Eds.)

Formal Methods for the Design of Real-Time Systems

International School on Formal Methods for the Design of
Computer, Communication and Software Systems, SFM-RT 2004
Bertinoro, Italy, September 13-18, 2004
Revised Lectures

 Springer

Volume Editors

Marco Bernardo
Università di Urbino "Carlo Bo", Istituto di Scienze e Tecnologie dell'Informazione
Piazza della Repubblica 13, 61029 Urbino, Italy
E-mail: bernardo@sti.uniurb.it

Flavio Corradini
Universitá di L'Aquila, Dipartimento di Informatica
E-mail: flavio@di.univaq.it

Library of Congress Control Number: 2004111362

CR Subject Classification (1998): D.2, D.3, F.3, C.3, C.2.4

ISSN 0302-9743
ISBN 3-540-23068-8 Springer Berlin Heidelberg New York

Springer is a part of Springer Science+Business Media

springeronline.com

© Springer-Verlag Berlin Heidelberg 2004
Printed in Germany

Typesetting: Camera-ready by author, data conversion by Olgun Computergrafik
Printed on acid-free paper   SPIN: 11315995   06/3142   5 4 3 2 1 0

Preface

A large class of computing systems can be specified and verified by abstracting away from the temporal aspects of their behavior. In *real-time systems*, instead, time issues become essential. Their correctness depends not only on which actions they can perform, but also on the action execution time. Due to their importance and design challenges, real-time systems have attracted the attention of a considerable number of computer scientists and engineers from various research areas.

This volume collects a set of papers accompanying the lectures of the fourth edition of the *International School on Formal Methods for the Design of Computer, Communication and Software Systems (SFM)*. The school addressed the use of formal methods in computer science as a prominent approach to the rigorous design of computer, communication and software systems. The main aim of the SFM series is to offer a good spectrum of current research in foundations as well as applications of formal methods, which can be of help for graduate students and young researchers who intend to approach the field.

SFM-04:RT was devoted to real-time systems. It covered formal models and languages for the specification, modeling, analysis, and verification of these time-critical systems, the expressiveness of such models and languages, as well as supporting tools and related applications in different domains.

The opening paper by Rajeev Alur and Parthasarathy Madhusudan provides a survey of the theoretical results concerning decision problems of reachability, language inclusion, and language equivalence for timed automata. The survey is concluded with a discussion of some open problems. Elmar Bihler and Walter Vogler's paper presents timed extensions of Petri nets with continuous and discrete time and a natural testing-based faster-than relation for comparing asynchronous systems. Several applications of the theory are also presented. Jos C.M. Baeten and Michel A. Reniers present the theory and application of classical process algebras extended with different notions of time and time passing and compare their expressiveness via embeddings and conservative extensions. The PAR communication protocol is considered as a case study. The expressiveness of existing timed process algebras that deal with temporal aspects by following very different interpretations is also the main theme of Diletta R. Cacciagrano and Flavio Corradini's paper. In addition, they compare the expressiveness of urgent, lazy and maximal progress tests. Mario Bravetti presents a theory of probabilistic timed systems where durations are expressed by generally distributed random variables. The theory supports the specification of both real-time and stochastic time during the design and analysis of concurrent systems. Bran Selic, instead, provides an overview of the foundations of the run-time semantics underlying the Unified Modeling Language (UML) as defined in revision 2.0 of the official OMG standard.

After these contributions on formal timed models, timed languages and their expressiveness, the volume includes the description of three significant tools supporting the specification, modeling, analysis and verification of real-time systems. Gerd Behrmann, Alexandre David and Kim G. Larsen's tutorial paper on the tool Uppaal provides an introduction to the implementation of timed automata in the tool, the user interface, and the usage of the tool. Reference examples and modeling patterns are also presented. Marius Bozga, Susanne Graf, Ileana Ober, Iulian Ober, and Joseph Sifak present an overview on the IF toolset, which is an environment for the modeling and validation of heterogeneous real-time systems. The toolset is built upon a rich formalism, the IF notation, allowing structured automata-based system representations. A case study concerning the Ariane-5 Flight Program is presented. Finally, Joost-Pieter Katoen, Henrik Bohnenkamp, Ric Klaren, and Holger Hermanns survey the language Modest, a modeling and description language for stochastic and timed systems, and its accompanying tool environment MOTOR. The modeling and analysis with this tool of a device-absence-detecting protocol in plug-and-play networks is reported in the paper.

We believe that this book offers a quite comprehensive view of what has been done and what is going on worldwide at present in the field of real-time models and languages for the specification, analysis, and verification of time-critical systems. We wish to thank all the lecturers and all the participants for a lively and fruitful school. We also wish to thank the whole staff of the University Residential Center of Bertinoro (Italy) for the organizational and administrative support, as well as the sponsors of the school – AICA and ONRG – for making it possible through the provision of grants to some of the participants.

September 2004   Marco Bernardo and Flavio Corradini

Table of Contents

Part I: Models and Languages

Part II: Tools and Applications

Author Index

Decision Problems for Timed Automata: A Survey[*]

Rajeev Alur and P. Madhusudan

University of Pennsylvania

Abstract. Finite automata and regular languages have been useful in a wide variety of problems in computing, communication and control, including formal modeling and verification. Traditional automata do not admit an explicit modeling of time, and consequently, *timed automata* [2] were introduced as a formal notation to model the behavior of real-time systems. Timed automata accept *timed languages* consisting of sequences of events tagged with their occurrence times. Over the years, the formalism has been extensively studied leading to many results establishing connections to circuits and logic, and much progress has been made in developing verification algorithms, heuristics, and tools. This paper provides a survey of the theoretical results concerning decision problems of reachability, language inclusion and language equivalence for timed automata and its variants, with some new proofs and comparisons. We conclude with a discussion of some open problems.

1 Timed Automata

A timed automaton is a finite automaton augmented with a finite set of (real-valued) *clocks*. The vertices of the automaton are called *locations*, and edges are called *switches*. While switches are instantaneous, time can elapse in a location. A clock can be reset to zero simultaneously with any switch. At any instant, the reading of a clock equals the time elapsed since the last time it was reset. With each switch we associate a clock constraint, and require that the switch may be taken only if the current values of the clocks satisfy this constraint. Timed automata accept (or, equivalently, generate) timed words, that is, strings of symbols tagged with occurrence times. Let $\mathbb{R}$ denote the set of nonnegative real numbers, and let $\mathbb{Q}$ denote the set of nonnegative rational numbers. A *timed word* over an alphabet Σ is a sequence $(a_0, t_0), (a_1, t_1) \cdots (a_k, t_k)$, where each $a_i \in \Sigma$, each $t_i \in \mathbb{R}$, and the occurrence times increase monotonically: $t_0 \leq t_1 \leq \cdots \leq t_k$. The set of all timed words over Σ is denoted $T\Sigma^*$. A *timed language* over Σ is a subset of $T\Sigma^*$.

The *untimed* word corresponding to a timed word $(a_0, t_0), (a_1, t_1) \cdots (a_k, t_k)$ is the word $a_0 a_1 \ldots a_k$ obtained by deleting the occurrence times. The untimed language *untime(L)* of a timed language L consists of all the untimed words corresponding to the timed words in L. For an alphabet Σ, we use Σ^ϵ to denote

---

[*] This research was partially supported by NSF award ITR/SY 0121431.

M. Bernardo and F. Corradini (Eds.): SFM-RT 2004, LNCS 3185, pp. 1–24, 2004.

$\Sigma \cup \{\epsilon\}$ (where ϵ is not in Σ), and for a subset $\Sigma' \subseteq \Sigma$, and a timed word $w = (a_0, t_0), (a_1, t_1) \cdots (a_k, t_k)$ over Σ, the projection of w over Σ' is obtained from w by deleting all (a_i, t_i) such that $a_i \notin \Sigma'$. The projection operation extends to timed languages as well.

To define timed automata formally, we need to say what type of clock constraints are allowed as guards. For a set X of clocks, the set $\Phi(X)$ of *clock constraints* g is defined by the grammar

$$g := x \le c \mid c \le x \mid x < c \mid c < x \mid g \wedge g$$

where $x \in X$ and $c \in \mathbb{Q}$. A *clock valuation* ν for a set X of clocks assigns a real value to each clock; that is, it is a mapping from X to $\mathbb{R}$. For $\delta \in \mathbb{R}$, $\nu + \delta$ denotes the clock valuation which maps every clock x to the value $\nu(x) + \delta$. For $Y \subseteq X$, $\nu[Y := 0]$ denotes the clock valuation for X which assigns 0 to each $x \in Y$, and agrees with ν over the rest of the clocks.

A *timed automaton* A over an alphabet Σ is a tuple $\langle V, V^0, V^F, X, E \rangle$, where

- V is a finite set of locations,
- $V^0 \subseteq V$ is a set of initial locations,
- $V^F \subseteq V$ is a set of final locations,
- X is a finite set of clocks,
- $E \subseteq V \times \Sigma^\epsilon \times \Phi(X) \times 2^X \times V$ is a set of switches. A switch $\langle s, a, g, \lambda, s' \rangle$ represents an edge from location s to location s' on symbol a. The *guard* g is a clock constraint over X that specifies when the switch is enabled, and the *update* $\lambda \subseteq X$ gives the clocks to be reset to 0 with this switch.

The semantics of a timed automaton A is defined by associating an infinite-state automaton S_A over the alphabet $\Sigma \cup \mathbb{R}$. A state of S_A is a pair (s, ν) such that s is a location of A and ν is a clock valuation for X. A state (s, ν) is an initial state if s is an initial location (i.e. $s \in V^0$) and $\nu(x) = 0$ for all clocks x. A state (s, ν) is a final state if s is a final location (i.e. $s \in V^F$). There are two types of transitions in S_A:

Elapse of time: for a state (s, ν) and a time increment $\delta \in \mathbb{R}$, $(s, \nu) \xrightarrow{\delta} (s, \nu + \delta)$.

Location switch: for a state (s, ν) and a switch $\langle s, a, g, \lambda, s' \rangle$ such that ν satisfies the guard g, $(s, \nu) \xrightarrow{a} (s', \nu[\lambda := 0])$.

For a timed word $w = (a_0, t_0), (a_1, t_1) \cdots (a_k, t_k)$ over Σ^ϵ, a *run* of A over w is a sequence

$$q_0 \xrightarrow{t_0} q_0' \xrightarrow{a_0} q_1 \xrightarrow{t_1 - t_0} q_1' \xrightarrow{a_1} q_2 \xrightarrow{t_2 - t_1} q_2' \xrightarrow{a_2} q_3 \rightarrow \cdots \xrightarrow{a_k} q_{k+1}$$

such that q_0 is an initial state of S_A. The run is *accepting* if q_{k+1} is a final state of S_A. The timed automaton A accepts a timed word w over Σ if there exists a timed word w' over Σ^ϵ such that A has an accepting run over w' and the projection of w' to Σ is w. The set of timed words accepted by A is denoted $L(A)$.

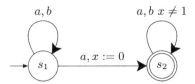

Fig. 1. A non-complementable timed automaton.

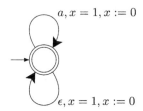

Fig. 2. ϵ-transitions increase expressiveness.

A timed language $L \subseteq T\Sigma^*$ is said to be *timed regular* if there exists a timed automaton A such that $L(A) = L$. The closure properties of timed regular languages are summarized below:

Theorem 1. *The set of timed regular languages is closed under union, intersection, and projection, but not under complementation [2].*

The closure under union and intersection is established by extending the classical product construction to timed automata. Closure under projection is immediate since switches can be labeled with ϵ.

For the non-closure under complementation, we give a new proof here. Let $\Sigma = \{a, b\}$. Let L be the timed language consisting of timed words w containing an a event at some time t such that no event occurs at time $t + 1$. The (non-deterministic) timed automaton shown in Figure 1 (with initial location s_1 and final location s_2) accepts L.

We claim that $\overline{L}$, the complement of L, is not timed regular. Consider the timed language L' consisting of timed words w such that the untimed word of w is in a^*b^*, all the a events happen before time 1, and no two a events happen at the same time. Verify that L' is timed regular. Observe that a word of the form $a^n b^m$ belongs to $untime(\overline{L} \cap L')$ iff $m \geq n$. Since timed regular languages are closed under intersection, the untimed language of a timed regular language is regular (see Section 2), and the language $\{a^n b^m \mid m \geq n\}$ is not regular, it follows that $\overline{L}$ is not timed regular.

Unlike classical automata, ϵ-labeled switches add to the expressive power of timed automata [10]. For example, the automaton of Figure 2 accepts timed words w over $\{a\}$ such that every occurrence time is an integer and no two a-events occur at the same time. This language cannot be accepted by a timed automaton if ϵ-labeled switches are disallowed: if the largest constant in a timed automaton A is c and A does not have ϵ-labeled switches, then A cannot distinguish between the words $(a, c + 1)$ and $(a, c + 1.1)$.

The more recent definitions of timed automata also admit labeling of each location with a clock constraint called its *invariant*, and require that time can elapse in a location only as long as its invariant stays true [23]. While this is a useful modeling concept to enforce upper bounds (without introducing "error" locations), it does not add to the expressive power.

Timed languages can also be defined using *timed state sequences*: a timed state sequence is a mapping from a prefix of the reals to a finite alphabet that can be represented by a sequence $(a_o, I_0)(a_1, I_1) \ldots (a_k, I_k)$, where $I_0, I_1, \ldots I_k$ is a sequence of adjoining intervals (e.g. $[0, 1.1)[1.1, 1.2](1.2, 1.7))$. Timed state sequences can be generated by timed automata in which locations are labeled with observations [23, 3]. This dual view does not change the core results, but some expressiveness results do differ in the two views [34].

2   Reachability and Language Emptiness

2.1   Region Automata

Given a timed automaton A, to check whether the language $L(A)$ is empty, we must determine if some final state is reachable from an initial state in the infinite-state system S_A. The solution to this reachability problem involves construction of a finite quotient. The construction uses an equivalence relation on the state-space that equates two states with the same location if they agree on the integral parts of all clock values and on the ordering of the fractional parts of all clock values. The integral parts of the clock values are needed to determine whether or not a particular clock constraint is met, whereas the ordering of the fractional parts is needed to decide which clock will change its integral part first. This is formalized as follows. First, assume that all the constants in the given timed automaton A are integers (if A uses rational constants, we can simply multiply each constant with the least-common-multiple of all the denominators to get an automaton with the same timed language modulo scaling). For any $\delta \in \mathbb{R}$, $\langle \delta \rangle$ denotes the fractional part of δ, and $\lfloor \delta \rfloor$ denotes the integral part of δ; $\delta = \lfloor \delta \rfloor + \langle \delta \rangle$. For each clock $x \in X$, let c_x be the largest integer c such that x is compared with c in some clock constraint appearing in a guard. The equivalence relation $\cong$, called the *region equivalence*, is defined over the set of all clock valuations for X. For two clock valuations ν and μ, $\nu \cong \mu$ iff all the following conditions hold:

1. For all clocks $x \in X$, either $\lfloor \nu(x) \rfloor$ and $\lfloor \mu(x) \rfloor$ are the same, or both $\nu(x)$ and $\mu(x)$ exceed c_x.
2. For all clocks x, y with $\nu(x) \leq c_x$ and $\nu(y) \leq c_y$, $\langle \nu(x) \rangle \leq \langle \nu(y) \rangle$ iff $\langle \mu(x) \rangle \leq \langle \mu(y) \rangle$.
3. For all clocks $x \in X$ with $\nu(x) \leq c_x$, $\langle \nu(x) \rangle = 0$ iff $\langle \mu(x) \rangle = 0$.

A *clock region* for A is an equivalence class of clock valuations induced by $\cong$. Note that there are only a finite number of regions, at most $k! \cdot 4^k \cdot \Pi_{x \in X}(c_x + 1)$, where k is the number of clocks. Thus, the number of clock regions is exponential in the encoding of the clock constraints.

The key property of region equivalence is its stability: for any location s, and clock valuations ν and ν' such that $\nu \cong \nu'$, (a) for any $\delta \in \mathbb{R}$, if $(s, \nu) \xrightarrow{\delta} (s, \nu+\delta)$ then there exists $\delta' \in \mathbb{R}$ such that $(s, \nu') \xrightarrow{\delta'} (s, \nu'+\delta')$ and $(\nu+\delta) \cong (\nu'+\delta')$, and (b) for every label $a \in \Sigma^\epsilon$ and state (t, μ), if $(s, \nu) \xrightarrow{a} (t, \mu)$ then there exists μ' such that $(s, \nu') \xrightarrow{a} (t, \mu')$ and $\mu \cong \mu'$. Thus, if two states are equivalent, then an a-labeled discrete switch from one can be matched by a corresponding discrete switch from the other leading to an equivalent target state, and if the automaton can wait for δ units in one state, then it can wait for δ' units, possibly different from δ, resulting in equivalent states. For this reason, the region equivalence is a *time-abstract* bisimulation.

For a timed automaton A, the quotient of S_A with respect to the region equivalence is called the *region automaton* of A, and is denoted $R(A)$: vertices of $R(A)$ are of the form (s, r), where s is a location and r is a clock region; there is an edge $(s, r) \xrightarrow{a} (s', r')$ in $R(A)$ for $a \in \Sigma^\epsilon$ iff for some clock valuations $\nu \in r$ and $\nu' \in r'$, $(s, \nu) \xrightarrow{a} (s', \nu')$ in S_A, or, $a = \epsilon$ and $(s, \nu) \xrightarrow{\delta} (s', \nu')$ for some $\delta \in \mathbb{R}$. The initial and final states of S_A are used to define the initial and final vertices of $R(A)$. Now, the language of $R(A)$ is the untimed language of $L(A)$.

Theorem 2. *For a timed regular language L, untime(L) is a regular language [2].*

Consequently, $R(A)$ can be used to solve language emptiness for A, and also to answer reachability queries for A. Thus, emptiness and reachability can be solved in time linear in the number of vertices and edges of the region automaton, which is linear in the number of locations and edges of A, exponential in the number of clocks, and exponential in the encoding of the constants. Technically, these problems are PSPACE-complete.

Theorem 3. *The language emptiness question for timed automata is PSPACE-complete, and can be solved in time $O(m \cdot k! \cdot 4^k \cdot (c \cdot c' + 1)^k)$, where m is the number of switches in A, k is the number of clocks in A, c is largest numerator in the constants in the clock constraints in A, and c' is the least-common-multiple of the denominators of all the constants in the clock constraints of A [2].*

In [15] it was also shown that for timed automata with three clocks, reachability is already PSPACE-complete. A recent result [28] shows that for timed automata with one clock, reachability is NLOGSPACE-complete and for timed automata with two clocks, it is NP-hard. The reachability problem remains PSPACE-hard even if we bound the magnitudes of constants [15].

2.2   Cycle Detection

A timed ω-word is an infinite sequence of the form $\alpha = (a_0, t_0)(a_1, t_1) \ldots (a_i, t_i), \ldots$, with $a_i \in \Sigma$, $t_i \in \mathbb{R}$, and $t_0 \leq t_1 \leq \cdots t_i \leq \cdots$, and timed ω-language is a set of timed ω-words. Reasoning in terms of infinite timed words, as in the untimed setting, is useful for checking liveness properties. The notion of a run of a timed automaton A naturally extends to timed ω-words. A timed ω-word α is accepted by A using the Büchi condition, if there is a run of A on α that repeatedly hits (infinitely often) some final location in V^F. The set of ω-words accepted by A is denoted by $L_\omega(A)$. Checking whether $L_\omega(A)$ is nonempty, for a given A, can be done by checking whether there is a cycle in the region graph of A which is reachable from an initial state and contains some state in V^F.

For infinite words, it is natural to require that time diverges, that is, the sequence $t_0, t_1, \ldots t_i, \ldots$ grows without bound. Timed words that do not diverge depict an infinite number of events that occur in a finite amount of time. To restrict $L_\omega(A)$ only to divergent words, we can transform the timed automaton by adding a new clock x which is reset to 0 whenever it becomes 1 (using an ϵ-edge) and the timed automaton hits the new final set V'_F only if the run had passed through V_F in the last one unit of time.

Theorem 4. *Given a timed automaton A, the problem of checking emptiness of $L_\omega(A)$ is* PSPACE-*complete.*

Most of the results in this survey hold for timed ω-languages also.

2.3   Sampled Semantics

In the discrete-time or sampled semantics for timed automata, the discrete switches, or the events, are required to occur only at integral multiples of a given sampling rate f. This can be formalized as follows. Given a timed automaton A and a sampling rate $f \in \mathbb{Q}$, we define an automaton S_A^f: the states, initial states and final states of S_A^f are the same as the states, initial states, and final states of S_A, and the transitions of S_A^f are the transitions of S_A that are labeled with either $a \in \Sigma^\epsilon$ or with $m.f$ (where $m \in \mathbb{N}$). The sampled timed language $L^f(A)$ is defined using the automaton S_A^f. Note that time of occurrence of any symbol in the timed words in $L^f(A)$ is an integral multiple of the sampling frequency f. To check emptiness of $L^f(A)$, observe that in any reachable state of S_A^f, the values of all clocks are integral multiples of f, and this can lead to a reduced search space compared to the region automata. However, the complexity class of the reachability and cycle-detection problems stays unchanged (here L_ω^f denotes the set of ω-words where events occur at sampling rate f):

Theorem 5. *Given a timed automaton A and a sampling rate $f \in \mathbb{Q}$, the problem of checking the emptiness of $L^f(A)$ (or $L_\omega^f(A)$) is* PSPACE-*complete.*

If the sampling rate f is unknown, the resulting problems are the discrete-time reachability and discrete-time cycle-detection problems with unknown sampling rate: given a timed automaton A, does there exist a rational number $f \in \mathbb{Q}$ such that $L^f(A)$ (or $L_\omega^f(A)$) is nonempty. Discrete-time reachability for unknown sampling rate is decidable since it is equivalent to the question of whether $L(A)$ is empty: if $L(A)$ is nonempty, we can find a word in $L(A)$ where events occur at

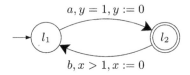

Fig. 3. Sampled semantics is different from the standard semantics.

rational times, and by choosing an appropriate f, show that it is an f-sampled word. However, the discrete-time cycle-detection problem with unknown sampling rate is undecidable:

Theorem 6. *Given* A, *the problem of checking whether* $\bigcup_{f \in \mathbb{Q}} L_\omega^f(A)$ *is nonempty, is undecidable [14].*

The undecidability proof is by reduction from the halting problem for two-counter machines. Given a two-counter machine M, one can construct a timed automaton A_M and a location s_F such that for any integer n, the location s_F is reachable in the discrete-time semantics with the sampling rate $1/n$ iff the two-counter machine M has a halting run in which both the counters do not exceed the value n.

To see that $L_\omega(A)$ can be nonempty while for each f, $L_\omega^f(A) = \emptyset$, consider the automaton in Figure 3. While the a-events occur at integer times, the b-events have to occur closer and closer to the a-events, and fixing any sampling rate f makes the ω-language empty.

2.4   Choice of Clock Constraints and Updates

The clock constraints in the guards of a timed automaton compare clocks with constants. Such constraints allow us to express (constant) lower and upper bounds on delays. Consider the following generalization of clock constraints: for a set X of clocks, the set $\Phi^d(X)$ of *clock constraints* g is defined by the grammar

$$g := x \leq c \mid c \leq x \mid x - y \leq c \mid x < c \mid c < x \mid x - y < c \mid g \wedge g$$

where x, y are clocks in X and $c \in \mathbb{Q}$. Including such "diagonal" clock constraints that compare clock differences with constants does not change the complexity of reachability. Similarly, we can relax the allowed updates on switches. In the original definition, each switch is tagged with a set λ which specifies which clocks should be reset to zero. A more general *update map* λ maps clocks in X to $\mathbb{Q} \cup X$ specifying the assignments $x := \lambda(x)$. Thus, x can be assigned to an arbitrary rational constant, or to the value of another clock. Both these modifications can be handled by modifying the region construction. In fact, both these extensions do not add to the expressive power.

Theorem 7. *If the clock constraints for guards are chosen from the set* $\Phi^d(X)$, *and the switches are annotated with the update maps, the expressive power of* *timed automata stays unchanged, and the language emptiness problem stays* PSPACE-*complete.*

However, a variety of extensions have been shown to allow definition of languages that are not timed regular, and lead to undecidability of the emptiness problem. We summarize some notable ones:

1. Allowing guards of the form $x = 2y$ renders reachability problem for timed automata undecidable [2].
2. Allowing guards of the form $x + y \sim c$, where $\sim \in \{<, \leq\}$ leads to undecidability if there are four or more clocks, but is decidable for automata with two clocks [9].
3. Allowing updates of the form $x := x - 1$ renders reachability problem for timed automata undecidable [13].
4. Allowing updates of the form $x := x + 1$ keeps the reachability problem PSPACE-complete if the clock constraints are chosen from $\Phi(X)$, but renders it undecidable if the guards are chosen from $\Phi^d(X)$ [13].
5. Allowing guards that compare clocks with irrational constants renders reachability problem for timed automata undecidable [30].

The first result above implies that allowing constraints involving addition of clock variables leads to undecidability of the reachability problem. With an enabling condition of the form $y = 2x$, one can express a constraint of the kind "the time delay between the symbols a and b is the same as the time delay between b and c" (reset a clock x while reading a, reset a clock y while reading b, and require $y = 2x$ while reading c). This can be exploited to copy the counter values, and encode configurations of a two-counter machine, leading to undecidability. The second result is of similar nature. The third result says that one cannot allow decrements. Since clocks increase with elapse of time, with decrements they can act as counters, and thus be used to encode counter machines. The fourth result says that explicit increments can be allowed in the original region construction, but in the presence of guards of the "diagonal" form $x - y \leq c$, such increments allow encoding of counter values using the differences between clocks. Bouyer et al have also studied nondeterministic updates (for example, x is reset to a value chosen nondeterministically from intervals such as $[0, c]$ or $[y, \infty)$), and their impact on the decidability with and without the "diagonal" constraints [13]. Finally, [30] considers timed automata where guard constraints compare clocks with *irrational constants*, and shows that if $\tau \in (0, 1)$ is an irrational number, then timed automata where the constants are taken from $\{0, 1, \tau, 3 - \tau\}$ have an undecidable emptiness problem.

2.5   Choice of Clock Rates

An interesting generalization of timed automata is *rectangular automata* in which clocks increase at a rate that is bounded by constants [21]. Such a clock can be used to approximate a continuous variable. A rectangular automaton A over an

Fig. 4. Clock drift, however small, influences reachability.

alphabet Σ is a tuple $\langle V, V^0, V^F, X, E, low, high \rangle$, where the components V, V^0, V^F, X, and E are as in a timed automaton, and low and $high$ are functions from X to $\mathbb{Q}$. When time elapses each clock x increases at a rate bounded by $low(x)$ from below, and by $high(x)$ from above. The transition system S_A associated with the rectangular automaton A is defined as in case of timed automata. The only difference is in the transitions corresponding to elapse of time: for a state (s, ν), a time increment $\delta \in \mathbb{R}$, and a clock valuation μ, $(s, \nu) \xrightarrow{\delta} (s, \mu)$ holds if for each clock $x \in X$, there exists a rate $low(x) \le r_x \le high(x)$ such that $\mu(x) = \nu(x) + \delta \cdot r_x$.

Theorem 8. *The language accepted by a rectangular automaton is timed regular, and the language emptiness problem for rectangular automata is* PSPACE-*complete [21].*

The emptiness problem for rectangular automata is solved by translating rectangular automata to equivalent timed automata. Consider a rectangular automaton A. We obtain an equivalent automaton B as follows. For every clock x of A, B has two clocks: x_l whose rate is $low(x)$ and x_h whose rate is $high(x)$. We would like x_l and x_h to track the lower and upper bounds, respectively, on the possible values of the clock x whose rate can vary in the interval $[low(x), high(x)]$. Consider a switch of A with guard $x \le c$. The corresponding switch in B has guard $x_l \le c$, and update $x_h := c$. Analogously, the guard $x \ge d$ is replaced by the constraint $x_h \ge d$, with an accompanying adjustment $x_l := d$. This transformation preserves answers to reachability questions, and in fact, timed languages. The automaton B has clocks that have fixed rates, and can easily be transformed into a timed automaton simply by scaling. Note that in rectangular automata, a variable does not change its rate from one location to another, the enabling conditions compare variables with constants, and updates reset variables to constants. Relaxing any of these restrictions results in undecidability [21].

Rectangular automata are also useful to introduce "errors" in the clocks. For a timed automaton A, and a constant ε, let A^ε be the rectangular automaton obtained from A by setting $low(x) = 1 - \varepsilon$ and $high(x) = 1 + \varepsilon$ for all clocks x. Thus, the clocks in A^ε have a drift bounded by ε. A location s of a timed automaton A is said to be *limit-reachable* if s is reachable in the perturbed automaton A^ε, for every $\varepsilon > 0$. Obviously, reachability implies limit reachability, but not vice versa [33]. For instance, the language of the automaton of Figure 4 is nonempty as long as the there is a non-zero drift for the two clocks. It is possible to compute the set of limit-reachable locations by modifying the search in the region automaton $R(A)$. For example, in Figure 4, in the initial location, the region $0 < x = y < 1$ is reachable. Since it touches the region $0 < x < y = 1$, which, in turn, touches the region $0 < x < 1 < y$, the latter is declared limit-reachable, and this makes the discrete switch to the final location possible. The computation, in general, requires identifying the so-called limit-cycles in the region graph [33].

Theorem 9. *Given a timed automaton A, the problem of deciding whether a location is limit reachable is* PSPACE-*complete [33].*

Instead of perturbing the clock rates, if we perturb the guards, that is, replace every $x \le c$ by $x \le c + \varepsilon$ and every $x \ge c$ by $x \ge c - \varepsilon$, and ask if a location is reachable for every positive perturbation ε of the guards, then the problem is solvable by similar techniques [17].

2.6   Weighted Automata and Optimal Reachability

A *weighted timed automaton* consists of a timed automaton A, a cost function J that maps every location and every switch to a nonnegative rational number. For a location $s \in V$, $J(s)$ is the cost of staying in s per unit time, and for a switch $e \in E$, $J(e)$ is the cost of a discrete switch corresponding to e. The cost function leads to costs on the edges of the underlying transition system S_A: the transitions of the form $(s, \nu) \xrightarrow{\delta} (s, \nu + \delta)$ have cost $\delta \cdot J(s)$, and transitions due to a switch e have cost $J(e)$. The *optimal reachability* problem for weighted timed automata is to determine the cost of the shortest path from an initial state to a final state, and thus, is a generalization of the classical shortest path problem in weighted automata. Formally, given a timed automaton A, and a cost function J, the optimal cost of reaching the final set V^F is the infimum over costs c such that there is a path of cost c from an initial state to a final state. The solution to this problem has been proposed in [7] (see also [8] for an alternative approach). Consider a path in the underlying graph of the timed automaton from an initial location to a final location. There can be many runs corresponding to the sequence of discrete switches specified by such a path, depending on the time spent between successive switches. However, since the constraints imposed by the resets and guards are linear, and so is the cost function, in an optimal run the times of switches will be at corner points (or arbitrarily close to corner points if the corner points are ruled out by the constraints).

In a more general version of the optimal reachability problem, we are given a source region (that is, some constraints on the initial values of the clocks), and we want to compute optimal costs for all the states in the source region. It is possible to construct a weighted graph whose nodes are "refined" regions and edges are annotated with parametric costs that are linear functions of the clock values in the source state. The size of this graph, like the region graph, is exponential in the timed automaton. Fixing a source state determines the costs on all the edges, and optimal cost to reach any of the locations (or regions) can be computed in PSPACE (see also [12]). However, the number of parameters is same as the number of clocks, and if wish to compute a symbolic representation of the optimal cost to reach a target as a function of the source state, this approach gives a doubly exponential solution.

Theorem 10. *Given a timed automaton A, and a cost function J, the optimal cost of reaching a final state can be computed in* PSPACE.

3 Inclusion, Equivalence and Universality

3.1 Undecidability

The *universality* problem for timed automata is to decide, given a timed automaton A, whether A accepts all timed traces, i.e. whether $L(A) = T\Sigma^*$. For automata on discrete words, this is decidable as one can complement the automaton A and check for emptiness. This approach does not work for timed automata since, as we saw earlier, timed automata are not closed under complementation. In fact, it turns out that the problem is undecidable:

Theorem 11. *The universality problem for timed automata is undecidable [2].*

The proof proceeds by encoding computations of a 2-counter machine (or a Turing machine) using timed words where every unit time interval encodes a configuration of the machine. Copying between successive configurations is achieved by requiring that every event in one interval has a matching event distance 1 apart in the next interval. While this requirement cannot be captured by a timed automaton, the complement can be accepted by a nondeterministic timed automaton that guesses the errors (that is, events with no matches in the following interval).

The inclusion problem is to check, given two timed automata A and B, whether $L(A) \subseteq L(B)$. This is an interesting question from the formal methods perspective as it corresponds to the model-checking problem: given a system modeled using A and a specification modeled as B, is the set of behaviors of A contained in the the the language defined by B?. The equivalence problem is to check, given A and B, whether $L(A) = L(B)$.

Since the set of all timed words is timed-regular, the universality problem reduces to both the inclusion and equivalence problems, and we have:

Corollary 1. *The inclusion and equivalence problems for timed automata are undecidable.*

Due to the interest in model-checking timed systems modeled as timed automata, there has been intense research over the years to find subclasses of timed automata for which the inclusion problem is decidable. We review some of them here.

3.2 Deterministic Timed Automata

A timed automaton A is *deterministic* if (1) V^0 contains only one location, (2) there are no switches labeled with ϵ, and (3) for every pair of distinct switches (s, a, g, λ, s') and $(s, a, g', \lambda', s'')$ with the same source location and label, the guards g and g' are disjoint (i.e. the sets of clock valuations that satisfy g and g'

are disjoint). These requirements ensure that A has at most one run on a given timed word, and consequently, complementation can be achieved by complementing the set of final states. The properties of deterministic timed automata are summarized below:

Theorem 12. *Deterministic timed automata are closed under union, intersection, and complementation, but not under projection. The language emptiness, universality, inclusion, and equivalence problems for deterministic timed automata are PSPACE-complete [2].*

Unlike classical automata, deterministic timed automata are strictly less expressive than the nondeterministic ones, and in particular, the language of the automaton of Figure 1 cannot be specified using a deterministic timed automaton. Given a timed automaton A, the problem of checking whether there exists an equivalent deterministic timed automaton is not known to be decidable (see [35] for a discussion).

An interesting extension of deterministic timed automata is *bounded 2-way deterministic timed automata* [5]. Automata in this class deterministically traverse a timed word from left to right, but can stop and reverse direction to read the word backwards from that point. For example, consider the language consisting of all words of the form $(a, t_0)(a, t_1) \ldots (a, t_k)(b, t')$ such that there exists some $i \le k$ with $t' = t_i + 1$ (i.e. there is some a-event which is exactly one unit of time before the b-event). This language is not accepted by a (forward) deterministic automaton, but can be accepted by an automaton that goes to the end of the word, sets a clock to the time of the last event, and traverses the word backwards looking for the matching a event. For decidability, it is required that there exists a bound n such that any symbol of any word is read at most n times. Such a bounded timed automaton (even a nondeterministic one) can be simulated by a single-pass forward nondeterministic automaton as it simply needs to guess the positions where the clocks are reset on the bounded number of passes. In the deterministic case, the expressive power strictly increases with the bound n. These deterministic bounded two-way automata also preserve the crucial property that there is at most one run on each timed word, and consequently, they are closed under all boolean operations, and checking whether $L(A) \subseteq L(B)$, where A is a timed automaton and B is a bounded 2-way deterministic automaton, is decidable.

3.3   Digitization

An important subclass of timed automata for which the inclusion problem is decidable involves the notion of *digitization*. A timed language L is said to be closed under digitization if discretizing a timed word $w \in L$ by approximating the events in w to the closest tick of a discrete clock results in a word that is also in L.

Formally, for any $t \in \mathbb{R}$ and for any $0 \le \varepsilon \le 1$, let $[t]_\varepsilon$ be $\lfloor t \rfloor$, if $t < \lfloor t \rfloor + \varepsilon$, and $\lceil t \rceil$ otherwise. We extend this to timed words: if $w = (a_0, t_0), \ldots (a_k, t_k)$, then $[w]_\varepsilon = (a_0, [t_0]_\varepsilon) \ldots (a_k, [t_k]_\varepsilon)$. Intuitively, $[w]_\varepsilon$ is the word obtained when events are observed using a discrete clock with offset ε. For a timed language L, $[L]_\varepsilon = \{[w]_\varepsilon \mid w \in L\}$.

A timed language L is *closed under digitization* [22] if for every $w \in L$ and for every $\varepsilon \in [0,1]$, $[w]_\varepsilon \in L$, i.e. if for every $\varepsilon \in [0,1]$, $[L]_\varepsilon \subseteq L$. L is said to be *closed under inverse digitization* if it is the case that whenever u is a timed word such that for every $\varepsilon \in [0,1]$, $[u]_\varepsilon \in L$, then u itself belongs to L.

For any timed language L, let $\mathbb{Z}(L)$ be the set of timed words in L in which every event happens at an integer time. Note the relation to the sampled semantics of Section 2.2: for a timed automaton A, $L^1(A) = \mathbb{Z}(L(A))$.

Lemma 1. *[22] Let L be closed under digitization and L' be closed under inverse digitization. Then $L \subseteq L'$ iff $\mathbb{Z}(L) \subseteq \mathbb{Z}(L')$.*

The proof of the above lemma runs as follows: Assume $\mathbb{Z}(L) \subseteq \mathbb{Z}(L')$. If $u \in L$, then $[u]_\varepsilon \in L$ for every $\varepsilon \in [0,1]$ (since L is closed under digitization); hence $[u]_\varepsilon \in \mathbb{Z}(L) \subseteq \mathbb{Z}(L')$, for every $\varepsilon \in [0,1]$, which in turn means that $u \in L'$ (since L' is closed under inverse digitization).

It is easy to see that timed languages over Σ in which events occur only at integral times are in one-to-one correspondence with untimed languages over $\Sigma \cup \{\sqrt{}\}$, where $\sqrt{}$ denotes the passage of one unit of time. For example, the trace $(a_0, 1)(a_1, 1)(a_2, 3)$ corresponds to the untimed word $\sqrt{}a_0 a_1 \sqrt{}\sqrt{}a_2$. For any timed word in which events occur at integral times, let $Tick(w)$ denote the corresponding word over $\Sigma \cup \{\sqrt{}\}$. Given a timed automaton A accepting L, we can effectively construct an automaton over $\Sigma \cup \{\sqrt{}\}$ accepting $Tick(\mathbb{Z}(L))$, using the region automaton for A. Hence, checking $\mathbb{Z}(L) \subseteq \mathbb{Z}(L')$ boils down to checking inclusion between two untimed languages, which is decidable. This gives:

Theorem 13. *[22] Given timed automata A and B, where $L(A)$ is closed under digitization and $L(B)$ is closed under inverse digitization, the problem of checking whether $L(A) \subseteq L(B)$ is decidable.*

Open timed automata are timed automata where all atomic clock constraints in guards are of the form $x < c$ or $x > c$, i.e. atomic guards of the form $x \leq c$ and $x \geq c$ are disallowed. Similarly, *closed timed automata* are those in which all atomic guards are of the form $x \leq c$ or $x \geq c$. The following is then true:

Proposition 1. *[22, 31] Closed timed automata are closed under digitization, and open timed automata are closed under inverse digitization.*

Corollary 2. *Given a closed timed automaton A and an open timed automaton B, the problem of checking if $L(A) \subseteq L(B)$ is decidable.*

Turning to the universality problem, since checking whether a timed automaton A accepts all timed words is the same as asking whether $T\Sigma^* \subseteq L(A)$, and since $T\Sigma^*$ is closed under digitization, it follows that:

Theorem 14. *[22, 31] The universality problem for open timed automata (or any class of timed automata that are closed under inverse digitization) is decidable.*

Note that the above crucially uses the fact that our definition of timed words allows several events to happen at the same time, i.e. the timed words are *weakly monotonic*. If this were disallowed and it was required that time strictly elapse between events, then we have as universe the set of all *strongly* monotonic words, which is not closed under digitization. It turns out that checking universality of open timed automata is undecidable in the domain of strongly monotonic words. Also, for closed timed automata, universality is undecidable regardless of whether the universe is weakly or strongly monotonic [31].

Note that open timed automata are defined syntactically by placing restrictions on the structure of the automata while closure under digitization is a semantic property of languages. Given automata A and B, one can always check whether $\mathbb{Z}(L(A)) \subseteq \mathbb{Z}(L(B))$. If we could decide whether A is closed under digitization and whether B is closed under inverse digitization, we would know whether we can use the above test to check language inclusion. It turns out that the former is decidable but the latter is not:

Theorem 15. *[31] Given a timed automaton A, checking whether $L(A)$ is closed under digitization is decidable, while the problem of checking whether $L(A)$ is closed under inverse digitization is undecidable (even if A is a closed timed automaton).*

3.4   Robust Timed Automata

Since the undecidability of universality and inclusion problems were shown using the fact that events that are precisely one unit (or an integral number of units) apart can be related, and hence used to count, this led to the belief that introducing some fuzziness in acceptance could alleviate the problem. Also, in practice, no timed system can be modeled and observed with such arbitrary accuracy a timed automaton provides.

The definition of robust timed automata addresses this. Given a timed automaton, under the robust semantics a word is accepted if and only if a dense subset "around" the word is accepted by the timed automaton. In this definition, a word that is accepted by the timed automaton may be rejected in the robust semantics if it is an isolated accepted trace, while a word that is rejected by the timed automaton can be accepted under the robust semantics if it is surrounded by a dense set of accepted traces.

Formally, let us first define a metric d on timed words. Let w and w' be two timed words. If $untime(w) \neq untime(w')$, then $d(w, w') = \infty$. Otherwise, if $w = (a_0, t_0) \ldots (a_k, t_k)$ and $w' = (a_0, t'_0) \ldots (a_k, t'_k)$, then $d(w, w') = \max\{|t_i - t'_i| \mid 0 \leq i \leq k\}$. In other words, the distance between two timed words (whose untimed components are identical) is the maximum difference in time between corresponding events in the two words. We refer to open and closed sets of timed words with regard to this metric.

The robust semantics can now be defined as follows. Given a timed automaton A accepting L, let L^c denote the smallest closed set containing L. Then the robust language accepted by the automaton, $L_R(A)$, is the interior of L^c, which is the largest open set contained within L^c.

In this subsection, to clearly distinguish between the standard semantics and the robust one, we refer to the former as *precise semantics*. In the original paper [20], the robust semantics of a timed automaton was defined as a collection of *tubes* as opposed to a collection of timed words. A tube is any set of timed words which is open (i.e. for each timed word in the tube, some ε-neighborhood should be contained in the tube). Here we adopt a slightly different semantics by defining the robust semantics to be the set of all timed words which belong to some tube that is robustly accepted.

The robust language of any timed automaton is, by definition, open. Also, it turns out that the (precise) languages accepted by open timed automata are also open. However, open timed automata and robust timed automata have incomparable expressive power (i.e. there are timed languages that are accepted by open timed automata which are not acceptable by robust timed automata and vice versa) [31].

Despite the involved definition of robust acceptance, emptiness for robust timed automata is decidable:

Theorem 16. *[20] The emptiness problem for robust timed automata is* PSPACE-*complete.*

The proof proceeds by showing that for any timed automaton A, we can construct an open timed automaton A^o such that both accept the same robust languages, i.e. $L_R(A) = L_R(A^o)$. Since the precise language of this open timed automaton is open, i.e. $L(A^o)$ is open, it follows that the robust language of A is nonempty iff the precise language of A^o is nonempty (i.e. $L_R(A) \neq \emptyset$ iff $L(A^o) \neq \emptyset$), which is decidable. One can in fact show that the untimed language corresponding to the robust language accepted by A is regular (as is true for the precise semantics).

However, it turns out that despite robustness, robust timed languages are not closed under complement (and hence not determinizable) [20, 26]. We give a new proof here. Consider the timed automaton A depicted in Figure 5, which accepts (in the precise semantics) the language L consisting of all timed words w such that the untimed word of w is in a^*b^* and there are two consecutive a-events at times t and t' such that there are no b-events in the range $[t + 1, t' + 1]$. It is easy to see that the robust language accepted by A is also L.

The robust complement of A, denoted by $\overline{L}$, consists of the set of all words w such that either the untimed word of w is not in a^*b^* or for every two consecutive a-events, there is at least one b-event in the *open* range $(t + 1, t' + 1)$. We show that $\overline{L}$ is not robustly acceptable by any timed automaton. We claim that a word is in the untimed language of $\overline{L}$ iff it is in $\Sigma^*.b.\Sigma^*.a.\Sigma^*$ or is of the form $a^m b^n$ where $n \geq m - 1$. This claim will show that $\overline{L}$ cannot be robustly accepted, since $untime(\overline{L})$ is non-regular. The only interesting part is to show that there is no word whose untimed word is $a^m b^n$ with $n < m - 1$. Assume there is such a word

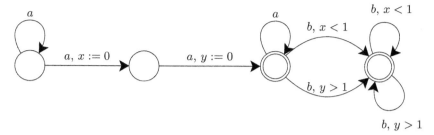

Fig. 5. A noncomplementable robust automaton.

τ. By robust acceptance, we can find a word τ' close to τ whose untimed word is the same as that of τ but where all a-events occur at different times. Then, it is easy to see that the a-events define $m-1$ intervals which cannot be filled by n b-events and hence τ' is not in the language, which is a contradiction.

The above mechanism of sandwiching a related event in an interval one unit away from a pair of consecutive events, gives a way to maintain counters. A similar mechanism is used to encode configurations of a Turing machine in [24], where the authors show that a robust timed automaton can accept all wrong configuration sequences of a Turing machine, making universality of robust timed automata undecidable.

Turning to the notions defined in the last subsection, the languages defined by robust automata are closed under inverse digitization [31]. However, unlike regular timed languages, checking whether the robust language of a timed automaton is closed under digitization is undecidable [31].

Also, in sharp contrast to the precise semantics of timed automata, it turns out that the discrete-time language accepted by robust timed automata need not be regular. That is, there are robust timed automata A such that $\mathbb{Z}(L_R(A))$ is not regular. Consequently, there are timed languages that can be accepted by timed automata under the robust semantics which cannot be accepted by timed automata under the precise semantics (and vice versa).

The nonregularity of $\mathbb{Z}(L_R(A))$ seems to render digitization techniques inapplicable for checking inclusion of robust timed automata. In fact, the decidability status of the integral language emptiness under the robust semantics (i.e. given an automaton A, to check whether $\mathbb{Z}(L_R(A)) \neq \emptyset$) is not known. Also, introducing imprecision using infinitesimal clock drift (recall the definition of A^ε from Section 2.4) as a way of defining semantics, and its relationship to the robust semantics has not been studied.

3.5 Restricting Resources

One approach to get a more tractable subclass is to restrict the resources a timed automaton can use. The original proof showing that inclusion of timed automata is undecidable also showed that timed automata with two clocks already renders the inclusion problem undecidable [2].

For timed automata with one clock, however, a recent result shows that checking inclusion (i.e. checking if $L(A) \subseteq L(B)$) is decidable when B has only one clock [32]. The proof is based on techniques used to solve problems on *infinite graphs* akin to those used to solve problems involving coverability in Petri nets.

The paper [32] also shows that the problem of checking whether $L(A) \subseteq L(B)$ is decidable if the only constant that appears in the guards of B is 0. The proof goes by showing that B can be determinized. The essence of the idea is this: Consider the region automaton for B. The only information we need to maintain is whether each clock is 0 or greater than 0 – the ordering of fractional parts of clocks need not be recorded as any region has at most one timed successor (the one with every clock greater than 0). Using now a clock, we can simulate a subset construction on the region automaton and turn it into a timed automaton where the clock is reset on every event and is used to check whether any amount of time has elapsed since the last event.

Theorem 17. *[32] The problem of checking, given two timed automata A and B, whether $L(A) \subseteq L(B)$, is decidable if B does not have any ϵ-labeled switches and either:*

- *B uses only one clock, or*
- *B uses guards involving the constant 0 only.*

The above results are the only known decidability results in this category. In fact, the following relaxations of these restrictions on a given automaton A, renders the universality problem undecidable [32]:

- A has two clocks and a one-event alphabet, or
- A has two clocks and uses a single non-zero constant in the guards, or
- A has a single location and a one-event alphabet, or
- A has a single location and uses a single non-zero constant in the guards.

3.6   Event Clock Automata

The essential power of nondeterminism in timed automata lies in its ability to reset clocks nondeterministically, as will become clear later in this subsection. The class of *event-recording automata* [4] are timed automata with a fixed set of clocks, a clock x_a for each $a \in \Sigma$, where x_a gets reset every time a occurs. There are no ϵ-labeled switches. Event-recording automata thus have switches labeled (a, g) instead of (a, g, λ), as it is implicitly assumed that $\lambda = \{x_a\}$.

An event-recording automaton A can be easily determinized. First, we can transform A to an automaton B such that if G is the set of guards used on the transitions, then G is "minimal" in the sense that for any two guards g and g' in G, there is no clock valuation that satisfies both g and g'. Then, we can do a subset construction on this automaton. Let $B = \langle V, V^0, V^F, X, E \rangle$. Then, we can build a deterministic event recording automaton $C = \langle 2^V, \{V^0\}, F, X, E' \rangle$ where for any $S \subseteq V$, $a \in \Sigma$, $g \in G$, $(S, a, g, S') \in E'$ where $S' = \{v' \in V \mid \exists v \in S.(v, a, g, v') \in E\}$. The set F contains the sets $S \subseteq V$ such that $S \cap V^F \neq \emptyset$.

It is easy to see that C is deterministic and accepts the same language as B does. Note that a similar construction fails for timed automata since for a set S, there could be two states $v, v' \in S$ with edges (v, g, λ, v_1) and (v', g, λ', v_1'), where $\lambda \neq \lambda'$.

An event-recording automaton at any point on the input word has access to a clock x_a, for each $a \in \Sigma$, whose value is the time that has elapsed since the last a-event. *Event clock automata* are an extension in which the automaton also has access to a *prophecy* clock y_a (for each $a \in \Sigma$) whose value at any point is the time that must elapse before the next a-event happens. For, example, in the timed word $(a, 0.4)(b, 0.5)(a, 0.7)(b, 0, 9)(a, 0.95)$, when reading the third event in the word, the clock $x_a = 0.3$ and $y_a = 0.25$.

Observe that prophecy clocks add to the expressiveness: the language of timed words such that the untimed word is in a^*b and there is some a event one time unit before b, is not accepted by any event recording automaton, or even any deterministic timed automaton, but can easily be accepted by an event clock automaton. For every event clock automaton, we can construct a (nondeterministic) timed automaton that accepts the same language. Event-recording clocks x_a do not cause any problem, of course, as we can reset the clock x_a at each a-event. To handle prophecy clocks is more tricky. The timed automaton simulates the event-clock automaton, and if at an event a guard demands $y_b < c$, then we can take the action and postpone the checking of this constraint. We do this by resetting a new clock $z_{y_b < c}$ and check at the next b-event that $z_{y_b < c} < c$ holds. If we meet another transition before the next b-event which also demands $y_b < c$ hold, then we can ignore it as checking $y_b < c$ at an earlier position is a stronger condition. Similarly, constraints of the form $y_b > c$ can be handled. Note that the resulting automaton can be nondeterministic as multiple edges that demand different constraints on the prophecy clocks can be enabled.

Since the values of any clock of an event clock automaton at any time depends only on the word w (and not on the run of the automaton), it turns out that event-clock automata can be complemented. Let A be an event clock automaton and let the guard constraints G used in A be "minimal". Also, let us assume that the guards of switches with identical source location and identical label cover the set of all clock valuations so that some guard is always enabled. Let Π be the set of all (a, g) where $a \in \Sigma$ and $g \in G$. Note that the transitions of A are labeled using symbols in Π and that Π is finite.

Consider words in Π^*. For any word $\pi \in \Pi^*$, we can associate a set of timed words $tw(\pi)$ corresponding to it. Formally, if $\pi = (a_0, g_0) \ldots (a_n, g_n)$, then $tw(\pi)$ contains the set of all timed words of the form $(a_0, t_0) \ldots (a_n, t_n)$ where, for any $i \leq n$, the set of event-recording and prophecy clocks at (a_i, t_i) satisfy the guard g_i.

In fact, if we denote the set of *symbolic* words accepted by A as $L_{sym}(A)$ (which is a regular subset of Π^*), it is easy to see that $L(A) = \bigcup_{\pi \in L_{sym}(A)} tw(\pi)$ [18].

Notice that for any timed word w, there is a word $\pi \in \Pi^*$ such that $w \in tw(\pi)$. In fact, this symbolic word is unique, by the minimality of the guards.

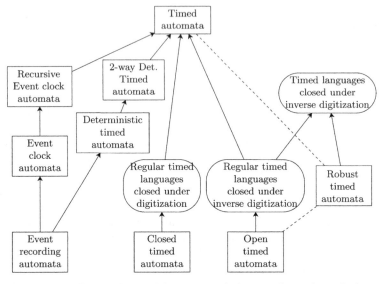

Fig. 6. The various classes of timed languages. An arrow from C to D denotes that the class defined by C is a subclass of that defined by D. Dotted lines emphasize that certain classes are not comparable.

Consequently, the timed words corresponding to words in $\Pi^* \setminus L_{sym}(A)$ form the complement of $L(A)$, i.e. $tw(\overline{L_{sym}(A)}) = \overline{L(A)}$. Hence we can complement the event clock automaton A by constructing an automaton A' accepting the complement of $L_{sym}(A)$ and by viewing A' as an event clock automaton. We can indeed even build a deterministic automaton for $L_{sym}(A)$ and by viewing it as an event-clock automaton we would get a *deterministic* event clock automaton equivalent to A. For event-recording automata A, this construction in fact yields a deterministic timed automaton equivalent to A.

We have the following results:

Theorem 18. *[4] Event clock automata are effectively closed under complementation. Further, given a timed automaton A and an event clock automaton B, the problem of checking whether $L(A) \subseteq L(B)$ is* PSPACE-*complete.*

Choosing recording clocks x_a and prophecy clocks y_a, for every symbol $a \in \Sigma$, is rather arbitrary, and one can generalize the notion of events with the corresponding recording and predicting clocks. For example, the occurrence of two a's exactly one unit of time apart can be an event for which we may want to keep recording and prophecy clocks. The property we would like to maintain is that the events are *determined* by the word, and not by a particular run of an automaton on the word.

The class of *recursive event clock automata* [25] are defined using this principle. These automata consist of a finite collection of automata, one at each level $\{1, \ldots, k\}$. The automaton at each level A_i uses events that are defined by the automaton at level A_{i-1} (A_1 is a simple event clock automaton). The notion of events is complex: essentially each automaton A_i comes as a pair of event clock automata (A_i^l, A_i^r) and an event is generated by A_i at time t if the prefix of the word till time t is accepted by A_i^l and the suffix from time t is accepted by A_i^r. The automaton at level i then uses clocks of the form x_j and y_j, $(j < i)$, where x_j and y_j are recording and prophecy clocks for events defined by the automaton A_j. The main result is that checking if $L(A) \subseteq L(B)$ is decidable, when A is a timed automaton and B is a recursive event-clock automaton. The class of languages defined by recursive event-clock automata has logical characterizations using real-time temporal logics [25, 34, 18], but its expressive power with respect to deterministic bounded two-way automata has not been studied. The relationship among various classes is summarized in Figure 6.

3.7   Resource-Bounded Inclusion

We present in this section a result that shows that checking whether a timed automaton with limited resources can exhibit an evidence to the fact that $L(A)$ is not a subset of $L(B)$, is decidable. This result is derived from ideas in [1, 19].

The *resources* of a timed automaton are the following: the number of clocks that it uses, the granularity $1/m$ with which it makes observations of the clocks, and the maximum constant it uses. The maximum constant, however, is not important, as for any timed automaton A, there exists an equivalent timed automaton B with ϵ-transitions which uses the same number of clocks, has the same granularity as A, but with maximum constant 1 in the guards. We can construct B such that it simulates A, except that it keeps track of $\lfloor x \rfloor$, for each clock x, in its control state, and uses the clock only to keep track of $x - \lfloor x \rfloor$.

The number of clocks and the granularity of observation are however important – increasing the number of clocks or decreasing the granularity from say $1/m$ to $1/2m$ strictly increases the class of languages a timed automaton can accept.

Given timed automata A and B, and resources $(k, 1/m)$, we now want to know whether there is an automaton C with granularity $(k, 1/m)$ which can be an evidence to the fact that $L(A)$ is not contained in $L(B)$. More precisely, is there such a C such that $L(A) \cap L(C) \neq \emptyset$ but $L(B) \cap L(C) = \emptyset$? We show that this is a decidable problem.

Let us fix resources $(k, 1/m)$. Let $X_k = \{x_1, \ldots, x_k\}$ be a set of k-clocks and let $G_{1/m}$ denote the set of all minimal guards formed using boolean combinations of constraints of the form $x_i \leq 1/m$ and $x_i < 1/m$, where $x_i \in X_k$. Let $\Pi = \{(a, g, \lambda) \mid a \in \Sigma', g \in G_{1/m}, \lambda \subseteq X_k\}$. Note that for any timed automaton C which has minimal guards on transitions, the symbolic language it accepts is a subset of Π^*.

Each word $\pi \in \Pi^*$ defines a set of timed words $tw(\pi)$ over Σ which is basically the set of timed words that would be accepted by a timed automaton along a run that is labeled with π. The question of the existence of a C that witnesses that $L(A)$ is not a subset of $L(B)$ boils down to finding whether there is some symbolic word $\pi \in \Pi^*$ such that $tw(\pi) \cap L(A) \neq \emptyset$ and $tw(\pi) \cap L(B) = \emptyset$.

The following lemma will help capture the set of all such witnesses:

Lemma 2. *[19] Let D be any timed automaton over Σ and let Π be a symbolic alphabet for granularity $(k, 1/m)$ as above. Then, the set of all $\pi \in \Pi^*$ such that $tw(\pi) \cap tw(D) \neq \emptyset$ is regular.*

The proof follows using the intersection construction for timed automata. Let E be the automaton accepting Π^*. Essentially, the automaton we are looking for is the region automaton accepting the product of D and E. When we take a product transition, however, we label this transition with the Π-label that was involved in the transition.

Consequently, R_A, the set of all words π in Π^* such that $tw(\pi) \cap L(A) \neq \emptyset$ is regular, and the set R_B of all words π in Π^* such that $tw(\pi) \cap L(B) = \emptyset$, is also regular. We can now check whether $R_A \cap R_B$ is empty, which is decidable, and we have:

Theorem 19. *Given timed automata A and B, and a resource constraint $(k, 1/m)$, the problem of checking whether there is an automaton C with granularity $(k, 1/m)$ such that $L(A) \cap L(C) \neq \emptyset$ and $L(B) \cap L(C) = \emptyset$ is decidable.*

4 Discussion

This survey attempts to collect, unify, and explain selected results concerning reachability and language inclusion for timed automata and its variants. The theoretical questions studied in the literature, but not addressed in this survey, include timed ω-languages, connections to monadic logics, regular expressions, and circuits, branching-time equivalences such as timed (bi)simulations, model checking of real-time temporal logics, analysis of parametric timed automata, and games and controller synthesis.

The reachability problem is the most relevant problem in the context of formal verification, and its complexity class is PSPACE. A large number of heuristics have been proposed to efficiently implement the reachability algorithm. All these involve searching the region automaton, either explicitly, or using symbolic encoding of regions using zones (see [6, 29, 16, 36, 11] for sample tools). Many of these optimizations have been devised so as to avoid enumerating all possible numerical combinations of the (integral) clock values. We believe that new insights can be obtained by exploring the following theoretical question [27]. Consider the special case when the graph formed by locations and edges of a timed automaton A is acyclic. Even in this case, the region automaton can be exponential, and the shortest path to a target region can be of exponential length. However, it is easy to see that the problem is in NP: the number of discrete switches along the path to the target is linear, it suffices to guess the regions when these discrete switches occur, and it is easy to verify the feasibility of the guess. The problem can also be shown to be NP-hard. The NP upper bound also holds if we allow a single self-loop switch on each location. We conjecture that this bound continues to hold when the strongly connected components in the graph are small: if the number of edges in each strongly-connected component of the graph formed by the locations and edges of a timed automaton is bounded, then the reachability problem is in NP.

The fact that the language "some two a symbols are distance 1 apart" is timed regular has led to the belief that timed automata are too powerful in terms of precision and unbounded nondeterminism, causing noncomplementability and undecidable language inclusion problem. The various solutions such as event clock automata, robust automata, open timed automata, have been proposed to address this issue. However, no solution has emerged as a convincing alternative, and research in obtaining a class of automata with properties more attractive than those of timed automata continues. We believe that introducing a small drift in the clocks of timed automata is a natural and simple way to introduce imprecision. Let us call a timed regular language L to be a *perturbed* language if there exists a timed automaton A and an error $\varepsilon > 0$ such that $L = L(A^{\varepsilon})$. We conjecture that the class of perturbed languages has a decidable language inclusion problem.

Acknowledgments

We thank Patricia Bouyer, Deepak D'Souza, Tom Henzinger, Joel Ouaknine and Jean-Francois Raskin for useful comments on the draft of this manuscript.

References

1. R. Alur, C. Courcoubetis, and T. Henzinger. The observational power of clocks. In *CONCUR '94: Fifth International Conference on Concurrency Theory*, LNCS 836, pages 162–177. Springer-Verlag, 1994.
2. R. Alur and D. Dill. A theory of timed automata. *Theoretical Computer Science*, 126:183–235, 1994.
3. R. Alur, T. Feder, and T. Henzinger. The benefits of relaxing punctuality. *Journal of the ACM*, 43(1):116–146, 1996.
4. R. Alur, L. Fix, and T. Henzinger. Event-clock automata: a determinizable class of timed automata. *Theoretical Computer Science*, 211:253–273, 1999. A preliminary version appears in *Proc. CAV'94*, LNCS 818, pp. 1–13.
5. R. Alur and T. Henzinger. Back to the future: Towards a theory of timed regular languages. In *Proceedings of the 33rd IEEE Symposium on Foundations of Computer Science*, pages 177–186, 1992.
6. R. Alur and R. Kurshan. Timing analysis in COSPAN. In *Hybrid Systems III: Control and Verification*, LNCS 1066, pages 220–231. Springer-Verlag, 1996.
7. R. Alur, S. La Torre, and G. Pappas. Optimal paths in weighted timed automata. In *Hybrid Systems: Computation and Control, Fourth International Workshop*, LNCS 2034, pages 49–62, 2001.
8. G. Behrman, T. Hune, A. Fehnker, K. Larsen, P. Petersson, J. Romijn, and F. Vaandrager. Minimum-cost reachability for priced timed automata. In *Hybrid Systems: Computation and Control, Fourth International Workshop*, LNCS 2034, pages 147–161, 2001.

9. B. Bérard and C. Dufourd. Timed automata and additive clock constraints. *Information Processing Letters*, 75(1–2):1–7, 2000.
10. B. Berard, P. Gastin, and A. Petit. On the power of non-obervable actions in timed automata. In *Proceedings of the 13th Annual Symposium on Theoretical Aspects of Computer Science*, LNCS 1046, pages 257–268, 1996.
11. P. Bouyer. Forward analysis of updatable timed automata. *Formal Methods in System Design*, 24(3):281–320, 2004.
12. P. Bouyer, E. Brinksma, and K. Larsen. Staying alive as cheaply as possible. In *Proc. 7th Int. Workshop on Hybrid Systems: Computation and Control (HSCC 2004)*, LNCS 2993, pages 203–218. Springer, 2004.
13. P. Bouyer, C. Dufourd, E. Fleury, and A. Petit. Are timed automata updatable? In *Computer Aided Verification, 14th International Conference*, LNCS 2404, pages 464–479, 2000.
14. F. Cassez, T. Henzinger, and J. Raskin. A comparison of control problems for timed and hybrid systems. In *Hybrid Systems: Computation and Control, Fifth International Workshop*, LNCS 2289, pages 134–148, 2002.
15. C. Courcoubetis and M. Yannakakis. Minimum and maximum delay problems in real-time systems. In *Proceedings of the Third Workshop on Computer-Aided Verification*, LNCS 575, pages 399–409. Springer-Verlag, 1991.
16. C. Daws, A. Olivero, S. Tripakis, and S. Yovine. The tool KRONOS. In *Hybrid Systems III: Verification and Control*, LNCS 1066, pages 208–219. Springer-Verlag, 1996.
17. M. De Wulf, L. Doyen, N. Markey, and J. Raskin. Robustness and implementability of timed automata. In *Proc. FORMATS*, 2004.
18. D. D'Souza. A logical characterisation of event recording automata. In *Proc. 6th Int. Symp. on Formal Techniques in Real-Time and Fault-Tolerant Systems (FTRTFT'00)*, LNCS 1926, pages 240–251. Springer, 2000.
19. D. D'Souza and P. Madhusudan. Timed control synthesis for external specifications. In *Proceedings of the 19th Symposium on Theoretical Aspects of Computer Science*, LNCS 2285, pages 571–582. Springer, 2002.
20. V. Gupta, T. Henzinger, and R. Jagadeesan. Robust timed automata. In *Hybrid and Real Time Systems: International Workshop (HART'97)*, LNCS 1201, pages 48–62. Springer, 1997.
21. T. Henzinger, P. Kopke, A. Puri, and P. Varaiya. What's decidable about hybrid automata. *Journal of Computer and System Sciences*, 57:94–124, 1998.
22. T. Henzinger, Z. Manna, and A. Pnueli. What good are digital clocks? In *ICALP 92: Automata, Languages, and Programming*, LNCS 623, pages 545–558. Springer-Verlag, 1992.
23. T. Henzinger, X. Nicollin, J. Sifakis, and S. Yovine. Symbolic model-checking for real-time systems. *Information and Computation*, 111(2):193–244, 1994.
24. T. Henzinger and J. Raskin. Robust undecidability of timed and hybrid systems. In *Hybrid Systems: Computation and Control, Third International Workshop*, LNCS 1790, pages 145–159, 2000.
25. T. Henzinger, J. Raskin, and P. Schobbens. The regular real-time languages. In *ICALP'98: Automata, Languages, and Programming*, LNCS 1443, pages 580–593. 1998.
26. P. Herrmann. Timed automata and recognizability. *Information Processing Letters*, 65(6):313–318, 1998.
27. S. La Torre, S. Mukhopadhyay, and R. Alur. Subclasses of timed automata with NP-complete reachability problem. Technical report, 2003. Unpublished.

28. F. Laroussinie, N. Markey, and P. Schnoebelen. Model checking timed automata with one or two clocks. In *Proceedings of the 15th International Conference on Concurrency Theory (CONCUR 2004)*. Springer, 2004.
29. K. Larsen, P. Pettersson, and W. Yi. UPPAAL in a nutshell. *Springer International Journal of Software Tools for Technology Transfer*, 1, 1997.
30. J. Miller. Decidability and complexity results for timed automata and semi-linear hybrid automata. In *Proceedings of the Third International Workshop on Hybrid Systems: Computation and Control (HSCC 2000)*, LNCS 1790, pages 296–309. Springer, 2000.
31. J. Ouaknine and J. Worrell. Revisiting digitization, robustness, and decidability for timed automata. In *Proceedings of the 18th IEEE Symposium on Logic in Computer Science*, 2003.
32. J. Ouaknine and J. Worrell. On the language inclusion problem for timed automata: Closing a decidability gap. In *Proceedings of the 19th IEEE Symposium on Logic in Computer Science*, 2004.
33. A. Puri. Dynamical properties of timed automata. In *Proceedings of the 5th International Symposium on Formal Techniques in Real Time and Fault Tolerant Systems*, LNCS 1486, pages 210–227, 1998.
34. J. Raskin and P. Schobbens. The logic of event clocks – decidability, complexity, and expressiveness. *Journal of Automata, Languages, and Combinatorics*, 4(3):247–286, 1999.
35. S. Tripakis. Folk theorems on determinization and minimization of timed automata. In *Proc. FORMATS*, 2003.
36. F. Wang. Efficient data structures for fully symbolic verification of real-time software systems. In *TACAS '00: Sixth International Conference on Tools and Algorithms for the Construction and Analysis of Software*, LNCS 1785, pages 157–171, 2000.

Timed Petri Nets:
Efficiency of Asynchronous Systems

Elmar Bihler and Walter Vogler

Institut für Informatik, Universität Augsburg
vogler@informatik.uni-augsburg.de

Abstract. We shortly discuss how Petri nets have been extended with timing constraints and then choose to associate clocks to tokens and time intervals to arcs from places to transitions. In this model, we present a timed testing approach derived from the testing scenario of De Nicola and Hennessy; timed testing gives rise to an implementation relation that requires an implementation to be at least as satisfactory as the specification regarding functionality and efficiency.
We show that we get the same implementation relation whether we regard time as continuous or as discrete; so we will work with discrete time, which is easier to handle, and nevertheless get results for continuous time, which is presumably more realistic. With our testing approach, we can show that timed refusal traces of a system are exactly the behaviour that can be observed by a user. Interestingly, this can already be observed by asynchronous observers, and this leads naturally to a faster-than relation for asynchronous systems. We close with a discussion of some examples.

1 Introduction

Petri nets are a formal model for concurrent systems with a graph-theoretic notation, which makes them attractive for practitioners. The vertices of a Petri net are *transitions* (representing activities) and *places*, representing local states; places can carry so-called *tokens*, and each distribution of tokens (a *marking*) describes a global system state, which consists of the marked local states. Transitions and places are connected by directed arcs; a transition is enabled under a marking according to the arcs from places to transitions, and the occurrence (or *firing*) of the transition changes the marking according to all its arcs.

Beginning with [MF76,Ram74], clocks and timing constraints have been associated in several ways to the items of a Petri net, and various definitions of timed net behaviour have been given. We give a short discussion of these issues in Section 2, and refer the reader to e.g. [CMS99] for more details and more references. In the area of Petri nets, the approach to efficiency of asynchronous systems that we present here has mostly been studied by associating with each transition a clock that starts running when the transition becomes enabled, and associating a timing constraint to the transition that must be satisfied by the clock value when the transition fires. In this tutorial, we follow [Bih98] to have a more flexible type of timed Petri net: we associate clocks to tokens (or to places,

M. Bernardo and F. Corradini (Eds.): SFM-RT 2004, LNCS 3185, pp. 25–58, 2004.
© Springer-Verlag Berlin Heidelberg 2004

which amounts to the same since we work with so-called safe nets) and intervals with integer bounds to place-transition arcs. The idea is that the token becomes available to the transition at some point in this interval, and the transition fires once all tokens it needs are available. In the larger part of the paper, we deal with general timed systems and not only with asynchronous ones.

To compare the efficiency of concurrent systems, we consider a variation of the classical testing approach of [DNH84]. This approach compares concurrent systems on the basis of their observable behaviour; to formalise this, systems are embedded – with a parallel composition operator $\parallel$ – in test environments that represent observers or users. One variant of testing (must-testing) considers worst-case behaviour: a system N performs successfully in an environment O if *every* run of $N \parallel O$ reaches success, which is signalled by a special action ω. If some system N_1 performs successfully whenever a second system N_2 does, then N_1 shows all the good behaviour described by N_2 and we call it an implementation of the specification N_2; of course, an implementation may be successful in more environments than specified.

The classical approach only takes into account the functionality of systems, i.e. which actions can be performed. To take also into account the efficiency of systems, we add a time bound D to our tests and require that every run reaches success within time D [Vog95]. In the resulting *timed testing* approach, an implementation can not only be successful in more environments than the specification, but also be successful faster; i.e. the implementation (or testing) preorder can serve as a faster-than relation. We introduce timed testing in Section 3, and as a first important result, we generalize a result of [JV01] and show that the implementation preorder does not depend on the time domain, i.e. it is the same for continuous and for discrete time. Therefore, we will work in the following with discrete time, which is easier to handle; at the same time, our results also hold for continuous time, which is presumably more realistic.

A testing scenario models behaviour observation in an intuitive fashion; the implementation relation compares systems on the basis of such observable behaviour. But in order to compare two systems with this relation, we have to consider all possible test environments and all test durations, so it is hard to work with the relation directly. What is needed is a characterization of this relation that only refers to the systems to be compared. Such a characterization is provided in Section 4 with a timed refusal trace semantics: the implementation relation corresponds to refusal trace inclusion. This characterization also allows another result: often, a testing approach gives rise to a precongruence for parallel composition, and also our implementation relation turns out to be one. This means that, if we replace a system component by an implementation, then the resulting system is an implementation of the original system. Such a result is the basis for building up systems from components, and therefore of utmost importance.

Due to our discretization, timed refusal traces can be described by a finite automaton; thus, our results allow to decide the faster-than relation automatically. Our tool FastAsy is described at the end of Section 5.

Considering the timed refusal trace semantics for an easy example, one can see that an implementation in our approach is maybe better described as being *more predictable* than the specification instead of being faster. In fact, Moller and Tofts have argued in their seminal paper [MT91], one cannot expect a relation for general timed systems to have some intuitive properties of a faster-than relation and to be a precongruence. The reason is that replacing a component by a faster one might destroy the coordination based on time, and thus the complete system might fail instead of being faster. Moller and Tofts suggest to restrict attention to asynchronous systems, and this is what we do in Section 5.

Characteristic for asynchronous systems is that they do not have time-outs. Components in asynchronous systems work with indeterminate relative speed, i.e. one component can perform many actions in sequence, while another one performs just one. This is the behaviour of an untimed Petri net: a sequence of transitions can fire, while another transition is enabled all the time but only fires after the sequence. How can we associate time to such unclocked systems in a meaningful way?

If we associate only lower or only upper time bounds to actions, all the characteristics of asynchronous systems are preserved. In [MT91], lower time bounds are studied, but these are not suitable for studying worst case efficiency, which is usually of primary interest: in the worst case, everything takes arbitrarily long. Therefore, we follow [Vog03,Vog02,BV98] and consider upper time bounds. Behaviour of timed Petri nets with only upper time bounds (*at-nets*) is asynchronous: if one transition fires within time d, a long sequence of transitions can quickly fire before time d; more formally, the sequences of transitions that can be performed if we abstract from time steps are the same as those of the net without time.

The characterization result for the implementation relation in Section 4 is based on specific test nets (or standard users). This result is not so difficult if the test nets are arbitrary timed nets; it is interesting (though more involved) that it suffices to consider at-nets as test nets: already asynchronous systems with their limited control of timing can observe all the behaviour timed systems can see. The involved version implies furthermore: if we restrict timed testing to at-nets as systems under observations and as observers, we get the same implementation relation. Intuitively, we study with this relation performance guarantees of systems under the assumption that we such guarantees (namely upper time bounds) for the basic building blocks of our systems, modelled as transitions. In Section 5, we show that we really have a suitable faster-than relation. We give some constructions that should intuitively slow down a system, and they indeed do in our theory. (If such a construction is applicable in reverse, we get a faster system.) As a realistic application, we compare several implementations of a bounded buffer. These implementations are given as Petri nets without explicit timing; for such nets, we take 1 as upper time bound for all transitions as a natural standard choice. Such at-nets are the ones that have been studied in most papers this tutorial is based on.

Section 5 closes with a summary of results regarding solutions to the MUTEX-problem (mutual-exclusion problem) and with a few words about our tool FastAsy; with some specific view, we have derived numerical values to measure the efficiency in our approach, which is a priori qualitative and not quantitative. Interestingly, we have used FastAsy also to prove the correctness of a presumably new solution.

We give a short conclusion in Section 6, pointing out closely related work in process algebra and some open questions.

2   Basic Notions of Timed Petri Nets

We first introduce untimed Petri nets as roughly explained in the introduction; additionally, the transitions are labelled with actions from some infinite alphabet Σ or with the empty word λ. In general, these actions are left uninterpreted; the labelling only indicates that two transitions with the same label from Σ represent the same action occurring in different internal situations, while λ-labelled transitions represent internal, unobservable actions. Σ contains a special action ω, which we will need in our tests to indicate success. For more information on Petri nets, the reader is referred to e.g. [Pet81,Rei85].

A (labelled) *untimed Petri net* $N = (S, T, W, l, M_N)$ (or just an *untimed net* for short) consists of finite disjoint sets S of *places* and T of *transitions*, the *weight function* $W : S \times T \cup T \times S \rightarrow \{0, 1\}$, the *labelling* $l : T \rightarrow \Sigma \cup \{\lambda\}$, and the *initial marking* $M_N : S \rightarrow \{0, 1\}$. Typically, elements of S are denoted by s, s', s_1 etc., elements of T by t, t', t_1 etc. When we introduce an untimed net N or N_1 etc., then we assume that implicitly this introduces its components S, T, W, ... or S_1, T_1, W_1, ... etc., and similar conventions apply later on.

If $W(x, y) = 1$, then (x, y) is called an *arc*; for each $x \in S \cup T$, the *preset* of x is $^\bullet x = \{y \mid W(y, x) = 1\}$ and the *postset* of x is $x^\bullet = \{y \mid W(x, y) = 1\}$.

A *marking* is a function $M : S \rightarrow \mathbb{N}_0$; $M(s)$ is the number of *tokens* on place s. E.g. $^\bullet t$ is sometimes understood as its characteristic function, i.e. as a function $S \rightarrow \{0, 1\}$.

Places are drawn as circles, transitions as boxes and arcs as arrows; cf. Figure 1 and ignore the intervals written there for the time being. Transition labels are inside the boxes, tokens are black dots inside the respective circles. So in Figure 1, e.g. $M_N(nc_2) = 1$, transition t is labelled λ and $^\bullet t = \{p_2, nc_2\}$. We say that t and nc_2 form a *loop*, since they are connected by arcs in both directions. This net represents a token-ring (with just two processes) that solves the MUTEX-problem (mutual exclusion); the transitions on the left represent the first process requesting, entering and leaving the critical section, and analogously the transitions on the right represent the actions of the second process. This token-ring is attributed to Le Lann, so we will call this net LL in the future.

A transition t is *enabled* under a marking M, denoted by $M[t\rangle$, if $^\bullet t \leq M$. If $M[t\rangle$ and $M' = M + t^\bullet - {}^\bullet t$, then we denote this by $M[t\rangle M'$ and say that t can *occur* or *fire* under M yielding the *follower marking* M'. In Figure 1, t is not enabled, while the other λ-transition is; firing it moves the token from p_1 to p_2.

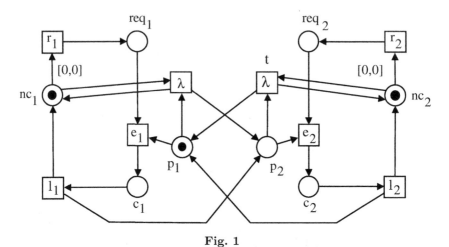

Fig. 1

This definition of enabling and occurrence can inductively be extended to sequences as usual: a sequence w of transitions is *enabled* under a marking M, denoted by $M[w\rangle$, and yields the follower marking M' when *occurring*, denoted by $M[w\rangle M'$, if $w = \lambda$ and $M = M'$ or $w = w't$, $M[w'\rangle M''$ and $M''[t\rangle M'$ for some marking M''. If w is enabled under the initial marking, then it is called a *firing sequence*.

We can extend the labelling of an untimed net to sequences of transitions as usual, i.e. $l(t_1 \ldots t_n) = l(t_1) \ldots l(t_n)$; this automatically deletes all unobservable transitions. Next, we lift the enabledness and firing definitions to the level of actions:

A sequence $v \in \Sigma^*$ is *enabled* under a marking M, denoted by $M[v\rangle\rangle$, if there is some $w \in T^*$ with $M[w\rangle$ and $l(w) = v$; note that there might be several such w. If $M = M_N$, then v is called a *trace*; the *language* $L(N)$ is the set of all traces of N, and *language equivalence* and *language inclusion* are defined accordingly. An enabled action sequence can *occur* yielding the follower marking M', $M[v\rangle\rangle M'$, if $M[w\rangle M'$ and $l(w) = v$ for some $w \in T^*$. Note that M and w determine a unique follower marking M', while M and v might not.

In Figure 1, after firing the λ-transition discussed above, we can fire two transitions on the right and see that $r_2 e_2 \in L(LL)$; then, c_2 is marked with a token, denoting that the second process is in its critical section. The token on p_1 represents the access-token: when the first process enters, it takes this token to c_1; when leaving, it hands the token over to the second process etc. This shows that never both process will be in their critical section at the same time; a more formal argument uses so-called *S-invariants*. When the access-token is on p_2, the second process can either use it and hand it back afterwards or hand it back directly via t; the latter only happens if the second process is not interested, i.e. has not requested access to the critical section and nc_2 is marked. Thus, in some sense each requesting process will eventually enter, so N really solves the MUTEX-problem.

Note that an arbitrary repetition of $r_1e_1l_1$ is a trace of LL; hence, there are numerous respective transition occurrences, while the r_2-transition is enabled at each stage but never fires. This shows that untimed nets model asynchronous systems as discussed in the introduction.

By their graphical nature, Petri nets clearly exhibit the concurrency of actions. Without making this formal here, we can see that e.g. the actions r_1 and r_2 can occur concurrently, since they need separate tokens for being enabled.

For a marking M the set $[M\rangle$ of markings *reachable* from M is defined as $\{M' \mid \exists w \in T^* : M[w\rangle M'\}$. A marking is called *reachable* if it is reachable from M_N. The *reachability graph* of N has the reachable markings as vertices, and a t-labelled arc from M to M' whenever $M[t\rangle M'$. The untimed net is *safe* if $M(s) \leq 1$ for all places s and reachable markings M; e.g. the net in Figure 1 is safe.

General assumption. All untimed nets considered in this paper are safe and without isolated transitions, i.e. ${}^\bullet t \cup t^\bullet \neq \emptyset$ for all transitions t.

We will now add timing information to untimed nets. In the first two papers where this was done, [Ram74] specified a fixed *duration* for each transition, while [MF76] specified an interval for the *delay* of each transition. So we have to make a number of design decisions.

Should our transitions have a duration or a delay? In the first case, an enabled transition starts firing immediately by removing tokens from its preset and delivers tokens to its postset some time later; in the second case, a transition stays enabled for a while and then fires instantaneously – as in the firing rule above. While a duration is maybe more realistic, delays are technically easier to handle and actually more flexible: we can model an activity with duration by two transitions in sequence (via a place), where the first represents the start of the activity and has no delay, while the second represents the end with a delay equal to the duration. Hence, we will specify delays.

As regards fixed numbers versus intervals, the latter are clearly more flexible since a fixed number d corresponds to the interval $[d, d]$. Also, we want to specify upper time bounds in order to add time to asynchronous systems; for this, we will use intervals $[0, d]$.

There is another issue concerning the interpretation of timing constraints: when we specify that a transition t should fire some time $\varepsilon \in [lb, ub]$ after enabling (with lb being the lower and ub the upper bound for the delay), then we usually expect that time will not exceed ub after enabling without t firing (or being disabled). This is sometimes called *strong timing*, in contrast to weak timing or soft time: the latter allows time to go on and simply disables the transition when time ub has passed. The latter is suitable for multimedia systems, where e.g. audio data must accompany video data or be suppressed. We stick with the former, which seems to be applicable more often and fits the idea of upper time bounds for asynchronous systems.

Finally, we have to decide how to add the timing constraints to our mathematical model. In [MF76] (and similarly in our previous papers), for each transition a clock is added, and a state or *instantaneous description* consists of a marking and a clock valuation that gives for each enabled transition the time that has elapsed since enabling. As in [Bih98], we will associate clocks to tokens (or to places) and intervals to place-transition arcs; the next example will show that the former approach can easily be captured with this modelling.

The idea is that a token becomes available to a transition after some delay in the respective interval, and the transition fires once all tokens it needs are available. Consider Figure 2, and assume that t_1 fires 1 time unit and t_2 3 time units after system start, i.e. at *absolute times* 1 and 3. The token produced first becomes available to t_3 between absolute times 1 and 4, the second token between 3 and 6. Clearly, both tokens are available between 3 and 6, i.e. between 0 and 3 time units after arrival of the second token which (time-abstractedly) enabled t_3. This holds generally: when all arcs into transition t have the same interval $[lb, ub]$, then the transition will fire some time $\varepsilon \in [lb, ub]$ after enabling.

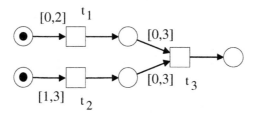

Fig. 2

Thus, instead of attaching $[lb, ub]$ to t as in [MF76], we can equivalently attach $[lb, ub]$ to each arc into t. But we can also specify that a token becomes available to some 'local' transition earlier than to some 'distant' transition. We now come to the formal definitions.

Definition 1. A *timed Petri net* $N = (S, T, W, l, M_N, lb, ub)$ (or just a *net* for short) consists of an untimed net (S, T, W, l, M_N) (satisfying our general assumption above) and two functions $lb, ub : S \times T \to \mathbb{N}_0$ with $lb(s, t) \leq ub(s, t)$ for all $(s, t) \in S \times T$.

A *continuously-timed instantaneous description* (*cid* for short) *CID* of a net N is a pair (M, cv) consisting of a marking M of N and a clock valuation $cv : S \to \mathbb{R}_0^+ \cup \{-\infty\}$ such that $\forall s \in S : cv(s) \geq 0 \Leftrightarrow M(s) = 1$. The *initial cid* is $CID_N = (M_N, cv_N)$, where $cv_N(s)$ is 0 if s is marked and $-\infty$ otherwise. □

We will only refer to $lb(s, t)$ or $ub(s, t)$, if (s, t) is an arc; note that these values are integers. Graphically, an arc is labelled with $[lb(s, t), ub(s, t)]$, where intervals $[0, 1]$ are omitted. Thus, Figure 1 shows a timed net. If N is a net, then e.g. a firing sequence of N is an (untimed) firing sequence of the untimed net N is built upon.

Clocks are associated with tokens or marked places, and they are started when the token is created (or at system start); in a cid, cv shows the current age of each token, while unmarked places get the default value $-\infty$. This implies that M can be derived from cv; still, it seems clearer to mention M explicitly.

Definition 2. We say that transition t is *time-enabled* under cid (M, cv), if $lb(s, t) \leq cv(s)$ for all $s \in {}^\bullet t$ (which implies $M[t\rangle$). For cid's (M, cv) and (M', cv'), we write $(M, cv)[\varepsilon\rangle_c(M', cv')$ if one of the following cases applies:

i) $\varepsilon = t \in T$ is time-enabled, $M[t\rangle M'$, and $\forall s$:

$$
cv'(s) = \begin{cases} -\infty & \text{if } s \in {}^\bullet t \setminus t^\bullet \\ 0 & \text{if } s \in t^\bullet \\ cv(s) & \text{otherwise} \end{cases}
$$

ii) $\varepsilon \in \mathbb{R}_0^+$, $\forall t \exists s : cv(s) + \varepsilon \leq ub(s, t)$ and $\forall s : cv'(s) = cv(s) + \varepsilon$

Extending this definition to sequences as usual, we get the set $CFS(N) = \{w \mid CID_N[w\rangle_c\}$ of *continuous firing sequences* of N; the cid reached by $w \in CFS(N)$ is *c-reachable*, and the set $CL(N) = \{l(w) \mid w \in CFS(N)\}$ is the *continuous language* of N, where we let l preserve *time steps*, i.e. $l((r)) = (r)$ for $r \in \mathbb{R}$.

For every w in $CL(N)$ ($CFS(N)$ resp.), $\alpha(w)$ is the *sequence* of *actions* (*transitions* resp.) in w, and $\zeta(w)$ is the *duration*, i.e. the sum of time steps in w. □

This definition formalizes our intuition from above: if all tokens in ${}^\bullet t$ are available then the age of each must have reached the respective lower bound – and they certainly all become available when the last age reaches the respective upper bound; in the latter case, some firing will occur before time goes on. All c-reachable cid's are consistent in the sense that $\forall t \exists s : cv(s) \leq ub(s, t)$. Note that the clocks for unmarked places are not changed when time goes on. Also note that firing of t resets the clock of place s to 0 if t and s are connected by a loop.

In Figure 2, we indeed get the continuous firing sequences $(1)t_1(2)t_2(r)t_3$ for all $r \in [0, 3]$. Also observe that $t_1 t_4$ is a firing sequence, but that there is no continuous firing sequence containing t_4; in general, the introduction of time restricts the behaviour of a net in this sense, or in other words there is more asynchronous than synchronous behaviour. This is formally stated in the following proposition, which is obvious since the conditions for ordinary firing are part of the conditions for timed firing.

Proposition 3. *If w is a continuous firing sequence of a net N, then $\alpha(w)$ is a firing sequence of N.*

Looking back at Figure 1, the r_1-transition is required to fire immediately; this is sensible, because this net is a scheduler that has to synchronize with the user processes. In particular, r_1 only occurs when both, the first user and the scheduler agree on it. To treat this formally, we introduce parallel composition.

Parallel composition $\|_A$ with synchronization inspired from TCSP. If we combine nets N_1 and N_2 with $\|_A$, then they run in parallel and have to synchronize

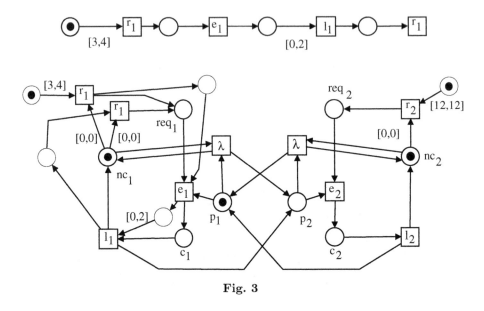

Fig. 3

on actions from A. To construct the composed net, we have to combine each a-labelled transition t_1 of N_1 with each a-labelled transition t_2 from N_2 if $a \in A$. Before giving the formal definition we show an example.

Figure 3 shows in the top part a possible first user U, who is willing to request after 3 to 4 time units, and after entering and leaving wants to request again. Below we show $U \parallel_{\{r_1, e_1, l_1\}} LL$; there is also an additional place on the right, representing the second user who will request after 12 time units – with the effect that we can ignore this user in the following. The two marked places in the top left corner represent the initial state of the first user and the scheduler. These have to agree on r_1, so despite the $[0,0]$-inscription r_1 will not occur before time 3. At this time, the access token might be on p_2, and it might return to p_1 only one time unit later, where it may age for a further time unit. So, r_1 occurs at time 3, the user then waits longer as expected and e_1 occurs at time 5. After l_1 the second r_1 occurs at most 1 time unit later, so this must be a different r_1-transition, representing a different communication.

The purpose of the $[0,0]$-inscription is that the scheduler continuously offers r_1 until it is performed. With a $[0,1]$-inscription instead, the scheduler might delay r_1 by time 1; then, the access-token might circulate and this puts the clock of nc_1 back to 0, giving rise to another delay etc. One can argue that LL (in principle) always offers the suitable action r_1, e_1 or l_1 after some delay and is therefore a correct MUTEX-solution.

[Vog02] shows that untimed ordinary nets cannot solve the MUTEX-problem under the assumption of weak fairness (which is also shown with a different formalization in [KW97]); it suggests to extend nets by so-called read arcs which allows to solve the problem. The timed behaviour of such extended nets, but with all inscriptions being $[0,1]$, is studied and related to fair behaviour.

In the formal definition of parallel composition, $*$ is used as a dummy element, which is formally combined e.g. with those transitions that do not have their label in the synchronization set A. (We assume that $*$ is not a transition or a place of any net.)

Definition 4. Let N_1, N_2 be nets, $A \subseteq \Sigma$. Then the *parallel composition* $N = N_1 \parallel_A N_2$ *with synchronization* over A is defined by

$$S = S_1 \times \{*\} \cup \{*\} \times S_2$$
$$T = \quad \{(t_1, t_2) \mid t_1 \in T_1, t_2 \in T_2, l_1(t_1) = l_2(t_2) \in A\}$$
$$\cup \{(t_1, *) \mid t_1 \in T_1, l_1(t_1) \notin A\}$$
$$\cup \{(*, t_2) \mid t_2 \in T_2, l_2(t_2) \notin A\}$$

$$W((s_1, s_2), (t_1, t_2)) = \begin{cases} W_1(s_1, t_1) & \text{if } s_1 \in S_1, t_1 \in T_1 \\ W_2(s_2, t_2) & \text{if } s_2 \in S_2, t_2 \in T_2 \\ 0 & \text{otherwise} \end{cases}$$

$$W((t_1, t_2), (s_1, s_2)) = \begin{cases} W_1(t_1, s_1) & \text{if } s_1 \in S_1, t_1 \in T_1 \\ W_2(t_2, s_2) & \text{if } s_2 \in S_2, t_2 \in T_2 \\ 0 & \text{otherwise} \end{cases}$$

$$l((t_1, t_2)) = \begin{cases} l_1(t_1) & \text{if } t_1 \in T_1 \\ l_2(t_2) & \text{if } t_2 \in T_2 \end{cases}$$

$$M_N = M_{N_1} \ \dot\cup \ M_{N_2}, \text{ i.e. } M_N((s_1, s_2)) = \begin{cases} M_{N_1}(s_1) & \text{if } s_1 \in S_1 \\ M_{N_2}(s_2) & \text{if } s_2 \in S_2 \end{cases}$$

lb, *ub* are defined on $S \times T$ in the same way as W.   □

Parallel composition is an important operator for the modular construction of nets. In the present paper, the main purpose of this operator is to combine a net N with a test net; this is a user or observer who can signal satisfaction with action ω. We use $\parallel$ to denote $\parallel_{\Sigma - \{\omega\}}$. Designing suitable test nets O and looking at the behaviour of $N \parallel O$, we can get information on the behaviour of N. For the classical approach of testing, see [DNH84].

3   Timed Testing in Continuous and Discrete Time

To see whether a system N performs successfully in a testing environment O even in the worst case, we have to check that in each run of $N \| O$ the success action ω is performed at some given time D at the latest. To be sure that we have seen everything that occurs up to time D, we only look at runs w with $\zeta(w) > D$.

Definition 5. A net is *testable* if none of its transitions is labelled with ω. A *continuously timed test* is a pair (O, D), where O is a net (the *test net*) and $D \in \mathbb{R}_0^+$ (the *test duration*). A testable net N *c-satisfies* a continuously timed test (O, D) ($N \ must_c \ (O, D)$), if each $w \in CL(N \| O)$ with $\zeta(w) > D$ contains some ω. For testable nets N_1 and N_2, we call N_1 a *continuously faster implementation* of N_2, $N_1 \sqsupseteq_c N_2$, if N_1 c-satisfies all continuously timed tests that N_2 c-satisfies.   □

We speak of a *faster* implementation, since the implementation might satisfy more tests and, in particular, some test net within a shorter time. Note that N $must_c$ (O, D) implies N $must_c$ (O, D') for all $D' > D$; hence, if N_1 c-satisfies the same O as N_2 but with a different time D, this must be a shorter time. As announced in the introduction, we will discuss this point again in Section 5.

Since our timed testing approach deals with worst case behaviour, we are only interested in the slowest firing sequences; these sequences will decide the success of a timed test (O, D). It turns out that we can restrict attention to the discretized sublanguage of the continuous language, i.e. those $w \in CL$ that contain only discrete time steps of one unit.

Definition 6. The *discrete firing* rule defines that $(M, cv)[w\rangle(M', cv')$ whenever $(M, cv)[w\rangle_c(M', cv')$ and all time steps r in w satisfy $r \in \mathbb{N}_0$. This gives rise to the *discrete firing sequences* $w \in DFS(N)$ of N (starting at CID_N), and the cid's reached by such w are called *d-reachable*. Clearly, such a cid (M, cv) satisfies $cv(s) \in \mathbb{N}_0 \cup \{-\infty\}$ for all $s \in S$, and we call it an *instantaneous description* or id; CID_N is now denoted by ID_N.

Applying l to the discrete firing sequences we get the *discrete traces*, which form the *discrete language* $DL(N)$ of N. Analogously, $(M, cv)[w\rangle(M', cv')$ and $l(w) = v$ imply $(M, cv)[v\rangle\rangle(M', cv')$.

Analogously to Definition 5 we define *(discretely) timed testing*: a *timed test* is a pair (O, D), where O is a net and $D \in \mathbb{N}_0$. A testable net N *satisfies* such a test (O, D), N *must* (O, D), if each $v \in DL(N\|O)$ with $\zeta(v) > D$ contains some ω, and write $N_1 \sqsupseteq N_2$ if for all (O, D) we have N_2 *must* $(O, D) \Rightarrow N_1$ *must* (O, D); then, N_1 is a *faster implementation* of N_2 or simply *faster*.   □

We now show that for every $w \in CFS$ we can find a $v \in DFS$ that has the same action sequence but is discrete in its time steps and slower: whenever the absolute (or cumulated) time in w exceeds some natural number, we let discrete time pass in v such that the next natural number is reached.

Lemma 7. *For a net N there is for each $w \in CFS(N)$ a $v \in DFS(N)$ such that $\alpha(v) = \alpha(w)$ and $\zeta(v) \geq \zeta(w)$.*

Proof. We will construct for each $w \in CFS(N)$ a suitable $v \in DFS(N)$ such that they and the cid's CID_w and CID_v reached after w and v satisfy the desired and some additional properties, namely:

1. $\alpha(v) = \alpha(w)$ (hence, $M_w = M_v$, shortly denoted by M)
2. $\zeta(v) \geq \zeta(w) > \zeta(v) - 1$
3. $cv_v + \zeta(w) - \zeta(v) \leq cv_w$
4. $cv_w(s) < cv_v(s) + \zeta(w) - \zeta(v) + 1$ for all s marked under M

The proof is by induction on $|w|$, where for $w = \lambda$ we can choose $v = w$. Hence, assume that for $w \in CFS(N)$ we have constructed $v \in DFS(N)$ as required and consider $w' = w\varepsilon \in CFS(N)$. We denote the cid's reached after w' and the corresponding v' by CID'_w and CID'_v.

If $\varepsilon = t \in T$, then we have for each $s \in {}^\bullet t$ that $lb(s,t) \le cv_w(s)$, and by induction and 4. and 2. we get $cv_w(s) < cv_v(s) + \zeta(w) - \zeta(v) + 1 \le cv_v(s) + 1$; since the latter and $lb(s,t)$ are integers, we conclude $lb(s,t) \le cv_v(s)$ and that t is enabled under CID_v. We put $v' = vt$, which immediately gives 1. and 2. For the remaining two items for a given s, we have three cases: s is unmarked under M', so 3. is obvious and 4. does not apply; or $s \notin {}^\bullet t \cup t^\bullet$, so $cv_v(s)$ and $cv_w(s)$ remain unchanged implying that 3. and 4. still hold; or $s \in t^\bullet$, i.e. $cv'_v(s) = cv'_w(s) = 0$, and 3. and 4. follow from 2.

Now let $\varepsilon = r$, and choose $n = \lceil \zeta(w) - \zeta(v) + r \rceil$. To check that $CID_v[n\rangle$, take any transition t; there is some $s \in {}^\bullet t$ with $cv_w(s) + r \le ub(s,t)$. If s is unmarked under M, the same holds for $cv_v(s)$; otherwise, we have by induction (3.) and choice of n that $cv_v(s) + n < cv_v(s) + \zeta(w) - \zeta(v) + r + 1 \le cv_w(s) + r + 1 \le ub(s,t) + 1$ and conclude $cv_v(s) + n \le ub(s,t)$ since these are integers. We put $v' = v(n)$, which immediately implies 1. for w' and v'.

For 2., observe that by choice of n we have $\zeta(v') = \zeta(v) + n \ge \zeta(v) + \zeta(w) - \zeta(v) + r > \zeta(v) + n - 1 = \zeta(v') - 1$ and that the middle term is $\zeta(w)$. For 3., apply induction (3.) to get $cv'_v + \zeta(w') - \zeta(v') = cv_v + n + \zeta(w) + r - \zeta(v) - n \le cv_w + r = cv'_w$. Finally for 4., take an s marked under $M' = M$; apply induction (4.) to get $cv'_w(s) = cv_w(s) + r < cv'_v(s) + \zeta(w') - \zeta(v') + r + 1 = cv'_v(s) + n + \zeta(w') + r - \zeta(v') - n + 1 = cv_v(s) + \zeta(w) - \zeta(v) + 1$. □

A similar result is shown in [Pop91], namely that all the markings that can be reached in continuous time can also be reached in discrete time (in a setting where intervals are attached to transitions. Whereas for us it is important that the continuous firing sequence is transformed to a longer discrete one (the length is rounded up to the next integer), this is of no concern in [Pop91], where the length is rounded down to the previous integer – which would be of no help to us.

Theorem 8. *The relations $\sqsupseteq_c$ and $\sqsupseteq$ coincide.*

Proof. For testable nets N_1 and N_2 we show $N_1 \sqsupseteq_c N_2 \Leftrightarrow N_1 \sqsupseteq N_2$.
"$\Rightarrow$": Assume a timed test (O, D) with $N_1 \not\!must (O, D)$. Since $DL(N_1\|O) \subseteq CL(N_1\|O)$, we have $N_1 \not\!must_c (O, D)$ and by hypothesis $N_2 \not\!must_c (O, D)$. Let $\zeta(w) > D$ for a $w \in CL(N_2\|O)$ that contains no ω. Using Lemma 7, from w we construct a $v \in DL(N_2\|O)$ with $\zeta(v) \ge \zeta(w) > D$ that contains no ω either and conclude $N_2 \not\!must (O, D)$.
"$\Leftarrow$": Assume a continuously timed test (O, D) with $N_1 \not\!must_c (O, D)$. Then there is a $w \in CL(N_1\|O)$ with $\zeta(w) > D$ that contains no ω. Using Lemma 7, we can find a $v \in DL(N_1\|O)$ with $\zeta(v) > D' = \lfloor D \rfloor$ that contains no ω, i.e. $N_1 \not\!must (O, D')$. From $N_1 \sqsupseteq N_2$ we conclude $N_2 \not\!must (O, D')$, i.e. there is a $v' \in DL(N_2\|O)$ with $\zeta(v') \ge D' + 1 > D$ that contains no ω. This v' shows $N_2 \not\!must_c (O, D)$. □

The construction of a *DFS*-sequence from a *CFS*-sequence has made it very obvious that several transitions can occur at the same moment, i.e. without any time passing in between. In particular, a long sequence of events where one event causes the next could occur in zero-time. Some readers might regard this as unrealistic. In contrast, we could require that between any two transitions a positive amount of time has to pass; at least for the setting in [JV01], this would not change the testing preorder, as shown there.

From now on, we will assume that all time steps in a discrete trace are of form 1, which we will write σ: time steps 0 can be omitted, and larger time steps n can be broken up in unit time steps; we might still write n, but regard it as shorthand for n σs. Furthermore, we observe that values $cv(s)$ that exceed $\max\{ub(s,t) \mid t \in s^\bullet\}$ are not relevant; we can assume that whenever $cv(s)$ exceeds this maximum according to the firing rule, it will immediately be replaced by it. This way, a net has only finitely many d-reachable id's: the markings correspond to subsets of S, and for each $s \in S$ $cv(s)$ has one of finitely many values. If we define the *d-reachability graph* of N analogously to the *reachability graph*, this graph will always be finite.

Definition 9. A transition t is *urgent* under an id (M, cv), if $cv(s) \geq ub(s,t)$ for all $s \in {}^\bullet t$. □

With this notion, we can describe the timed behaviour as follows: whenever there is no urgent transition, a time step σ can occur; otherwise, transitions (urgent or not) have to fire until no urgent transition is left. A discrete trace is an ordinary trace subdivided into *rounds* by σ's; cf. Proposition 3.

4   Characterization of the Timed Testing Preorder

The faster-than-relation or testing-preorder $\sqsupseteq$ formalizes observable difference in efficiency; even though the discretization allows us to work with finite d-reachability graphs, $\sqsupseteq$ refers by definition to all possible tests, and one can hardly work with it directly. Therefore, our aim is now to characterize $\sqsupseteq$ internally, i.e. by only looking at the nets themselves that are compared. In the classical case [DNH84], the must-testing preorder can be characterized using failure semantics which contains pairs (w, X) where w is an executable action sequence and X is a set of actions that can be refused by the system in some state reached after w. In a refusal trace this refusal information is also given for intermediate states encountered during execution of an action sequence, [Phi87].

When we discussed the MUTEX-solution LL above, we already came across this idea: it is very important that the scheduler offers certain actions at certain times and does not refuse them. Hence, similar to refusal traces, we replace the σ's in a discrete trace by sets of actions (called refusal sets) which now indicate the time steps. A refusal set contains actions that are not urgent when the time step occurs; these actions are not possible or can at least be delayed, i.e. they can be refused at this moment. Note that our treatment of internal actions is very different from ordinary refusal traces; in particular, all internal actions must be refused, i.e. they must not be urgent when the time step occurs.

The time steps indicated by a refusal set might be impossible if we regard the net on its own; they are just *potential time steps* that occur in an appropriate environment. E.g. LL cannot perform a σ initially, but has to perform the urgent actions r_1 and r_2; in the environment shown in Figure 3, an initial σ is possible. Correspondingly, LL can perform a potential time step, where neither r_1 nor r_2 are refused – but possibly all other actions of LL.

Definition 10. We write $(M, cv)[\varepsilon\rangle_r(M', cv')$ for id's (M, cv) and (M', cv'), if one of the following cases applies:

1. $\varepsilon = t \in T$ and $(M, cv)[t\rangle(M', cv')$ as in Definitions 6 and 2.
2. $\varepsilon = X \subseteq \Sigma$, for each urgent transition t we have $l(t) \notin X \cup \{\lambda\}$, and $cv' = cv + 1$; X is called a *refusal set*.

The corresponding sequences (starting at ID_N) are called *(timed) refusal firing sequences*, their set is denoted by $RFS(N)$, and the id's reached by them are called *r-reachable*. $RT(N) = \{l(w) \mid w \in RFS(N)\}$ is the set of *(timed) refusal traces* where $l(X) = X$. If $ID[w\rangle_r ID'$, we write $ID[l(w)\rangle\rangle_r ID'$.

The definition of refusal firing sequences can be extended to infinite refusal firing sequences in an obvious way. We also extend the definition of α in the obvious way: for every w in $RT(N)$ ($RFS(N)$ resp.), $\alpha(w)$ is the *sequence* of *actions* (*transitions* resp.) in w.   □

The RT-semantics is more detailed than the DL-semantics, since the occurrence of Σ exactly corresponds to that of σ; cf. the last paragraph of the preceding section. Other usual properties for refusal sets also hold in our setting and are not difficult to see: refusal sets are closed under inclusion, and we can always add actions that cannot possibly occur – like actions not occurring in the respective net.

Proposition 11. *For nets N_1 and N_2, $RT(N_1) \subseteq RT(N_2)$ implies $DL(N_1) \subseteq DL(N_2)$. If $vXw \in RT(N_1)$ with $X \subseteq \Sigma$, then $Y \subseteq X$ implies $vYw \in RT(N_1)$ and $Z \cap l(T) = \emptyset$ implies $v(X \cup Z)w \in RT(N_1)$.*

Before we continue our study of testing and the RT-semantics, we have to come back to transitions that are immediately urgent when becoming enabled, so-called zero-transitions. We have seen that a zero-transition labelled with an observable action might still delay in a composition (cf. the r_1-transition of LL). This is not so for internal transitions, and this can create the following problem: if we can fire an infinite sequence of internal zero-transitions, then not even a partial time-step is possible at any id reached along this sequence. We regard a net that allows this sort of behaviour as inconsistent, and we will exclude such nets for some results. Vice versa, if we cannot fire such an infinite sequence, we can fire urgent internal transitions as long as there are any; this reaches an id where a partial time-step is possible. Formally:

Definition 12. A transition t of a net N is a *zero-transition* if for all $s \in {}^\bullet t$ $lb(s, t) = ub(s, t) = 0$. An id of N is an *internal timestop* if it enables an infinite sequence of internal zero-transitions. N does not *have internal timestops*, if no r-reachable id is an internal timestop.   □

Lemma 13. *If a net N does not have internal timestops and $w \in RT(N)$, then $w\emptyset \in RT(N)$.*

Thus, if N does not have internal timestops, then time can always go on, which we clearly expect in reality. [Bih98] argues in detail that a net cannot have an internal timestop if it does not have any cycles consisting of internal zero-transitions only.

A touchstone for a behaviour notion is whether it supports compositional reasoning by inducing a congruence or precongruence for some suitable operations. We will show that the RT-semantics induces a precongruence for parallel composition. This result will also be used for the characterization we are aiming at. Furthermore, the characterization does not only show that refusal traces are observable, but also that they give just the right precongruence if we regard discrete traces as a basic behaviour: inclusion of refusal traces will turn out to be the coarsest precongruence for parallel composition refining discrete-language inclusion.

To show the precongruence result, we define $\|_A$ for refusal traces. Applying this operation, actions from A are merged, while others are interleaved. Furthermore, a combined transition (t_1, t_2) of some $N_1 \|_A N_2$ is enabled, if t_1 is enabled in N_1 and t_2 is enabled in N_2, and analogously (t_1, t_2) is urgent if t_1 and t_2 are urgent; essentially due to this similarity between enabledness and urgency, refusal sets are combined as in ordinary failure semantics.

Definition 14. Let $u, v \in (\Sigma \cup \mathcal{P}(\Sigma))^*$, $A \subseteq \Sigma$. Then $u \|_A v$ is the set of all $w \in (\Sigma \cup \mathcal{P}(\Sigma))^*$ such that for some n we have $u = u_1 \ldots u_n$, $v = v_1 \ldots v_n$, $w = w_1 \ldots w_n$ and for $i = 1, \ldots, n$ one of the following cases applies:

1. $u_i = v_i = w_i \in A$
2. $u_i = w_i \in (\Sigma - A)$ and $v_i = \lambda$
3. $v_i = w_i \in (\Sigma - A)$ and $u_i = \lambda$
4. $u_i, v_i, w_i \subseteq \Sigma$ and $w_i \subseteq ((u_i \cup v_i) \cap A) \cup (u_i \cap v_i)$ $\square$

In this definition, λ's are inserted into the decomposition of u and v to describe the interleaving of actions from $\Sigma - A$. An instantaneous description of a composition of nets can obviously be regarded as the (pairwise) disjoint union of instantaneous descriptions of the component nets; cf. the treatment of the initial markings in Definition 4. This is a much easier relation than the one that had to be used e.g. in [JV01]; also, the following technical lemma is easier to see than its variant in e.g. [JV01].

Lemma 15. *Let N_1, N_2 be nets, $A \subseteq \Sigma$, and $N = N_1 \|_A N_2$. Let (M_1, cv_1), (M_2, cv_2) and $(M, cv) = (M_1 \mathbin{\dot{\cup}} M_2, cv_1 \mathbin{\dot{\cup}} cv_2)$ be reachable instantaneous descriptions of N_1, N_2, N, respectively. In the following, we treat $*$ like λ in formulas like $(M_1, cv_1)[*\rangle_r$.*

1. If $(M, cv)[\varepsilon\rangle_r$ in N according to Definition 10.1 or 10.2, then there are ε_1, ε_2 such that $(M_1, cv_1)[\varepsilon_1\rangle_r$ in N_1, $(M_2, cv_2)[\varepsilon_2\rangle_r$ in N_2 and one of the following cases applies:
   (a) $\varepsilon = (t_1, t_2) \in T$, $\varepsilon_1 = t_1$ and $\varepsilon_2 = t_2$
   (b) $\varepsilon = X$, $\varepsilon_1 = X_1$, $\varepsilon_2 = X_2$ and $X \subseteq ((X_1 \cup X_2) \cap A) \cup (X_1 \cap X_2)$
2. Let $(M_1, cv_1)[\varepsilon_1\rangle_r$ and $(M_2, cv_2)[\varepsilon_2\rangle_r$ according to Definition 10.1 or 10.2 or with $\varepsilon_1 = *$ or $\varepsilon_2 = *$.
   (a) If $\varepsilon_1 = t_1$ and $\varepsilon_2 = t_2$ with $(t_1, t_2) \in T$, then $(M, cv)[\varepsilon\rangle_r$ for $\varepsilon = (t_1, t_2)$.
   (b) If $\varepsilon_1 = X_1$ and $\varepsilon_2 = X_2$, then $(M, cv)[\varepsilon\rangle_r$ for all $\varepsilon = X$ with $X \subseteq ((X_1 \cup X_2) \cap A) \cup (X_1 \cap X_2)$

Furthermore we have for each of these subcases: if $(M, cv)[\varepsilon\rangle_r (M', cv')$ as well as $(M_1, cv_1)[\varepsilon_1\rangle_r(M_1', cv_1')$ and $(M_2, cv_2)[\varepsilon_2\rangle_r(M_2', cv_2')$ for the respective ε, ε_1 and ε_2, then $(M', cv') = (M_1' \cup M_2', cv_1' \cup cv_2')$.

This lemma implies in the usual fashion the first part of the following theorem, which immediately implies that RT-inclusion is a precongruence (second part) and also gives us one half of the characterization result in the theorem after.

Theorem 16. For nets N, N_1 and N_2 and $A \subseteq \Sigma$ we have

$$RT(N_1 \|_A N_2) = \bigcup \{u \|_A v \mid u \in RT(N_1), v \in RT(N_2)\}.$$

If $RT(N_1) \subseteq RT(N_2)$, then $RT(N_1 \|_A N) \subseteq RT(N_2 \|_A N)$.

Theorem 17. Let N_1 and N_2 be testable nets without internal timestops. Then $N_1 \sqsupseteq N_2$ if and only if $RT(N_1) \subseteq RT(N_2)$.

Proof. "if": Let (O, D) be a timed test. By Theorem 16 and Proposition 11, $RT(N_1) \subseteq RT(N_2)$ implies $DL(N_1 \| O) \subseteq DL(N_2 \| O)$. Thus, if N_1 fails the test due to some $w \in DL(N_1 \| O)$, then so does N_2.

"only if": In this proof upper indices are used; e.g. a_1^2 is an item with two indices in the following and *not* the string $a_1 a_1$. We assume $N_1 \sqsupseteq N_2$ and take some $w = a_1^1 \ldots a_{n_1}^1 X^1 \ldots a_1^k \ldots a_{n_k}^k X^k \in RT(N_1)$, where $k, n_i \in \mathbb{N}_0$. (All refusal traces of N_1 can be extended to end with a set according to Lemma 13, hence it is enough to consider traces of this form.) We may assume that $X^j \subseteq l_1(T_1) \cup l_2(T_2)$, i.e. X^j is finite $(j = 1, \ldots, k)$, since any $RT(N)$ is closed under addition and removal of actions that do not appear in N at all to resp. from the refusal sets, see Proposition 11. We construct a test (O, D) that a net fails if and only if it has w as refusal trace. Then N_1 fails (O, D), hence N_2 does and we are done. We choose $D = k$ and define O as follows; see Figure 4 for the case $w = ab\{x\}a\{y\}$.

$$S_O = \{s_i^j \mid j = 1, \ldots, k+1; i = 0, 1, 2\} \cup \{s_1^{k+2}\}$$
$$\cup \{s_{ai}^j \mid j = 1, \ldots, k; i = 1, \ldots, n_j + 1\}$$
$$\cup \{s_{rx}^j \mid j = 1, \ldots, k; x \in X^j\}$$
$$T_O = \{t_i^j \mid j = 1, \ldots, k+1; i = 0, 1, 2\} \cup \{t_1^{k+2}\}$$
$$\cup \{t_{ai}^j \mid j = 1, \ldots, k; i = 1, \ldots, n_j\}$$
$$\cup \{t_{rx}^j \mid j = 1, \ldots, k; x \in X^j\}$$

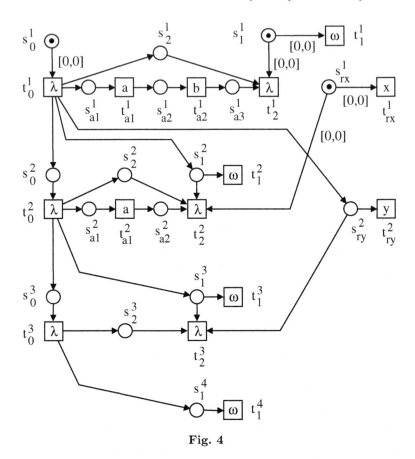

Fig. 4

O has arcs for the following pairs:

$(s_0^j, t_0^j), j = 1, \ldots, k+1;$
$(t_0^j, s_0^{j+1}), j = 1, \ldots, k;$
$(t_0^j, s_1^{j+1}), j = 1, \ldots, k+1;$
$(t_0^j, s_2^j), j = 1, \ldots, k+1;$
$(s_2^j, t_2^j), j = 1, \ldots, k+1;$
$(s_1^j, t_1^j), j = 1, \ldots, k+2;$
$(s_1^j, t_2^j), j = 1, \ldots, k+1;$

$(t_0^j, s_{a1}^j), j = 1, \ldots, k;$
$(s_{ai}^j, t_{ai}^j), j = 1, \ldots, k, i = 1, \ldots, n_j;$
$(t_{ai}^j, s_{a(i+1)}^j), j = 1, \ldots, k, i = 1, \ldots, n_j;$
$(s_{a(n_j+1)}^j, t_2^j), j = 1, \ldots, k;$

$(t_0^j, s_{rx}^{j+1}), j = 1, \ldots, k-1, x \in X^{j+1};$
$(s_{rx}^j, t_{rx}^j), j = 1, \ldots, k, x \in X^j;$
$(s_{rx}^j, t_2^{j+1}), j = 1, \ldots, k, x \in X^j.$

Initially, the places s_0^1, s_1^1 and s_{rx}^1 with $x \in X^1$ are marked. For the arcs (s,t) outgoing from these places, we have $[lb(s,t), ub(s,t)] = [0,0]$, for all other arcs (s,t) outgoing from some place s, we have $[lb(s,t), ub(s,t)] = [0,1]$. The labelling is as follows:

$$l_O(t_0^j) = l_O(t_2^j) = \lambda, \; j = 1, \ldots, k+1;$$
$$l_O(t_1^j) = \omega, \; j = 1, \ldots, k+2;$$
$$l_O(t_{ai}^j) = a_i^j, \; j = 1, \ldots, k; \; i = 1, \ldots, n_j;$$
$$l_O(t_{rx}^j) = x, \; j = 1, \ldots, k; \; x \in X^j.$$

The subnet consisting of the s_i^j, t_i^j with $i = 0, 1, 2$ for $j = 1, \ldots, k+1$ and s_1^{k+2}, t_1^{k+2} acts as a clock. It ends with an ω-transition (t_1^{k+2}), and in order to fail the test, the clock must proceed as slowly as possible but still respect the firing discipline, i.e it must work with a fixed speed. Assume some N fails the test for $D = k$, i.e. $k+1$ rounds with $k+1$ σ's occur in $N \parallel O$.

We now describe how such a failing discrete trace must look like. First, consider the sequence of the s_0^j, t_0^j with $j = 1, \ldots, k+1$ finished by s_1^{k+2}, t_1^{k+2}. Before the $(k+1)$-th σ occurs, t_1^{k+2} must not be urgent, i.e. t_0^{k+1} must fire after the k-th σ. Inductively, we see for $j = k+1$ down to 2 that t_0^j must fire after the $(j-1)$-th σ. As t_0^1 is initially urgent, it must fire before the first σ. Inductively, t_0^j must fire before the j-th σ. Altogether, t_0^j must fire in the j-th round.

As a result, t_1^j is urgent in the j-th round, for $j = 1, \ldots, k+1$, and must be deactivated by t_2^j; since s_2^j is only marked in the j-th round, t_2^j fires in the j-th round.

The t_{ai}^j are sequenced in between t_0^j and t_2^j, and by the above argument, they all must fire in zero time in the j-th round. By the synchronization discipline, N must be able to perform $a_1^j \ldots a_{n_j}^j$ in round j.

The occurrence of some t_{rx}^j would make t_2^{j+1} impossible; hence, t_{rx}^j does not fire but is urgent in round j because s_{rx}^j (for $j > 1$) was marked one round before. We conclude that N must not offer an urgent x (or have an urgent internal transition) at the end of round j, i.e. it can refuse X^j at this stage.

In other words, as desired, N must perform w to fail the test (O, k), and it will indeed fail the test if it performs w.   □

Observe that a faster system has less refusal traces, i.e. such a trace is a witness for slow behaviour, it is something 'bad' due to the refusal information it contains. Also observe that, for Theorem 17, we only need test nets without internal timestops. It will become important in the next section, that all lower bounds in our test nets are 0.

Above, we have already announced the following corollary and also explained its intuitive importance: it is a way to state that our RT-semantics is just right.

Corollary 18. *Inclusion of RT-semantics (i.e. $\sqsupseteq$) is fully abstract w.r.t. DL-inclusion and parallel composition for nets without internal timestops, i.e. it is the coarsest precongruence for parallel composition that respects DL-inclusion.*

Proof. follows from Proposition 11, Theorem 16 and Theorem 17. Theorem 16 and Proposition 11 show that RT-inclusion is a precongruence that respects discrete-language inclusion. If $RT(N_1) \not\sqsubseteq RT(N_2)$, then the proof of Theorem 17 exhibits a test net O without internal timestops such that $DL(N_1\|O) \not\sqsubseteq DL(N_2\|O)$. (If N_1 or N_2 contain the special action ω, then its rôle in O must be played by some other action a not occurring in N_1 or N_2; in this case, consider $DL(N_i\|_{\Sigma-\{a\}}O)$.)   □

The testing preorder $\sqsupseteq$ is also compatible with some other interesting operations for the construction of nets as system models, namely relabelling, hiding and restriction; see [Vog02].

As at the end of Section 3, we can introduce the *r-reachability graph*; again, bounding the clock values we only have finitely many r-reachable id's – also due to time being discrete. The only small problem is that the refusal sets X can be arbitrarily large; but when comparing N_1 and N_2 it is obviously sufficient to draw these sets from the finite set $l_1(T_1) \cup l_2(T_2)$; compare Proposition 11 and the respective argument in the above proof. Hence, when comparing N_1 and N_2 we can take their r-reachability graphs to be finite automata: Theorem 17 reduces $\sqsupseteq$ to an inclusion of regular languages.

Thus, $\sqsupseteq$ is in particular decidable, which is not obvious from the start, where we have an infinite (even uncountable) state space according to Definitions 1 and 2. In the literature, similar results exist that reduce an infinite state space arising from the use of dense time to a finite one, starting with [AD94]; but it seems that these results are not applicable to our setting.

Based on the decidability result, we have developed the tool FastAsy to check the faster-than relation. We come back to FastAsy at the end of the next section.

5   Application of the Timed Testing Preorder for Asynchronous Systems

We start with a well-known technique to prove language-inclusion, that we can use for checking our faster-than relation; this technique is particularly useful when we want to compare infinite families of systems, where we need symbolic proofs instead of a tool that explores the complete state space. We will use this technique in this section.

Definition 19. For nets N_1 and N_2, a relation $\mathcal{S}$ between some id's of N_1 and some of N_2 is a *(forward) simulation* from N_1 to N_2 if the following hold:

1. $(ID_{N_1}, ID_{N_2}) \in \mathcal{S}$
2. If $(ID_1, ID_2) \in \mathcal{S}$ and $ID_1[t\rangle_r ID_1'$ or $ID_1[X\rangle_r ID_1'$, then for some ID_2' with $(ID_1', ID_2') \in \mathcal{S}$ we have $ID_2[l_1(t)\rangle\rangle_r ID_2'$ or $ID_2[X\rangle\rangle_r ID_2'$. Observe that these moves from ID_2 to ID_2' may involve several transitions.

The following theorem is straightforward; compare e.g. [LV95] for a similar result and a survey on the use of simulations; note that a simulation does not have to exist in each case where $N_1 \sqsupseteq N_2$.

Theorem 20. *If there exists a simulation from N_1 to N_2, then $N_1 \sqsupseteq N_2$.*

It is clear that this result also holds, when we do not start N_1 and N_2 in their standard initial id's derived from their initial markings, but instead in arbitrary id's ID^1 of N_1 and ID^2 of N_2; we only have to replace $(ID_{N_1}, ID_{N_2}) \in \mathcal{S}$ in the definition above by $(ID^1, ID^2) \in \mathcal{S}$. The respective variant of Theorem 20 then tells us that, whenever $ID^1[v\rangle\rangle_r$, it also holds that $ID^2[v\rangle\rangle_r$.

Now consider the net N_1 in Figure 5; in the lower part of the figure, we have indicated its r-reachability graph, where we only give the maximal refusal sets – recall that refusal sets are closed under inclusion as stated in Proposition 11. Now consider N_2 for various values of n and m; it should be clear that the r-reachability graph will look very similar to the one of N_1 in every case. E.g. for $[n, m] = [2, 3]$, N_2 is strictly faster than N_1: it does not have any additional refusal traces, and it does not have Σa or $\Sigma\Sigma\Sigma$ as refusal trace. This is maybe slightly surprising, since the lower bound n is larger than 1 as in N_1; but we can accept this easily since our approach is focussed on the worst case complexity and the upper bound m is less than 4.

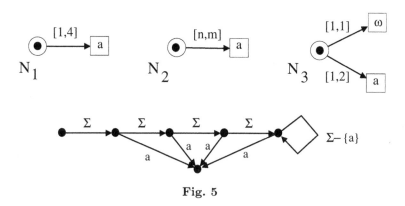

Fig. 5

Things become harder to accept when we consider $[n, m] = [2, 4]$: again, N_2 is strictly faster than N_1 – it does not have Σa as refusal trace. For intuition, we have to imagine a system with N_1 as a component; the additional behaviour Σa of N_1 can lead to additional behaviour in another component, which in turn can bring down the worst-case efficiency. As a concrete example, $N_2 \| N_3$ will certainly perform ω at time 1, while $N_1 \| N_3$ might also perform a at time 1 and completely fail to ever perform ω.

The other side of the same coin is, that N_2 for $[n, m] = [0, 2]$ is not faster than N_1 in contrast to what one might expect: it has the additional refusal trace a. As a consequence, one might find the expression 'more predictable than' preferable to 'faster than'. In fact, a testing scenario (for a process algebra) is developed in [NC96b] where to a system N and a test O a predictability measure is associated: it is the difference between the worst-case and the best-case time for reaching success in $N \| O$. Then, system N_1 is more predictable than system

N_2 if, for each test O, the predictability measure of N_1 and O is at most the predictability measure of N_2 and O. Roughly speaking, this relation turns out to be the same as our faster-than relation.

But these qualms are only related to differences in the lower bound, and they vanish when we only consider nets where all lower bounds are 0, which we will do now.

Our approach of [Vog03,JV01,Vog02,BV98] aimed at comparing the efficiency of asynchronous systems; as already argued in the introduction, adding just upper time bounds leaves the system with its full functionality: timing is just added for measuring efficiency, it does not restrict the occurrence of actions. Also in the area of distributed algorithms, upper time bounds are added to asynchronous systems for efficiency considerations, see e.g. [Lyn96]; there, one measures the time a system needs to obtain a desired result, whereas in our testing approach we consider reactive systems that repeatedly interact with their environment.

Definition 21. A net is called an *asynchronously timed* or *at-net* if lb is constantly 0. □

Thus, we view asynchronous systems as a subclass of general timed systems. Therefore, it is e.g. absolutely obvious that inclusion of RT-semantics is also a precongruence for at-nets. But in principle, the timed testing preorder could change when we restrict ourselves to a subclass, because we then also have fewer test environments. Here it becomes important that the test nets we used in the proof of Theorem 17 were in fact at-nets. Because of this feature, the timed testing preorder does not change when working in the class of at-nets, and Theorem 17 and Corollary 18 carry over to this class.

It would have been significantly easier to prove Theorem 17 using test nets that are not at-nets; these nets could check for refusal sets by offering the respective actions for just one moment in time. On the one hand, this is actually not very realistic; on the other hand, we regard the proof with only at-nets as quite some achievement: it shows that these nets, which intuitively speaking have so little control over time, already can observe all the timed behaviour that synchronous systems can see.

Before we show some results demonstrating that we really have developed a sensible faster-than relation, we will prove for the approach of this tutorial that indeed with only upper time bounds timing is intuitively speaking orthogonal to functionality, i.e. that at-nets are really asynchronous systems.

Proposition 22. *Let N be an at-net.*

1. *For an id (M, cv) of N, $(M, cv)[t\rangle$ if and only if $M[t\rangle$.*
2. *Let $v \in RT(N)$ and let v' be obtained from v by removing some refusal sets. Then $v' \in RT(N)$.*

Proof. 1. By definition, $(M, cv)[t\rangle$ iff $lb(s, t) \leq cv(s)$ for all $s \in {}^\bullet t$; since $lb(s, t) = 0$ and by definition of an id, this is equivalent to $1 \leq M(s)$ for all $s \in {}^\bullet t$, i.e. to $M[t\rangle$.

2. It suffices to consider $v = wXw'$ and $v' = ww'$. Let (M, cv) be the id that is reached by w and enables X, thus $(M, cv)[X\rangle_r(M, cv + 1)$. We have $(M, cv + 1)[w'\rangle\rangle_r$ and want to prove $(M, cv)[w'\rangle\rangle_r$. According to Theorem 20 and the consideration thereafter, this is achieved when we find a simulation that relates N with initial id $(M, cv + 1)$ to N with initial id (M, cv).

Consider the relation $\{((M_1, cv_1), (M_1, cv_2) \mid cv_1 \geq cv_2\}$ on id's of N; we check that it satisfies 19.2: The case of a transition firing follows from Part 1, since both id's have the same marking and the clock valuations are changed to the same value for $s \in {}^\bullet t \cup t^\bullet$ and stay unchanged otherwise. If a transition is urgent under the smaller clock valuation cv_2, it is certainly urgent under cv_1 as well; hence, $(M_1, cv_1)[Y\rangle_r(M_1, cv_1 + 1)$ implies $(M_1, cv_2)[Y\rangle_r$ and $(M_1, cv_2)[Y\rangle_r(M_1, cv_2 + 1)$, and clearly $(M_1, cv_1 + 1), (M_1, cv_2 + 1)$ is in the relation again. $\square$

From this proposition, we can derive the announced result that at-nets cover the full functionality of the respective underlying untimed net.

Corollary 23. *For an at-net N, $L(N) = \alpha(RT(N))$, where α is extended to sets pointwise.*

Proof. Inclusion follows, since by 22.1 each firing sequence of N is also a refusal firing sequence. Inverse inclusion is implied by 22.2; also compare 3. $\square$

Now we consider two modifications of at-nets, where in both cases we have a clear intuition how the modification influences efficiency. We show that our theory agrees with this intuition, which increases the plausibility of our approach.

Definition 24. *A speed-up modification of an at-net N is obtained by decreasing some value $ub(s, t)$ for an arc (s, t).* $\square$

Theorem 25. *If a net N_2 is a speed-up modification of an at-net N_1, then $N_2 \sqsupseteq N_1$*

Proof. Consider the identity relation on the id's of N_1; it satisfies Definition 19.1, and the case of a transition in Part 2 is treated as in the proof of Proposition 22.2. If a transition t is urgent in N_1, $cv(s)$ is at least as large as $ub_N(s, t)$, which is at least as large as $ub_{N'}(s, t)$; hence, the transition is also urgent in N_2. Therefore, if a refusal set X occurs in N_2, it can also occur in N_1 – and it changes the clock valuation in the same way in both nets. $\square$

Considering variations of N_1 in Figure 5 should make clear that in many cases a speed-up modification will be even strictly faster. The next modification changes a net by disallowing the concurrent firing of two transitions; after the change, when firing one of the transitions, the other may always delay one time unit afterwards.

Definition 26. *A sequentialization of an at-net N is obtained by adding a new marked place s and connecting it to two transitions by loops, where the respective arcs are labelled $[0, 1]$. (Generalization to arbitrary $[0, m]$ is possible.)* $\square$

Theorem 27. *If a net N_2 is a sequentialization of an at-net N_1, then $N_1 \sqsupseteq N_2$.*

Proof. Consider the relation where the first id coincides with the second, if we ignore the new place and its clock value in the latter. This relates the initial id's of N_1 and N_2. If a transition can fire in N_1, it can also fire in N_2 where the new place is always marked; so the treatment of this case is as above. If a transition t is urgent in N_2, then $cv(s)$ is at least as large as $ub(s,t)$ for all places s of N_2 which comprise the places of N_1; hence, transition t is also urgent in N_1. Thus, also the treatment of refusal sets is as above. $\square$

If we add a marked loop place for a zero-transition, this can already slow down the net; consider N_1 in Figure 6, which would not have the refusal trace Σa without the loop place. If we add a marked loop place for a transition that is not a zero-transition, then the resulting net is RT-equivalent, as one can show. If we sequentialize two such transitions, the resulting net can be strictly slower: N_2 in Figure 6 is strictly faster than N_3 due to $\Sigma a \Sigma b \in RT(N_3)$.

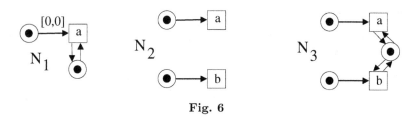

Fig. 6

[JV01] also considers two other operations on nets, which add an internal initialisation transition or make a transition last longer by splitting it in two; both operations are shown to slow a system down.

As a realistic application of our theory, we will now compare three implementations of a bounded buffer with respect to $\sqsupseteq$; this example has also been discussed in [AKH92]. The first implementation *PIPE* is the usual sequence of buffers of capacity 1; the other two, *BUFFC* and *BUFFD*, use a buffer controller and an array as a circular queue to store the items. These two implementations differ only in a small detail making the buffer controller centralized in the first case and distributed (between input and output) in the second. Both variants are mentioned in [AKH92], but only *BUFFC* is studied and shown to be faster than *PIPE*; and indeed, *BUFFC* and *BUFFD* are equivalent with respect to the efficiency preorder of [AKH92]. This is a consequence of the interleaving approach taken in [AKH92], which ignores that actions can be performed in parallel – which should take less time than performance one after the other.

One would expect that in reality *BUFFD* – being more distributed – is faster than *BUFFC*; also, an item should in the worst case take a long time to move through *PIPE*, so one might expect both *BUFF*-variants to be faster than *PIPE*. In our approach, it turns out that indeed *BUFFD* $\sqsupseteq$ *BUFFC* and *BUFFD* $\sqsupseteq$ *PIPE*, but that – surprisingly – *BUFFC* is not (i.e. not always) faster than *PIPE* (nor the other way round). We will exhibit a refusal trace as a witness of slow behaviour of *BUFFC* that *PIPE* cannot show; it will turn out that this slow behaviour indeed is a realistic possibility. Thus, our theory can help to find out facts about reality one might otherwise overlook.

For the rest of the section, we fix some $n \geq 4$ as capacity of the buffers. For simplicity, we assume that the items to be stored are from the set $\{0,1\}$. We formally define *PIPE*, *BUFFC* and *BUFFD* as at-nets where all arc inscriptions are $[0,1]$. But in the figures, we draw them as some sort of high-level net and hope that the translation will be clear: places are annotated with the type of tokens they store, and V stands for $\{\bullet, 0, 1\}$; arcs without annotation refer to ordinary tokens ($\bullet$), while we always have $x \in \{0,1\}$.

To explain a little the translation from the high-level net in Figure 7 to the at-net defined below, consider e.g. the first high-level place in Figure 7: this is a 'cell' s_1 that stores a token to indicate that the cell is free or stores a value 0 or 1; it corresponds to the three places $(s_1, \bullet)$, $(s_1, 0)$ and $(s_1, 1)$ of the at-net. The first internal high-level transition t_1 in Figure 7 moves a value 0 or 1 from the first to the second cell; it corresponds to the transition $(t_1, 0)$ with incoming arcs from $(s_1, 0)$ and $(s_2, \bullet)$ and to the transition $(t_1, 1)$ with incoming arcs from $(s_1, 1)$ and $(s_2, \bullet)$.

Fig. 7

PIPE: The first implementation, *PIPE*, is shown in Figure 7 and defined as follows:
$S_{PIPE} = \{(s_i, v) \mid i = 1, \ldots, n, \ v \in V\}$
$T_{PIPE} = \{(t_i, x) \mid i = 0, \ldots, n, \ x \in \{0,1\}\}$
We have arcs for the following pairs with $i = 1, \ldots, n, \ x \in \{0,1\}$:

$$((s_i, \bullet), (t_{i-1}, x)), \ ((t_{i-1}, x), (s_i, x)), \ ((s_i, x), (t_i, x)), \ ((t_i, x), (s_i, \bullet))$$

Initially, the places $(s_i, \bullet)$, $i = 1, \ldots, n$, are marked. The transitions (t_0, x) are labelled *inx*, $x \in \{0,1\}$, the transitions (t_n, x) are labelled *outx*, $x \in \{0,1\}$, and all other transitions are internal.

The other two implementations, *BUFFC* and *BUFFD*, use one 'cell' for the recent input, one 'cell' for the next output and $n - 2$ 'cells' indexed from 0 to $n - 3$ for the other items in store. These 'cells' are used as a queue in a circular fashion; in *BUFFD*, *first* gives the index of the next item to be moved to the 'output cell', *last* gives the index of the next free 'cell' in the circular queue. Alternatively, *BUFFC* uses *first* and a 'variable' *length*, which gives the length of the circular queue. For the following, we put $I = \{0, \ldots, n-3\}$ and let $\oplus$ and $\ominus$ denote addition and subtraction modulo $n - 2$.

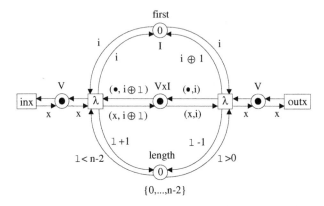

Fig. 8

BUFFC: For the translation of Figure 8 to the following formal description of an at-net, observe e.g. that the middle place represents the array: for each index $i \in I$, we have a cell with value $v \in V$, i.e. this place is translated to the places (s_i, v). Similarly, the variable *length* has value $l \in \{0, \dots, n-2\}$ and corresponds to the places $length_l$. The internal transition on the left is the input controller; it reads the value i of *first*, the value l of *length* and moves the value x from the input cell s to the cell with index $i \oplus l$, provided this is free – which is indicated by a $\bullet$ in this cell; the transition corresponds to the transitions $(t_{i,l}, x)$ in the at-net. On the right, we have the analogous situation for the output controller and the output cell s'. In general, each parameterized place, transition or arc in the formal definition corresponds one-to-one to a place, transition or arc in the figure.

$$
\begin{aligned}
S_{BUFFC} = \;& \{(s,v),\ (s',v) \mid v \in V\} \\
& \cup \{(s_i, v) \mid i \in I,\ v \in V\} \\
& \cup \{first_i \mid i \in I\} \\
& \cup \{length_l \mid l = 0, \dots, n-2\} \\
T_{BUFFC} = \;& \{(t,x),\ (t',x) \mid x = 0,1\} \\
& \cup \{(t_{i,l}, x) \mid i \in I,\ l = 0, \dots, n-3,\ x = 0,1\} \\
& \cup \{(t'_{i,l}, x) \mid i \in I,\ l = 1, \dots, n-2,\ x = 0,1\}
\end{aligned}
$$

We have arcs for the following pairs with $x = 0, 1$ and $i \in I$:

$$
\begin{aligned}
&((s, \bullet), (t,x)),\ ((t,x), (s,x)) \\
&((s,x), (t_{i,l}, x)),\ ((t_{i,l}, x), (s, \bullet)) && \text{with } l = 0, \dots, n-3 \\
&(first_i, (t_{i,l}, x)),\ ((t_{i,l}, x), first_i) && \text{with } l = 0, \dots, n-3 \\
&(length_l, (t_{i,l}, x)),\ ((t_{i,l}, x), length_{l+1}) && \text{with } l = 0, \dots, n-3 \\
&((s_{i \oplus l}, \bullet), (t_{i,l}, x)),\ ((t_{i,l}, x), (s_{i \oplus l}, x)) && \text{with } l = 0, \dots, n-3 \\
&((s', \bullet), (t'_{i,l}, x)),\ ((t'_{i,l}, x), (s', x)) && \text{with } l = 1, \dots, n-2 \\
&(first_i, (t'_{i,l}, x)),\ ((t'_{i,l}, x), first_{i \oplus 1}) && \text{with } l = 1, \dots, n-2 \\
&(length_l, (t'_{i,l}, x)),\ ((t'_{i,l}, x), length_{l-1}) && \text{with } l = 1, \dots, n-2 \\
&((s_i, x), (t'_{i,l}, x)),\ ((t'_{i,l}, x), (s_i, \bullet)) && \text{with } l = 1, \dots, n-2 \\
&((s', x), (t', x)),\ ((t', x), (s', \bullet))
\end{aligned}
$$

Initially, the places $(s, \bullet)$, $(s', \bullet)$, $first_0$, $length_0$ and $(s_i, \bullet)$, $i \in I$, are marked. The transitions (t, x) are labelled inx, $x \in \{0, 1\}$, the transitions (t', x) are labelled $outx$, $x \in \{0, 1\}$, and all other transitions are internal.

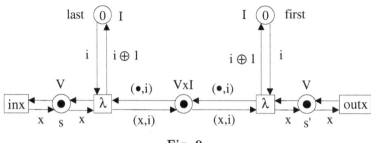

Fig. 9

BUFFD: Figure 9 can be translated similarly as above; here, the input controller accesses the input cell s, one cell of the array and only the variable $last$, and similarly for the output controller, the output cell s' and $first$.

$$S_{BUFFD} = \{(s, v), (s', v) \mid v \in V\}$$
$$\cup \{(s_i, v) \mid i \in I, \, v \in V\}$$
$$\cup \{last_i, first_i \mid i \in I\}$$
$$T_{BUFFD} = \{(t, x), (t', x) \mid x = 0, 1\}$$
$$\cup \{(t_i, x), (t'_i, x) \mid i \in I, \, x = 0, 1\}$$

We have arcs for the following pairs with $x = 0, 1$ and $i \in I$:

$$((s, \bullet), (t, x)), \, ((t, x), (s, x))$$
$$((s, x), (t_i, x)), \, ((t_i, x), (s, \bullet))$$
$$(last_i, (t_i, x)), \, ((t_i, x), last_{i \oplus 1})$$
$$((s_i, \bullet), (t_i, x)), \, ((t_i, x), (s_i, x))$$
$$((s', \bullet), (t'_i, x)), \, ((t'_i, x), (s', x))$$
$$(first_i, (t'_i, x)), \, ((t'_i, x), first_{i \oplus 1})$$
$$((s_i, x), (t'_i, x)), \, ((t'_i, x), (s_i, \bullet))$$
$$((s', x), (t', x)), \, ((t', x), (s', \bullet))$$

Initially, the places $(s, \bullet)$, $(s', \bullet)$, $first_0$, $last_0$ and $(s_i, \bullet)$, $i \in I$, are marked. The transitions (t, x) are labelled inx, $x \in \{0, 1\}$, the transitions (t', x) are labelled $outx$, $x \in \{0, 1\}$, and all other transitions are internal.

E.g. [AKH92]) prefers $BUFFC$ over $BUFFD$, presumably because the variable $length$ helps to distinguish a full queue from an empty one. In $BUFFD$, $last = first$ if and only if the array is completely empty or completely full; observe that $BUFFD$ only works because a token on $(s_i, \bullet)$ indicates that the cell s_i is free.

Comparing the three implementations, we first note that $PIPE$ can be slow when transporting an item from input to output. Formally, since $n \geq 4$, we have $(in0)\emptyset\emptyset\emptyset\{out0\} \in RT(PIPE) \setminus (RT(BUFFC) \cup RT(BUFFD))$ as a witness of slow behaviour: item 0, input in the first round, can still not be delivered in the fourth round in $PIPE$. This only shows that sometimes – i.e. for some behaviour of the environment or user – $PIPE$ is slower than $BUFFC$ and $BUFFD$; it does not show that e.g. $BUFFC$ is always faster.

In $BUFFC$, all internal transitions access 'variable' $last$ and $length$, hence input and output controller block each other. This has the surprising effect that $BUFFC$ is in fact not faster than $PIPE$: we will exhibit a trace $w \in RT(BUFFC) \setminus RT(PIPE)$ as a witness of slow behaviour. It demonstrates that with some user behaviour the blocking leads to a slowdown – not only w.r.t $BUFFD$ but also to $PIPE$.

This trace starts $(in0)\emptyset^{n-1}$; each refusal set $\emptyset$ requires the occurrence of at least one internal transition unless none is enabled; hence, after $(in0)\emptyset^{n-1}$ the first item 0 is in $BUFFC$ stored in cell s', i.e. $(s', 0)$ is marked, and in $PIPE$ in cell s_n. The next part is $(in1)\emptyset^{n-2}$, after which the second item 1 is in $BUFFC$ in the queue in s_0 and in $PIPE$ in s_{n-1}. The third part is $(out0)\emptyset$, i.e. 0 is removed from s', s_n resp. Now, in $PIPE$ item 1 is moved to s_n in the next round and, henceforth, $out1$ is enabled – no matter what else happens; in particular, in $PIPE$ output cannot be blocked by input. But in $BUFFC$, $in0$ might be performed, followed by a transport of 0 to s_1 which blocks the output controller for this round; consequently, 1 is not moved from s_0 to s' in this round due to blocking, and $out1$ may be refused in the next round. Hence, for $BUFFC$ – but not for $PIPE$ – we can continue with $(in0)\emptyset\{out1\}$ giving $w = (in0)\emptyset^{n-1}(in1)\emptyset^{n-2}(out0)\emptyset(in0)\emptyset\{out1\} \in RT(BUFFC) \setminus RT(PIPE)$. This trace shows: if the environment inputs two items and waits a long time (presumably doing something else), and afterwards requires output of the two items while inputting another one, then the second output can be blocked by the input in $BUFFC$ but not in $PIPE$. This blocking in $BUFFC$ and its absence in $PIPE$ closely correspond to reality.

Actually, the above sort of behaviour can be repeated as long as there is space in the circular queue, and $out1$ is blocked for several rounds. Hence, we have $(in0)\emptyset^{n-1}(in1)\emptyset^{n-2}(out0)\emptyset((in0)\{out1\})^{n-3}\{out1\}$ as another refusal trace as desired above, and it is in general even longer. In contrast, in a setting where all arcs are inscribed with $[1,1]$, the resulting strictly clocked system cannot have a behaviour where $out1$ is blocked for several rounds; only in our asynchronous setting, the fast performance of input can block the output for an extended period.

In $BUFFD$, the buffer controller has an input and an output part, which communicate via the common store: the input part can store an item x in the circular queue only if the current cell s_{last} is marked as free with $\bullet$; the output part can remove an item from the circular queue only if the current cell s_{first} stores an item $x \in \{0, 1\}$. With this pattern of communication, the two parts can work in parallel and the input cannot block the output as above.

In [Vog03], it is shown that $BUFFD \sqsupseteq PIPE$ and $BUFFD \sqsupseteq BUFFC$, exhibiting two suitable simulations from $BUFFD$ to $PIPE$ and $BUFFC$. The setting there is actually significantly different from ours, since there actions have a duration of at most one time unit instead of delay. In [JV01], this setting with durations, called the a-variant, and two other settings are studied, where the setting of this tutorial is almost the same as the so-called i-variant. In general, the three different faster-than relations are incomparable, but for some classes a faster-than result in one variant implies the same faster-than result in another variant. In particular, these results imply that $BUFFD \sqsupseteq PIPE$ and $BUFFD \sqsupseteq BUFFC$ do not only hold in the a- but also in the i-variant. One can argue that the latter result carries over to the present setting.

As another application, we have studied solutions to the MUTEX-problem that are based on a token-ring in [BV98]. One is the token-ring attributed to Le Lann, which for two users is shown in Figure 1: the access-token travels around the ring, and whenever it reaches one user (or more precisely, the part of the ring that is 'responsible' for one user), the user either sends the token on or in case of interest he enters the critical section and sends it on upon leaving. The more intricate solution of Dijkstra [Dij85] is tuned to a scenario with low competition: here the token stays after leaving the critical section; the price to pay is that a user who wants to access the critical section, but does not have the token, has to order it.

Both solutions have their advantages if we consider the overall behaviour of all users. But from the point of view of one user who wants to minimize his worst-case access time, Le Lann's token-ring is preferable. To demonstrate this, the two types of token-rings for several numbers of users and varying communication delays are compared according to our faster-than relation with a family of standard interaction patterns for one user; these patterns describe how long a user who is ready to enter might be delayed. This comparison leads to a numerical value, the so-called enter-delay: the enter-delay corresponds (for the values studied) to the length of the ring for the first, and to twice the length of the ring for the second solution.

The comparison of a solution with an interaction pattern was performed with our tool FastAsy; in case the solution is not faster, FastAsy produces a responsible refusal trace. For the second solution, these traces demonstrate that in the worst case the order of a user might travel almost around the complete ring followed by the token travelling in the opposite direction again almost around the complete ring. This behaviour is an intuitively convincing explanation for the enter-delay we derived.

An advantage of Dijkstra's token-ring, which is not taken into account in our temporal efficiency, is that it produces no communication load in the ring if no user wants to enter the critical section. We propose a (presumably) new solution which combines the advantages of the two solutions above: in our solution, the token also has to be ordered, but order and token travel in the same direction. A drawback is that in our solution users must be distinguished by unique identifiers.

It is in no way obvious that this solution is correct, but surprisingly we can use our efficiency approach and FastAsy to prove it correct – at least for up to three users. (The main reason that this works is that we have a theory for asynchronous systems, and that the behaviour with upper time bounds is closely related to fair behaviour.) It is also surprising that in our correctness proofs we could abstract away large parts of the functional behaviour; this abstraction improved the tool performance significantly, and in fact made the correctness proof with FastAsy (in the version of 98) possible at all.

Furthermore, [Vog01] studies correctness of infinite families of symmetric nets like MUTEX-solutions based on a token-ring; the results imply that e.g. for the correctness of Le Lann's token-ring it is enough to check rings with two and three users – and the proof obligations could be checked again with FastAsy! Unfortunately, the theory does not cover our new solution; it has to be extended to deal with data like the unique identifiers, and this has remained an open problem.

We close this section with a few words about FastAsy. The basic stages for deciding $N_1 \sqsupseteq N_2$ in FastAsy are as follows. In stage 1, the r-reachability graphs R_1 and R_2 of N_1 and N_2 respectively are computed. Recall that these are finite since we work with discrete time, bound the clock values, and restrict the refusal sets to actions of N_1 and N_2 as discussed above.

In stage 2, a finite automaton DR_2 with the same language as R_2 is computed that is deterministic and has no internal transitions. (In principle, this is the well-known construction of the power set automaton.) Optionally, the same can be done for R_1, which usually is a good idea: despite the exponential worst-case complexity, it turns out that DR_1 may well be much smaller in size than R_1, even without putting effort in minimizing DR_1. (Interestingly, if DR_1 was not smaller during our experiments, this often indicated erratic behaviour of the system, typically a typo in an input file.)

In stage 3, a simulation S from N_1 to N_2, i.e. between R_1 (or DR_1) and DR_2 is built iteratively, starting from the pair consisting of the initial id's. Since DR_2 is deterministic, we get a characterization: N_1 is faster than N_2 if and only if stage 3 is successful.

If N_1 is faster than N_2 and we want a proof for this, FastAsy can output the simulation relation; this is usually quite large and therefore not so useful. Far more interestingly, if stage 3 fails, we can get a refusal trace $v \in RT(N_1) \setminus RT(N_2)$, or even better a refusal firing sequence w underlying v as diagnostic information. To build such a trace, we modify stage 1 to store the Petri net transition associated with an action for every step of the automaton, and stage 3 to store an immediate predecessor for every element in S (except the initial element of course) according to Definition 19.2, and then perform the following additional stages:

Going backwards from the element of S where the simulation failed, the trace v is built in reverse order using the additional information. This v is an observable behaviour that N_1 has and N_2 has not. (Note that v does not exhibit any internal behaviour, since internal transitions have been eliminated in stage 2.) In order to regain information about internal transitions, we now have to find a run in R_1 which produces this v. This can be done in more than one way, either using a modified DFS algorithm or performing a more intricate backward matching as described in [Bih98]. A suitable firing sequence w is then constructed as the sequence of Petri net transitions associated with the automaton transitions in the run of R_1.

With w, the user can now reproduce the 'slow' behaviour of N_1 on the transition level. This may help to identify avoidable bottlenecks in N_1 – or again, typos or mistakes in the modelling of the conceptual MUTEX-solution as a Petri net. Unfortunately, it is not so easy to understand why N_2 is 'fast': v is a short element in $RT(N_1) \setminus RT(N_2)$ in the sense that only its last item brings it into this set difference; if $v = lead(v)last(v)$, then $lead(v) \in RT(N_1) \cap RT(N_2)$, and to understand why N_2 is 'fast', we would have to look at all possible ways how N_2 can produce $lead(v)$ and then in every case examine why $last(v)$ is not possible for N_2.

FastAsy has been developed in three phases. An early prototype from 1996 used naive internal representations of the mathematical objects and was strictly fixed on the particular semantics of the variant of timed nets with additional read-arcs used in [BV98]. With this prototype, we obtained the results sketched above and also considered Peterson's and Dekker's MUTEX-solutions. Although this initial proof-of-concept lacked the potential for more involved extensions, many minor improvements were added up to spring 2000, e.g. commands to apply net modifications as in Definitions 24 and 26. These additional features were used extensively in the preparations of [BV98]. As it became obvious that we wanted to extend automated proofs to other timed Petri net semantics, from 1998 on we worked on an intermediate version of FastAsy, which used more abstracted representations of mathematical objects. It also featured a convenient GUI. The algorithms however were still not parameterized in the sense of modern generic programming as outlined in e.g. [Ale01].This became a problem as further theoretical work provided conceptual refinements that made it necessary to introduce behavioural degrees of freedom into the algorithms - something that is easily done in functional programming, but is to some degree unnatural in traditional object oriented programming.

So in 2001, yet another design for FastAsy took shape and has since been (almost) implemented. It makes extensive use of parameterized algorithms to implement the refinements mentioned above. An interesting example of an optimization is the following: r-reachability graphs have usually numerous arcs, since refusal sets are closed under set inclusion; one could leave this subset closure implicit and just represent maximal refusal sets. But one cannot make such a compressed representation of a finite automaton deterministic in the usual fashion, and also the computation of a simulation is not directly possible. We have developed methods which allow to perform these tasks without the need to restore the original representations first.

The use of Petri nets has been abstracted to general models of timed systems: essentially, a description of such a general model consists of a set of rules how to derive a directed graph as timed operational semantics (analogous to d- or r-reachability graphs). It can e.g. be used to handle timed process algebras.

Logical dependencies between the different stages of the computation (see above) that were present in the earlier version have been eliminated, so partial results from other tools can be imported and used as input for further processing. E.g. instead of building a reachability graph with FastAsy, this graph can be built by any other tool and then be processed further with FastAsy.

The concept of a graphical user interface was revoked, mainly because experience had shown in the meantime that command-line scripting as an easy way to automate bulk jobs (e.g. for parameterized nets) was by far preferable. Other major changes include the use of the Boost Graph Library [SLL02] as a foundation for graph representations and the introduction of automated regression testing to support code correctness.

6 Conclusion

In this tutorial, we have shortly discussed how to add timing to Petri nets, and then chosen to attach timing intervals to place-transition arcs. We have looked at timed testing, where test durations are added to tests; thus, the testing preorder can naturally be regarded as a faster-than relation, and we have shown that this faster-than relation can equivalently be based on continuous or discrete time. It can be characterized as inclusion of refusal traces, which implies its decidability. We have presented some applications to validate our faster-than relation, and we have shortly discussed our tool FastAsy.

Studies of timed systems most often concentrate on synchronous systems; since, as already argued in [MT91], it can be dangerous to replace a component of a synchronous system by a faster one, these studies almost never consider faster-than preorders. We will recall a few exceptions here; all these model systems within a process algebra, so a detailed direct comparison is not so easy in any case. As already mentioned, [NC96b] considers synchronous systems and test durations, and systems are compared on the basis of their predictability. Abstracting from small technical details, one can say that the predictability relation in [NC96b] is the same as ours – and the same as the relation derived from durationless must-testing for the timed process algebra TPL in [HR95].

Efficiency of untimed processes have been compared by counting internal actions either within a testing framework [CZ91,NC96a] or a bisimulation-based setting [AKH92,AKN95]. While [CZ91] does not consider parallel composition at all, internal actions of different components are interleaved in the other three papers; thus, two internal actions count the same in parallel as in sequence. This is clearly not the case, if we associate a duration or a delay to such actions and consider timewise efficiency. Hence, these approaches are incomparable to ours.

Another very different idea for relating processes with respect to speed is investigated in [CGR97] within the so-called ill-timed-but-well-caused approach [AM96,GRS95]. In this approach, components attach local time stamps to actions; however, actions occur as in an untimed algebra. Hence, in a sequence of actions exhibited by different processes running in parallel, local time stamps might decrease. This way, the timed algebra technically stays very close to untimed ones, but the "ill-timed" runs make the faster-than preorder of Corradini et al. difficult to relate to our approach.

The approach presented in this tutorial has been translated to a process algebra PAFAS (process algebra for fast asynchronous systems) in [CVJ02]: a corresponding timed-testing preorder is defined and characterized with refusal traces, and the discretization result is shown – with a technically quite different proof. The buffer example we have seen in Section 5 has been studied with PAFAS in [CDBV01].

The idea of upper time bounds for studying the efficiency of asynchronous systems has been taken up in a bisimulation setting in [LV04a]. A standard development with weak and strong bisimulation, compositionality results and an axiomatization for a fragment is presented. The definition of the strong bisimulation-preorder is particularly simple: it is simply bisimulation on actions and simulation on time steps. Technically, this simplicity is of course a big advantage. But the intuition behind the definition is not immediately clear; thus, an important and quite original contribution of [LV04a] is an intuitive justification: it is shown that the preorder is the same as some others that are intuitively convincing immediately, but technically rather involved.

For the same purpose of studying the efficiency of asynchronous systems, lower time bounds have been considered very early in a bisimulation setting in [MT91]. This approach has been improved very recently in [LV04b]: an intuitive justification for the bisimulation-type preorder defined in [MT91] is given; its compositionality result is generalized; the axioms for processes without recursion or parallel composition are corrected; finally, in contrast to claims in [MT91], it is shown that an expansion law does hold for processes without recursion.

Finally, we want to mention some further topics to expand the approach presented in this tutorial. It is very important that other realistic examples are worked out. Actually, for describing realistic examples with nets, some form of high-level nets should be used; it would be useful to extend the tool support to these nets. So far, FastAsy does not use any advanced techniques for state space generation like BDD's or partial order reductions; such additions are clearly needed.

To mention a concrete realistic example one could tackle, it is to be expected that a sliding window protocol becomes faster if the window size is increased – an example suggested by Arend Rensink. An obvious problem is that the buffering capacities of the processes involved increase with a larger window size; in order to come to useful results, one has therefore to modify the processes slightly – in this case, giving the processes with smaller window additional buffering capacity that is not needed for the protocol.

Also in our studies in [BV98], we had to modify the MUTEX-solutions in some ways. It is to be expected that this might happen regularly; with more experience, one might identify patterns in these modifications that could evolve to a theory. A related problem, already mentioned in Section 5, is to generalize the results of [Vog01] in order to cover the new MUTEX-solution presented in [BV98].

It is not so easy to find two systems solving the same task where one is faster than the other for *all* possible users. E.g. [CV02] studies pipelining, using PAFAS: one would expect that pipelining two sequential subtasks would give a speed-up compared to performing them atomically. But these two systems are functionally incomparable, since the first can buffer two tasks, while the second can only buffer one. In [CV02], it is suggested to consider only restricted test environments that are not sensitive to this functional difference. A very specific theory for very specific test environments with nice quantitative results concerning efficiency is developed. It is open how to generalize these results; it is to be expected that other case studies will suggest other restrictions on the test environments, and eventually one could hope for a general theory how to deal with such situations.

At last, it would also be very interesting to develop an elegant temporal logic that fits our faster-than relation; the optimal result would be that a system is faster than another if and only if it satisfies all formulas of the logic the other satisfies.

References

[AD94]   R. Alur and D. Dill. A theory of timed automata. *Theoret. Comput. Sci.*, 126:183–235, 1994.

[AKH92]   S. Arun-Kumar and M. Hennessy. An efficiency preorder for processes. *Acta Informatica*, 29:737–760, 1992.

[AKN95]   S. Arun-Kumar and V. Natarajan. Conformance: a precongruence close to bisimilarity. In J. Desel, editor, *Structures in Concurrency Theory*, Worksh. in Computing, 55–68. Springer, 1995.

[Ale01]   A. Alexandrescu. *Modern C++ Design – Applied Generic and Design Patterns*. C++ In-Depth Series. 2001.

[AM96]   L. Aceto and D. Murphy. On the ill–timed but well–caused. *Acta Informatica*, 33:317–350, 1996.

[Bih98]   E. Bihler. Effizienzvergleich bei verteilten Systemen – eine Theorie und ein Werkzeug. Diplomarbeit an der Uni. Augsburg, 1998.

[BV98]   E. Bihler and W. Vogler. Efficiency of token-passing MUTEX-solutions – some experiments. In J. Desel et al., editors, *Applications and Theory of Petri Nets 1998*, Lect. Notes Comp. Sci. 1420, 185–204. Springer, 1998.

[CDBV01]   F. Corradini, M. Di Berardini, and W. Vogler. PAFAS at work: comparing the worst-case efficiency of three buffer implementations. In Y.T .Yu and T.Y. Chen, editors, *2nd Asia-Pacific Conference on Quality Software APAQS 2001*, pages 231–240, IEEE, 2001.

[CGR97]   F. Corradini, R. Gorrieri, and M. Roccetti. Performance preorder and competitive equivalence. *Acta Informatica*, 34:805–835, 1997.

[CMS99]   A. Cerone and A. Maggiolo-Schettini. Time-based expressivity of time Petri nets for system specification. *Theoret. Comput. Sci.*, 216:1–53, 1999.

[CV02]   F. Corradini and W. Vogler. Measuring the performance of asynchronous systems with PAFAS. Technical Report 2002-4, University of Augsburg, http://www.Informatik.Uni-Augsburg.DE/skripts/techreports/, 2002. to appear in Theoretical Computer Science.

[CVJ02]   F. Corradini, W. Vogler, and L. Jenner. Comparing the worst-case efficiency of asynchronous systems with PAFAS. *Acta Informatica*, 38:735–792, 2002.

[CZ91]   R. Cleaveland and A. Zwarico. A theory of testing for real-time. In *Proc. 6th Symp. on Logic in Computer Science*, pages 110–119. IEEE Computer Society Press, 1991.

[Dij85]   E.W. Dijkstra. Invariance and non-determinacy. In C.A.R. Hoare and J.C. Sheperdson, editors, *Mathematical Logic and Programming Languages*, 157–165. Prentice-Hall, 1985.

[DNH84]   R. De Nicola and M.C.B. Hennessy. Testing equivalence for processes. *Theoret. Comput. Sci.*, 34:83–133, 1984.

[GRS95]   R. Gorrieri, M. Roccetti, and E. Stancampiano. A theory of processes with durational actions. *Theoret. Comput. Sci.*, 140:73–294, 1995.

[HR95]   M. Hennessy and T. Regan. A process algebra for timed systems. *Information and Computation*, 117:221–239, 1995.

[JV01]   L. Jenner and W. Vogler. Fast asynchronous systems in dense time. *Theoret. Comput. Sci.*, 254:379–422, 2001.

[KW97]   E. Kindler and R. Walter. Mutex needs fairness. *Inf. Proc. Letter*, 62:31–39, 1997.

[LV95]   N. Lynch and F. Vaandrager. Forward and backward simulations I: Untimed systems. *Information and Computation*, 121:214–233, 1995.

[LV04a]   G. Lüttgen and W. Vogler. Bisimulation on speed: Worst-case efficiency. *Information and Computation*, 191:105–144, 2004.

[LV04b]   G. Lüttgen and W. Vogler. Bisimulation on speed: Lower time bounds. In I. Walukiewicz, editor, *FOSSACS 2004*, Lect. Notes Comp. Sci. 2987, 333–347. Springer, 2004.

[Lyn96]   N. Lynch. *Distributed Algorithms*. Morgan Kaufmann Publishers, San Francisco, 1996.

[MF76]   P. Merlin and D.J. Farber. Recoverability of communication protocols. *IEEE Trans. Communications*, COM-24:1036–1043, 1976.

[MT91]   F. Moller and C. Tofts. Relating processes with respect to speed. In J. Baeten and J. Groote, editors, *CONCUR '91*, Lect. Notes Comp. Sci. 527, 424–438. Springer, 1991.

[NC96a]   V. Natarajan and R. Cleaveland. An algebraic theory of process efficiency. In *11th Ann. Symp. Logic in Computer Science (LICS '96)*, 63–72. IEEE, 1996.

[NC96b]   V. Natarajan and R. Cleaveland. Predictability of real-time systems: A process-algebraic approach. In *11th IEEE Real-Time Systems Symp. (RTSS '96)*, IEEE, 1996.

[Pet81]   J.L. Peterson. *Petri Net Theory*. Prentice-Hall, 1981.

[Phi87]   I. Phillips. Refusal testing. *Theoret. Comput. Sci.*, 50:241–284, 1987.

[Pop91]   L. Popova. On time Petri nets. *J. Inform. Process. Cybern. EIK*, 27:227–244, 1991.

[Ram74]   C. Ramchandi. Analysis of asynchronous concurrent systems by timed Petri nets. Technical Report TR 120, Project MAC, MIT, 1974.

[Rei85]   W. Reisig. *Petri Nets*. EATCS Monographs on Theoretical Computer Science 4. Springer, 1985.

[SLL02]   J.G. Siek, L.-Q. Lee, and A. Lumsdaine. *The Boost Graph Library*. C++ In-Depth Series. 2002.

[Vog95]   W. Vogler. Timed testing of concurrent systems. *Information and Computation*, 121:149–171, 1995.

[Vog01]   W. Vogler. Partial s-invariants for the verification of infinite systems families. In J.-M. Colom and M. Koutny, editors, *Applications and Theory of Petri Nets 2001*, Lect. Notes Comp. Sci. 2075, 382 – 401. Springer, 2001.

[Vog02]   W. Vogler. Efficiency of asynchronous systems, read arcs, and the mutex-problem. *Theoret. Comput. Sci.*, 275:589–631, 2002.

[Vog03]   W. Vogler. Faster asynchronous systems. *Information and Computation*, 184:311–342, 2003.

Timed Process Algebra
(With a Focus on Explicit Termination
and Relative-Timing)

J.C.M. Baeten and M.A. Reniers

Department of Mathematics and Computing Science
Eindhoven University of Technology
{J.C.M.Baeten,M.A.Reniers}@tue.nl

Abstract. We treat theory and application of timed process algebra.
We focus on a variant that uses explicit termination and action prefixing.
This variant has some advantages over other variants. We concentrate on
relative timing, but the treatment of absolute timing is similar. We treat
both discrete and dense timing. We build up the theory incrementally.
The different algebras are interrelated by embeddings and conservative
extensions. As an example, we consider the PAR communication protocol.

1 Introduction

Process algebras that incorporate some form of timing, enabling quantitative
analysis of time performance, have been studied extensively by now (see e.g.
[1–5]), and successfully applied in a number of case studies (see e.g. [6, 7]).

For different purposes and applications different versions of describing timing
have been presented in the literature. The following fundamental choices have
to be made:

1. The nature of the time domain.
   (a) Discrete time versus dense time. This choice is with respect to which type
       of time domain, timing is described. Usually, two types of time domains
       are distinguished. These are *discrete time*, where the time domain is of a
       discrete nature, and *dense time*, where the time domain is of a continuous
       nature, i.e. between every two moments in time there is another moment
       in time.
   (b) Linear time versus branching time. In a linear time domain each two
       moments in time are ordered by some total ordering $\leq$, in a branching
       time domain this is only a partial ordering.
   (c) Least element available or not.
   For example in timed μCRL [8], the user of the language can specify his own
   time domain by means of algebraic specifications as long as it has a least
   element and a total order. In this process algebra both discrete and dense
   time domains can be used.
   In the present work, we consider both the natural numbers N and the non-
   negative reals $R^{\geq 0}$ as the time domain.

M. Bernardo and F. Corradini (Eds.): SFM-RT 2004, LNCS 3185, pp. 59–97, 2004.

2. The way time is described syntactically.
   (a) Time-stamped description versus two-phase description. If the description of time is attached to the atomic actions, we speak of a time-stamping mechanism. If, on the other hand, time delay is decoupled from action execution, we have a two-phase approach.

   In the present work, we start out from a two-phase approach. This is the syntax the overwhelming majority of literature uses, both when giving axioms and when giving operational semantics. We stick to this approach in the axiom systems, but surprisingly, we find that giving operational rules for the dense-time case works better if in the transition steps, actions and time, and termination and time, are combined.

3. The way time is incorporated semantically.
   (a) Absolute timing versus relative timing. Sometimes, it is convenient to describe the passage of time with respect to a global clock, sometimes, it is convenient to describe passage of time relative to the previous action. The first is called *absolute timing*, the second *relative timing*. The combination of these two notions is called *parametric timing* [9, 10]. Here, we focus on relative-timing, but the theory with absolute timing is similar.
   (b) Time-determinism versus time-nondeterminism. A choice to be made with far reaching consequences is whether a delay may determine a choice. In the literature three versions are encountered. Firstly, if the delay by itself may not determine any choice we speak of *strong time-determinism*. Secondly, if a delay of t time by itself cannot determine a choice between alternatives that allow a delay of t time we speak of *weak time-determinism*. Finally, if a delay can determine a choice we speak of *time-nondeterminism*. Strong time-determinism is found in ATP [4], weak time-determinism in many ACP-like timed process algebras (also in the present work), and time-nondeterminism in $ACP^t_{\tau\epsilon}$ [11]. In the literature, time-determinism is also referred to as time-factorisation.
   (c) Duration of actions. One can either assume that actions have no duration, and hence are instantaneous, or that they do have a duration. In the latter case, the duration can be specified or unspecified. Here, we assume actions have no duration, and so we explicitly have to model delays between actions.
   (d) Urgent actions versus multi-actions. If actions occurring at the same time can be ordered these are called urgent actions, otherwise these are called multi-actions. Here, we use urgent actions.

In [12], several process algebras are treated in a common framework, and related by embeddings and conservative extension relations. These process algebras, ACP^{sat}, ACP^{srt}, ACP^{dat} and ACP^{drt}, allow the execution of two or more actions consecutively at the same point in time, separate the execution of actions from the passage of time, adhere to the principle of weak time-determinism, and consider actions to have no duration. The process algebra ACP^{sat} is a real-time process algebra with absolute time, ACP^{srt} is a real-time process algebra with relative time. Similarly, ACP^{dat} and ACP^{drt} are discrete-time process algebras with absolute time and relative time respectively. In these process algebras, considerable attention was given to the inaction constant δ, standing for unsuccessful termination or deadlock and the different roles it plays in the untimed theory.

In this paper, we extend the framework of [12] with a constant representing successful termination for the relative-time case. We consider a linear-time process algebra with urgent actions which have no duration. Furthermore, we will adopt the principle of weak time-determinism. It is not necessary to include the deadlocked process $\dot{\delta}$ as in [12]. The discrete-time part is taken from [13], the dense-time part is from [14].

Explicit termination is denoted by the constant ϵ, called *empty process*. This process ϵ denoting successful termination or *skip* has not been studied nearly as well as the unsuccessful termination constant δ. The untimed theory was investigated in [15–17]. In the context of ACP-like process algebras the empty process in a timed setting is mentioned in [11, 18, 19]. In [18, 19] a relative-time, discrete-time process algebra has been extended with both a non-delayable and a delayable successful termination constant.

As is the case for deadlock in the untimed theory, also the empty process has more roles. On the one hand, it serves as the neutral element for sequential composition (and parallel composition), on the other hand, it stands for the process that executes no actions but terminates at some unspecified time.

Thus, we have extended the integrated framework of process algebras with timing from [12] with a relative-time process algebra with the empty process. We show that the various subtheories are still related by means of embeddings and conservative extensions. This extension with the empty process, in itself needed for a clear understanding of termination in timed process algebra, is also needed in order to give semantics for programming languages and specification languages that involve skip: examples are CSP (see [20, 7]), χ (see [21]) and MSC (see [22]).

This article is structured as follows. In Section 2, we review the basic theory of relative-time process algebra with explicit termination, first discrete-time, and then dense-time. In Section 3, we extend with sequential composition, in Section 4 with parallel composition. In Section 5, we discuss various embeddings of different time-free process algebras. In Section 6, we discuss a couple of extra operators and notations that we will use in the examples to come. As examples, we use buffers with various timing behaviours in Section 7, and the PAR communication protocol in Section 8. We conclude in Section 9 with a short description of related work.

2   Minimal Process Algebra for Relative Timing

2.1   Minimal Process Algebra: MPA$_{drt}$

In this section we give a short overview of the process algebra MPA$_{drt}$ from [13] as it is the process algebra that is closest to the process algebra that we introduce. It is a process algebra that uses relative timing and discrete time. Further, it is two-phase and has weak time-determinism.

The process algebra MPA$_{drt}$ is parametrised by a set A of actions. The signature of MPA$_{drt}$ contains the following constants:

- *undelayable deadlock* $\underline{\delta}$. This is the process that cannot perform any action, cannot terminate and cannot let time progress beyond the current time slice (it cannot 'tick'). Operationally, it is characterized by having no operational rules at all. Undelayable deadlock is the neutral element of alternative composition (discussed below).
- *undelayable termination* $\underline{\epsilon}$. This is the process that cannot perform any action and cannot let time progress beyond the current time slice (cannot 'tick'). It can only terminate successfully in the current time slice. Undelayable termination is the neutral element of sequential composition (to be discussed in a later section).

More complex processes are constructed using the following operators:

- for each action $a \in A$, the *current time slice action prefix* operator $\underline{a}.\_$. The process $\underline{a}.x$ executes action a in the current time slice (it cannot progress to the next time slice) and next starts the execution of x in the current time slice.
- the *next time slice prefix* operator $\sigma.\_$. The process $\sigma.x$ can 'tick' (can let time progress to the next time slice), and can then continue with x (in the next time slice). Since we have explicit termination, we can consider this operator as a prefix operator. Often, it is written σ_{rel} to emphasize the fact that we have relative timing. As we will not consider absolute timing in this work, it is not necessary to write the subscript here.
- alternative composition $+$. The process $x + y$ executes either x or y, but not both. The choice is resolved upon execution of the first action.

We have omitted from the signature of MPA$_{drt}$ the delayable counterparts of $\underline{\epsilon}$, $\underline{\delta}$ and $\underline{a}.\_$. We consider such extensions later in Section 5 when embedding untimed process algebras into the timed process algebras introduced in this paper.

The axioms of MPA$_{drt}$ are presented in Table 1. Axioms A1-A3 explain that alternative composition is commutative, associative and idempotent. Axiom A6DR states that undelayable deadlock is the neutral element of alternative composition. Finally, Axiom DRTD (Discrete Relative Time Determinism) expresses

Table 1. Axioms of MPA$_{drt}$.

$x + y = y + x$	A1
$(x + y) + z = x + (y + z)$	A2
$x + x = x$	A3
$x + \underline{\delta} = x$	A6DR
$\sigma.x + \sigma.y = \sigma.(x + y)$	DRTD

weak time-determinism: passage of time cannot introduce non-determinism, so passage of time leads to a unique remaining process. This indicates that passage of time is different from action execution, which can introduce non-determinism (upon execution of an action, different processes can result).

In [13], by means of the operational rules of Table 2, an operational semantics is given for closed MPA$_{drt}$-terms defining binary relations $\_ \xrightarrow{a} \_$ (for $a \in A$) and $\_ \xmapsto{1} \_$, and a unary relation (predicate) $\_ \downarrow$. Intuitively, these have the following meaning:

- $x \xrightarrow{a} x'$ means that x evolves into x' by executing atomic action a (in the current time slice);
- $x \xmapsto{1} x'$ means that x evolves into x' by passing to the next time slice;
- $x \downarrow$ means that x has an option to terminate successfully (in the current time slice).

Deduction rules (8 – 10) clearly state that in an alternative composition a choice is made by passing to the next time slice only in case the other alternative is not able to proceed to this time slice. In case both alternatives allow a passage to the next time slice, no choice is made (yet).

Table 2. Deduction rules for MPA$_{drt}$ ($a \in A$).

$$\underline{\epsilon} \downarrow (1) \qquad \underline{a}.x \xrightarrow{a} x \ (2) \qquad \sigma.x \xmapsto{1} x \ (3)$$

$$\frac{x \downarrow}{x + y \downarrow} (4) \qquad \frac{y \downarrow}{x + y \downarrow} (5) \qquad \frac{x \xrightarrow{a} x^\square}{x + y \xrightarrow{a} x^\square} (6) \qquad \frac{y \xrightarrow{a} y^\square}{x + y \xrightarrow{a} y^\square} (7)$$

$$\frac{x \xmapsto{1} x^\square \quad y \xmapsto{1} y^\square}{x + y \xmapsto{1} x^\square + y^\square} (8) \qquad \frac{x \xmapsto{1} x^\square \quad y \xcancel{\xmapsto{1}}}{x + y \xmapsto{1} x^\square} (9) \qquad \frac{x \xcancel{\xmapsto{1}} \quad y \xmapsto{1} y^\square}{x + y \xmapsto{1} y^\square} (10)$$

Observe that for enforcing weak time-determinism, in the deduction rules for time transitions of process terms in the form of a sum, negative premises are used. For deduction systems in which negative premises are used, it is not obvious which set of positive formulas can be deduced. If a stratification[1] can be provided for the deduction system, it is well-defined in the sense that a set of positive formulas is defined by it. In this case, it is not difficult to come up with a stratification.

The axioms introduced before are meant to identify processes that are strongly bisimilar.

Definition 1 (Strong bisimilarity). *A symmetric, binary relation R on processes is called a strong bisimulation relation if for all process terms p, q such that $(p, q) \in R$ we have*

---

[1] See [23] for a definition of stratification.

- *if $p \downarrow$ then $q \downarrow$;*
- *for all $a \in A$ and process terms p': if $p \xrightarrow{a} p'$, then there exists a process term q' such that $q \xrightarrow{a} q'$ and $(p', q') \in R$;*
- *for all process terms p': if $p \xmapsto{1} p'$, then there exists a process term q' such that $q \xmapsto{1} q'$ and $(p', q') \in R$.*

Two processes p and q are strongly bisimilar, notation $p \leftrightarrow q$, if there exists a strong bisimulation relation R such that $(p, q) \in R$. If a relation R is given that witnesses the strong bisimilarity of processes p and q, then we write $R : p \leftrightarrow q$.

The notion of strong bisimilarity on closed MPA_{drt}-terms is both an equivalence and a congruence for all the operators of the process algebra MPA_{drt}. As we have used the standard definition of strong bisimilarity, equivalence is for free (follows from the format of the deduction rules).

Theorem 1 (Equivalence). *Strong bisimilarity is an equivalence relation.*

Theorem 2 (Congruence). *Strong bisimilarity is a congruence for the operators of the process algebra MPA_{drt}.*

Proof. The deduction system is stratifiable and in panth format and hence strong bisimilarity is a congruence [24, 25].

We establish that the structure of transition systems modulo strong bisimilarity is a model for our axioms, or, put differently, that our axioms are sound with respect to the set of closed terms modulo strong bisimilarity. We also state that the axiomatisation is complete, a proof of this fact is outside the scope of this survey.

Theorem 3 (Soundness). *The process algebra MPA_{drt} is a sound axiomatisation of strong bisimilarity on closed MPA_{drt}-terms.*

Theorem 4 (Completeness). *The process algebra MPA_{drt} is a complete axiomatization of strong bisimilarity on closed MPA_{drt}-terms.*

The next time slice prefix σ allows the passage of one unit of time. It can be generalized to an operator $\sigma^n._-$ for $n \in N$, that allows the passage of n units of time. This relative delay prefix operator $\sigma^n._-$ can be added to MPA_{drt} by considering the axioms given in Table 3. In specifications, this operator is very useful. In fact, in [12], it is taken as a basic operator.

Table 3. Axioms of relative delay prefix ($n \in N$).

$\sigma^0.x = x$	DRDP1
$\sigma^{n+1}.x = \sigma.\sigma^n.x$	DRDP2

The emphasis of the present work is to present variants of this discrete time theory and its extensions to dense time theories. It will turn out that discrete time and dense time theories have very much in common, the axioms look more or the less the same. In order to bring out these similarities sharply, we present the axiomatization of this basic discrete time theory based on the σ^n prefix rather than the σ prefix.

In the next section, we introduce such a process algebra, called MPT_{drt}.

2.2   Relative Delay Prefix Operator

The axioms of MPT_{drt} are given in Table 4. Axiom DRT1 states that a delay of zero time units has no effect on the following process. Axiom DRT2 captures the relative-time nature of the relative delay prefix operators: two consecutive delays can be added to obtain a single delay. Axiom DRT3 is a generalization of axiom DRTD from MPA_{drt} to capture weak time-determinism for any delay, not just for one time unit. The resulting theory is called MPT_{drt}.

Table 4. Axioms of MPT_{drt} $(a \in A, n, m \in N)$.

$x + y = y + x$	A1	$\sigma^0.x = x$	DRT1
$(x + y) + z = x + (y + z)$	A2	$\sigma^n.(\sigma^m.x) = \sigma^{n+m}.x$	DRT2
$x + x = x$	A3	$\sigma^n.x + \sigma^n.y = \sigma^n.(x + y)$	DRT3
$x + \underline{\underline{\delta}} = x$	A6DR		

The theory MPA_{drt} can be embedded into MPT_{drt} by interpreting $\sigma.\_$ as $\sigma^1.\_$. Observe that Axiom DRTD is obtained (modulo notations) by instantiating axiom DRT3 with $n = 1$. This embedding is discussed in more detail in Section 5.4.

An operational semantics of MPT_{drt} can be found relatively easily by using the same relations and predicate $\_ \xrightarrow{a} \_$ and $\_ \xmapsto{1} \_$ and $\_ \downarrow$. Alternatively, we can use relations $\_ \xmapsto{n} \_$ (for all $n \in N$) instead of $\_ \xmapsto{1} \_$. We give neither approach here, as they cannot be generalized to dense time theories, for reasons to be explained later.

Now for this discrete time theory MPT_{drt}, it is very easy to obtain a dense time counterpart MPT_{srt}. All that needs to be done is to change the time slice syntax to time point syntax, and change the range of the delay superscripts from N to $R^{\geq 0}$. We spell this out in the following.

The process algebra MPT_{srt} is a minimal process theory with real-time relative timing. It is parametrised by a set A of actions. The signature of MPT_{srt} contains the following constants:

− *undelayable deadlock* $\tilde{\tilde{\delta}}$. This is the process that cannot execute any action, cannot terminate, and cannot let time progress beyond the current point of time.

– *undelayable termination* $\widetilde{\widetilde{\epsilon}}$. The process that cannot execute any action, cannot let time progress beyond the current point of time, but can terminate at the current point of time.

More complex processes are constructed using the following operators:

– for each action $a \in A$, the *urgent action prefix* operator $\widetilde{\widetilde{a}}\,._-$. The process $\widetilde{\widetilde{a}}\,.x$ can only execute a at the current point in time and then continue with x at the current point of time.
– for $t \in R^{\geq 0}$, the *relative delay prefix* operator $\sigma^t._-$. The process $\sigma^t.x$ can only delay for an amount of time t and then continues with x (at time t after the current point of time);
– alternative composition $+$. The process $x + y$ executes either x or y, but not both. The choice is resolved upon execution of the first action.

Observe that the signatures and the axioms of $\mathrm{MPT}_{\mathrm{drt}}$ and $\mathrm{MPT}_{\mathrm{srt}}$ only differ in their notations for the constants and the action prefix operators.

The axioms of $\mathrm{MPT}_{\mathrm{srt}}$ are presented in Table 5. It turns out that these are the same as the axioms of $\mathrm{MPT}_{\mathrm{drt}}$ except for the notations as mentioned before.

Table 5. Axioms of $\mathrm{MPT}_{\mathrm{srt}}$ $(t, s \in R^{\blacksquare 0})$.

$x + y = y + x$	A1	$\sigma^0.x = x$	SRT1
$(x + y) + z = x + (y + z)$	A2	$\sigma^t.(\sigma^s.x) = \sigma^{t+s}.x$	SRT2
$x + x = x$	A3	$\sigma^t.x + \sigma^t.y = \sigma^t.(x + y)$	SRT3
$x + \widetilde{\widetilde{\delta}} = x$	A6SR		

For both $\mathrm{MPT}_{\mathrm{drt}}$ and $\mathrm{MPT}_{\mathrm{srt}}$ an operational semantics can easily be obtained by generalizing the time transition relation $\_ \overset{1}{\mapsto} \_$ of MPA_{drt} to the time transitions $\_ \overset{t}{\mapsto} \_$ (for $t \in N^{>0}$ and $t \in R^{>0}$ respectively). The deduction rules are then simple reformulations of the deduction rules of MPA_{drt} from Table 2.

Given these similarities between a discrete-time and a real-time process algebra with relative timing, we only consider process algebras with real-time relative timing in the remainder of this paper. The corresponding discrete-time variants can be derived easily by changing the range of the delay parameter and changing time slice constants and prefixes to time point constants and prefixes.

In the next section we extend $\mathrm{MPT}_{\mathrm{srt}}$ with an operator for sequential composition. Due to the presence of a constant for explicit termination and our desire to have weak time-determinism, the formulation of deduction rules for time transitions of sequential composition turn out to be difficult (see [26] and the next section). For this reason we present a different operational semantics for $\mathrm{MPT}_{\mathrm{srt}}$. Instead of the two-phase operational approach used in the previous section, we now integrate passage of time with action transitions and termination in the operational semantics. We define binary relations $\_ \overset{a}{\to}_t \_$ and unary relations $\_ \downarrow_t$

and $\Delta_t(\_)$ on closed terms (for $a \in A$ and $t \in R^{\geq 0}$). Intuitively, they have the following meaning:

1. $x \xrightarrow{a}_t x'$ means that x evolves into x' at time t after the current point of time upon the execution of the atomic action a at that time;
2. $x \downarrow_t$ means that x has an option to terminate successfully at time t after the current point of time.
3. $\Delta_t(x)$ means that x has the possibility of delaying for t time.

The predicate $\downarrow_0$ discriminates between $\widetilde{\widetilde{\delta}}$ and $\widetilde{\widetilde{\epsilon}}$. The predicate $\Delta_{\max(t,t')}$ discriminates between $\sigma^t(\widetilde{\widetilde{\delta}})$ and $\sigma^{t'}(\widetilde{\widetilde{\delta}})$ for different t and t'. The deduction rules for MPT$_{\text{srt}}$ are given in Table 6. Note that in these deduction rules no negative premises appear. This is due to the decision to integrate time passage with action transitions and termination. Note that the predicate Δ_0 holds for all processes. This predicate does not hold for the process $\dot{\delta}$ of [12] that is not considered here.

Table 6. Deduction rules for MPT$_{\text{srt}}$ ($a \in A$, $t, s \in R^{\blacksquare 0}$).

$$\widetilde{\widetilde{\epsilon}} \downarrow_0 (1) \qquad \Delta_0(x) (2) \qquad \widetilde{\widetilde{a}}.x \xrightarrow{a}_0 x (3)$$

$$\frac{x \downarrow_t}{\sigma^s.x \downarrow_{t+s}} (4) \qquad \frac{x \xrightarrow{a}_t x^\blacksquare}{\sigma^s.x \xrightarrow{a}_{t+s} x^\blacksquare} (5) \qquad \frac{t \leq s}{\Delta_t(\sigma^s.x)} (6) \qquad \frac{\Delta_t(x)}{\Delta_{t+s}(\sigma^s.x)} (7)$$

$$\frac{x \downarrow_t}{x + y \downarrow_t} (8) \qquad \frac{y \downarrow_t}{x + y \downarrow_t} (9) \qquad \frac{x \xrightarrow{a}_t x^\blacksquare}{x + y \xrightarrow{a}_t x^\blacksquare} (10) \qquad \frac{y \xrightarrow{a}_t y^\blacksquare}{x + y \xrightarrow{a}_t y^\blacksquare} (11)$$

$$\frac{\Delta_t(x)}{\Delta_t(x + y)} (12) \qquad \frac{\Delta_t(y)}{\Delta_t(x + y)} (13)$$

Since we have replaced the relations and predicates that are used in the operational semantics, the notion of strong bisimilarity must be adapted accordingly.

Definition 2 (Strong bisimilarity). *A symmetric, binary relation R on process terms is called a strong bisimulation relation if for all process terms p, q such that $(p, q) \in R$ we have*

- *for all $t \in R^{\geq 0}$: if $p \downarrow_t$ then $q \downarrow_t$;*
- *for all $a \in A$, $t \in R^{\geq 0}$, and process terms p': if $p \xrightarrow{a}_t p'$, then there exists process term q' such that $q \xrightarrow{a}_t q'$ and $(p', q') \in R$;*
- *for all $t \in R^{\geq 0}$: if $\Delta_t(p)$ then $\Delta_t(q)$.*

Two processes p and q are strongly bisimilar, notation $p \leftrightarrow q$, if there exists a strong bisimulation relation R such that $(p, q) \in R$. If a relation R is given that witnesses the strong bisimilarity of processes p and q, then we write $R : p \leftrightarrow q$.

The notion of strong bisimilarity on closed MPT$_{\text{srt}}$-terms is both an equivalence and a congruence for all the operators of the process algebra MPT$_{\text{srt}}$. As we have used the standard definition of strong bisimilarity, equivalence is for free.

Theorem 5 (Equivalence). *Strong bisimilarity is an equivalence relation.*

Theorem 6 (Congruence). *Strong bisimilarity is a congruence for the operators of the process algebra* MPT_{srt}.

Proof. The deduction system is in path format and hence strong bisimilarity is a congruence [27, 25].

We establish that the structure of transition systems modulo strong bisimilarity is a model for our axioms, or, put differently, that our axioms are sound with respect to the set of closed terms modulo strong bisimilarity. We also state that the axiomatisation is complete. The proof of the latter fact (not given here) relies on the elimination theorem stated first.

Theorem 7 (Soundness). *The process algebra* MPT_{srt} *is a sound axiomatisation of strong bisimilarity on closed* MPT_{srt}*-terms.*

We define a notion of *basic terms*. These are useful in the proofs to come. It turns out that every closed MPT_{srt}-term is derivably equal to a basic term. This provides us with an easier to use means of induction: instead of proving properties by induction on the structure of closed terms, it suffices to prove these properties by induction on the structure of basic terms. The proof that the axiomatization is complete with respect to the set of closed terms modulo strong bisimilarity uses this induction principle.

Definition 3 (Basic terms). *The set of all basic terms is the smallest set* $\mathcal{B}$ *that satisfies*

1. *for* $t \in R^{\geq 0}$: $\sigma^t . \tilde{\tilde{\epsilon}} \in \mathcal{B}$;
2. *for* $t \in R^{\geq 0}$: $\sigma^t . \tilde{\tilde{\delta}} \in \mathcal{B}$;
3. *for* $a \in A$, $t \in R^{\geq 0}$ *and* $x \in \mathcal{B}$: $\sigma^t . \tilde{\tilde{a}} . x \in \mathcal{B}$;
4. *for* $x, y \in \mathcal{B}$: $x + y \in \mathcal{B}$.

Theorem 8 (Elimination). *Every closed* MPT_{srt}*-term* p *is derivably equal to a basic term* $q \in \mathcal{B}$, *i.e. for all process term* p *there is a basic term* q *with* $MPT_{\mathrm{srt}} \vdash p = q$.

Proof. By induction on the structure of closed MPT_{srt}-term p.

Theorem 9 (Completeness). *The process algebra* MPT_{srt} *is a complete axiomatization of strong bisimilarity on closed* MPT_{srt}*-terms.*

3   Sequential Composition

In this section we extend the process algebra MPT_{srt} from the previous section with sequential composition. The sequential composition of two processes p and

q is denoted $p \cdot q$. The process $p \cdot q$ starts with the execution of p, and upon termination of p continues with the execution of q. Sequential composition binds stronger than alternative composition and weaker than action prefix. The axioms of TSP_{srt} are the axioms of MPT_{srt}, and in addition the axioms presented in Table 7.

Table 7. Axioms of TSP_{srt} $(a \in A, t \in R^{\blacksquare \, 0})$.

$$(x + y) \cdot z = x \cdot z + y \cdot z \qquad \text{A4} \qquad \tilde{\tilde{\delta}} \cdot x = \tilde{\tilde{\delta}} \qquad \text{A7SR}$$

$$(x \cdot y) \cdot z = x \cdot (y \cdot z) \qquad \text{A5} \qquad \tilde{\tilde{\epsilon}} \cdot x = x \quad \text{A8SDR}$$

$$\tilde{\tilde{a}} . x \cdot y = \tilde{\tilde{a}} .(x \cdot y) \qquad \text{A10SR} \qquad x \cdot \tilde{\tilde{\epsilon}} = x \quad \text{A9SR}$$

$$\sigma^t . x \cdot y = \sigma^t .(x \cdot y) \qquad \text{SRSEQ}$$

The axioms A4 and A5 describe straightforward properties of alternative and sequential composition: sequential composition distributes over alternative composition from the right, and sequential composition is associative. Notice that the other distributive law does not hold, as the moment of choice in $x \cdot (y + z)$ is after the execution of x, whereas in $x \cdot y + x \cdot z$ it is before the execution of x. The axiom A7SR explains that undelayable deadlock is a left-zero element for sequential composition. As $\tilde{\tilde{\delta}}$ cannot terminate, nothing of a following process can occur. The axioms A8SR-A9SR explain that undelayable termination is a neutral element for sequential composition. This is because $\tilde{\tilde{\epsilon}}$ terminates immediately and successfully, so a following process can be started at the same point in time, and possible termination of a previous process is not affected. The axioms A10SR and SRSEQ describe the interplay between the action prefix operators and sequential composition and between the delay prefix operators and sequential composition, respectively.

Compared to [12], we can present the delay operators as prefix operators rather than a general unary operator, and we have no need of a special deadlocked process constant $\dot{\delta}$. This simplifies the set of axioms and operational rules.

We present the deduction rules for sequential composition in Table 8. The operational semantics of TSP_{srt} consists of the deduction rules of MPT_{srt} and in addition the deduction rules for sequential composition from Table 8.

Table 8. Deduction rules for sequential composition $(a \in A, t, s \in T)$.

$$\frac{x \downarrow t, y \downarrow s}{x \cdot y \downarrow t+s} \ (1) \qquad \frac{x \xrightarrow{a}_t x^{\blacksquare}}{x \cdot y \xrightarrow{a}_t x^{\blacksquare} \cdot y} \ (2) \qquad \frac{x \downarrow t, y \xrightarrow{a}_s y^{\blacksquare}}{x \cdot y \xrightarrow{a}_{t+s} y^{\blacksquare}} \ (3)$$

$$\frac{\Delta_t(x)}{\Delta_t(x \cdot y)} \ (4) \qquad \frac{x \downarrow t \quad \Delta_s(y)}{\Delta_{t+s}(x \cdot y)} \ (5)$$

Intermezzo: One-phase versus two-phase operational semantics. At this point, it is possible to further explain our switch from the two-phase approach in defining operational semantics for MPA_{drt} with (generalized) time transitions $\_ \overset{1}{\mapsto} \_$ (or $\_ \overset{n}{\mapsto} \_$) to the current setting. For discrete time theories, in the two-phase approach using the single time-unit time transitions gives the following deduction rules for sequential composition (see [13], note that the second deduction rule is missing in [13]):

$$\frac{x \overset{1}{\mapsto} x' \quad x \not\downarrow}{x \cdot y \overset{1}{\mapsto} x' \cdot y} \quad \frac{x \overset{1}{\mapsto} x' \quad y \not\overset{1}{\mapsto}}{x \cdot y \overset{1}{\mapsto} x' \cdot y} \quad \frac{x \not\overset{1}{\mapsto} \quad x \downarrow \quad y \overset{1}{\mapsto} y'}{x \cdot y \overset{1}{\mapsto} y'} \quad \frac{x \overset{1}{\mapsto} x' \quad x \downarrow \quad y \overset{1}{\mapsto} y'}{x \cdot y \overset{1}{\mapsto} x' \cdot y + y'}$$

Observe that the premises of these deduction rules exclude each other in cases where the result of the conclusion differs. Consequently, time-determinism is preserved by these deduction rules. In a dense setting, where there is no smallest unit of time, this approach can not be used at all.

Using generalized time transitions in a discrete or dense setting is already impossible without introducing additional syntax as in order to consider a possible delay of $x \cdot y$, it is required to consider all combinations: the delay can come completely from x, it can come partly from x followed by termination of x and the rest of the delay from y, and in case x can terminate immediately, the delay can come completely from y. In [26], saturation of the transition systems was proposed as a solution, thereby allowing the transition systems to be time-nondeterministic.

The notion of strong bisimilarity on closed TSP_{srt}-terms is both an equivalence and a congruence for all the operators of the process algebra TSP_{srt}. As we have used the standard definition of strong bisimilarity, equivalence is for free.

Theorem 10 (Equivalence). *Strong bisimilarity is an equivalence relation.*

Theorem 11 (Congruence). *Strong bisimilarity is a congruence for the operators of the process algebra TSP_{srt}.*

Proof. The deduction system is in path format and hence strong bisimilarity is a congruence [27, 25].

Next, we establish that the structure of transition systems modulo strong bisimilarity is a model for our axioms, or, put differently, that our axioms are sound with respect to the set of closed terms modulo strong bisimilarity. We also prove that the axiomatisation is complete.

Theorem 12 (Soundness). *The process algebra TSP_{srt} is a sound axiomatisation of strong bisimilarity on closed TSP_{srt}-terms.*

The following theorem states that every closed TSP_{srt}-term is derivably equal to a closed MPT_{srt}-term, i.e., that every occurrence of sequential composition in a closed term can be eliminated. The virtue of this theorem is that in future proofs about closed TSP_{srt}-terms we are allowed to apply induction on the structure of closed MPT$_{\text{srt}}$-terms or even basic terms instead of on the structure of closed TSP$_{\text{srt}}$-terms, thereby limiting the number of cases to be considered. An example of a proof in which this reduction of the number of cases to be considered is applied, is the proof of the completeness theorem (Theorem 15).

Theorem 13 (Elimination). *For every closed TSP$_{\text{srt}}$-term p there exists a closed MPT$_{\text{srt}}$-term q such that TSP$_{\text{srt}} \vdash p = q$.*

Proof. The only difference between closed TSP$_{\text{srt}}$-terms and closed MPT$_{\text{srt}}$-terms is that sequential composition cannot occur in the latter. For proving that all occurrences of sequential composition can be eliminated, it suffices to prove the following property: for every two closed MPT$_{\text{srt}}$-terms p_1 and p_2 there exists a closed MPT$_{\text{srt}}$-term q such that $p_1 \cdot p_2 = q$. This property is easily proven with induction on the structure of closed MPT$_{\text{srt}}$-term p_1.

Repeated application of this property to the smallest subterms of the form $p_1 \cdot p_2$ that occur in a closed TSP$_{\text{srt}}$-term, eventually results in a closed MPT$_{\text{srt}}$-term.

Theorem 14 (Conservativity). *The process algebra TSP$_{\text{srt}}$ is a conservative extension of the process algebra MPT$_{\text{srt}}$, i.e., for all closed MPT$_{\text{srt}}$-terms p and q: MPT$_{\text{srt}} \vdash p = q$ iff TSP$_{\text{srt}} \vdash p = q$.*

Proof. This theorem follows, using the meta-theory of [28], from the completeness of MPT$_{\text{srt}}$ (Theorem 9), from the soundness of TSP$_{\text{srt}}$ (Theorem 12), and from the observation that the term deduction system of TSP$_{\text{srt}}$ is an operationally conservative extension of the term deduction system of MPT$_{\text{srt}}$. This last observation follows from the observations that both term deduction systems are in path format and that the term deduction system for MPT$_{\text{srt}}$ is pure (see, e.g., [28] for a definition of pure deduction systems) and well-founded.

Theorem 15 (Completeness). *The process algebra TSP$_{\text{srt}}$ is a complete axiomatization of strong bisimilarity on closed TSP$_{\text{srt}}$-terms.*

Proof. This theorem follows, using the meta-theory of [28], from the fact that TSP$_{\text{srt}}$ is a conservative extension of MPT$_{\text{srt}}$ (Theorem 14) and the elimination theorem (Theorem 13).

4 Parallelism and Communication

In this section, we extend the process algebra TSP$_{\text{srt}}$ with the parallel composition operator $\parallel$. We also add the encapsulation operator ∂_H, which is well-known from standard process algebra. The operator ∂_H will block all actions from the set of actions H ($H \subseteq A$). The operator is used to enforce communication between parallel components. The resulting process algebra is denoted TCP$_{\text{srt}}$.

The parallel composition of two processes x and y, notation $x \parallel y$, describes the interleaving of their behaviour. An action can be executed by $x \parallel y$ if and only if one of the operands can execute this action or this action is the result

Table 9. Axioms of TCP_{srt} $(a, b \in A,\ t \in R^{\blacksquare\,0},\ u \in R^{>0})$.

$$
\begin{aligned}
&x \parallel y = (x \lfloor\!\lfloor y + y \lfloor\!\lfloor x) + x \mid y & &x \mid y = y \mid x \\[4pt]
&\widetilde{\widetilde{\delta}} \lfloor\!\lfloor x = \widetilde{\widetilde{\delta}} & &\widetilde{\widetilde{\delta}} \mid x = \widetilde{\widetilde{\delta}} \\[4pt]
&\widetilde{\widetilde{\epsilon}} \lfloor\!\lfloor x = \widetilde{\widetilde{\delta}} & &\widetilde{\widetilde{\epsilon}} \mid \widetilde{\widetilde{\epsilon}} = \widetilde{\widetilde{\epsilon}} \\[4pt]
&\widetilde{\widetilde{a}} .x \lfloor\!\lfloor y = \widetilde{\widetilde{a}} .(x \parallel y) & &\widetilde{\widetilde{a}} .x \mid \widetilde{\widetilde{\epsilon}} = \widetilde{\widetilde{\delta}} \\[4pt]
&(x+y) \lfloor\!\lfloor z = x \lfloor\!\lfloor z + y \lfloor\!\lfloor z & &\widetilde{\widetilde{a}} .x \mid \widetilde{\widetilde{b}} .y = \widetilde{\widetilde{c}} .(x \parallel y) \quad \text{if } \gamma(a,b) = c \\[4pt]
&\sigma^u .x \lfloor\!\lfloor y = \widetilde{\widetilde{\delta}} & &\widetilde{\widetilde{a}} .x \mid \widetilde{\widetilde{b}} .y = \widetilde{\widetilde{\delta}} \qquad\ \text{otherwise} \\[4pt]
&\partial_H(\widetilde{\widetilde{\delta}}) = \widetilde{\widetilde{\delta}} & &\widetilde{\widetilde{a}} .x \mid \sigma^u .y = \widetilde{\widetilde{\delta}} \\[4pt]
&\partial_H(\widetilde{\widetilde{\epsilon}}) = \widetilde{\widetilde{\epsilon}} & &\sigma^u .x \mid \widetilde{\widetilde{\epsilon}} = \sigma^u .x \\[4pt]
&\partial_H(\widetilde{\widetilde{a}} .x) = \widetilde{\widetilde{a}} .\partial_H(x) \quad \text{if } a \notin H & &\sigma^u .x \mid \sigma^u .y = \sigma^u .(x \parallel y) \\[4pt]
&\partial_H(\widetilde{\widetilde{a}} .x) = \widetilde{\widetilde{\delta}} \qquad \text{if } a \in H & &(x+y) \mid z = x \mid z + y \mid z \\[4pt]
&\partial_H(\sigma^t .x) = \sigma^t .\partial_H(x) \\[4pt]
&\partial_H(x+y) = \partial_H(x) + \partial_H(y)
\end{aligned}
$$

of the simultaneous execution of an action from x and an action from y. This last possibility is called synchronisation or communication. The possible communications are specified by the *communication* function $\gamma : A \times A \rightarrow A$. This function is a parameter of the process algebra and can be chosen dependent on the application. The function γ is partial, commutative and associative.

A parallel composition $x \parallel y$ can only terminate successfully if both x and y have an option to terminate successfully.

The timing behaviour of $x \parallel y$ is as follows: a delay can take place only if both components allow this delay, or if one of the components can terminate successfully and the other can delay. The axiomatisation is now as follows, using two auxiliary operators $\lfloor\!\lfloor$ (left merge) and $\mid$ (communication merge). The left-merge will capture that part of the behaviour of the merge where one components can execute an action independently and immediately, and the communication merge will capture that part of the behaviour of the merge where the initial activity is a termination, a delay or a synchronisation.

The axioms are given in Table 9. For the left operand of a left-merge operator the axioms are based on the structure of MPT_{srt}-terms. The axioms for the communication merge operator are based on the structure of MPT_{srt}-terms in both operands. Note that if both processes involved in communication merge can delay, the delays are synchronised.

In the operational rules we encounter a difficulty. Because of earlier decisions, we have to give an expression for a process after a certain delay has occurred. We find we have a need for an extra operator in order to express this. This is the time shift operator $t \gg \_$. The process $t \gg x$ is the process that results after

Table 10. Deduction rules for parallel composition, encapsulation and time shift $(a, b, c \in A, H \subseteq A, t, s \in R^{\blacksquare \, 0})$.

$$\frac{x \downarrow_t \quad y \downarrow_s}{x \parallel y \downarrow_{\max(t,s)}} \; [1] \qquad \frac{x \xrightarrow{a}_t x^{\blacksquare} \quad \Delta_t(y)}{x \parallel y \xrightarrow{a}_t x^{\blacksquare} \parallel (t \gg y)} \; [2] \qquad \frac{x \xrightarrow{a}_t x^{\blacksquare} \quad y \downarrow_s \quad s \leq t}{x \parallel y \xrightarrow{a}_t x^{\blacksquare}} \; [3]$$

$$\frac{\Delta_t(x) \quad y \xrightarrow{a}_t y^{\blacksquare}}{x \parallel y \xrightarrow{a}_t (t \gg x) \parallel y^{\blacksquare}} \; [4] \qquad \frac{x \downarrow_s \quad s \leq t \quad y \xrightarrow{a}_t y^{\blacksquare}}{x \parallel y \xrightarrow{a}_t y^{\blacksquare}} \; [5]$$

$$\frac{x \xrightarrow{a}_t x^{\blacksquare} \quad y \xrightarrow{b}_t y^{\blacksquare} \quad \gamma(a,b) = c}{x \parallel y \xrightarrow{c}_t x^{\blacksquare} \parallel y^{\blacksquare}} \; [6]$$

$$\frac{\Delta_t(x) \quad \Delta_t(y)}{\Delta_t(x \parallel y)} \; [7] \qquad \frac{\Delta_t(x) \quad y \downarrow_s \quad s \leq t}{\Delta_t(x \parallel y)} \; [8] \qquad \frac{x \downarrow_s \quad \Delta_t(y) \quad s \leq t}{\Delta_t(x \parallel y)} \; [9]$$

$$\frac{x \downarrow_t}{\partial_H(x) \downarrow_t} \; [10] \qquad \frac{x \xrightarrow{a}_t x^{\blacksquare} \quad a \notin H}{\partial_H(x) \xrightarrow{a}_t \partial_H(x^{\blacksquare})} \; [11] \qquad \frac{\Delta_t(x)}{\Delta_t(\partial_H(x))} \; [12]$$

$$\frac{x \downarrow_{t+s}}{s \gg x \downarrow_t} \; [13] \qquad \frac{x \xrightarrow{a}_{t+s} x^{\blacksquare}}{s \gg x \xrightarrow{a}_t x^{\blacksquare}} \; [14] \qquad \frac{\Delta_{t+s}(x)}{\Delta_t(s \gg x)} \; [15]$$

a delay has occurred of t time units starting at the current time. We present the operational rules in Table 10.

Rules for the left-merge and communication merge are given in Table 11.

In the axiomatisation of parallel composition, the time shift operator is not needed. It is not difficult to give axioms anyway. In this way, the signatures of the process algebra and the term deduction system will be equal. See Table 12.

Strong bisimilarity (Definition 2) is a congruence for the operators of the process algebra TCP$_{\mathrm{srt}}$.

Theorem 16 (Congruence). *Strong bisimilarity is a congruence for the operators of the process algebra TCP$_{\mathrm{srt}}$.*

Proof. The term deduction is in path format. Therefore congruence follows immediately.

It is a routine exercise to check that the axioms of TCP$_{\mathrm{srt}}$ are sound for our model of transition systems modulo strong bisimilarity.

Theorem 17 (Soundness). *The process algebra TCP$_{\mathrm{srt}}$ is a sound axiomatisation of strong bisimilarity on closed TCP$_{\mathrm{srt}}$-terms.*

The newly introduced operators can be eliminated from every closed term. We skip the (quite elaborate!) proof.

Theorem 18 (Elimination). *For every closed TCP$_{\mathrm{srt}}$-term p there exists a closed TSP$_{\mathrm{srt}}$-term q such that TCP$_{\mathrm{srt}} \vdash p = q$.*

It is not hard to prove that the process algebra TCP$_{\mathrm{srt}}$ is a conservative extension of the process algebra TSP$_{\mathrm{srt}}$. Combining this result with the elimination

Table 11. Deduction rules for left-merge and communication merge ($a, b, c \in A$, $t, s \in R^{\square \geq 0}$, $u, v \in R^{>0}$).

$$\frac{x \xrightarrow{a}_0 x^{\square}}{x \lfloor\!\lfloor y \xrightarrow{a}_0 x^{\square} \parallel y} \ [1] \qquad \frac{x \downarrow_t \quad y \downarrow_s}{x \mid y \downarrow_{\max(t,s)}} \ [2]$$

$$\frac{x \xrightarrow{a}_u x^{\square} \quad \Delta_u(y)}{x \mid y \xrightarrow{a}_u x^{\square} \parallel (u \gg y)} \ [3] \qquad \frac{x \xrightarrow{a}_u x^{\square} \quad y \downarrow_v \quad v \leq u}{x \mid y \xrightarrow{a}_u x^{\square}} \ [4]$$

$$\frac{\Delta_u(x) \quad y \xrightarrow{a}_u y^{\square}}{x \mid y \xrightarrow{a}_u (u \gg x) \parallel y^{\square}} \ [5] \qquad \frac{x \downarrow_v \quad v \leq u \quad y \xrightarrow{a}_u y^{\square}}{x \mid y \xrightarrow{a}_u y^{\square}} \ [6]$$

$$\frac{x \xrightarrow{a}_t x^{\square} \quad y \xrightarrow{b}_t y^{\square} \quad \gamma(a,b) = c}{x \mid y \xrightarrow{c}_t x^{\square} \parallel y^{\square}} \ [7]$$

$$\frac{\Delta_t(x) \quad \Delta_t(y)}{\Delta_t(x \mid y)} \ [8] \qquad \frac{\Delta_t(x) \quad y \downarrow_s \quad s \leq t}{\Delta_t(x \mid y)} \ [9] \qquad \frac{x \downarrow_s \quad \Delta_t(y) \quad s \leq t}{\Delta_t(x \mid y)} \ [10]$$

Table 12. Axioms of time shift ($a \in A, t, s \in R^{\square \geq 0}, u \in R^{>0}$).

$0 \gg x = x$	$t \gg \sigma^{t+s}.x = \sigma^s.x$
$t \gg \tilde{\tilde{\delta}} = \tilde{\tilde{\delta}}$	$(t+s) \gg \sigma^s.x = t \gg x$
$u \gg \tilde{\tilde{\epsilon}} = \tilde{\tilde{\delta}}$	$t \gg (x+y) = t \gg x + t \gg y$
$u \gg \tilde{\tilde{a}}.x = \tilde{\tilde{\delta}}$	

theorem, the completeness of TSP$_{\mathrm{srt}}$ gives that TCP$_{\mathrm{srt}}$ is complete. Note that we can also prove that TCP$_{\mathrm{srt}}$ is a conservative extension of MPT$_{\mathrm{srt}}$.

Theorem 19 (Conservativity). *The process algebra TCP$_{\mathrm{srt}}$ is a conservative extension of the process algebra TSP$_{\mathrm{srt}}$, i.e., for all closed TSP$_{\mathrm{srt}}$-terms p and q: TSP$_{\mathrm{srt}} \vdash p = q$ iff TCP$_{\mathrm{srt}} \vdash p = q$.*

Proof. This theorem follows, using the meta-theory of [28], from the completeness of TSP$_{\mathrm{srt}}$ (Theorem 15), from the soundness of TCP$_{\mathrm{srt}}$ (Theorem 17), and from the observation that the term deduction system of TCP$_{\mathrm{srt}}$ is an operationally conservative extension of the term deduction system of TSP$_{\mathrm{srt}}$. This last observation follows from the observations that both term deduction systems are in path format and that the term deduction system for TSP$_{\mathrm{srt}}$ is pure and well-founded.

Theorem 20 (Completeness). *The process algebra TCP$_{\mathrm{srt}}$ is a complete axiomatization of strong bisimilarity on closed TCP$_{\mathrm{srt}}$-terms.*

Proof. This theorem follows, using the meta-theory of [28], from the fact that TCP$_{\mathrm{srt}}$ is a conservative extension of TSP$_{\mathrm{srt}}$ (Theorem 19) and the elimination theorem (Theorem 18).

Table 13. Axioms of Standard Concurrency.

$$x \parallel \tilde{\tilde{\epsilon}} = x$$
$$(x \parallel y) \parallel z = x \parallel (y \parallel z)$$
$$(x \mid y) \mid z = x \mid (y \mid z)$$
$$(x \lfloor\!\lfloor y) \lfloor\!\lfloor z = x \lfloor\!\lfloor (y \parallel z)$$
$$(x \mid y) \lfloor\!\lfloor z = x \mid (y \lfloor\!\lfloor z)$$

It is quite common to add to the axioms for TCP$_{\text{srt}}$ the axioms of Table 13. These are called the *Axioms of Standard Concurrency*. For closed TCP$_{\text{srt}}$-terms these are derivable from the axioms of TCP$_{\text{srt}}$. This fact requires a quite lengthy proof.

Theorem 21. *For closed TCP$_{\text{srt}}$-terms x, y, and z, the equalities of Table 13 are derivable from the axioms of TCP$_{\text{srt}}$.*

Using the axioms of Standard Concurrency, we can derive the Expansion Theorem, generalizing the merge axiom to a parallel composition of a number of processes.

5   Relation with Other Process Algebras

In the previous sections, the notion of conservative extension has already been used for comparing the process algebras we introduced. Conservative extension results can only be applied in case the syntax of one of the process algebras is fully included in the syntax of the other process algebra. For comparison of our process algebras with existing process algebras this is in general not the case. Therefore, we first introduce another means of comparing process algebras: embeddings.

Then, we first consider the embedding of the discrete-time process algebras into the real-time process algebras. Second, we consider the relation of the real-time versions of the process algebras we have introduced with some existing untimed process algebras. Finally, we relate our process algebras to some timed variants found in literature which do not have a constant for successful termination.

5.1   Comparing Process Algebras

A process algebra $T' = (\Sigma', E')$ is a *conservative extension* of the process algebra $T = (\Sigma, E)$ if (1) $\Sigma \subseteq \Sigma'$ and (2) for all closed terms s and t over the signature Σ: $(\Sigma, E) \vdash s = t$ if and only if $(\Sigma', E') \vdash s = t$. This is an interesting notion of comparing process algebras as it says that the smaller process algebra is contained precisely in the larger process algebra. No identities are lost and none are added.

An *explicit definition* of an operator or constant f in the process algebra (Σ, E) is an equation $f(x_1, \cdots, x_n) = t$ where t is a term over the signature Σ that does not contain other free variables than $x_1, \cdots, x_n$. An extension of (Σ, E) with only explicitly defined operators and constants is called a *definitional extension* of (Σ, E). The following theorem states that a definitional extension is a special type of conservative extension.

Theorem 22. *If the process algebra T' is a definitional extension of the process algebra T, then T' is a conservative extension of T.*

An *embedding* of a process algebra $T = (\Sigma, E)$ in a process algebra $T' = (\Sigma', E')$ is a term structure preserving injective mapping $\hbar$ from the terms of T to the terms of T' such that for all closed terms s, t of T, $T \vdash s = t$ implies $T' \vdash \hbar(s) = \hbar(t)$.

Theorem 23 (Baeten and Middelburg). *Let $T = (\Sigma, E)$ and $T' = (\Sigma', E')$ be process algebras such that all operators from the signature Σ that are not in the signature Σ' can be defined in T' by explicit definitions. Let $T'' = (\Sigma'', E'')$ be the resulting definitional extension of T'. If the axioms of T are derivable for closed terms in T'', then T can be embedded in T' as follows: $\hbar(x) = x$, $\hbar(f(t_1, \ldots, t_n)) = f(\hbar(t_1), \ldots, \hbar(t_n))$ if f in the signature of T', and finally $\hbar(f(t_1, \ldots, t_n)) = t[\hbar(t_1), \ldots, \hbar(t_n)/x_1, \ldots, x_n]$ if the explicit definition of f is $f(x_1, \ldots, x_n) = t$.*

5.2   Embedding Discrete Relative Timing into Continuous Relative Timing

The discrete relative timing process algebras are easily embedded into their continuous relative timing counterparts by interpreting $\underline{\delta}$, $\underline{\epsilon}$ and $\underline{a}._\_$ as $\widetilde{\underline{\delta}}$, $\widetilde{\underline{\epsilon}}$ and $\widetilde{\underline{a}}._\_$, respectively.

However, this is not the embedding that conforms to our intuition. The embedding that does that, is the following:

- discrete time process $\underline{\delta}$ is mapped to the real time process that allows any delay from the current point of time up to the end of the current time slice (up to the next integer value), and no further activity;
- discrete time process $\underline{\epsilon}$ is mapped to the real time process that allows any delay from the current point of time up to the end of the current time slice followed by immediate termination ($\widetilde{\underline{\epsilon}}$);
- discrete time process $\underline{a}.x$ is mapped to the real time process that allows any delay from the current point of time up to the end of the current time slice followed by the execution of a followed by the translation of x.

However, in order to define this embedding formally, we need to know the position of the current point of time in the current time slice, so that we can calculate the upper bound of the possible delay. This requires knowledge of absolute timing. This point was already noted in [12], section 4.3.2. Note that it is an advantage of absolute timing over relative timing, that such an embedding can be written down explicitly. There, such an embedding is eventually achieved by extending the theory first to parametric timing, a variant in which relative and absolute timing coexist. We refrain from doing this here, and just remark a similar approach works in the present setting.

5.3 Embedding Untimed Process Algebras with Explicit Termination

Minimal Process Algebra. We compare the real-time process algebra with relative timing MPT_{srt} with the process algebra MPA from [13]. The signature of the process algebra MPA consists of constants for deadlock δ and termination ϵ, action prefix operators $a.\_$ (for $a \in A$), and alternative composition $+$. In this process algebra, where timing is only implicitly available in the interpretation of the action prefix operators, deadlock is a unit for alternative composition. The axioms of MPA are given in Table 14.

Table 14. Axioms of MPA.

$x + y = y + x$	A1
$(x + y) + z = x + (y + z)$	A2
$x + x = x$	A3
$x + \delta = x$	A6

One embedding of MPA is where $a.\_$ is mapped to $\widetilde{\widetilde{a}}.\_$, and where δ, ϵ are mapped to $\widetilde{\widetilde{\delta}}, \widetilde{\widetilde{\epsilon}}$. This is an embedding as all axioms remain valid. But it is a not very interesting embedding as any untimed process is interpreted as a timed process where all behaviour takes place at time 0. In such a setting, one might as well stick with the time-free theory. For this reason, we will not consider embeddings based on this interpretation anymore.

Thus, this leads us to interpret a process $a.x$ as a process where action a can be executed at any moment of time, i.e. a is executed after an arbitrary delay. Operationally, this means we have:

$$\Delta_t(a.x) \qquad a.x \xrightarrow{a}_t \ldots$$

for any $t \in R^{\geq 0}$.

Now it is still to be decided what remains of process $a.x$ after a is executed. There are two possibilities.

1. In the timed setting, the process $a.x$ executes the action a after an arbitrary delay and upon the execution of a the process x starts executing immediately.
2. In the timed setting, the process $a.x$ executes the action a after an arbitrary delay and upon the execution of a the process x starts after an arbitrary delay.

Both of these interpretations yield embeddings, but we have a strong preference to use the first possibility and not the second. This can be motivated as follows.

Having realised the embedding, we want to use the arbitrary delay prefix $a.\_$ and the urgent action prefix $\tilde{\tilde{a}}.\_$ both together in the description of processes. This will be apparent in the examples further on. Thus, we will have terms of the form $a.b.x$ and terms of the form $a.\tilde{\tilde{b}}.x$. In the first term, execution of b is some time after the execution of a (after an arbitrary delay), whereas in the second term, we intend to say that execution of b is immediately after the execution of a (after no delay). This forces us to use the first interpretation, so we have

$$\Delta_t(a.x) \qquad a.x \xrightarrow{a}_t x$$

for any $t \in R^{\geq 0}$.

Note that the process algebra MPA_{drt} from [13] also uses this interpretation.

It remains now to give the embedding of the constants δ, ϵ. An important operator in process algebra is the encapsulation operator ∂_H, that blocks the execution of actions in H (usually to enforce communication). If $a \in H$, the time-free theory contains the axiom $\partial_H(a.x) = \delta$ in cases where $a \in H$ as it limits choices of embedding the time-free theory in the real-time theory. As the action prefix operator allows an initial arbitrary delay, we are forced to also interpret δ as having an initial arbitrary delay, i.e. the process δ cannot execute any action, but does not block time. For this reason, this process can be called livelock. For more details, see [13]. Next, $x + \delta = x$ is an axiom of the time-free theory (A6), i.e. this axiom holds for all time-free processes. Thus, it holds in particular for ϵ, and thus, also the process ϵ should allow an initial arbitrary delay. It turns out the time-free processes are characterized by the fact that before any action execution and before any termination, an arbitrary delay can occur.

In order to make things explicit, let us extend the real-time process algebra MPT_{srt} with the arbitrary delay prefix operator $\sigma^*.\_$. The process $\sigma^*.x$ describes an arbitrary delay before x starts executing. The deduction rules for the arbitrary delay prefix operator are given in Table 15 and axioms can be found in Table 16.

Table 15. Deduction rules for arbitrary delay prefix operator $(t, s \in R^{\blacksquare\, 0})$.

$$\frac{x \downarrow_t}{\sigma^{\blacksquare}.x \downarrow_{t+s}}\ [1] \qquad \frac{x \xrightarrow{a}_t x^{\blacksquare}}{\sigma^{\blacksquare}.x \xrightarrow{a}_{t+s} x^{\blacksquare}}\ [2] \qquad \Delta_t(\sigma^{\blacksquare}.x)\ [3]$$

Thus, we now have the following definitional extension:

- $a.x = \sigma^*.\tilde{\tilde{a}}.x$
- $\delta = \sigma^*.\tilde{\tilde{\delta}}$
- $\epsilon = \sigma^*.\tilde{\tilde{\epsilon}}.$

Table 16. Axioms of arbitrary delay prefix operator ($t \in R^{\blacksquare \geq 0}$).

$$
\begin{array}{l}
\sigma^{\blacksquare}.\sigma^{\blacksquare}.x = \sigma^{\blacksquare}.x \\
\sigma^{\blacksquare}.\sigma^{t}.x = \sigma^{t}.\sigma^{\blacksquare}.x \\
\sigma^{\blacksquare}.x + \sigma^{t}.x = \sigma^{\blacksquare}.x \\
\sigma^{\blacksquare}.x + \sigma^{\blacksquare}.y = \sigma^{\blacksquare}.(x + y) \\
\sigma^{\blacksquare}.x \cdot y = \sigma^{\blacksquare}.(x \cdot y) \\
\partial_H(\sigma^{\blacksquare}.x) = \sigma^{\blacksquare}.\partial_H(x)
\end{array}
$$

In order to show we have an embedding, we need to derive the axioms of MPA for closed MPA-terms. We proceed to do this. The axioms A1-A3 are also part of $\mathrm{MPT_{srt}}$ and need therefore not be considered. For axiom A6 we use induction on the structure of closed MPA-terms:

- $x \equiv \epsilon$. Then $x + \delta = \epsilon + \delta = \sigma^*.\widetilde{\widetilde{\epsilon}} + \sigma^*.\widetilde{\widetilde{\delta}} = \sigma^*.(\widetilde{\widetilde{\epsilon}} + \widetilde{\widetilde{\delta}}) = \sigma^*.\widetilde{\widetilde{\epsilon}} = \epsilon = x$.
- $x \equiv \delta$. Then $x + \delta = \delta + \delta = \delta = x$.
- $x \equiv a.x'$ for some $a \in A$ and closed MPA-term x'. Then $x + \delta = a.x' + \delta = \sigma^*.\widetilde{\widetilde{a}}.x' + \sigma^*.\widetilde{\widetilde{\delta}} = \sigma^*.(\widetilde{\widetilde{a}}.x' + \widetilde{\widetilde{\delta}}) = \sigma^*.\widetilde{\widetilde{a}}.x' = a.x'$.
- $x \equiv x_1 + x_2$. By induction we have $x_1 + \delta = x_1$ and $x_2 + \delta = x_2$. Then $x + \delta = (x_1 + x_2) + \delta = x_1 + (x_2 + \delta) = x_1 + x_2 = x$.

Sequential Process Algebra. Next, we briefly consider the embedding of SPA into $\mathrm{TSP_{srt}}$. The process algebra SPA [13], is the extension of MPA with sequential composition. It has the axioms of Table 17 in addition to those from MPA.

Table 17. Axioms of SPA.

$$
\begin{array}{ll}
(x + y) \cdot z = x \cdot z + y \cdot z & \text{A4} \\
(x \cdot y) \cdot z = x \cdot (y \cdot z) & \text{A5} \\
\delta \cdot x = \delta & \text{A7} \\
\epsilon \cdot x = x & \text{A8} \\
x \cdot \epsilon = x & \text{A9} \\
a.x \cdot y = a.(x \cdot y) & \text{A10}
\end{array}
$$

The axioms A4 and A5 are also part of $\mathrm{TSP_{srt}}$ and need therefore not be considered to show we have an embedding. Axiom A7 is easily derived as follows:

$$\delta \cdot x = (\sigma^*.\widetilde{\widetilde{\delta}}) \cdot x = \sigma^*.(\widetilde{\widetilde{\delta}} \cdot x) = \sigma^*.\widetilde{\widetilde{\delta}} = \delta.$$

The proof for axiom A6, again for both interpretations, is extended with the case that $x \equiv x_1 \cdot x_2$ as follows, using the fact that axiom A7 can be derived for closed SPA-terms:

$$x + \delta = x_1 \cdot x_2 + \delta = x_1 \cdot x_2 + \delta \cdot x_2 = (x_1 + \delta) \cdot x_2 = x_1 \cdot x_2 = x.$$

Axiom A10 is derived as follows:

$$a.x \cdot y = \sigma^*.\tilde{\tilde{a}}\,.x \cdot y = \sigma^*.(\tilde{\tilde{a}}\,.x \cdot y) = \sigma^*.\tilde{\tilde{a}}\,.(x \cdot y) = a.(x \cdot y),$$

Next, the equality $\sigma^*.x = x$ can be derived for closed SPA-terms by induction. The proof goes as follows:

- $x \equiv \epsilon$. Then $\sigma^*.x = \sigma^*.\epsilon = \sigma^*.\sigma^*.\tilde{\tilde{\epsilon}} = \sigma^*.\tilde{\tilde{\epsilon}} = \epsilon = x$.
- $x \equiv \delta$. Then $\sigma^*.x = \sigma^*.\delta = \sigma^*.\sigma^*.\tilde{\tilde{\delta}} = \sigma^*.\tilde{\tilde{\delta}} = \delta = x$.
- $x \equiv a.x'$ for some $a \in A$ and closed SPA-term x'. Then $\sigma^*.x = \sigma^*.a.x' = \sigma^*.\sigma^*.\tilde{\tilde{a}}\,.x' = \sigma^*.\tilde{\tilde{a}}\,.x' = a.x' = x$.
- $x \equiv x_1 + x_2$ for some closed SPA-terms x_1 and x_2. Then, using the induction hypotheses $\sigma^*.x_1 = x_1$ and $\sigma^*.x_2 = x_2$, we have $\sigma^*.x = \sigma^*.(x_1 + x_2) = \sigma^*.x_1 + \sigma^*.x_2 = x_1 + x_2 = x$.
- $x \equiv x_1 \cdot x_2$ for some closed SPA-terms x_1 and x_2. Then, using the induction hypothesis $\sigma^*.x_1 = x_1$, we have $\sigma^*.x = \sigma^*.(x_1 \cdot x_2) = \sigma^*.x_1 \cdot x_2 = x_1 \cdot x_2 = x$.

Then, Axiom A8 is derived for closed SPA-terms x as follows:

$$\epsilon \cdot x = \sigma^*.\tilde{\tilde{\epsilon}} \cdot x = \sigma^*.(\tilde{\tilde{\epsilon}} \cdot x) = \sigma^*.x = x$$

Finally, Axiom A9 is obtained by induction on the structure of closed SPA-term x as follows.

- $x \equiv \epsilon$. Then $x \cdot \epsilon = \epsilon \cdot \epsilon = \sigma^*.\tilde{\tilde{\epsilon}} \cdot \epsilon = \sigma^*.(\tilde{\tilde{\epsilon}} \cdot \epsilon) = \sigma^*.\epsilon = \epsilon = x$.
- $x \equiv \delta$. Then $x \cdot \epsilon = \delta \cdot \epsilon = \sigma^*.\tilde{\tilde{\delta}} \cdot \epsilon = \sigma^*.(\tilde{\tilde{\delta}} \cdot \epsilon) = \sigma^*.\tilde{\tilde{\delta}} = \delta = x$.
- $x \equiv a.x'$ for some $a \in A$ and closed SPA-term x'. Then using the induction hypothesis $x' \cdot \epsilon = x'$, we get $x \cdot \epsilon = a.x' \cdot \epsilon = \sigma^*.\tilde{\tilde{a}}\,.x' \cdot \epsilon = \sigma^*.(\tilde{\tilde{a}}\,.x' \cdot \epsilon) = \sigma^*.\tilde{\tilde{a}}\,.(x' \cdot \epsilon) = \sigma^*.\tilde{\tilde{a}}\,.x' = a.x' = x$.
- $x \equiv x_1 + x_2$ for some closed SPA-terms x_1 and x_2. Then, using the induction hypotheses $x_1 \cdot \epsilon = x_1$ and $x_2 \cdot \epsilon = x_2$, we have $x \cdot \epsilon = (x_1 + x_2) \cdot \epsilon = x_1 \cdot \epsilon + x_2 \cdot \epsilon = x_1 + x_2 = x$.
- $x \equiv x_1 \cdot x_2$ for some closed SPA-terms x_1 and x_2. Then, using the induction hypothesis $x_2 \cdot \epsilon = x_2$, we have $x \cdot \epsilon = (x_1 \cdot x_2) \cdot \epsilon = x_1 \cdot (x_2 \cdot \epsilon) = x_1 \cdot x_2 = x$.

Interaction Process Algebra. The extension of SPA with parallel composition and communication, called IPA, from [13] cannot be embedded into TCP_{srt}. The reason for this, perhaps unexpected, result is that the intended meaning of the auxiliary operators $\|$ and $|$ in these theories is fundamentally different. We conjecture that the subalgebras that are obtained by removing these auxiliary operators from the signature, allow for embeddings similar to the embeddings from MPA and SPA into MPT_{drt} and TSP_{drt}.

Basic Process Algebra. We consider the process algebra $BPA_{\delta\epsilon}$ of [29], which is similar to SPA with the difference that is does not have action prefix operators, but action constants instead. The axioms of $BPA_{\delta\epsilon}$ are A1-A9.

The same reasoning as above leads us to interpret δ as $\sigma^* . \widetilde{\widetilde{\delta}}$ and ϵ as $\sigma^* . \widetilde{\widetilde{\epsilon}}$. But now, we have to interpret the constant a. If we interpret a as $\sigma^* . \widetilde{\widetilde{a}} . \widetilde{\widetilde{\epsilon}}$, the axiom $x \cdot \epsilon = x$ cannot be derived as $a \cdot \epsilon = \sigma^* . \widetilde{\widetilde{a}} \cdot \sigma^* . \widetilde{\widetilde{\epsilon}} \neq \sigma^* . \widetilde{\widetilde{a}} = a$. On the other hand, if we interpret a as $\sigma^* . \widetilde{\widetilde{a}} . \sigma^* . \widetilde{\widetilde{\epsilon}}$, then we run into problems with the interpretation of terms of the form $a \cdot \widetilde{\widetilde{b}} .x$.

This observation has been the reason to redesign the hierarchy of ACP-related process algebras replacing action constants by action prefix in [13], [30].

5.4   Embedding MPA$_{drt}$ into MPT$_{\mathrm{drt}}$

In this section, we formalize the intuition that the process algebra MPA$_{drt}$ from Section 2.1 can be embedded into the process algebra MPT$_{\mathrm{drt}}$ from Section 2.2. We interpret, as mentioned before, the next time slice prefix operator from MPA$_{drt}$ as the relative delay prefix operator with relative delay 1. Thereto we add the relative delay prefix operator to MPT$_{\mathrm{drt}}$ by means of the following explicit definition:

$$\sigma.x = \sigma^1.x.$$

Using Theorem 23, we only need to derive the axioms of MPA$_{drt}$, for closed MPA$_{drt}$-terms, in this definitional extension of MPT$_{\mathrm{drt}}$. The only axiom of MPA$_{drt}$ that is not also an axiom of MPT$_{\mathrm{drt}}$ is axiom DRTD from Table 1. It can be derived as follows:

$$\sigma.x + \sigma.y = \sigma^1.x + \sigma^1.y = \sigma^1.(x + y) = \sigma.(x + y).$$

5.5   Embedding Timed Process Algebras
Without Explicit Termination

In this section, we compare the process algebra TSP$_{\mathrm{drt}}$ with a relative timing process algebra from the literature that is very similar to TSP$_{\mathrm{drt}}$, but does not contain a constant for undelayable termination. One of the few examples of such process algebras is the process algebra BPA$^{\mathrm{drt}} - $ID from [12]. The signature of this process algebra consists of the urgent actions $\underline{a}$ (for $a \in A$), undelayable deadlock $\underline{\delta}$, alternative and sequential composition, and the unary relative delay operator $\overline{\sigma}^n(\_)$ (for $n \in N$) . The axioms of this process algebra are given in Table 18.

The undelayable actions $\underline{a}$ (for $a \in A$) and the unary relative delay operator σ^n of BPA$^{\mathrm{drt}} - $ID can be defined explicitly on TSP$_{\mathrm{drt}}$ by the equations $\underline{a} = \underline{a.\epsilon}$ and $\sigma^n(x) = \sigma^n.x$, respectively.

We show that, for closed terms over the signature of BPA$^{\mathrm{drt}} - $ID, the axioms of BPA$^{\mathrm{drt}} - $ID are derivable from this definitional extension of TSP$_{\mathrm{drt}}$.

Thereto, we have to consider each of the axioms of BPA$^{\mathrm{drt}} - $ID. The axioms A1-A5, and A7DR of BPA$^{\mathrm{drt}} - $ID are also axioms of TSP$_{\mathrm{drt}}$ and need therefore not be considered. For the other axioms we have the following derivations (for $n, m \in N$):

Table 18. Axioms of $\text{BPA}^{\text{drt}}_{-} - \text{ID}$ $(m, n \in N)$.

$x + y = y + x$	A1	$\sigma^0_{\text{rel}}(x) = x$	DRT1
$(x + y) + z = x + (y + z)$	A2	$\sigma^m_{\text{rel}}(\sigma^n_{\text{rel}}(x)) = \sigma^{m+n}_{\text{rel}}(x)$	DRT2
$x + x = x$	A3	$\sigma^n_{\text{rel}}(x) + \sigma^n_{\text{rel}}(y) = \sigma^n_{\text{rel}}(x + y)$	DRT3
$(x + y) \cdot z = x \cdot z + y \cdot z$	A4	$\sigma^n_{\text{rel}}(x) \cdot y = \sigma^n_{\text{rel}}(x \cdot y)$	DRT4
$(x \cdot y) \cdot z = x \cdot (y \cdot z)$	A5	$\underline{a} + \underline{\delta} = \underline{a}$	A6DRa
		$\sigma^{n+1}_{\text{rel}}(x) + \underline{\underline{\delta}} = \sigma^{n+1}_{\text{rel}}(x)$	A6DRb
		$\underline{\underline{\delta}} \cdot x = \underline{\underline{\delta}}$	A7DR

(DRT1) $\sigma^0(x) = \sigma^0.x = x$,

(DRT2) $\sigma^n(\sigma^m(x)) = \sigma^n.\sigma^m.x = \sigma^{n+m}.x = \sigma^{n+m}(x)$,

(DRT3) $\sigma^n(x) + \sigma^n(y) = \sigma^n.x + \sigma^n.y = \sigma^n.(x + y) = \sigma^n(x + y)$,

(DRT4) $\sigma^n(x) \cdot y = (\sigma^n.x) \cdot y = \sigma^n.(x \cdot y) = \sigma^n(x \cdot y)$,

(A6DRa) $\underline{a} + \underline{\delta} = \underline{a}$,

(A6DRb) $\sigma^{n+1}(x) + \underline{\underline{\delta}} = \sigma^{n+1}(x)$.

Then, as a consequence of Theorem 23, we have that $\text{BPA}^{\text{drt}} - \text{ID}$ can be embedded in TSP_{srt} using $\hbar$ defined by $\hbar(\underline{\delta}) = \underline{\delta}$, $\hbar(\underline{a}) = \underline{a}.\underline{\epsilon}$, $\hbar(x_1 + x_2) = \hbar(x_1) + \hbar(x_2)$, $\hbar(x_1 \cdot x_2) = \hbar(x_1) \cdot \hbar(x_2)$, $\hbar(\sigma^t(x)) = \sigma^t.\hbar(x)$.

6   Time-Free Projection, Abstraction and Recursion, $\sum$-Notations

In this section, we discuss some additional operators that will be used in the examples we discuss in the following section.

6.1   Time-Free Projection

First of all, we discuss an operator that abstracts from all timing information. This means a process is turned into a process in time-free process algebra. As we saw in the previous section, in time-free process algebra, there are arbitrary delays between all activities. We introduce the *time-free projection* operator π_{tf}, with the axioms in Table 19. The process $\pi_{\text{tf}}(x)$ has the same action and termination behaviour as the process x, but it also allows arbitrary time steps in between.

Table 19. Axioms for time-free projection ($a \in A$, $t \in R^{\blacksquare\,0}$).

$$\pi_{\mathrm{tf}}(\widetilde{\widetilde{\delta}}) = \delta$$
$$\pi_{\mathrm{tf}}(\widetilde{\widetilde{\epsilon}}) = \epsilon$$
$$\pi_{\mathrm{tf}}(\widetilde{\widetilde{a}}\,.x) = a.\pi_{\mathrm{tf}}(x)$$
$$\pi_{\mathrm{tf}}(x + y) = \pi_{\mathrm{tf}}(x) + \pi_{\mathrm{tf}}(y)$$
$$\pi_{\mathrm{tf}}(\sigma^t.x) = \pi_{\mathrm{tf}}(x)$$

6.2 Abstraction

In the calculations to come, abstraction from internal activity will play an important role. In time-free process algebra, abstraction and internal steps are often approached by use of the notion of *branching bisimulation*, see [31]. This notion can be formulated by analogy in timed theories also, see e.g. [12]. We will refrain from doing this here, however, because we will have reason to change this notion in the sequel, Instead, at this point we just give an axiomatization of timed branching bisimulation, adapted from [12]. This axiomatization uses an auxiliary operator ν ("now"), that strips away any possible initial delay behaviour of a process. This operator is used in the timed variants of the branching axiom (the first two axioms), in order to ensure that a term starting with a delay is not split.

The axioms are given in Table 20. Obviously, the now operator and the abstraction operator can easily be eliminated from every closed term.

6.3 Recursion

A recursive specification over $\mathrm{TCP}_{\mathrm{srt}}$ is a set of recursive equations $E = \{X = t_X \mid X \in V\}$ where V is a set of variables and each t_X is a $\mathrm{TCP}_{\mathrm{srt}}$-term that only contains variables from V.

A recursive specification is called a *completely guarded* recursive specification if all occurrences of variables in terms t_X (for $X \in V$) occur in the context of an action prefix operator or a time prefix operator with positive delay. A recursive specification is called a *guarded* recursive specification if it can be rewritten into a completely guarded recursive specification using the axioms of $\mathrm{TCP}_{\mathrm{srt}}$ and the equations from the recursive specification.

We can assume that we work in a setting where all guarded recursive specifications have unique solutions. The necessary theory underpinning this assumption can be found e.g. in [12].

6.4 Generalized Alternative Composition

For a finite set D we define $\sum_{d \in D} p$ recursively as follows: for $v \notin D$

$$\sum_{d \in \emptyset} p = \widetilde{\widetilde{\delta}} \qquad \sum_{d \in D \cup \{v\}} p = p[d := v] + \sum_{d \in D} p.$$

Table 20. Axioms for abstraction $(a \in A_\tau,\ I \subseteq A,\ t \in R^{\blacksquare\,0},\ u \in R^{>0})$.

$$\tilde{\tilde{a}}\,.(\tilde{\tilde{\tau}}\,.(\nu(x) + y) + \nu(x)) = \tilde{\tilde{a}}\,.(\nu(x) + y)$$
$$\tilde{\tilde{a}}\,.(\tilde{\tilde{\tau}}\,.(\nu(x) + y) + y) = \tilde{\tilde{a}}\,.(\nu(x) + y)$$
$$\tilde{\tilde{a}}\,.(\sigma^u.\tilde{\tilde{\tau}}\,.x + \nu(y)) = \tilde{\tilde{a}}\,.(\sigma^u.x + \nu(y))$$

$$\nu(\tilde{\tilde{\delta}}) = \tilde{\tilde{\delta}}$$
$$\nu(\tilde{\tilde{\epsilon}}) = \tilde{\tilde{\epsilon}}$$
$$\nu(\tilde{\tilde{a}}\,.x) = \tilde{\tilde{a}}\,.x$$
$$\nu(x + y) = \nu(x) + \nu(y)$$
$$\nu(\sigma^u.x) = \tilde{\tilde{\delta}}$$

$$\tau_I(\tilde{\tilde{\delta}}) = \tilde{\tilde{\delta}}$$
$$\tau_I(\tilde{\tilde{\epsilon}}) = \tilde{\tilde{\epsilon}}$$
$$\tau_I(\tilde{\tilde{a}}\,.x) = \tilde{\tilde{\tau}}\,.\tau_I(x) \quad \text{if } a \in I$$
$$\tau_I(\tilde{\tilde{a}}\,.x) = \tilde{\tilde{a}}\,.\tau_I(x) \quad \text{if } a \notin I$$
$$\tau_I(x + y) = \tau_I(x) + \tau_I(y)$$
$$\tau_I(\sigma^t.x) = \sigma^t.\tau_I(x)$$

For simplicity, we only consider the case here where we use the sum notation for a finite set of data, or a finite set of time units. A generalization to an infinite set of data, or even an uncountable set of time points, will require additional theory.

7   Some Simple Calculations: Communicating Buffers

In this section, we give some simple calculations in order to illustrate the use of our relative-time theory.

In the calculations to come we use the so called *standard communication function*. Suppose we have given two finite sets, the set of messages or data D, and the set of ports P. For each $d \in D$ and $i \in P$, we have atomic actions $s_i(d)$, $r_i(d)$ and $c_i(d)$ (denoting send, receive and communication of datum d along port i) and the only defined communications are

$$\gamma(s_i(d), r_i(d)) = \gamma(r_i(d), s_i(d)) = c_i(d).$$

for any $d \in D$ and $i \in P$.

In time-free process algebra, there is the following standard specification of a one-place buffer with input port i and output port j:

$$B^{ij} = \sum_{d \in D} r_i(d).s_j(d).B^{ij}.$$

A straightforward computation shows that the parallel composition of two such buffers placed in sequence (connecting the output port of the first with the input port of the second) with the corresponding encapsulation of internal send and receive events and abstraction from internal communication events results in a two-place buffer:

$$\tau_I \circ \partial_H(B^{ij} \parallel B^{jk}) = B_2^{ik}$$

where $H = \{s_j(d), r_j(d) \mid d \in D\}$ and $I = \{c_j(d) \mid d \in D\}$.

In the remainder of this section we consider timed versions of such buffers. It is possible to use the discrete time theory, as all points of interest can be discussed. The unit of time is chosen in such a way that at most one input per time slice is possible.

In time-free process algebra, combining two one-place buffers yields a two-place buffer. This is the case when arbitrary delays are added at each point. Adding timing constraints in different ways can yield instead a one-place or a two-place buffer in different ways, as we will see.

7.1   No-Delay One-Place Buffers

The first type of one-place buffer with input port i and output port j we consider allows at most one input in every time slice, and outputs with no delay:

$$C^{ij} = \sum_{d \in D} r_i(d).\underline{s_j(d)}.\sigma.C^{ij},$$

or equivalently

$$C^{ij} = \sum_{d \in D} \underline{r_i(d).s_j(d)}.\sigma.C^{ij} + \sigma.C^{ij}.$$

If we consider the time-free projection of C^{ij}, i.e., $\pi_{\mathrm{tf}}(C^{ij})$ we obtain

$$\pi_{\mathrm{tf}}(C^{ij}) = \sum_{d \in D} r_i(d).s_j(d).\pi_{\mathrm{tf}}(C^{ij})$$

which satisfies the specification of the time-free one-place buffer. Hence, this timed one-place buffer can be considered an implementation of the time-free one-place buffer.

With $H = \{s_j(d), r_j(d)\}$ we can derive

$$
\begin{aligned}
&\partial_H(C^{ij} \parallel C^{jk}) \\
&= \partial_H(C^{ij} \lfloor\!\!\!\underline{} C^{jk}) + \partial_H(C^{jk} \lfloor\!\!\!\underline{} C^{ij}) + \partial_H(C^{ij} \mid C^{jk}) \\
&= \sum_{d \in D} \underline{r_i(d)}.\partial_H(\underline{s_j(d)}.\sigma.C^{ij} \parallel C^{jk}) + \sigma.\partial_H(C^{ij} \parallel C^{jk}) \\
&= \sum_{d \in D} \underline{r_i(d).c_j(d)}.\partial_H(\sigma.C^{ij} \parallel \underline{s_k(d)}.\sigma.C^{jk}) \\
&= \sum_{d \in D} \underline{r_i(d).c_j(d).s_k(d)}.\partial_H(\sigma.\overline{C^{ij}} \parallel \sigma.C^{jk}) \\
&= \sum_{d \in D} \underline{r_i(d).c_j(d).s_j(d)}.\sigma.\partial_H(C^{ij} \parallel C^{jk})
\end{aligned}
$$

Next, abstracting from the internal communication actions over port 2 using $I = \{c_j(d) \mid d \in D\}$ gives:

$$
\begin{aligned}
&\tau_I \circ \partial_H(C^{ij} \parallel C^{jk}) \\
&= \tau_I(\textstyle\sum_{d \in D} r_i(d).c_j(d).\underline{s_k(d)}.\sigma.\partial_H(C^{ij} \parallel C^{jk})) \\
&= \textstyle\sum_{d \in D} r_i(d).\underline{\underline{\tau}}.\underline{s_k(d)}.\sigma.\tau_I \circ \partial_H(C^{ij} \parallel C^{jk}) \\
&= \textstyle\sum_{d \in D} r_i(d).\underline{s_k(d)}.\sigma.\tau_I \circ \partial_H(C^{ij} \parallel C^{jk})
\end{aligned}
$$

Observe that the composition again behaves as a no-delay channel, with input port i and output port k, i.e.,

$$
\tau_I \circ \partial_H(C^{ij} \parallel C^{jk}) = C^{ik}.
$$

We see that this is very different behaviour from the time-free case.

7.2   Unit-Delay One-Place Buffers

Consider

$$
D^{ij} = \sum_{d \in D} r_i(d).\sigma.s_j(d).D^{ij}.
$$

This specification describes a buffer with capacity one and a delay between input and output of one time unit. Again, if we consider the time-free projection of D^{ij}, i.e., $\pi_{\mathrm{tf}}(D^{ij})$ we obtain

$$
\pi_{\mathrm{tf}}(D^{ij}) = \sum_{d \in D} r_i(d).s_j(d).\pi_{\mathrm{tf}}(D^{ij})
$$

which satisfies the specification of the time-free one-place buffer. Hence, this timed one-place buffer can be considered as a different implementation of the time-free one-place buffer. Now define $X = \partial_H(D^{ij} \parallel D^{jk})$ and $X_d = \partial_H(D^{ij} \parallel \sigma.\underline{s_k(d)}.D^{jk})$ for $d \in D$. Then the following recursive specification can be derived for variables X, X_d:

$$
\begin{aligned}
&X \\
&= \partial_H(D^{ij} \parallel D^{jk}) \\
&= \partial_H(D^{ij} \underline{\lfloor} D^{jk}) + \partial_H(D^{jk} \underline{\lfloor} D^{ij}) + \partial_H(D^{ij} \mid D^{jk}) \\
&= \textstyle\sum_{d \in D} r_i(d).\partial_H(\sigma.s_j(d).D^{ij} \parallel D^{jk}) + \sigma.\partial_H(D^{ij} \parallel D^{jk}) \\
&= \textstyle\sum_{d \in D} \overline{r_i(d)}.\sigma.\partial_H(\overline{s_j(d)}.D^{ij} \parallel D^{jk}) \\
&= \textstyle\sum_{d \in D} r_i(d).\sigma.c_j(d).\partial_H(D^{ij} \parallel \sigma.\underline{s_k(d)}.D^{jk}) \\
&= \textstyle\sum_{d \in D} r_i(d).\sigma.\underline{c_j(d)}.X_d
\end{aligned}
$$

and, for $d \in D$

$$X_d$$
$$= \partial_H(D^{ij} \parallel \sigma.s_k(d).D^{jk})$$
$$= \sum_{e \in D} \overline{r_i(e)}.\partial_H(\sigma.s_j(e).D^{ij} \parallel \sigma.s_k(d).D^{jk}) + \sigma.\partial_H(D^{ij} \parallel \underline{s_k(d).D^{jk}})$$
$$= \sum_{e \in D} \overline{r_i(e)}.\sigma.\partial_H(\overline{s_j(e)}.D^{ij} \parallel \underline{s_k(d).D^{jk}}) +$$
$$\quad \sigma.(\sum_{e \in D} \overline{r_i(e)}.\partial_H(\sigma.s_j(e).D^{ij} \parallel \underline{s_k(d).D^{jk}}) + \underline{s_k(d)}.\partial_H(D^{ij} \parallel D^{jk}))$$
$$= \sum_{e \in D} \overline{r_i(e)}.\sigma.\underline{s_k(d)}.\partial_H(\overline{s_j(e)}.D^{i\overline{j}} \parallel D^{jk}) +$$
$$\quad \sigma.(\sum_{e \in D} \overline{r_i(e)}.\underline{s_k(d)}.\partial_H(\overline{\sigma.s_j(e)}.D^{ij} \parallel D^{jk}) + \underline{s_k(d)}.X)$$
$$= \sum_{e \in D} \overline{r_i(e)}.\sigma.\underline{s_k(d)}.c_j(e).\partial_H(D^{ij} \parallel \overline{\sigma.s_k(e)}.D^{j\overline{k}}) +$$
$$\quad \sigma.(\sum_{e \in D} \overline{r_i(e)}.\underline{s_k(d)}.\sigma.\partial_H(\overline{s_j(e)}.D^{ij} \parallel \overline{D^{jk}}) + \underline{s_k(d)}.X)$$
$$= \sum_{e \in D} \overline{r_i(e)}.\sigma.\underline{s_k(d)}.c_j(e).X_e +$$
$$\quad \sigma.(\sum_{e \in D} \overline{r_i(e)}.\underline{s_k(d)}.\sigma.\overline{c_j(e)}.\partial_H(D^{ij} \parallel \overline{\sigma.s_k(e)}.D^{jk}) + \underline{s_k(d)}.X)$$
$$= \sum_{e \in D} \overline{r_1(e)}.\sigma.\underline{s_k(d)}.\overline{c_2(e)}.X_e +$$
$$\quad \sigma.(\sum_{e \in D} \overline{r_i(e)}.\underline{s_k(d)}.\sigma.\overline{c_j(e)}.X_e + \underline{s_k(d)}.X)$$

Abstraction from the internal communications gives:

$$\tau_I(X) = \sum_{d \in D} r_i(d).\sigma.\underline{\tau}.\tau_I(X_d)$$
$$= \sum_{d \in D} r_i(d).\sigma.\tau_I(X_d)$$

$$\tau_I(X_d) = \sum_{e \in D} \overline{r_i(e)}.\sigma.\underline{s_k(d)}.\underline{\tau}.\tau_I(X_e) +$$
$$\quad \sigma.(\sum_{e \in D} \overline{r_i(e)}.\underline{s_k(d)}.\sigma.\underline{\tau}.\tau_I(X_e) + \underline{s_k(d)}.\tau_I(X))$$
$$= \sum_{e \in D} \overline{r_i(e)}.\sigma.\underline{s_k(d)}.\tau_I(X_e) +$$
$$\quad \sigma.(\sum_{e \in D} \overline{r_i(e)}.\underline{s_k(d)}.\sigma.\tau_I(X_e) + \underline{s_k(d)}.\tau_I(X))$$

Observe that this denotes a two-place buffer with a delay of two time units. Thus, in this case we do obtain a result in accordance with the time-free theory. It can be claimed that this is a more faithful timed variant of the time-free buffer as in this version, each transportation from input to output takes one unit of time.

7.3 Unit-Delay One-Place Buffers II

To conclude this section, consider yet another variant of a one-place buffer.

$$E^{ij} = \sum_{d \in D} r_i(d).\sigma. \left(\underline{s_j(d).\underline{\epsilon}} \parallel E^{ij} \right)$$

Again, transportation from input to output take one unit of time, but now, a new input can be accepted in every time slice. Thus, it can be said that this implementation is *input-enabled*.

The composition $\tau_I(\partial_H(E^{ij} \parallel E^{jk}))$ now satisfies the following recursive specification:

$$Y = \sum_{d\in D} r_i(d).\sigma.Y_d'$$
$$Y_d' = \sigma.\left(s_k(d).Y + \sum_{e\in D} r_i(e).s_k(d).\sigma.Y_e'\right) + \sum_{e\in D} r_i(e).\sigma.Y_{de}''$$
$$Y_{de}'' = \underline{s_k(d).Y_e'} + \sum_{f\in D} \underline{r_i(f).s_k(d).\sigma.Y_{ef}''}$$

We see that it is possible that three data elements reside in this composition at the same time.

The time-free abstraction of this process gives:

$$\pi_{\mathrm{tf}}(Y) = \sum_{d\in D} r_i(d).\pi_{\mathrm{tf}}(Y_d')$$
$$\pi_{\mathrm{tf}}(Y_d') = s_k(d).X + \sum_{e\in D} r_i(e).s_k(d).\pi_{\mathrm{tf}}(Y_e') + \sum_{e\in D} r_i(e).\pi_{\mathrm{tf}}(Y_{de}'')$$
$$\pi_{\mathrm{tf}}(Y_{de}'') = s_k(d).\pi_{\mathrm{tf}}(Y_e') + \sum_{f\in D} r_i(f).s_k(d).\pi_{\mathrm{tf}}(Y_{ef}'')$$

8 Case Study: PAR Protocol

In the following example, we describe a simple communication protocol. A communication protocol concerns the transmission of data through an unreliable channel, such that no data will get lost. The example shows that with the basic concepts for timing introduced so far, we are able to describe the protocol in a satisfactory way. This is not possible with the concepts around which ACP (without timing) has been set up.

8.1 Description of the PAR Protocol

We consider a simple version of the communication protocol known as the *PAR* (Positive Acknowledgement with Retransmission) protocol.

The configuration of the PAR protocol is shown in Fig. 1 by means of a connection diagram. The sender waits for an acknowledgement before a new

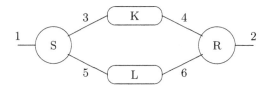

Fig. 1. Connection diagram for PAR protocol.

datum is transmitted. If an acknowledgement is not received within a complete protocol cycle, the old datum is retransmitted. In order to avoid duplicates due to retransmission, data are labeled with an alternating bit from $B = \{0, 1\}$.

We have a sender process S, a receiver process R, and two channels K and L. The process S waits until a datum d is offered at an external port (port 1). When a datum, say d, is offered at this port, S consumes it, packs it with an alternating bit b in a frame (d, b), and then delivers the frame at an internal port used for sending (port 3). Next, S waits until an acknowledgement ack is offered at an internal port used for receiving (port 5). When the acknowledgement does not arrive within a certain time period, S delivers the same frame again and goes back to waiting for an acknowledgement. When the acknowledgement arrives within that time period, S goes back to waiting for a datum. The process R waits until a frame with a datum and an alternating bit (d, b) is offered at an internal port used for receiving (port 4). When a frame is offered at this port, R consumes it, unpacks it, and then delivers the datum d at an external port (port 2) if the alternating bit b is the right one and in any case delivers an acknowledgement ack at an internal port used for sending (port 6). After that, R goes back to waiting for a frame, but the right bit changes to $(1 - b)$ if the alternating bit was the right one. The processes K and L pass on frames from an internal port of S to an internal port of R and acknowledgements from an internal port of R to an internal port of S, respectively. Because the channels are supposed to be unreliable, they may produce an error instead of passing on frames or acknowledgements. The times $t_1, \ldots, t_4$ are the times that it takes the different processes to pack and deliver, to unpack and deliver or simply to deliver what they consume. The time t_1' is the time-out time of the sender, i.e., the time after which it retransmits a datum in case it is still waiting for an acknowledgement. The time t_2' is the time that it takes the receiver to produce and deliver an acknowledgement.

We assume a finite set of data D. Let $F = D \times B$ be the set of frames. For $d \in D$ and $b \in B$, we write d, b for the frame (d, b).

Again, we use the standard communication function, so assuming a finite set of data D, the communication function is defined such that

$$\gamma(s_i(d), r_i(d)) = \gamma(r_i(d), s_i(d)) = c_i(d)$$

for all $d \in D$, and it is undefined otherwise. The recursive specification of the sender consists of the following equations: for every $b \in B$ and $d \in D$

$$
\begin{aligned}
S &= S_0 \\
S_b &= \sum_{d \in D} r_1(d).\sigma^{t_1}.SF_{d,b}
\end{aligned}
$$

$$SF_{d,b} = \underline{s_3(d,b)}.\left(\sum_{k<t_1'} \sigma^k.\underline{r_5(ack)}.S_{1-b} + \sigma^{t_1'}.SF_{d,b} \right)$$

The recursive specification of the receiver consists of the following equations: for every $b \in B$

$$
\begin{aligned}
R &= R_0 \\
R_b &= \sum_{d \in D} r_4(d,b).\sigma^{t_2}.\underline{s_2(d)}.\sigma^{t_2'}.\underline{s_6(ack)}.R_{1-b} \\
&\quad + \sum_{d \in D} r_4(d, 1-b).\sigma^{t_2'}.\underline{s_6(ack)}.R_b
\end{aligned}
$$

Each of the channels is recursively defined by a single equation:

$$K = \sum_{f \in F} r_3(f).\left(\sigma^{t_3}.\underline{s_4(f).K} + \sum_{k \leq t_3} \sigma^k.\underline{error.K} \right)$$

$$L = r_6(ack).\left(\sigma^{t_4}.\underline{s_5(ack).L} + \sum_{k \leq t_4} \sigma^k.\underline{error.L} \right).$$

The whole system is described by the following term:

$$\partial_H(S \parallel K \parallel L \parallel R),$$

where

$$H = \{s_i(f) \mid i \in \{3,4\}, f \in F\} \cup \{r_i(f) \mid i \in \{3,4\}, f \in F\}$$
$$\cup \{s_i(ack) \mid i \in \{5,6\}\} \cup \{r_i(ack) \mid i \in \{5,6\}\}.$$

This protocol is only correct if the time-out time t_1' is longer than a complete protocol cycle, i.e., if $t_1' > t_2 + t_2' + t_3 + t_4$. If the time-out time is shorter than a complete protocol cycle, the time-out is called premature. In that case, while an acknowledgement is still on the way, the sender will retransmit the current frame. When the acknowledgement finally arrives, the sender will treat this acknowledgement as an acknowledgement of the retransmitted frame. However, an acknowledgement of the retransmitted frame may be on the way. If the next frame transmitted gets lost and the latter acknowledgement arrives, no retransmission of that frame will follow and the protocol will fail.

There have been attempts to describe this protocol using process algebra without timing. These attempts are unsatisfactory. In most attempts the premature time-out of an acknowledgement is excluded by inhibiting a time-out so long as it does not lead to deadlock! In [32], two ways in which that can be established are described: by means of a priority operator (not treated here) and by means of communication between three processes. In other attempts, the premature time-out of an acknowledgement is not excluded at all.

8.2 Analysis of the PAR Protocol

We now have all we need to analyze the PAR protocol.

We use the expansion theorem in order to derive a recursive specification of the process $\partial_H(S \parallel K \parallel L \parallel R)$.

We introduce some auxiliary variables in order to facilitate expansion. We rewrite the recursive specifications of S, R, K and L as follows. We refrain from mentioning after each equation schema that there is an instance for every $d \in D$ and/or $b \in B$.

$$S = S_0,$$
$$S_b = \sum_{d \in D} r_1(d).S_{d,b}',$$
$$S_{d,b}' = \sigma^{t_1}.\underline{s_3(d,b).S_{d,b}''},$$
$$S_{d,b}'' = \sum_{k < t_1'} \sigma^k.\underline{r_5(ack).S_{1-b}} + \sigma^{t_1'}.\underline{s_3(d,b).S_{d,b}''},$$

$$R \quad = R_0,$$
$$R_b \quad = \sum_{d \in D} r_4(d, b).R'_{d,b} + \sum_{d \in D} r_4(d, 1-b).R''_b,$$
$$R'_{d,b} = \sigma^{t_2}.\underline{s_2(d)}.R''_{1-b},$$
$$R''_b = \sigma^{t'_2}.\underline{s_6(ack)}.R_b,$$
$$K \quad = \sum_{(d,b) \in D \times B} \underline{r_3(d, b)}.K'_{d,b} + \sigma.K,$$
$$K'_{d,b} = \sigma^{t_3}.\underline{s_4(d, b)}.K + \sum_{k \le t_3} \sigma^k.\underline{error}.K,$$
$$L \quad = \underline{r_6(ack)}.L' + \sigma.L,$$
$$L' \quad = \overline{\sigma^{t_4}.\underline{s_5(ack)}}.L + \sum_{k \le t_4} \sigma^k.\underline{error}.L.$$

Secondly, we expand the term $\partial_H(S_b \parallel K \parallel L \parallel R_b)$ by repeated application of the expansion theorem. We remove in each step immediately those alternatives that are known to be equal to $\sigma^n(\underline{\delta})$ (for some $n \ge 0$) because of incapability to communicate, encapsulation or timing conflict, provided the removal is justified by the fact that $\sigma^m(t) + \sigma^n(\underline{\delta}) = \sigma^m(t)$ is derivable for all closed terms t and for all $m \ge n$. In the expansion, we will use the following abbreviation for every $d \in D$, $b \in B$ and $t > 0$:

$$S''_{d,b,t} \text{ for } \sum_{k<t} \sigma^k.\underline{r_5(ack)}.S_{1-b} + \sigma^t.\underline{s_3(d, b)}.S''_{d,b}.$$

Again, we refrain from mentioning after each equation schema that there is an instance for every $d \in D$ and/or $b \in B$.

$$\partial_H(S_b \parallel K \parallel L \parallel R_b)$$
$$= \sum_{d \in D} r_1(d).\partial_H(S'_{d,b} \parallel K \parallel L \parallel R_b),$$

$$\partial_H(S'_{d,b} \parallel K \parallel L \parallel R_b) = \sigma^{t_1}.\underline{c_3(d, b)}.\partial_H(S''_{d,b} \parallel K'_{d,b} \parallel L \parallel R_b),$$

$$\partial_H(S''_{d,b} \parallel K'_{d,b} \parallel L \parallel R_b)$$
$$= \sigma^{t_3}.\underline{c_4(d, b)}.\partial_H(S''_{d,b,t'_1-t_3} \parallel K \parallel L \parallel R'_{d,b})$$
$$+ \sum_{k \le t_3} \sigma^k.\underline{error}.\partial_H(S''_{d,b,t'_1-k} \parallel K \parallel L \parallel R_b),$$

$$\partial_H(S''_{d,b,t} \parallel K \parallel L \parallel R'_{d,b}) = \sigma^{t_2}.\underline{s_2(d)}.\partial_H(S''_{d,b,t-t_2} \parallel K \parallel L \parallel R''_{1-b})$$
(for every $t > t_2$),

$$\partial_H(S''_{d,b,t} \parallel K \parallel L \parallel R''_{1-b})$$
$$= \sigma^{t'_2}.\underline{c_6(ack)}.\partial_H(S''_{d,b,t-t'_2} \parallel K \parallel L' \parallel R_{1-b})$$
(for every $t > t'_2$),

$$\partial_H(S''_{d,b,t} \parallel K \parallel L' \parallel R_{1-b})$$
$$= \sigma^{t_4}.\underline{c_5(ack)}.\partial_H(S_{1-b} \parallel K \parallel L \parallel R_{1-b})$$
$$+ \sum_{k \le t_4} \sigma^k.\underline{error}.\partial_H(S''_{d,b,t-k} \parallel K \parallel L \parallel R_{1-b})$$
(for every $t > t_4$),

$$\partial_H(S''_{d,b,t} \parallel K \parallel L \parallel R_b) = \sigma^t.\underline{c_3(d,b)}.\partial_H(S''_{d,b} \parallel K'_{d,b} \parallel L \parallel R_b)$$
(for every $t > 0$),

$$\partial_H(S''_{d,b,t} \parallel K \parallel L \parallel R_{1-b})$$
$$= \sigma^t.\underline{c_3(d,b)}.\partial_H(S''_{d,b} \parallel K'_{d,b} \parallel L \parallel R_{1-b})$$
(for every $t > 0$),

$$\partial_H(S''_{d,b} \parallel K'_{d,b} \parallel L \parallel R_{1-b})$$
$$= \sigma^{t_3}.\underline{c_4(d,b)}.\partial_H(S''_{d,b,t'_1-t_3} \parallel K \parallel L \parallel R''_{1-b})$$
$$+ \sum_{k \le t_3} \sigma^k.\underline{error}.\partial_H(S''_{d,b,t'_1-k} \parallel K \parallel L \parallel R_{1-b}).$$

If the terms on the left-hand sides of these equations include all unexpanded terms on the right-hand sides, we have that the terms on the left-hand sides make up a solution of the guarded recursive specification obtained by replacing all occurrences of these terms in the equations by occurrences of corresponding variables. It is easy to see that this is the case iff $t'_1 > t_2 + t'_2 + t_3 + t_4$. Hence, we derive that $\partial_H(S_b \parallel K \parallel L \parallel R_b)$ is the solution for its corresponding variable of this guarded recursive specification. The guarded recursive specification concerned can easily be rewritten, using its equations and the axioms of process algebra, to the following sender-oriented guarded recursive specification:

$$X_b = \sum_{d \in D} r_1(d).\sigma^{t_1}.Y_{d,b},$$

$$Y_{d,b} = \underline{c_3(d,b)}.\left(\sigma^{t_3}.\underline{c_4(d,b)}.\sigma^{t_2}.\underline{s_2(d)}.\sigma^{t'_2}.\underline{c_6(ack)}.Z_{d,b}\right.$$
$$\left. + \sum_{k \le t_3} \sigma^k.\underline{error}.\sigma^{t'_1-k}.Y_{d,b}\right),$$

$$Z_{d,b} = \sigma^{t_4}.\underline{c_5(ack)}.X_{1-b} + \sum_{k \le t_4} \sigma^k.\underline{error}.\sigma^{t'_1-(t_2+t'_2+t_3+k)}.U_{d,b},$$

$$U_{d,b} = \underline{c_3(d,b)}.\left(\sigma^{t_3}.\underline{c_4(d,b)}.\sigma^{t'_2}.\underline{c_6(ack)}.V_{d,b}\right.$$
$$\left. + \sum_{k \le t_3} \sigma^k.\underline{error}.\sigma^{t'_1-k}.U_{d,b}\right),$$

$$V_{d,b} = \sigma^{t_4}.\underline{c_5(ack)}.X_{1-b} + \sum_{k \le t_4} \sigma^k.\underline{error}.\sigma^{t'_1-(t'_2+t_3+k)}.U_{d,b}.$$

This recursive specification shows that, if we abstract from all actions other than the send and receive actions at the external ports 1 and 2 and in addition from the timing of actions, the whole PAR protocol is a buffer with capacity 1 as described in the previous section.

In the previous calculations, we obtained useful results by just applying the branching laws of Table 20. If we consider the PAR protocol, things become much more difficult, however. We want to hide the actions in the set

$$I = \{error, c_5(ack), c_6(ack)\} \cup \{c_i(d,b) \mid i \in \{3,4\}, d \in D, b \in \{0,1\}\}.$$

Now we can proceed in different ways. First of all, we can focus on functional correctness. This means that we abstract from all timing of actions by means of the time free projection operator of Sect. 6 before we abstract from internal actions. In that case, we can apply the abstraction operator in the theory without timing. Starting from the specification of $\partial_H(S_b \parallel K \parallel L \parallel R_b)$ just given, we can easily calculate that $\pi_{\mathrm{tf}}(\partial_H(S_b \parallel K \parallel L \parallel R_b))$ is the solution of the guarded recursive specification that consists of the following equations:

$$
\begin{aligned}
X'_b &= \sum_{d \in D} r_1(d).Y'_{d,b}, \\
Y'_{d,b} &= c_3(d,b).(c_4(d,b).s_2(d) \cdot c_6(ack).Z'_{d,b} + error.Y'_{d,b}), \\
Z'_{d,b} &= c_5(ack).X'_{1-b} + error.U'_{d,b}, \\
U'_{d,b} &= c_3(d,b).(c_4(d,b).c_6(ack).V'_{d,b} + error.U'_{d,b}), \\
V'_{d,b} &= c_5(ack).X'_{1-b} + error.U'_{d,b}.
\end{aligned}
$$

We see immediately that $Z'_{d,b} = V'_{d,b}$. The branching law as given in [31] is in this case not sufficient to obtain, starting from this specification, a guarded recursive specification of $\tau_I(\pi_{\mathrm{tf}}(\partial_H(S_b \parallel K \parallel L \parallel R_b)))$, as this process can get into performing cycles of silent steps, and a fair abstraction rule like KFAR [29] is needed. However, it is straightforward to exhibit a branching bisimulation between the process $\tau_I(\pi_{\mathrm{tf}}(\partial_H(S_b \parallel K \parallel L \parallel R_b)))$ and the buffer with capacity one recursively specified by the equation

$$
B = \sum_{d \in D} r_1(d) \cdot s_2(d) \cdot B.
$$

Thus, we see the PAR protocol is functionally correct. We want to stress that, in order to achieve this result, it was necessary to calculate first the time-dependent behavior of the whole protocol, because the PAR protocol is only correct if the timing parameters are set correctly. A complete verification in process algebra without timing is not possible without resorting to artificial tricks such as excluding the premature time-out of an acknowledgement by inhibiting a time-out so long as it does not lead to deadlock (see e.g., [32]).

Next, we can have a look at the timing aspects. Starting from the specification of $\partial_H(S_b \parallel K \parallel L \parallel R_b)$ obtained, we can easily calculate that $\tau_I(\partial_H(S_b \parallel K \parallel L \parallel R_b))$ is the solution of the guarded recursive specification that consists of the following equations:

$$
\begin{aligned}
X'' &= \sum_{d \in D} r_1(d).\sigma^{t_1}.Y''_d, \\
Y''_d &= \sigma^{t_3}.\underline{\tau}.\sigma^{t_2}.\underline{s_2(d)}.\sigma^{t'_2}.Z'' + \sum_{k \le t_3} \sigma^k.\underline{\tau}.\sigma^{t'_1-k}.Y''_d, \\
Z'' &= \sigma^{t_4}.\underline{\tau}.X'' + \sum_{k \le t_4} \sigma^k.\underline{\tau}.\sigma^{t'_1-(t_2+t'_2+t_3+k)}.U'', \\
U'' &= \sigma^{t_3}.\underline{\tau}.\sigma^{t'_2}.V'' + \sum_{k \le t_3} \sigma^k.\underline{\tau}.\sigma^{t'_1-k}.U'', \\
V'' &= \sigma^{t_4}.\underline{\tau}.X'' + \sum_{k \le t_4} \sigma^k.\underline{\tau}.\sigma^{t'_1-(t'_2+t_3+k)}.U''.
\end{aligned}
$$

Not many simplifications can be achieved, mainly because branching bisimulation does not allow us to leave out silent steps that occur in between delays. In effect, all internal choices made, e.g., whether or not a channel forwards a datum correctly, remain visible. More research is needed in this matter. For some initial observations concerning this matter, we refer to [33]. In this paper, a more distinguishing equivalence is investigated, which is similar to rooted branching tail bisimulation equivalence, but treats silent steps in the midst of time steps under all circumstances as redundant.

Indeed, as a result the following extra τ-law can be applied:

$$\underline{\tau}.\sigma.x = \sigma.\underline{\tau}.x.$$

With the help of this law, the specification above can be simplified to the following:

$$
\begin{aligned}
A &= \sum_{d \in D} r_1(d).\sigma^{t_1 + t_2 + t_3}.B_d, \\
B_d &= \underline{s_2(d)}.\sigma^{t_2'}.C + \sigma^{t_1'}.B_d, \\
C &= \sigma^{t_4}.(A + \sigma^{t_1' - t_2 - t_4}.D), \\
D &= \sigma^{t_4}.(A + \sigma^{t_1' - t_4}.D).
\end{aligned}
$$

Based on this final specification, we can see that the protocol takes at least $t_1 + t_2 + t_3$ time slices between consumption and delivery of a datum, and in general, between consumption and delivery we have $t_1 + t_2 + t_3 + n \cdot t_1'$ time slices, where $n \geq 0$. After delivery, at least $t_2' + t_4$ time slices must pass before the next datum can be consumed, and in general, we have $t_2' + t_4$ or $t_2' + t_4 + m \cdot t_1' - t_2$ time slices, where $m > 0$. Thus, we have a complete throughput analysis of the protocol.

9   Related Work

In [18], an attempt to introduce the undelayable empty process into the realm of process algebra with discrete relative timing has been described. Three design goals were formulated for the extension: (i) the undelayable empty process should be a unit element w.r.t. both sequential composition and parallel composition; (ii) commutativity and associativity of parallel composition should remain valid; (iii) the time-determinism property should be maintained.

Despite the elaborate and rather convincing discussions presented in [18] regarding the unavoidability of strange intuitions involving the undelayable empty process, we have presented such an extension that avoids the unintuitive examples described in [18] while realizing the three design goals formulated before. We contribute this succes to the design decision to only capture synchronization aspects of parallel processes (such as termination and time-synchronization) in the communication merge and not in the left-merge.

In the theory of [18], the following derivations can be made (presented in the syntax used in this paper):

$$
\begin{aligned}
&- \ (\underline{a}.\underline{\epsilon} + \underline{\epsilon}) \parallel \underline{b}.\underline{\epsilon} = \underline{a}.\underline{b}.\underline{\epsilon} + \underline{b}.(\underline{a}.\underline{\epsilon} + \underline{\epsilon}) \\
&- \ (\sigma.\underline{a}.\underline{\epsilon} + \underline{\epsilon}) \parallel \sigma.\underline{b}.\underline{\epsilon} = \sigma.\underline{a}.\underline{\epsilon} \parallel \sigma.\underline{b}.\underline{\epsilon} \\
&- \ (\underline{a}.\underline{\epsilon} + \underline{\epsilon}) \parallel \sigma.\underline{b}.\underline{\epsilon} = \underline{a}.\sigma.\underline{b}.\underline{\epsilon} + \sigma.\underline{b}.\underline{\epsilon}
\end{aligned}
$$

In the theory presented in this paper we obtain the following equalities:

- $(\underline{a}.\underline{\epsilon} + \underline{\epsilon}) \parallel \underline{b}.\underline{\epsilon} = \underline{a}.(\underline{\epsilon} \parallel \underline{b}.\underline{\epsilon}) + \underline{b}.(\underline{\epsilon} \parallel (\underline{a}.\underline{\epsilon} + \underline{\epsilon})) = \underline{a}.\underline{b}.\underline{\epsilon} + \underline{b}.(\underline{a}.\underline{\epsilon} + \underline{\epsilon})$
- $(\sigma.\underline{a}.\underline{\epsilon} + \underline{\epsilon}) \parallel \sigma.\underline{b}.\underline{\epsilon} = \sigma.\underline{a}.\underline{\epsilon} \parallel \sigma.\underline{b}.\underline{\epsilon} + \sigma.\underline{b}.\underline{\epsilon}$
- $(\underline{a}.\underline{\epsilon} + \underline{\epsilon}) \parallel \sigma.\underline{b}.\underline{\epsilon} = \underline{a}.\sigma.\underline{b}.\underline{\epsilon} + \sigma.\underline{b}.\underline{\epsilon}$

10   Conclusion

Using our theory, we can replace the delay operators of timed ACP by delay prefixing, thus simplifying axioms and calculations. We have a clear separation of action execution and termination in our operational rules. All states in transition systems correspond to process terms. In order to ensure that the axiom of weak time-determinism holds in our operational model, we use a different set of relations generating the transition systems. This avoids the use of bisimulations relating sets of states and allows to use the results that are based on the format of the SOS rules. This is an improvement in the treatment of time steps.

On the basis of the material presented here, we can extend also the other timed process algebras of the framework of [12] with explicit termination. To reach this goal, first define a variant of the present theory using absolute timing instead of relative timing. Both absolute and relative timing can be integrated using parametric timing ([9, 10]). Then, absolute-time discrete-time process algebra is a subtheory of absolute-time dense-time process algebra as in [12]. Finally, relative-time discrete-time process algebra and parametric time discrete-time process algebra can be developed.

The combination of the empty process and discrete, relative time process algebra has been studied in [18, 19]. Among the conclusions in [18, 19] are the following two: the empty process cannot be straightforwardly combined with the deadlocked process of [9, 10, 34], and the behaviour of the empty process is not always into accordance with one's first intuition. In this paper we present a combination of the empty process with standard real-time process algebra in relative timing with the deadlocked process in which the behaviour of the empty process is clear in all cases.

Acknowledgments

We like to thank Sjouke Mauw, Kees Middelburg and Tim Willemse for their various useful suggestions.

References

1. Baeten, J., Bergstra, J.: Real time process algebra. Formal Aspects of Computing **3** (1991) 142–188
2. Hennessy, M., Regan, T.: A process algebra for timed systems. Information and Computation **177** (1995) 221–239

3. Moller, F., Tofts, C.: A temporal calculus of communicating systems. In Baeten, J., Klop, J., eds.: CONCUR'90 - Theories of Concurrency: Unification and Extension. Volume 458 of Lecture Notes in Computer Science., Amsterdam, Springer-Verlag (1990) 401–415

4. Nicollin, X., Sifakis, J.: The algebra of timed processes, ATP: Theory and application. Information and Computation **114** (1994) 131–178

5. Quemada, J., de Frutos, D., Azcorra, A.: TIC: A TImed calculus. Formal Aspects of Computing **5** (1993) 224–252

6. Bos, S., Reniers, M.: The I^2C-bus in discrete-time process algebra. Science of Computer Programming **29** (1997) 235–258

7. Schneider, S., Davies, J., Jackson, D., Reed, G., Reed, J., Roscoe, A.: Timed CSP: Theory and practice. In de Bakker, J., Huizing, C., de Roever, W., Rozenberg, G., eds.: Real Time: Theory and Practice. Volume 600 of Lecture Notes in Computer Science., Springer-Verlag (1991) 640–675

8. Groote, J.: The syntax and semantics of timed μCRL. Technical Report SEN-R9709, CWI, Amsterdam (1997)

9. Baeten, J., Bergstra, J.: Discrete time process algebra. Formal Aspects of Computing **8** (1996) 188–208

10. Baeten, J., Bergstra, J.: Discrete time process algebra: absolute time, relative time and parametric time. Fundamenta Informaticae **29** (1997) 51–76

11. Groote, J.: Process Algebra and Structured Operational Semantics. PhD thesis, University of Amsterdam (1991)

12. Baeten, J., Middelburg, C.: Process Algebra with Timing. Springer Verlag (2002)

13. Baeten, J.: Embedding untimed into timed process algebra: the case for explicit termination. Mathematical Structures in Computer Science **13** (2003) 589–618

14. Baeten, J., Reniers, M.: Explicit termination in timed process algebra with relative-timing. Formal Aspects of Computing (2004) To appear.

15. Koymans, C., Vrancken, J.: Extending process algebra with the empty process ε. Technical Report Logic Group Preprint Series 1, University Utrecht, Department of Philosophy (1985)

16. Baeten, J., Glabbeek, R.v.: Merge and termination in process algebra. In Nori, K., ed.: Foundations of Software Technology and Theoretical Computer Science VII. Volume 287 of Lecture Notes in Computer Science., Pune, Springer-Verlag (1987) 153–172

17. Vrancken, J.: The algebra of communicating processes with empty process. Theoretical Computer Science **177** (1997) 287–328

18. Vereijken, J.: Discrete-time process algebra. PhD thesis, Eindhoven University of Technology (1997)

19. Baeten, J., Vereijken, J.: Discrete-time process algebra with empty process. In Bruné, M., van Deursen, A., Heering, J., eds.: Dat is dus heel interessant, CWI (1997) 5–24 Liber Amicorum dedicated to Paul Klint.

20. Hoare, C.: Communicating Sequential Processes. International Series in Computer Science. Prentice-Hall International (1985)

21. Bos, V., Kleijn, J.: Formalisation of a production system modelling language: the operational semantics of χ Core. Fundamenta Informaticae **41** (2000) 367–392

22. Reniers, M.: Message Sequence Chart: Syntax and Semantics. PhD thesis, Eindhoven University of Technology (1999)

23. Groote, J.: Transition system specifications with negative premises. In Baeten, J., Klop, J., eds.: CONCUR'90 - Theories of Concurrency: Unification and Extension. Volume 458 of Lecture Notes in Computer Science., Amsterdam, Springer-Verlag (1990) 332–341

24. Verhoef, C.: A congruence theorem for structured operational semantics with predicates and negative premises. Nordic Journal of Computing **2** (1995) 274–302
25. Fokkink, W.: The tyft/tyxt format reduces to tree rules. In Hagiya, M., Mitchell, J., eds.: Proceedings 2nd International Symposium in Theoretical Aspects of Computer Software (TACS'94). Volume 789 of Lecture Notes in Computer Science., Springer-Verlag (1994) 440–453
26. Baeten, J., Reniers, M.: Termination in timed process algebra. Technical Report CSR 00-13, Eindhoven University of Technology, Department of Computing Science (2000)
27. Baeten, J., Verhoef, C.: A congruence theorem for structured operational semantics with predicates. In Best, E., ed.: CONCUR'93, International Conference on Concurrency Theory. Volume 715 of Lecture Notes in Computer Science., Springer-Verlag (1993) 477–492
28. Baeten, J., Verhoef, C.: Concrete process algebra. In Abramsky, S., Gabbay, D.M., Maibaum, T., eds.: Semantic Modelling. Volume 4 of Handbook of Logic in Computer Science. Oxford University Press (1995) 149–268
29. Baeten, J., Weijland, W.: Process Algebra. Volume 18 of Cambridge Tracts in Theoretical Computer Science. Cambridge University Press (1990)
30. Baeten, J., Basten, T., Reniers, M.: Algebra of Communicating Processes. Cambridge University Press (2004) To appear.
31. van Glabbeek, R., Weijland, W.: Branching time and abstraction in bisimulation semantics. Journal of the ACM **43** (1996) 555–600
32. Vaandrager, F.: Two simple protocols. In Baeten, J., ed.: Applications of process algebra. Volume 17 of Cambridge Tracts in Theoretical Computer Science., Cambridge University Press (1990) 23–44
33. Baeten, J., Middelburg, C., Reniers, M.: A new equivalence for processes with timing. Technical Report CSR 02-10, Eindhoven University of Technology, Department of Computing Science (2002)
34. Baeten, J., Bergstra, J., Reniers, M.: Discrete time process algebra with silent step. In Plotkin, G., Stirling, C., Tofte, M., eds.: Proof, Language, and Interaction: Essays in Honour of Robin Milner. Foundations of Computing Series. MIT Press (2000) 535–569

Expressiveness of Timed Events
and Timed Languages*

Diletta R. Cacciagrano and Flavio Corradini

Università di Camerino, Dipartimento di Matematica e Informatica,
Camerino, 62032, Italy
{diletta.cacciagrano,flavio.corradini}@unicam.it

Abstract. Timed process algebras are useful tools for the specification
and verification of real-time systems. We study the expressiveness of
(classes of) these algebras which deal with temporal aspects of concurrent
systems by following very different interpretations: durational actions
versus durationless actions, absolute time versus relative time, timed
functional behavior versus time and functional behavior, local clocks versus global clocks, eagerness versus laziness versus maximal progress.
The aim of this study is manifold. It permits to gain confidence on how
time and time passing are modelled in the different approaches to timed
process algebras. It shows that some different design decisions are not
irreconcilable by presenting simple semantic-preserving mappings from
an algebra to another so that techniques and analytic concepts can be
transferred from one theory to the other. It allows a better understanding
of the technical details and of the definitions in the different approaches
in order to speculatively detect advantages/disadvantages of the used
methodologies.

1 Introduction

Timed process algebras (see, for example, [AM95], [BB91], [Cor98], [CN96],
[CZ91], [FM95], [GRS95], [HR95], [MT90], [RR88], [Yi90]) are useful tools for the
specification and verification of timed systems. They extend the classic process
algebras such as *CCS* [Mil89], *CSP* [Hoa85], *ACP* [BK89] in order to take into
account, besides the *functional behavior* of concurrent systems (which actions
the concurrent systems can do), also the *temporal aspects* of their executions.

Because of the several temporal properties of interest, there has been in
the last years a great proliferation of such timed calculi. These extensions differ,
mainly, in the way *time* and *time passing* are modelled. There are, indeed, several
parameters which have influenced the choice in the literature:

---

* This work was supported by the Center of Excellence for Research 'DEWS: Architectures and Design Methodologies for Embedded Controllers, Wireless Interconnect
and System-on-chip' and by the MURST project 'Sahara: Software Architectures for
Heterogeneous Access Networks infrastructures'.

M. Bernardo and F. Corradini (Eds.): SFM-RT 2004, LNCS 3185, pp. 98–131, 2004.

– *Durational or Durationless Actions*: Basic actions take a fixed amount of time to be performed and time passes in a system only due to the execution of real "programmable" actions. In other approaches, instead, basic actions are instantaneous events and "time passes in between them" via explicit global synchronizations.
– *Absolute or Relative Time*: During a system execution time stamps are associated with the observed events. These time stamps are referred to either the starting time of the system execution (and, in this case, time features as *absolute time*) or the time instant of the previous observation (and, in this case, time features as *relative time*).
– *Timed Functional Behavior or Time and Functional Behavior*: The study of the functional and temporal behavior of a concurrent system is done by integrating these two views together, or by separating the functional and temporal descriptions into two orthogonal parts.
– *Local Clocks or Global Clocks*: A local clock is associated with each of the parallel components of a concurrent system. These local clocks elapse independently of each other, although they define a unique notion of global time. Alternatively, the notions of global time and unique global clock are made explicit.

Another significant difference among the different proposals is on the different interpretation of basic actions and, in particular, on how processes can delay the execution of their basic actions.

– Processes are *eager* (or *urgent*) to perform basic actions; namely, actions must be performed as soon as they become available.
– Processes are *lazy*; namely, action can be delayed arbitrarily long before their execution.
– Processes can delay action execution arbitrarily long. However, if the environment is willing to communicate no further delay is allowed. This notion of urgency of synchronizations is known in the literature as *maximal progress*.

In this paper we study the expressiveness of well-known timed process algebras that suitably implement the above mentioned parameters and assumptions. The aim of this study is manifold:

– It permits to gain confidence on how time and time passing are modelled in the different approaches to timed process algebras;
– It shows that some different design decisions are not irreconcilable by presenting simple semantic-preserving mappings from an algebra to another. This permits techniques and analytic concepts to be transferred from one theory to the other;
– It shows that the inessential differences among the timed process algebras are indeed inessential, while the essential ones are are indeed essential;
– It allows a better understanding of the technical details and of the definitions in the different approaches in order to speculatively detect advantages/disadvantages of the used methodologies.

Our comparison is only limited to the core of such languages; that is, we have taken into account the operators that these algebras have in common together with those characterizing the underlying notion of time and time passing. Operators such as timeouts or watchdogs are not taken into account here since, in our view, they do not have any impact on the design decisions described above and on how abstract time is modelled. For a nice overview of several process algebras we are interested in, including the above mentioned operators, see [NS91].

In the first part of the paper we compare two classes of timed process algebras. Those that are known in the literature as two-phase functioning principle - where actions are instantaneous and "time passes between them", time features as relative, functional and temporal system behaviors are studied by separating them into two orthogonal parts and there exists a unique global clock - and those that can be classified as one-phase functioning principle. In this latter setting, actions are durational, time is absolute (that is, referred to the starting time of the system execution), functional and temporal system behaviors are integrated into a unique framework and, likewise distributed systems, local clocks are associated to the parallel components of a system.

As a representative for the two-phase functioning principle we consider $TCCS$ ('Temporal CCS') [MT90,MT91] while as a representative for the one-phase principle we consider cIPA ('Closed Interval Process Algebra') [AM95,CP01].

We compare the expressiveness of these two languages under the different interpretations of basic actions; namely when they are interpreted as eager, lazy or behave according to the maximal progress principle. Our comparison is technically based on studying semantic-preserving syntactic mappings from a timed process algebra to the another.

We show that cIPA and $TCCS$ are strictly related. If "Ill-Timed"[1] traces are disallowed in cIPA, then there exists a very simple mapping from cIPA to $TCCS$ which preserves (strong) bisimulation-based equivalence defined over the two timed calculi. This result holds when actions are interpreted as eager [AM93,MT90] or as lazy [CP96,MT91] or as maximal progress. The lazy and maximal progress cases are particularly interesting because they allow us to overcome a problem we have when mapping cIPA into $TCCS$ in the presence of the restriction operator and urgency. Nevertheless, cIPA is interesting of its own. Besides the original motivations on the theory of processes with durational actions that can be found in [AM93,FM95,GR93,GRS95], we present in [Cor00] another interesting property of this theory. The behavioral equivalence of cIPA allows a (finite) alternative characterization which can be checked more efficiently than the behavioral equivalence of $TCCS$. To show this property we prove that the labelled transition system describing the transitional semantics of a cIPA process is strictly smaller (in terms of the number of transitions and states) than the one associated with its translation.

---

[1] cIPA presents the so-called "Ill-Timed phenomenon" [AM93,AM95] that allows the performed actions to be observed in an order which is not necessarily the one given by time.

The second part of this work concentrates instead on the semantic relationships among the different interpretations of basic actions and, hence, on the expressiveness of actions when interpreted as eager, lazy or maximal progress. To this aim we focus on a common language (cIPA) and study the discriminating power of eagerness, laziness and maximal progress. In other words, we contrast the three strong bisimulation-based equivalences that are defined on top of the transitional semantics obtained by interpreting actions as eager, lazy or maximal progress on different language features that are significant from the point of view of the expressiveness of eager, lazy and maximal progress tests. The study is conducted by showing how the bisimulation-based equivalences relate when the base language changes according to these significant features. It also shows that the three equivalences may behave differently according to these restrictions. The language features have to do with process synchronization, with the non deterministic composition, with the relabelling functions [Mil89], with the number of actions a process can perform at a given time. In more detail:

- The language allows process synchronization or only "visible" actions are performed.
- The language allows choices at the same time or also at different times. In other words, we are distinguishing between "timed alternative compositions" and "alternative timed compositions". In the former case the non deterministic composition only involves the functionality of the process while in the latter one it involves both functionality and timing. E.g., I can choose at time t between a snack and a full lunch ((snack+lunch)@t) or I can choose between a snack at noon and a dinner eight hours after ((snack@t) + (dinner@t'), where $t' > t$).
- The language allows relabelling functions which preserve the duration of the actions (that is, they rename actions having the same duration) or also rename actions with (possibly) different durations.
- The language allows the description of processes which can perform finitely many actions (though of unbounded number) at a fixed time or also infinitely many[2].

Note that these different languages do not constitute a hierarchy but a classification of specific language features which are significant when comparing the discriminating power of the urgent and patient actions.

It turns out that *only* when the language allows (a) only visible actions, (b) only processes which can perform finitely many actions at a fixed time, (c) only choices at the same time and (d) only duration preserving relabelling functions, then eager tests, lazy tests and maximal progress tests have the same discriminating power.

The rest of the paper is organized as follows. The next section briefly recalls the basic assumptions behind $TCCS$ while Section 3 introduces cIPA. Section 4 presents a simple mapping from $TCCS$ to cIPA (when actions are interpreted as

---

[2] This permits the construction of processes which can do infinitely many actions in a finite interval of time, also called *Zeno*-processes.

eager). Section 5 introduces lazy actions and lazy equivalence in $TCCS$ and cIPA and shows how to map the former into the latter. Section 6 shows that the same result holds under the hypothesis of maximal progress. Section 7 concentrate on a single language and studies the discriminant power of eagerness, laziness and maximal progress over different language features.

2   A Theory of Timed Processes with Durationless Actions

2.1   The Calculus $TCCS$

The $TCCS$ process algebra [MT90] is a variant of Milner's CCS. A (ranged over by α) denotes an infinite set of basic actions from which the set of co-actions $\bar{A} = \{\bar{\alpha} \mid \alpha \in A\}$ is obtained. Act (ranged over by $a, b, \ldots$) is used to denote $A \cup \bar{A}$, the set of visible actions, with the convention that if $a \in Act$ then $\bar{\bar{a}} = a$. $\tau \notin Act$ denotes an invisible action while Act_τ (ranged over by μ) denotes the set of all actions $Act \cup \{\tau\}$. $\mathbb{N}$ denotes the set of natural numbers, while $\mathbb{N}^+$ denotes the positive ones. Process *variables*, used for recursive definitions, are ranged over by $x, y, \ldots$.

Let $Open\ \mathcal{P}_{MT}$ be the set of terms generated by the following grammar:

$$ p := 0 \ \Big| \ \mu.p \ \Big| \ (n).p \ \Big| \ p+p \ \Big| \ p|p \ \Big| \ p\backslash C \ \Big| \ p[\varPhi] \ \Big| \ x \ \Big| \ \text{rec } x.p $$

where $\mu \in Act_\tau$, $C \subseteq Act$ and $n \in \mathbb{N}^+$. Assume the usual notions of free and bound variables in terms, with rec $x.\_$ as the binding operator. Given $p \in Open\ \mathcal{P}_{MT}$, $\mathcal{F}(p)$ denotes the set of its free variables. The notation $p[q/y]$, where p and q are $Open\ \mathcal{P}_{MT}$ terms and y is a process variable, is used to denote the $Open\ \mathcal{P}_{MT}$ term obtained from p by simultaneously replacing each free occurrence of y by q.

The set of guarded (i.e., variable x in a rec $x.p$ term can only appear within a $\mu.\_$ prefix or a $(n)\_$ prefix) and closed (i.e., without free variables) $Open\ \mathcal{P}_{MT}$ terms, also called *processes*, is denoted by $\mathcal{P}_{MT}$ (ranged over by $p, q, \ldots$). In the rest of this paper we concentrate on $\mathcal{P}_{MT}$ terms, unless differently specified.

Process 0 represents the nil process; it cannot perform any action and cannot proceed through time. $\mu.p$ is the process that can perform an instantaneous action μ and then evolves into process p. $(n).p$ is the process which will evolve into process p after exactly n units of time. $p+q$ denotes alternative composition of p and q. $p|q$, the parallel composition of p and q, is the process which can perform any interleaving of the actions of p and q or synchronizations whenever p and q can perform complementary actions. $p\backslash C$ is a process which behaves like p but actions in C, or their co-actions, are forbidden. $p[\varPhi]$ behaves like p but its actions are relabelled according to relabelling function Φ. Finally, rec x. P is used for recursive definitions[3].

For the sake of simplicity, terminal nil's can be omitted; e.g. $a + b.c$ stands for $a.0 + b.c.0$.

2.2   The $TCCS$ Operational Semantics

The operational semantics of $TCCS$ is given through two transition relations: $p \xrightarrow{\mu} p'$ and $p \overset{t}{\rightsquigarrow} p'$. The former transition relation is concerned with the execution of basic actions. It is the least relation which satisfies the inference rules in Table 1 (it is the standard CCS transition relation). A transition $p \xrightarrow{\mu} p'$ intuitively means that process p becomes process p' by performing a basic action μ. The latter transition relation, $p \overset{t}{\rightsquigarrow} p'$, is concerned with the elapsing of time. It is the least relation which satisfies the inference rules in Table 2. A transition $p \overset{t}{\rightsquigarrow} p'$ intuitively means that p lets t units of time pass and, after that, it becomes p'.

Table 1. The Structural Rules for Action Execution in $TCCS$.

$$BAct \ \frac{}{a.p \xrightarrow{a} p} \qquad BTau \ \frac{}{\tau.p \xrightarrow{\tau} p}$$

$$BSum_1 \ \frac{p \xrightarrow{\mu} p^\blacksquare}{p+q \xrightarrow{\mu} p^\blacksquare} \qquad BSum_2 \ \frac{q \xrightarrow{\mu} q^\blacksquare}{p+q \xrightarrow{\mu} q^\blacksquare}$$

$$BPar_1 \ \frac{p \xrightarrow{\mu} p^\blacksquare}{p \,|\, q \xrightarrow{\mu} p^\blacksquare \,|\, q} \qquad BPar_2 \ \frac{q \xrightarrow{\mu} q^\blacksquare}{p \,|\, q \xrightarrow{\mu} p \,|\, q^\blacksquare} \qquad BSynch \ \frac{p \xrightarrow{a} p^\blacksquare, \ q \xrightarrow{\bar{a}} q^\blacksquare}{p \,|\, q \xrightarrow{\tau} p^\blacksquare \,|\, q^\blacksquare}$$

$$BRec \ \frac{p[rec \ x. \, p/x] \xrightarrow{\mu} p^\blacksquare}{rec \ x. \, p \xrightarrow{\mu} p^\blacksquare} \qquad BRes \ \frac{p \xrightarrow{\mu} p^\blacksquare}{p\backslash C \xrightarrow{\mu} p^\blacksquare\backslash C} \mu, \bar{\mu} \notin C \qquad BRel \ \frac{p \xrightarrow{\mu} p^\blacksquare}{p[\Phi] \xrightarrow{\Phi(\mu)} p^\blacksquare[\Phi]}$$

Transition relation $\overset{t}{\rightsquigarrow}$ holds what Wang Yi calls "time continuity" in [Yi90]. He has proven time continuity in a calculus implementing the so-called "maximal progress". Maximal progress forces only invisible actions to be performed urgently. We will formally introduce and study maximal progress in Section 6.

Proposition 1. Let p be a $\mathcal{P}_{MT}$ term and $s, t \geq 1$. Then: $p \overset{s+t}{\rightsquigarrow} q$ if and only if there exists p_1 such that $p \overset{s}{\rightsquigarrow} p_1$ and $p_1 \overset{t}{\rightsquigarrow} q$.

---

[3] The whole $TCCS$ process algebra (as defined in [MT90]) is obtained by extending the introduced syntax with two further process constructors: $\delta.p$ and $p \oplus q$. $\delta.p$ denotes a process which can delay the execution of process p arbitrarily long, while $p \oplus q$ is another non-deterministic composition where the choice between p and q can be solved by both basic actions and time passing. We do not introduce these operators here; the present syntax is enough for our codings.

Table 2. The Structural Rules for Time Passing in $TCCS$.

$$TSum \ \frac{p \stackrel{t}{\leadsto} p^\square \text{ and } q \stackrel{t}{\leadsto} q^\square}{p + q \stackrel{t}{\leadsto} p^\square + q^\square} \qquad TPar \ \frac{p \stackrel{t}{\leadsto} p^\square \text{ and } q \stackrel{t}{\leadsto} q^\square}{p \mid q \stackrel{t}{\leadsto} p^\square \mid q^\square}$$

$$TDec \ \frac{}{(s+t).p \stackrel{s}{\leadsto} (t).p} \qquad TFin \ \frac{}{(t).p \stackrel{t}{\leadsto} p} \qquad TFur \ \frac{p \stackrel{s}{\leadsto} p^\square}{(t).p \stackrel{s+t}{\leadsto} p^\square}$$

$$TRec \ \frac{p[rec \ x. \ p/x] \stackrel{t}{\leadsto} p^\square}{rec \ x. \ p \stackrel{t}{\leadsto} p^\square} \qquad TRes \ \frac{p \stackrel{t}{\leadsto} p^\square}{p \backslash C \stackrel{t}{\leadsto} p^\square \backslash C} \qquad TRel \ \frac{p \stackrel{t}{\leadsto} p^\square}{p[\Phi] \stackrel{t}{\leadsto} p^\square[\Phi]}$$

A corollary of the above proposition is the following:

Corollary 1. Let p be a $\mathcal{P}_{MT}$ term and $t \geq 2$. Then: $p_1 \stackrel{t}{\leadsto} p_{t+1}$ if and only if there are $p_2, \ldots, p_t$ such that $p_1 \stackrel{1}{\leadsto} p_2 \ldots p_t \stackrel{1}{\leadsto} p_{t+1}$.

Another useful property of the $TCCS$ operational semantics states that $rec \ x.(1).x$ can let every amount of time $t \in \mathbb{N}^+$ to pass.

Lemma 1. For every $t \in \mathbb{N}^+$, $rec \ x.(1).x \stackrel{t}{\leadsto} rec \ x.(1).x$

2.3   The $TCCS$ Observational Semantics

On top of the transition relations $p \stackrel{\mu}{\longrightarrow} p'$ and $p \stackrel{t}{\leadsto} p'$ a strong bisimulation-based relation over $\mathcal{P}_{MT}$ is defined [MT90].

Definition 1. ($\mathcal{T}$-Equivalence)

1. A binary relation $\Re$ over $\mathcal{P}_{MT}$ is a $\mathcal{T}$-bisimulation if and only if for each $(p, q) \in \Re$:
   a) $p \stackrel{\mu}{\longrightarrow} p'$ implies $q \stackrel{\mu}{\longrightarrow} q'$ and $(p', q') \in \Re$;
   b) $q \stackrel{\mu}{\longrightarrow} q'$ implies $p \stackrel{\mu}{\longrightarrow} p'$ and $(p', q') \in \Re$;
   c) $p \stackrel{t}{\leadsto} p'$ implies $q \stackrel{t}{\leadsto} q'$ and $(p', q') \in \Re$;
   d) $q \stackrel{t}{\leadsto} q'$ implies $p \stackrel{t}{\leadsto} p'$ and $(p', q') \in \Re$.
2. Two $\mathcal{P}_{MT}$ processes p and q are $\mathcal{T}$-equivalent, $p \sim_{MT} q$, if and only if there exists a $\mathcal{T}$-bisimulation $\Re$ such that $(p, q) \in \Re$.

Let $\simeq$ denote the least congruence over $\mathcal{P}_{MT}$ which satisfies the axioms in Table 3. It will be useful in the rest of this paper. Clearly, congruence $\simeq$ preserves process transitions.

Lemma 2. Let p and q be $\mathcal{P}_{MT}$ terms such that $p \simeq q$. Then:

(1) $p \stackrel{\mu}{\longrightarrow} p'$ implies $q \stackrel{\mu}{\longrightarrow} q' \simeq p'$;
(2) $p \stackrel{t}{\leadsto} p'$ implies $q \stackrel{t}{\leadsto} q' \simeq p'$.

Table 3. Time Distribution Equations and Unfolding.

$$
\begin{array}{l}
(n).(p \mid q) = (n).p \mid (n).q \\
(n).(p \backslash C) = ((n).p) \backslash C \\
(n).(p \ + \ q) = (n).p \ + \ (n).q \\
(n).(p[\varPhi]) = ((n).p)[\varPhi] \\
\text{rec } x.p = p[\text{rec } x.p \, / x]
\end{array}
$$

3 A Theory of Processes with Durational Actions

3.1 The Calculus CIPA

The basic assumptions behind the theory of processes with durational actions proposed in [AM93,AM95] are the following:

1) *maximal parallelism:* whenever a new sequential subprocess is activated, there is always a processor free, ready to execute it. In other words, there is never the need of serializing parallel computations;
2) *eagerness:* there is no time-passing in between the execution of actions from the same subprocess; equivalently actions happen as soon as possible;
3) *static duration:* the amount of time needed for the execution of a particular action is fixed once and for all on the basis of the features of the chosen machine. *Action duration functions* (ranged over by $\varDelta, \varGamma, ...$) $\varDelta : A \to \mathbb{N}^+$ ($\varDelta : A \to \mathbb{R}^+$ in the original CIPA), are introduced which associate to each action the positive natural number of time units needed for its execution. The duration $\varDelta(a)$ of action $a \in A$ will be assumed to be nonzero[4] and constant over all occurrences of a. $\varDelta$ is extended to Act by defining $\varDelta(\bar{a}) = \varDelta(a)$;
4) *duration-preserving relabelling function:* if $\varPhi$ is a relabelling function then it preserves action duration; namely, $\varDelta(a) = \varDelta(\varPhi(a))$, for every $a \in Act$.

Let *Open* $\mathcal{P}_{AM}$ be the set of terms generated by the following grammar:

$$
P := nil \ \Big| \ a.P \ \Big| \ \text{wait } n.\, P \ \Big| \ P+P \ \Big| \ P|P \ \Big| \ P\backslash C \ \Big| \ P[\varPhi] \ \Big| \ x \ \Big| \ \text{rec } x.P
$$

where $a \in Act$, $C \subseteq Act$, $n \in \mathbb{N}^+$ and x is a process variable[5].

The set of processes, denoted by $\mathcal{P}_{AM}$ (ranged over by $P, Q, \ldots$), are the closed (i.e., without free variables) and guarded (i.e., variable x in a term rec $x.P$ can only appear within an $a.\_$ prefix or a wait $n.\_$ prefix) *Open* $\mathcal{P}_{AM}$ terms. We concentrate on $\mathcal{P}_{AM}$ terms, unless differently specified.

Process *nil* denotes a terminated process. By prefixing a term P with an action a, we get a process term $a.P$ which can do an action a and then behaves

---

[4] Hence, processes which can do an infinite number actions in a finite interval of time, also called *Zeno*-processes, cannot be built in CIPA.

[5] It has to be noted that CIPA is originally defined over a dense time domain, namely $n \in \mathbb{R}^+$ (where $\mathbb{R}^+$ denotes the positive reals). We restrict attention to natural numbers because we are going to compare CIPA with $TCCS$ which is a discrete-time process algebra (with time domain $\mathbb{N}$).

like P. wait $n. P$ denotes a process which can internally evolve for $n \in \mathbb{N}^+$ time units and then behaves like process P. $P + Q$ denotes alternative composition of P and Q while $P|Q$ their parallel composition. $P \backslash C$ denotes restriction and $P[\Phi]$ relabelling - where, Φ is a duration preserving relabelling function. rec $x. P$ is used for recursive definitions.

Remark 1. There is a substantial difference between the *TCCS* $(t).p$ operator and the CIPA wait $t.P$. This is because wait $t.P$ is just a timed version of the *CCS* untimed $\tau.P$ and, in fact, it is possible to think of wait $t.P$ as an abbreviation for $(a|\bar{a}.P) \backslash \{a\}$ (where a is not "free" in P and $\Delta(a) = t$). This immediately leads to distinguish "a choice followed by a wait" and "a wait followed by a choice"; i.e., wait $t.P +$ wait $t.Q$ is different from wait $t.(P+Q)$ (the timed version of the distinction between $\tau.P + \tau.Q$ and $\tau.(P + Q)$). *TCCS*, instead, does not allow the "passage of time to decide a choice" and, hence, we will have $(n).p + (n).q$ equivalent to $(n).(p + q)$ because any initial passage of time must be allowed by both p and q.

3.2   The CIPA Operational Semantics

$\mathcal{P}_{AM}$ is equipped with an *SOS* semantics in terms of labelled transition systems the states of which are terms of a syntax extending that of processes with a local *clock prefixing* operator, $n \Rightarrow \_$, which records the evolution of different parts of a distributed state.

Definition 2. The states are terms generated by the following syntax:

$$d ::= n \Rightarrow nil \mid n \Rightarrow a.P \mid n \Rightarrow \text{wait } n'.P \mid n \Rightarrow \text{rec } x.P \mid d+d \mid d|d \mid d\backslash C \mid d[\Phi]$$

where P, rec $x. P \in \mathcal{P}_{AM}$, $n \in \mathbb{N}$, $n' \in \mathbb{N}^+$ and $C \subseteq Act$. The set of states is denoted by $\mathcal{S}_{AM}$ (ranged over by $d_1, d_2 \dots$).

In order to define a simple operational semantics the shorthand expression $n \Rightarrow P$ is used to mean that n distributes over the operators, till the sequential components. The equations in Table 4, called *clock distribution equations*, show that a term $n \Rightarrow P$ can be reduced to a canonical state, when interpreting these equations as rewrite rules from left to right.

Table 4. Clock Distribution Equations.

$n \Rightarrow (P \mid Q) = (n \Rightarrow P) \mid (n \Rightarrow Q)$
$n \Rightarrow (P \backslash C) = (n \Rightarrow P) \backslash C$
$n \Rightarrow (P + Q) = (n \Rightarrow P) + (n \Rightarrow Q)$
$n \Rightarrow (P[\Phi]) = (n \Rightarrow P)[\Phi]$

Each transition is of the form $d \xrightarrow[\delta]{\langle \mu,t \rangle} d'$, meaning that timed state d becomes timed state d' by performing an action μ, of duration δ, at time t. This transition relation is given through the set of inference rules listed in Table 5.

Table 5. The Timed Transition Rules for cIPA.

$$Act \quad \frac{}{n \Rightarrow a.P \xrightarrow[\Delta(a)]{\langle a,n\rangle} (n + \Delta(a)) \Rightarrow P}$$

$$Wait \quad \frac{}{n \Rightarrow \text{wait } n'.P \xrightarrow[n']{\langle \tau,n\rangle} (n + n') \Rightarrow P}$$

$$Sum_1 \quad \frac{d_1 \xrightarrow[\delta]{\langle \mu,t\rangle} d, \ \neg(d_2 \xrightarrow[\delta']{\langle \gamma,t'\rangle} d', \ t' < t)}{d_1 + d_2 \xrightarrow[\delta]{\langle \mu,t\rangle} d} \qquad Sum_2 \quad \frac{d_2 \xrightarrow[\delta]{\langle \mu,t\rangle} d, \ \neg(d_1 \xrightarrow[\delta']{\langle \gamma,t'\rangle} d', \ t' < t)}{d_1 + d_2 \xrightarrow[\delta]{\langle \mu,t\rangle} d}$$

$$Par_1 \quad \frac{d_1 \xrightarrow[\delta]{\langle \mu,t\rangle} d'_1, \ \neg(d_2 \xrightarrow[\delta']{\langle \gamma,t'\rangle} d'_2, \ t' < t)}{d_1 \mid d_2 \xrightarrow[\delta]{\langle \mu,t\rangle} d'_1 \mid d_2} \qquad Par_2 \quad \frac{d_2 \xrightarrow[\delta]{\langle \mu,t\rangle} d'_2, \ \neg(d_1 \xrightarrow[\delta']{\langle \gamma,t'\rangle} d'_1, \ t' < t)}{d_1 \mid d_2 \xrightarrow[\delta]{\langle \mu,t\rangle} d_1 \mid d'_2}$$

$$Synch \quad \frac{d_1 \xrightarrow[\Delta(a)]{\langle a,n\rangle} d'_1, \ d_2 \xrightarrow[\Delta(a)]{\langle \bar{a},n\rangle} d'_2}{d_1 \mid d_2 \xrightarrow[\Delta(a)]{\langle \tau,n\rangle} d'_1 \mid d'_2}$$

$$Res \quad \frac{d \xrightarrow[\delta]{\langle \mu,t\rangle} d'}{d\backslash C \xrightarrow[\delta]{\langle \mu,t\rangle} d'\backslash C} \mu, \bar{\mu} \notin C \qquad Rel \quad \frac{d \xrightarrow[\delta]{\langle \mu,t\rangle} d'}{d[\Phi] \xrightarrow[\delta]{\langle \Phi(\mu),t\rangle} d'[\Phi]}$$

$$Rec \quad \frac{n \Rightarrow P[\text{rec } x.\, P/x] \xrightarrow[\delta]{\langle \mu,t\rangle} d}{n \Rightarrow \text{rec } x.\, P \xrightarrow[\delta]{\langle \mu,t\rangle} d}$$

It is worthwhile observing that these rules are parametric w.r.t. the chosen duration function Δ. Hence, to be precise, we should write $\rightarrow_\Delta$. For the sake of simplicity, the subscript will always be omitted whenever clear from the context. Moreover, we often write $d \xrightarrow[\delta]{\langle \mu,t\rangle}$ to mean that there is d' such that $d \xrightarrow[\delta]{\langle \mu,t\rangle} d'$.

A few comments on the rules in Table 5 are now in order. The rule for action prefixing Act, states that state $n \Rightarrow a.P$ starts the execution of action a at time n and ends at time $n + \Delta(a)$. A state $n \Rightarrow \text{wait } n'.P$ starts the execution of a τ at time n and ends at time $n + n'$; n' being the duration of the performed invisible action. Rules Sum_1, Sum_2, Par_1 and Par_2 deal with non deterministic and parallel composition and are quite standard. The negative premises in these rules say that a component of a non-deterministic or parallel composition can evolve by performing some action at a certain time provided that other components cannot evolve earlier. In the case of non-deterministic composition, however, early actions can always disable later conflicting actions. *Synch* rule, dealing with synchronization, says that two partners can synchronize if they are able to perform complementary actions exactly at the same time. Rules for restriction, relabelling and recursive definitions are as expected.

The negative premises in the structural rules in Table 5 permits avoiding the Ill-Timed phenomenon which allows observation traces that do not respect the order given by time. It is present in the original CIPA [AM93,AM95] operational semantics. We can explain better this phenomenon with an example.

Consider $\mathcal{P}_{AM}$ process $a.b \mid c$ where $\Delta(a) = 2$, $\Delta(b) = 1$ and $\Delta(c) = 3$. When the two parallel components are performed by two different processors an external observer can see the execution of action a from time 0 to 2, the execution of action b from time 2 to 3 and the execution of action c from time 0 to 3. According to the original CIPA operational semantics (the rules in Table 5 without negative premises), after observing the starting of action a at time 0 and then the starting of action b at time 2, one can observe the starting of action c at time 0 so that, in some sense, "time goes backward".

According to the operational semantics in Table 5, process $a.b \mid c$ has the transition system in Figure 1 - where, ill-timed paths are not present.

Remark 2. It has to be noted that the negative premises in rules Sum_1, Sum_2, Par_1 and Par_2 of Table 5 do not introduce inconsistencies and define a transition relation in a natural way.

The stratification technique in the sense of Groote [Gro93] is a general method developed for proving these properties. In [Cor00], it has been shown that our set of rules are stratified. Hence, they are consistent and define a transition relation according to Groote's algorithm.

The following proposition establishes some nice properties of the CIPA transition relation. We state that the time increases as the computation proceeds (so that only well-timed traces are considered) and that actions in our calculus are urgent (they are performed as soon as they can). Detailed proofs of these statements can be found in [Cor00].

Proposition 2. Let $d \in \mathcal{S}_{AM}$. Then:

(1) $d \xrightarrow[\delta_1]{\langle \mu_1, t_1 \rangle} d'$ and $d' \xrightarrow[\delta_2]{\langle \mu_2, t_2 \rangle} d''$ imply $t_1 \leq t_2$ (*Well-Timedness*)

(2) $d \xrightarrow[\delta]{\langle \mu, t \rangle} d'$ implies $\neg(d \xrightarrow[\delta']{\langle \gamma, t' \rangle} d''$ with $t' < t)$ (*Urgency*)

3.3   Timed Bisimulation

On top of the CIPA operational semantics a strong bisimulation-based equivalence can be defined. This equivalence relates processes that can perform the same actions at the same time.

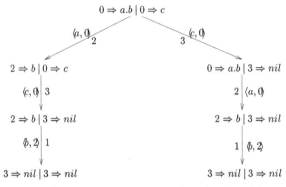

Fig. 1. The Timed Transition System for $a.b \mid c$.

Definition 3. (*Timed Equivalence*)

1. A binary relation $\Re$ over $\mathcal{S}_{AM}$ is a *timed (or eager) bisimulation* if and only if for each $(d_1, d_2) \in \Re$:

   a) $d_1 \xrightarrow[\delta]{\langle \mu, t \rangle} d_1'$ implies $d_2 \xrightarrow[\delta']{\langle \mu, t \rangle} d_2'$ and $(d_1', d_2') \in \Re$;

   b) $d_2 \xrightarrow[\delta]{\langle \mu, t \rangle} d_2'$ implies $d_1 \xrightarrow[\delta']{\langle \mu, t \rangle} d_1'$ and $(d_1', d_2') \in \Re$.

2. Two timed states d_1 and d_2 are *timed equivalent*, $d_1 \sim_{AM} d_2$, if and only if there exists a timed bisimulation $\Re$ such that $(d_1, d_2) \in \Re$.

3. Two $\mathcal{P}_{AM}$ processes P, Q are *timed equivalent*, $P \sim_{AM} Q$, if and only if $0 \Rightarrow P \sim_{AM} 0 \Rightarrow Q$.

4   Translating $\mathcal{P}_{AM}$ Processes into $\mathcal{P}_{MT}$ Processes

We are now ready to state our main results. We prove that CIPA and *TCCS*, different in several respects, are actually strictly related. We first introduce a mapping $\Pi[\![\_]\!]$ from $\mathcal{P}_{AM}$ terms to $\mathcal{P}_{MT}$ terms, and then we prove that two $\mathcal{P}_{AM}$ processes are timed equivalent if and only if their translations are $\mathcal{T}$-equivalent. More in detail, we prove the following statement:

Let P, $Q \in \mathcal{P}_{AM}$. Then, $P \sim_{AM} Q$ if and only if $\Pi[\![P]\!] \sim_{MT} \Pi[\![Q]\!]$.

We start by defining our mapping $\Pi[\![\_]\!] : \mathcal{P}_{AM} \to \mathcal{P}_{MT}$. This will be exploited to define a mapping from timed states to $\mathcal{P}_{MT}$ processes.

Definition 4. Let $\Pi[\![\_]\!] : \mathcal{P}_{AM} \to \mathcal{P}_{MT}$ be defined by the following rules:

$$\Pi[\![nil]\!] = \text{rec } x.\,(1).x$$
$$\Pi[\![a.P]\!] = a.(\Delta(a)).\Pi[\![P]\!]$$
$$\Pi[\![\text{wait } n.\,P]\!] = \tau.(n).\Pi[\![P]\!]$$

$$\Pi[P + Q] = \Pi[P] + \Pi[Q]$$
$$\Pi[P \mid Q] = \Pi[P] \mid \Pi[Q]$$
$$\Pi[P \backslash C] = \Pi[P] \backslash C$$
$$\Pi[P[\Phi]] = \Pi[P][\Phi]$$
$$\Pi[x] = x$$
$$\Pi[\text{rec } x.P] = \text{rec } x.\Pi[P]$$

A few words on the mapping are now in order. $\mathcal{P}_{AM}$ process nil cannot be mapped into $\mathcal{P}_{MT}$ process 0. The former process, indeed, behaves as the unit for parallel composition and non-deterministic choice, while the latter one behaves as an annihilator when composed in parallel or in choice with time-guarded processes. This is because 0 can perform neither basic actions, nor time passing actions. To give an example, consider $\mathcal{P}_{AM}$ process $nil \mid a.b$. When starting at time 0, it performs an action a (of duration $\Delta(a)$) at time 0 followed by an action b (of duration $\Delta(b)$) at time $\Delta(a)$. By mapping nil into 0 we would have $\Pi[nil \mid a.b] = 0 \mid a.(\Delta(a)).b.(\Delta(b)).0$. This process can only perform an action a. Indeed, after the execution of such an action, it reaches a deadlock state[6]. In order to find a $\mathcal{P}_{MT}$ process that behaves like $\mathcal{P}_{AM}$ process nil, we need a process which allows any amount of time to pass and cannot perform any basic action. This is the reason why we have chosen rec $x.(1).x$ (see Lemma 1). Alternatively, we could take $\delta.0$ (see Footnote 3) which has the same intended behavior ($\delta.0 \overset{t}{\rightsquigarrow} \delta.0$) but, since CIPA is an eager calculus, we are interested in mapping CIPA into the purely eager fragment of $TCCS$.

Consider now $\mathcal{P}_{AM}$ process $a.P$. This process can perform an action a, of duration $\Delta(a)$, at time 0. Then, at time $\Delta(a)$, it starts the execution of P. We map $a.P$ into a process that can perform a durationless action a followed by a relative delay of $\Delta(a)$ time units after which it becomes $\Pi[P]$. Hence, $\Pi[a.P] = a.(\Delta(a)).\Pi[P]$. Similarly, a wait of n time units followed by a process P, wait $n.P$, is mapped into a process that performs an instantaneous τ action followed by a relative delay of n time units after which it becomes $\Pi[P]$. Hence, $\Pi[\text{wait } n.P] = \tau.(n).\Pi[P]$. Mapping $\Pi[\_]$ is then extended homomorphically over all the others operators.

Example 1. Consider process $a.b \mid c$ where $\Delta(a) = 2$, $\Delta(b) = 1$ and $\Delta(c) = 3$. Function $\Pi[\_]$ applied to this process gives $a(2).b(1).\text{rec } x(1).x \mid c.(3).\text{rec } x(1).x$, the transition system of which is reported in Figure 2.

Unfortunately, our main statement does not hold for the whole $\mathcal{P}_{AM}$ language but for the subset of restriction-free $\mathcal{P}_{AM}$ processes. The following proposition shows a pair of processes P and Q such that $\Pi[P]$ and $\Pi[Q]$ are related by $\mathcal{T}$-equivalence while P and Q are not related by timed equivalence. The reasons for this drawback are similar to those for which process nil cannot be mapped into 0.

---

[6] This would lead our main statement to fail because, for instance, processes $nil \mid a.b$ and $nil \mid a$ are such that $\Pi[nil \mid a.b] \sim_{MT} \Pi[nil \mid a]$ while, clearly, $nil \mid a.b \not\sim_{AM} nil \mid a$.

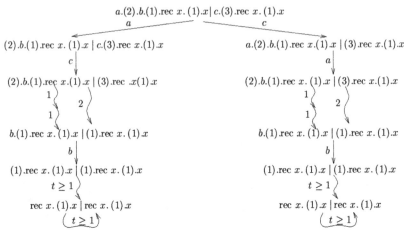

Fig. 2. The Transition System of $\mathcal{P}_{MT}$ process $\varPi[\![a.b \mid c]\!]$.

Proposition 3. There are $\mathcal{P}_{AM}$ processes P and Q such that $\varPi[\![P]\!] \sim_{MT} \varPi[\![Q]\!]$ but not $P \sim_{AM} Q$.

Proof. Consider the pair of processes $P = a\backslash\{a\} \mid b.c$ and $Q = a\backslash\{a\} \mid b$ that are such that $\varPi[\![P]\!] \sim_{MT} \varPi[\![Q]\!]$ but not $P \sim_{AM} Q$.

In the rest of this section, due to Proposition 3, we will concentrate on the subset of restriction-free $\mathcal{P}_{AM}$ (*Open* $\mathcal{P}_{AM}$) processes, denoted by $\mathcal{P}_{AM}^{rf}$ (*Open* $\mathcal{P}_{AM}^{rf}$), and hence also on the corresponding subset of restriction-free timed states, denoted by $\mathcal{S}_{AM}^{rf}$.

Since $\sim_{AM}$ is defined over timed states ($\mathcal{S}_{AM}$ terms) we need to translate timed states into $\mathcal{P}_{MT}$ processes. The next definition introduces this further mapping which exploits $\varPi[\![\_]\!]$.

Definition 5. Let $\mathcal{D}[\![\_]\!] : \mathcal{S}_{AM}^{rf} \to \mathcal{P}_{MT}$ be the least relation which satisfies the following rules:

$$
\begin{aligned}
\mathcal{D}[\![n \Rightarrow nil]\!] &= (n).\varPi[\![nil]\!] & n > 0 \qquad \mathcal{D}[\![d_1 + d_2]\!] &= \mathcal{D}[\![d_1]\!] + \mathcal{D}[\![d_2]\!] \\
\mathcal{D}[\![0 \Rightarrow nil]\!] &= \varPi[\![nil]\!] & \mathcal{D}[\![d_1 \mid d_2]\!] &= \mathcal{D}[\![d_1]\!] \mid \mathcal{D}[\![d_2]\!] \\
\mathcal{D}[\![n \Rightarrow a.P]\!] &= (n).\varPi[\![a.P]\!] & n > 0 \qquad \mathcal{D}[\![d[\varPhi]]\!] &= \mathcal{D}[\![d]\!][\varPhi] \\
\mathcal{D}[\![0 \Rightarrow a.P]\!] &= \varPi[\![a.P]\!] \\
\mathcal{D}[\![n \Rightarrow \text{wait } n'.\, P]\!] &= (n).\varPi[\![\text{wait } n'.\, P]\!] & n > 0 \\
\mathcal{D}[\![0 \Rightarrow \text{wait } n'.\, P]\!] &= \varPi[\![\text{wait } n'.\, P]\!] \\
\mathcal{D}[\![n \Rightarrow \text{rec } x.P]\!] &= (n).\varPi[\![\text{rec } x.P]\!] & n > 0 \\
\mathcal{D}[\![0 \Rightarrow \text{rec } x.P]\!] &= \varPi[\![\text{rec } x.P]\!]
\end{aligned}
$$

Then we need a little more terminology to relate the states of the transition system associated to a timed state $d \in \mathcal{S}_{AM}^{rf}$ and those corresponding to its translated version $\mathcal{D}[\![d]\!]$. This will be a significant progress in proving our main statement. Consider the transition systems in Figure 1 and that in Figure 2.

Note that states and transitions are strictly related. For instance, it is easy to convince that state $(2).b.(1).\text{rec } x.(1).x \mid (3).\text{rec } x.(1).x$ in the leftmost path of the transition system in Figure 2 corresponds to state $2 \Rightarrow b \mid 3 \Rightarrow nil$ in the leftmost path of the transition system in Figure 1; and, indeed, $\mathcal{D}[\![2 \Rightarrow b \mid 3 \Rightarrow nil]\!] = (2).b.(1).\text{rec } x.(1).x \mid (3).\text{rec } x.(1).x$.

However, also $b.(1).\text{rec } x.(1).x|(1).\text{rec } x.(1).x$ is in some way related to $\mathcal{D}[\![2 \Rightarrow b \mid 3 \Rightarrow nil]\!]$ (even if $\mathcal{D}[\![2 \Rightarrow b \mid 3 \Rightarrow nil]\!]$ is not $b.(1).\text{rec } x.(1).x \mid (1).\text{rec } x.(1).x)$: the latter state can be obtained by the former one by performing a $\overset{2}{\leadsto}$-transition (or, equivalently, two subsequent $\overset{1}{\leadsto}$-transitions). Note that 2 in $2 \Rightarrow b \mid 3 \Rightarrow nil$ corresponds to the least local clock for which a transition is enabled (a b-transition, in this case).

The following two definitions allow us to properly relate timed states and $\mathcal{P}_{MT}$ processes as $2 \Rightarrow b \mid 3 \Rightarrow nil$ and $b.(1).\text{rec } x.(1).x \mid (1).\text{rec } x.(1).x$. First of all we say when a timed state and a natural number are related. Roughly speaking, $d \in \mathcal{S}_{AM}^{rf}$ and $n \in \mathbb{N}$ are related if after decreasing each local clock $m \Rightarrow \_$ appearing in d of exactly n time units, we still have a term in $\mathcal{S}_{AM}^{rf}$ (i.e., a timed state). Since nil, in CIPA, does not stop the time, $n \Rightarrow nil$ is related with each natural number.

Definition 6. Let $wf \subseteq \mathcal{S}_{AM}^{rf} \times \mathbb{N}$ be the least relation which satisfies the following inference rules:

$$\frac{t \in \mathbb{N}}{wf(n \Rightarrow nil, t)} \qquad \frac{t \leq n}{wf(n \Rightarrow a.P, t)} \qquad \frac{t \leq n}{wf(n \Rightarrow \text{wait } n'.\, P, t)}$$

$$\frac{t \leq n}{wf(n \Rightarrow \text{rec } x.P, t)} \qquad \frac{wf(d, n)}{wf(d[\Phi], n)}$$

$$\frac{wf(d_1, n) \text{ and } wf(d_2, n)}{wf(d_1 + d_2, n)} \qquad \frac{wf(d_1, n) \text{ and } wf(d_2, n)}{wf(d_1 \mid d_2, n)}$$

Then an updating function $up : \mathcal{S}_{AM}^{rf} \times \mathbb{N} \to \mathcal{S}_{AM}^{rf}$ is defined which given a timed state $d \in \mathcal{S}_{AM}^{rf}$ and a natural number n such that $wf(d, n)$, returns the timed state d' obtained by decreasing each local clock $m \Rightarrow \_$ appearing in d of n time units.

Definition 7. Let $up : \mathcal{S}_{AM}^{rf} \times \mathbb{N} \to \mathcal{S}_{AM}^{rf}$ be the least function which satisfies the following inference rules:

$$up(n \Rightarrow nil, t) = (n - t) \Rightarrow nil, \ n \geq t$$
$$up(n \Rightarrow nil, t) = 0 \Rightarrow nil, \ n < t$$
$$up(n \Rightarrow a.P, t) = (n - t) \Rightarrow a.P, \ n \geq t$$
$$up(n \Rightarrow \text{wait } n'.\, P, t) = (n - t) \Rightarrow \text{wait } n'.\, P, \ n \geq t$$
$$up(n \Rightarrow \text{rec } x.P, t) = (n - t) \Rightarrow \text{rec } x.P, \ n \geq t$$

$$up(d_1 \mid d_2, t) = up(d_1, t) \mid up(d_2, t)$$
$$up(d_1 + d_2, t) = up(d_1, t) + up(d_2, t)$$
$$up(d[\Phi], t) = up(d, t)[\Phi]$$

This up function is such that if $d \in \mathcal{S}_{AM}^{rf}$ and $t \in \mathbb{N}$ such that $wf(d, t)$ then $\mathcal{D}[\![up(d, t)]\!] \in \mathcal{P}_{MT}$.

4.1   The Main Statement

In this section we present our main result showing that CIPA and $TCCS$ are strictly related. Its formal proof can be found in [Cor00]; here we just report three key propositions. The first one relates transitions out of $\mathcal{D}[\![up(d, t)]\!]$ and out of d. In particular, we show that $\mathcal{D}[\![up(d, t)]\!]$ can perform a basic action μ if and only if timed state d can perform an action μ at time t and duration δ.

Proposition 4. Let $d \in \mathcal{S}_{AM}^{rf}$ and $t \in \mathbb{N}$ such that $wf(d, t)$. Then:

(1) $\mathcal{D}[\![up(d, t)]\!] \xrightarrow{\mu} p$ implies $d \xrightarrow[\delta]{\langle \mu, t \rangle} d'$, $wf(d', t)$ and $p \simeq \mathcal{D}[\![up(d', t)]\!]$;

(2) $d \xrightarrow[\delta]{\langle \mu, t \rangle} d'$ implies $\mathcal{D}[\![up(d, t)]\!] \xrightarrow{\mu} p$, $wf(d', t)$ and $p \simeq \mathcal{D}[\![up(d', t)]\!]$.

We then show that if process $\mathcal{D}[\![up(d, t)]\!]$ in $\mathcal{P}_{MT}$ can let a unit of time to pass, $\mathcal{D}[\![up(d, t)]\!] \xrightarrow{1} p$, then (i) $\mathcal{D}[\![up(d, t)]\!]$ cannot perform any basic action γ and (ii) timed state d cannot perform basic actions at a time $t' \le t$.

Proposition 5. Let $d \in \mathcal{S}_{AM}^{rf}$ and $t \in \mathbb{N}$ such that $wf(d, t)$. Then $\mathcal{D}[\![up(d, t)]\!] \xrightarrow{1} p$ implies $\mathcal{D}[\![up(d, t)]\!] \xrightarrow{\gamma} \!\!\!\!/ \ p'$ for any γ and p', and $d \xrightarrow[\delta]{\langle \mu, t' \rangle} \!\!\!\!\!\!/ \ d'$ for any μ, d' and $t' \le t$. Moreover, $wf(d, t+1)$ and $p \simeq \mathcal{D}[\![up(d, t+1)]\!]$.

The reverse of the previous proposition states that if $d \xrightarrow[\delta]{\langle \mu, t' \rangle} \!\!\!\!\!\!/ \ d'$ for any μ and $t' \le t$, then $\mathcal{D}[\![up(d, t)]\!]$ can only evolve by performing a $\xrightarrow{1}$-transition.

Proposition 6. Let $d \in \mathcal{S}_{AM}^{rf}$ and $t \in \mathbb{N}$. If $d \xrightarrow[\delta]{\langle \mu, t' \rangle} \!\!\!\!\!\!/ \ d'$ for any $t' \le t$, $\mu \in Act_\tau$ and $d' \in \mathcal{S}_{AM}^{rf}$ then $wf(d, t)$, $wf(d, t+1)$ and $\mathcal{D}[\![up(d, t)]\!] \xrightarrow{1} \mathcal{D}[\![up(d, t+1)]\!]$.

Hence, we have the main statement:

Theorem 1. Let P and Q be $\mathcal{P}_{AM}^{rf}$ processes. Then $P \sim_{AM} Q$ if and only if $\Pi[\![P]\!] \sim_{MT} \Pi[\![Q]\!]$.

Proof. It is sufficient to prove that:

Let d_1 and d_2 be $\mathcal{S}_{AM}^{rf}$ terms. Then $d_1 \sim_{AM} d_2$ if and only if $\mathcal{D}[\![d_1]\!] \sim_{MT} \mathcal{D}[\![d_2]\!]$.

To prove that $d_1 \sim_{AM} d_2$ implies $\mathcal{D}[\![d_1]\!] \sim_{MT} \mathcal{D}[\![d_2]\!]$ we prove that relation

$$\mathfrak{R}_{AM}^{MT} = \{(p,q) \mid \exists t \in \mathbb{N}, \ \exists d_1, d_2 \in \mathcal{S}_{AM}^{rf} \text{ such that } wf(d_1,t), \ wf(d_2,t),$$
$$p \simeq \mathcal{D}[\![up(d_1,t)]\!], \ q \simeq \mathcal{D}[\![up(d_2,t)]\!] \text{ and } d_1 \sim_{AM} d_2\}$$

is a MT-bisimulation.

To prove $\mathcal{D}[\![d_1]\!] \sim_{MT} \mathcal{D}[\![d_2]\!]$ implies $d_1 \sim_{AM} d_2$ we show that relation

$$\mathfrak{R}_{MT}^{AM} = \{(d_1,d_2) \mid \exists t \in \mathbb{N}, \ \exists p_1, p_2 \in \mathcal{P}_{MT} \text{ such that } wf(d_1,t), \ wf(d_2,t),$$
$$p \simeq \mathcal{D}[\![up(d_1,t)]\!], \ q \simeq \mathcal{D}[\![up(d_2,t)]\!] \text{ and } p \sim_{MT} q\}$$

is an AM-bisimulation.

The formal details of the proof can be found in [Cor00]. Of course, it heavily relies on Propositions 4, 5 and 6.

4.2   On the Size of Timed Transition Systems

A serious drawback of the CIPA operational semantics is that the timed transition systems associated with processes are (in general) infinite state structures because local clocks are explicitly represented within the states. In [Cor00], we introduce a notion a compact state, $\widehat{d}$, and of compact bisimulation, $\sim_c$, as finite alternative representations of the infinite models. This in order to apply standard verification techniques on finite structures.

Once compact timed bisimulation is proven to be a finite alternative characterization of timed equivalence (see [Cor00], for the formal details) it is interesting to contrast the size of the compact transition system associated with a CIPA process and that associated with its translation. We have shown that the former is strictly smaller (in terms of the number of states and transitions) than the latter. Since the (time) complexity of standard algorithms for checking bisimulation-based equivalences over finite states processes depends on the number of states and transitions, compact timed bisimulations can be checked more efficiently than $\mathcal{T}$-equivalence. To show that the number of states and transitions to be visited when checking compact bisimulation of two CIPA processes is less or equal than the number of states and transitions to be visited when checking $\mathcal{T}$-bisimulation of their translations, we show the following two statements:

- A compact state $\widehat{d}$ can only perform transitions at time 0 (so that we actually "ignore" time in timed transitions);

- If the compact representation of a state, $\widehat{d}$, can perform an action μ, $\widehat{d} \xrightarrow[\delta]{\langle \mu, 0 \rangle} d'$, then the $\mathcal{D}[\![\_]\!]$-translation of $\widehat{d}$, $\mathcal{D}[\![\widehat{d}]\!]$, can perform an action μ leading to p, $\mathcal{D}[\![\widehat{d}]\!] \xrightarrow{\mu} p$ such that $\mathcal{D}[\![d']\!] \simeq p$. Moreover either $p \simeq \mathcal{D}[\![\widehat{d'}]\!]$ or $\mathcal{D}[\![\widehat{d'}]\!] \simeq q$ where q is such that $p \overset{t}{\leadsto} q$ for some $t > 0$. The vice versa also holds;

- If the translation of a compact state $\mathcal{D}[\![\widehat{d}]\!]$ can let time pass, then $\widehat{d}$ cannot perform any basic action at any time; namely, $\mathcal{D}[\![\widehat{d}]\!] \overset{1}{\leadsto} p$ implies $p = \mathcal{D}[\![\widehat{d}]\!]$ and $\widehat{d} \xrightarrow[\delta]{\langle \mu, t \rangle} \!\!\!\!\!/ \ \ d'$ for any $\mu \in Act_\tau$ and $t, \delta \in \mathbb{N}$.

The diagram in Fig. 3 summarizes the relationships among transitions out of a compact state $\widehat{d}$ and those out of its translation $\mathcal{D}[\![\widehat{d}\,]\!]$.

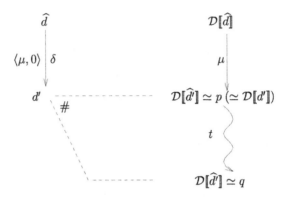

Fig. 3. Relating Timed Transitions to Timing and Action Transitions.

Note that only transitions performing basic actions are taken into account in the durational setting. Moreover, the mapping of the compact representations of the target states (which are the significant ones when looking at a compact timed bisimulation relating two compact states, possibly $0 \Rightarrow P$ and $0 \Rightarrow Q$ for P and Q cIPA terms), are $\overset{t}{\leadsto}$-derivatives of the corresponding target states in the $TCCS$ setting. Thus, the number of states and transitions to be visited when looking for a compact timed bisimulation relating $0 \Rightarrow P$ and $0 \Rightarrow Q$, are strictly smaller than the number of states and transitions to be visited when looking for a $\mathcal{T}$-bisimulation relating $\mathcal{D}[\![0 \Rightarrow P]\!]$ and $\mathcal{D}[\![0 \Rightarrow Q]\!]$. In Fig. 3, # means "either a branch or the other one is taken".

5   Dealing with Lazy Systems

In the previous sections we have presented a mapping from cIPA to $TCCS$ which preserves the behavioral equivalences over these two timed calculi. This result holds only for restriction-free processes. A $TCCS$ restriction operator, indeed, may cause a local deadlock; i.e., the deadlock of a component of a global system. A local deadlock may cause, in turn, the deadlock of the whole system. More in detail, the deadlock of a system may cause the stop of the passage of time. Every system which can cause a time stop, can consequently cause the deadlock of all the other systems which are in parallel composition or in alternative composition with the system itself (see rules $TSum$ and $TPar$ in Table 2).

In this section we show that when the *lazy* versions of $TCCS$ and cIPA are taken into account, the mapping is fully abstract also in presence of the restriction operator. Lazy means that actions can be delayed arbitrarily long before their execution. A consequence of this fact is that every $TCCS$ process can let every amount of time to pass even if it cannot perform any basic action. This permits avoiding the problems discussed in Section 4 (see Proposition 3).

5.1 The Lazy *TCCS*

Lazy *TCCS*, also known as *loose TCCS* and denoted by *lTCCS*, has been proposed by Moller and Tofts in [MT91].

The syntax of *lTCCS* is the same as the syntax of *TCCS* we considered in Section 2. Thus, we still use $\mathcal{P}_{MT}$ to denote the set of *lTCCS* processes. Add the rules *Zero* and *PAct* in Table 6 to the rules in Table 2 to give a lazy interpretation to the basic actions. By convention it is also assumed that $p \overset{0}{\rightsquigarrow} p$, for every process $p \in lTCCS$. The rules describing the functional behavior of *lTCCS* are, instead, those in Table 1.

A notion of $\mathcal{T}$-*Equivalence* can be given as in Definition 1 - we use $\sim_{lMT}$ for the new equivalence. Similar properties of the *TCCS* transitional semantics and equivalence relation are satisfied by the lazy interpretation. In particular, Corollary 1, Lemma 1 and Lemma 2 still hold in the lazy setting. In addition, the following important Proposition 7 holds (see Proposition 3.1 in [MT91]). It says that every *lTCCS* process can let every amount of time to pass. Thus the counterexample in Proposition 3 does not hold. In a lazy setting, $a \backslash \{a\}$ cannot perform any basic action but can let every amount of time to pass. Hence, it does not behave as an annihilator for the others parallel components.

Table 6. Structural Rules for Laziness in *lTCCS*.

$$Zero \; \frac{}{0 \overset{t}{\rightsquigarrow} 0} \qquad\qquad PAct \; \frac{}{\mu.p \overset{t}{\rightsquigarrow} \mu.p}$$

Proposition 7. For every $\mathcal{P}_{MT}$ process p and for every $t \in \mathbb{N}^+$, there exits a (unique) q such that $p \overset{t}{\rightsquigarrow} q$.

5.2 The Lazy cIPA

Lazy cIPA, LCIPA, has been proposed by Corradini and Pistore in [CP96]. The syntax of LCIPA is the same as the syntax of cIPA (see Section 3). We still use $\mathcal{P}_{AM}$ to denote the set of LCIPA processes, but give a different interpretation to basic actions. These actions are not forced to be performed as soon as they become available but can be delayed arbitrarily long before firing. Thus, the central rule for Lazy cIPA is something like

$$n \Rightarrow a.P \xrightarrow[\Delta(a)]{\langle a, n+r \rangle} (n + r + \Delta(a)) \Rightarrow P, \text{ for every delay } r \in \mathbb{N}.$$

This is not the only modification that CIPA needs in order to model actions which can be delayed. The syntax of timed states, indeed, must be extended to explicitly record the value of the global clock (the global observation time for execution). Consider timed state

$$d = 10 \Rightarrow a.nil \mid 50 \Rightarrow b.nil \mid 100 \Rightarrow c.nil,$$

where the duration of a, b and c is 1. Assume that the value of the global clock is 10 and suppose that d performs a delayed action a at starting time 60 leading to timed state

$$d' = 61 \Rightarrow nil \mid 50 \Rightarrow b.nil \mid 100 \Rightarrow c.nil.$$

At this point we explicitly need to record that 60 is the value of the global clock in order to solve ambiguities[7].

For this reason we consider timed states of the form

$$d \rhd n,$$

where d is a timed state as defined in Section 3 and n denotes the value of the global clock. We use $\mathcal{S}_{GT}$ to denote the new set of timed states.

The operational semantics of $\mathcal{S}_{GT}$ terms is given in Table 7. The only rule worth of note is $LAct$. It says that timed state $(n \Rightarrow a.P) \rhd m$ can perform an action a at every time t, provided that t is greater than the global clock and, clearly, greater than the local clock. The rule for $LWait$ is similar. The other rules are now standard.

The definition of *lazy timed equivalence* is similar to Definition 3.

Definition 8. (*Lazy Timed Equivalence*)

1. A binary relation $\mathfrak{R}$ over $\mathcal{S}_{GT}$ is a *lazy timed bisimulation* if and only if for each $(d_1 \rhd n, d_2 \rhd n) \in \mathfrak{R}$:
   a) $d_1 \rhd n \xrightarrow[\delta]{\langle \mu, t \rangle} d_1' \rhd t$ implies $d_2 \rhd n \xrightarrow[\delta']{\langle \mu, t \rangle} d_2' \rhd t$ and $(d_1' \rhd t, d_2' \rhd t) \in \mathfrak{R}$;
   b) $d_2 \rhd n \xrightarrow[\delta']{\langle \mu, t \rangle} d_2' \rhd t$ implies $d_1 \rhd n \xrightarrow[\delta]{\langle \mu, t \rangle} d_1' \rhd t$ and $(d_1' \rhd t, d_2' \rhd t) \in \mathfrak{R}$.
2. Two timed states $d_1 \rhd n$ and $d_2 \rhd n$ are *lazy timed equivalent*, $d_1 \rhd n \sim_{lAM} d_2 \rhd n$, if and only if there exists a lazy timed bisimulation $\mathfrak{R}$ such that $(d_1 \rhd n, d_2 \rhd n) \in \mathfrak{R}$.
3. Two $\mathcal{P}_{AM}$ processes P, Q are *lazy timed equivalent*, $P \sim_{lAM} Q$, if and only if $(0 \Rightarrow P) \rhd 0 \sim_{lAM} (0 \Rightarrow Q) \rhd 0$.

To prove that LCIPA and $lTCCS$ are strictly related we need further notation. Consider timed state

$$(1000 \Rightarrow a.nil \mid 500 \Rightarrow b.nil \mid 0 \Rightarrow c.nil) \rhd 998.$$

---

[7] Note that this problem does not arise in CIPA where actions must be performed as soon as they can. The value of the global clock in a timed state, indeed, coincides with the value of the minimum local clock associated with a (non-deadlock) sequential process within the state.

Table 7. The Structural Rules for LCIPA.

$$LAct \quad \frac{t \geq max(m,n)}{(n \Rightarrow a.P) \rhd m \xrightarrow[\Delta(a)]{\square a,t\square} ((t + \Delta(a)) \Rightarrow P) \rhd t}$$

$$LWait \quad \frac{t \geq max(m,n)}{(n \Rightarrow \text{wait } n^{\square}.P) \rhd m \xrightarrow[n']{\square \tau,t\square} ((t + n^{\square}) \Rightarrow P) \rhd t}$$

$$LSum_1 \quad \frac{d_1 \rhd m \xrightarrow[\delta]{\square \mu,t\square} d \rhd t}{(d_1 + d_2) \rhd m \xrightarrow[\delta]{\square \mu,t\square} d \rhd t} \qquad LSum_2 \quad \frac{d_2 \rhd m \xrightarrow[\delta]{\square \mu,t\square} d \rhd t}{(d_1 + d_2) \rhd m \xrightarrow[\delta]{\square \mu,t\square} d \rhd t}$$

$$LPar_1 \quad \frac{d_1 \rhd m \xrightarrow[\delta]{\square \mu,t\square} d_1^{\square} \rhd t}{(d_1 \mid d_2) \rhd m \xrightarrow[\delta]{\square \mu,t\square} (d_1^{\square} \mid d_2) \rhd t} \qquad LPar_2 \quad \frac{d_2 \rhd m \xrightarrow[\delta]{\square \mu,t\square} d_2^{\square} \rhd t}{(d_1 \mid d_2) \rhd m \xrightarrow[\delta]{\square \mu,t\square} (d_1 \mid d_2^{\square}) \rhd t}$$

$$LSynch \quad \frac{d_1 \rhd m \xrightarrow[\Delta(a)]{\square a,t\square} d_1^{\square} \rhd t, \; d_2 \rhd m \xrightarrow[\Delta(a)]{\square \bar{a},t\square} d_2^{\square} \rhd t}{(d_1 \mid d_2) \rhd m \xrightarrow[\Delta(a)]{\square \tau,t\square} (d_1^{\square} \mid d_2^{\square}) \rhd t}$$

$$LRes \quad \frac{d \rhd m \xrightarrow[\delta]{\square \mu,t\square} d^{\square} \rhd t}{d \backslash C \rhd m \xrightarrow[\delta]{\square \mu,t\square} d^{\square} \backslash C \rhd t} \mu, \bar{\mu} \notin C \qquad LRel \quad \frac{d \rhd m \xrightarrow[\delta]{\square \mu,t\square} d^{\square} \rhd t}{d[\Phi] \rhd m \xrightarrow[\delta]{\square \Phi(\mu),t\square} d^{\square}[\Phi] \rhd t}$$

$$LRec \quad \frac{(n \Rightarrow P[\text{rec } x.\, P/x]) \rhd m \xrightarrow[\delta]{\square \mu,t\square} d \rhd t}{(n \Rightarrow \text{rec } x.\, P) \rhd m \xrightarrow[\delta]{\square \mu,t\square} d \rhd t}$$

Since the value of the global clock is 998, by a simple inspection of the operational rules in Table 7, we can conclude that no action can be performed at a time less than 998. Thus, intuitively, the above timed state behaves like

$$(1000 \Rightarrow a.nil \mid 998 \Rightarrow b.nil \mid 998 \Rightarrow c.nil) \rhd 998,$$

where each local clock less than 998 is increased to the value of the global clock.

In order to update those local clocks in a state which are less than the value of the global clock, we introduce function aug.

Definition 9. Let $aug : \mathcal{S}_{AM} \times \mathbb{N} \to \mathcal{S}_{AM}$ be the least function which satisfies the following inference rules:

$$aug(n \Rightarrow nil, t) = t \Rightarrow nil, \ t \geq n$$
$$aug(n \Rightarrow nil, t) = n \Rightarrow nil, \ n > t$$
$$aug(n \Rightarrow \text{wait } n'. \ P, t) = t \Rightarrow \text{wait } n'. \ P, \ t \geq n$$
$$aug(n \Rightarrow \text{wait } n'. \ P, t) = n \Rightarrow \text{wait } n'. \ P, \ n > t$$
$$aug(n \Rightarrow a.P, t) = t \Rightarrow a.P, \ t \geq n$$
$$aug(n \Rightarrow a.P, t) = n \Rightarrow a.P, \ n > t$$
$$aug(n \Rightarrow \text{rec } x.P, t) = t \Rightarrow \text{rec } x.P, \ t \geq n$$
$$aug(n \Rightarrow \text{rec } x.P, t) = n \Rightarrow \text{rec } x.P, \ n > t$$
$$aug(d_1 + d_2, t) = aug(d_1, t) + aug(d_2, t)$$
$$aug(d_1 \mid d_2, t) = aug(d_1, t) \mid aug(d_2, t)$$
$$aug(d[\varPhi], t) = aug(d, t)[\varPhi]$$
$$aug(d \backslash C, t) = aug(d, t) \backslash C$$

Remark 3. The intended behavior of a given state $d \triangleright n$ does not change if we increase to n all those local clocks in d which are less than n. In particular, it can be proven that $d \triangleright n \sim_{lAM} (aug(d, n)) \triangleright n$.

5.3   Mapping Lazy cIPA into Lazy *TCCS*

In this section we contrast Lazy cIPA and Lazy *TCCS* via behavioral equivalences. As in Section 4, we show that there exists a simple mapping $\Pi[\![\_]\!]$: $\mathcal{P}_{AM} \to \mathcal{P}_{MT}$ such that $P \sim_{lAM} Q$ if and only if $\Pi[\![P]\!] \sim_{lMT} \Pi[\![Q]\!]$, where P and Q are $\mathcal{P}_{AM}$ processes. Note that, in this case, we consider the whole Lazy cIPA, not only the restriction-free fragment.

The mapping $\Pi[\![\_]\!]$: $\mathcal{P}_{AM} \to \mathcal{P}_{MT}$ coincides with that in Definition 4[8].

In order to map a $\mathcal{S}_{GT}$ process into a $\mathcal{P}_{MT}$ process consider the function $\mathcal{D}[\![\_]\!]$ given in Definition 5, extended with rule

$$\mathcal{D}[\![d \backslash C]\!] = \mathcal{D}[\![d]\!] \backslash C.$$

Now let

$$\mathcal{D}[\![d \triangleright n]\!] = \mathcal{D}[\![up(aug(d, n), n)]\!],$$

where up is the updating function given in Definition 7. Given a state $d \triangleright n$ we first increase each local clock in d less than n to n (the value of the global clock). This implies that the minimum local clock in $aug(d, n)$ is greater or equal than n. Then, decrease every local clock appearing in $aug(d, n)$ of n time units. At this point we translate state $up(aug(d, n))$ into a $\mathcal{P}_{MT}$ process. To give an example consider state:

$$d \triangleright 98 = (100 \Rightarrow a.nil \mid 0 \Rightarrow b.nil) \triangleright 98.$$

Then,

$$aug(d, 98) = 100 \Rightarrow a.nil \mid 98 \Rightarrow b.nil$$

and

$$up(aug(d, 98), 98) = 2 \Rightarrow a.nil \mid 0 \Rightarrow b.nil.$$

---

[8] In this case we could also map *nil* directly into 0. Indeed, by rule *Zero* in Table 6 it is $0 \overset{t}{\leadsto} 0$.

Finally,

$$\mathcal{D}[\![up(aug(d,98),98)]\!] = (2).a.(\Delta(a)).\text{rec } x. (1).x \mid b.(\Delta(b)).\text{rec } x. (1).x.$$

Before stating the relationships among transitions out of $d \rhd n$ and those out of $\mathcal{D}[\![d \rhd n]\!]$ we need a further proposition.

Proposition 8. Let $d \rhd n \in \mathcal{S}_{GT}$. Then $\mathcal{D}[\![d \rhd n]\!] \overset{t}{\leadsto} q$ and $q \simeq \mathcal{D}[\![d \rhd n+t]\!]$.

The relationships among transitions out of $d \rhd n$ and those out of $\mathcal{D}[\![d \rhd n]\!]$ can now be stated. The first item states that $d \rhd n \xrightarrow[\delta]{\langle \mu, t \rangle} d' \rhd t$ implies that $\mathcal{D}[\![up(aug(d,n),n)]\!]$ can first let $t - n$ time units to pass (the idling time), and then it can perform an action μ. The target states are also related. The second item is essentially the reverse of the second one. Below, $\simeq$ denotes the congruence in Table 3.

Proposition 9. Let $d \rhd n$ be a $\mathcal{S}_{GT}$ timed state.

(i) $d \rhd n \xrightarrow[\delta]{\langle \mu, t \rangle} d' \rhd t$ then $\mathcal{D}[\![d \rhd n]\!] \overset{t-n}{\leadsto} q \xrightarrow{\mu} q'$ with $q \simeq \mathcal{D}[\![d \rhd t]\!]$ and $q' \simeq \mathcal{D}[\![d' \rhd t]\!]$;

(ii) if $t \geq n$ and $\mathcal{D}[\![d \rhd n]\!] \overset{t-n}{\leadsto} q \xrightarrow{\mu} q'$ then $d \rhd n \xrightarrow[\delta]{\langle \mu, t \rangle} d' \rhd t$ with $q \simeq \mathcal{D}[\![d \rhd t]\!]$ and $q' \simeq \mathcal{D}[\![d' \rhd t]\!]$.

Then we prove that the equivalence of states is not altered by the elapsing of time.

Proposition 10. Let $d_1 \rhd n$ and $d_2 \rhd n$ be $\mathcal{S}_{GT}$ timed states and $t \geq n$. Then $d_1 \rhd n \sim_{lAM} d_2 \rhd n$ implies $d_1 \rhd t \sim_{lAM} d_2 \rhd t$.

Proof. Let $\Re_n$ be the lazy timed bisimulation such that $(d_1 \rhd n, d_2 \rhd n) \in \Re_n$. Define relation

$$\Re_t = \Re_n \cup \{(d_1 \rhd t, d_2 \rhd t), (d_2 \rhd t, d_1 \rhd t)\}$$

and prove that $\Re_t$ is a lazy timed bisimulation.

The main statement of this section immediately follows.

Theorem 2. Let P and Q be $\mathcal{P}_{AM}$ processes. Then $P \sim_{lAM} Q$ if and only if $\Pi[\![P]\!] \sim_{lMT} \Pi[\![Q]\!]$.

Proof. By Definition 8, $P \sim_{lAM} Q$ if and only if $(0 \Rightarrow P) \rhd 0 \sim_{lAM} (0 \Rightarrow Q) \rhd 0$. Moreover, $\mathcal{D}[\![(0 \Rightarrow P) \rhd 0]\!] \sim_{lMT} \mathcal{D}[\![(0 \Rightarrow Q) \rhd 0]\!]$ if and only if (since $up(aug(0 \Rightarrow P, 0), 0) = 0 \Rightarrow P$) $\mathcal{D}[\![0 \Rightarrow P]\!] \sim_{lMT} \mathcal{D}[\![0 \Rightarrow Q]\!]$ if and only if $\Pi[\![P]\!] \sim_{lMT} \Pi[\![Q]\!]$. Thus in order to prove our statement we actually state the following statement. Let $d_1 \rhd n$, $d_2 \rhd n$ be $\mathcal{S}_{GT}$ terms. Then:

$$d_1 \rhd n \sim_{lAM} d_2 \rhd n \text{ iff } \mathcal{D}[\![d_1 \rhd n]\!] \sim_{lMT} \mathcal{D}[\![d_2 \rhd n]\!].$$

To prove that $d_1 \triangleright n \sim_{lAM} d_2 \triangleright n$ implies $\mathcal{D}[\![d_1 \triangleright n]\!] \sim_{lMT} \mathcal{D}[\![d_2 \triangleright n]\!]$ define relation

$$\mathfrak{R}_{AM}^{MT} = \{(p, q) \mid \exists d_1 \triangleright n, \, d_2 \triangleright n \in \mathcal{S}_{GT}, \, p \simeq \mathcal{D}[\![d_1 \triangleright n]\!], \, q \simeq \mathcal{D}[\![d_2 \triangleright n]\!],$$

$$d_1 \triangleright n \sim_{lAM} d_2 \triangleright n\}$$

and prove that it is a $\mathcal{T}$-bisimulation.

To prove that $\mathcal{D}[\![d_1 \triangleright t]\!] \sim_{lMT} \mathcal{D}[\![d_2 \triangleright t]\!]$ implies $d_1 \triangleright t \sim_{lAM} d_2 \triangleright t$ define relation

$$\mathfrak{R}_{MT}^{AM} = \{(d_1 \triangleright n, d_2 \triangleright n) \mid \exists p, q \in \mathcal{P}_{MT}, \, p \simeq \mathcal{D}[\![d_1 \triangleright n]\!], q \simeq \mathcal{D}[\![d_2 \triangleright n]\!] \text{ and } p \sim_{lMT} q\}$$

and prove that it is a lazy timed bisimulation.

6   Dealing with Maximal Progress

In Section 2 and Section 3 we have presented (urgent) $TCCS$ and (urgent) cIPA, while in Section 4 these two calculi have been contrasted by presenting simply semantic-preserving mappings from the restriction-free fragment of the latter language to the former one. In Section 5 similar results were stated for the lazy versions of (the full) cIPA and $TCCS$.

In this section we consider *maximal progress* that implements a form of urgency of synchronizations. Processes can delay their execution arbitrarily long but if the environment is willing to communicate no further delay is possible. This notion of urgency has been introduced in [Yi90] and [HR95].

6.1   TCCS and cIPA with Maximal Progress

As usual in the two-phase functioning principle, the operational semantics of $TCCS$ processes with maximal progress relies on the functional behavior and the temporal one. The rules describing the functional behavior are the same as those in Table 1, while the rules describing the temporal one are described in Table 8.

The only rule worth of note is $TPar$ that allows time to elapse only if processes cannot synchronize. The other rules are standard.

The operational rules for cIPA with maximal progress are, instead, those in Table 9.

On top of the $TCCS$ with maximal progress and cIPA with maximal progress operational semantics we can define bisimulation-based observational equivalences, $\sim_{mpMT}$ and $\sim_{mpAM}$, similarly to Definition 1 and Definition 8, respectively.

Then, by considering the mapping in Section 5 for the lazy versions of cIPA and $TCCS$, we obtain the expected language embedding result from cIPA with maximal progress to $TCCS$ with maximal progress.

Table 8. The Structural Rules for Maximal Progress in $TCCS$.

$$Zero \; \frac{}{0 \overset{t}{\leadsto} 0} \qquad\qquad PAct \; \frac{}{a.p \overset{t}{\leadsto} a.p}$$

$$TSum \; \frac{p \overset{t}{\leadsto} p^{\square} \text{ and } q \overset{t}{\leadsto} q^{\square}}{p + q \overset{t}{\leadsto} p^{\square} + q^{\square}}$$

$$TPar \; \frac{p \overset{t}{\leadsto} p^{\square} \text{ and } q \overset{t}{\leadsto} q^{\square} \text{ and } \forall m < t, \; p \overset{m}{\leadsto} p^{\blacksquare}, \; q \overset{m}{\leadsto} q^{\blacksquare}, \; \neg(p^{\blacksquare} \,|\, q^{\blacksquare} \overset{\tau}{\longrightarrow})}{p \,|\, q \overset{t}{\leadsto} p^{\square} \,|\, q^{\square}}$$

$$TDec \; \frac{}{(s+t).p \overset{s}{\leadsto} (t).p} \qquad TFin \; \frac{}{(t).p \overset{t}{\leadsto} p} \qquad TFur \; \frac{p \overset{s}{\leadsto} p^{\square}}{(t).p \overset{s+t}{\leadsto} p^{\square}}$$

$$TRec \; \frac{p[\text{rec } x.\, p/x] \overset{t}{\leadsto} p^{\square}}{\text{rec } x.\, p \overset{t}{\leadsto} p^{\square}} \qquad TRes \; \frac{p \overset{t}{\leadsto} p^{\square}}{p\backslash C \overset{t}{\leadsto} p^{\square}\backslash C} \qquad TRel \; \frac{p \overset{t}{\leadsto} p^{\square}}{p[\Phi] \overset{t}{\leadsto} p^{\square}[\Phi]}$$

7 The Discriminating Power of Eagerness, Lazyness and Maximal Progress

In this section we focus on a common language and study the discriminating power of eagerness, laziness and maximal progress. Namely, we consider CIPA as basic language and take into account the three different interpretations of basic actions. In other words, we contrast eager equivalence ($\sim_{AM}$), lazy equivalence ($\sim_{lAM}$) and maximal progress equivalence ($\sim_{mpAM}$) by concentrating on different language features that are significant from the point of view of the expressiveness of eager, lazy and maximal progress tests. The study is conducted by showing how the bisimulation-based equivalences relate when the base language changes according to some significant features and proving that the violation of one of these restrictions makes the three equivalences to behave differently. The language features have to do with process synchronization, with the non deterministic composition, with the relabelling functions [Mil89], with the number of actions a process can perform at a given time. Consider the following restrictions over the base language:

$\mathcal{P}_v$ – *The language that contains processes that can perform visible actions,*
$\mathcal{P}_c$ – *The language that contains processes where choices are made at the same time,*
$\mathcal{P}_r$ – *The language that contains processes where relabelling functions are duration preserving,*
$\mathcal{P}_a$ – *The language that contains processes which can perform finitely many actions at a fixed time,*

Table 9. The Structural Rules for CIPA with maximal progress.

$$
MPAct \quad \frac{t \geq max(m,n)}{(n \Rightarrow a.P) \rhd m \xrightarrow[\Delta(a)]{\square a,t\square} ((t + \Delta(a)) \Rightarrow P) \rhd t}
$$

$$
MPWait \quad \frac{n \geq m}{(n \Rightarrow \text{wait } n^{\square}.P) \rhd m \xrightarrow[n']{\square \tau, n\square} ((n + n^{\square}) \Rightarrow P) \rhd n}
$$

$$
MPSum_1 \quad \frac{d_1 \rhd m \xrightarrow{\square \mu, t\square}_{\delta} d \rhd t, \ \neg(d_2 \rhd m \xrightarrow{\square \tau, t'\square}_{\delta'}, t^{\square} < t)}{d_1 + d_2 \rhd m \xrightarrow{\square \mu, t\square}_{\delta} d \rhd t}
$$

$$
MPSum_2 \quad \frac{d_2 \rhd m \xrightarrow{\square \mu, t\square}_{\delta} d \rhd t, \ \neg(d_1 \rhd m \xrightarrow{\square \tau, t'\square}_{\delta'}, t^{\square} < t)}{d_1 + d_2 \rhd m \xrightarrow{\square \mu, t\square}_{\delta} d \rhd t}
$$

$$
MPPar_1 \quad \frac{d_1 \rhd m \xrightarrow{\square \mu, t\square}_{\delta} d_1^{\square} \rhd t, \ \neg((d_1 \mid d_2) \rhd m \xrightarrow{\square \tau, t'\square}_{\delta}, t^{\square} < t)}{(d_1 \mid d_2) \rhd m \xrightarrow{\square \mu, t\square}_{\delta} (d_1^{\square} \mid d_2) \rhd t}
$$

$$
MPPar_2 \quad \frac{d_2 \rhd m \xrightarrow{\square \mu, t\square}_{\delta} d_2^{\square} \rhd t, \ \neg((d_1 \mid d_2) \rhd m \xrightarrow{\square \tau, t'\square}_{\delta}, t^{\square} < t)}{(d_1 \mid d_2) \rhd m \xrightarrow{\square \mu, t\square}_{\delta} (d_1 \mid d_2^{\square}) \rhd t}
$$

$$
MPSynch \quad \frac{d_1 \rhd m \xrightarrow[\Delta(a)]{\square a, t\square} d_1^{\square} \rhd t, \ d_2 \rhd m \xrightarrow[\Delta(a)]{\square \bar{a}, t\square} d_2^{\square} \rhd t, \ \neg((d_1 \mid d_2) \rhd m \xrightarrow{\square \tau, t'\square}_{\delta}, t^{\square} < t)}{(d_1 \mid d_2) \rhd m \xrightarrow[\Delta(a)]{\square \tau, t\square} (d_1^{\square} \mid d_2^{\square}) \rhd t}
$$

$$
MPRes \quad \frac{d \rhd m \xrightarrow{\square \mu, t\square}_{\delta} d^{\square} \rhd t}{d \backslash C \rhd m \xrightarrow{\square \mu, t\square}_{\delta} d^{\square} \backslash C \rhd t} \mu, \bar{\mu} \notin C
\qquad
MPRel \quad \frac{d \rhd m \xrightarrow{\square \mu, t\square}_{\delta} d^{\square} \rhd t}{d[\Phi] \rhd m \xrightarrow{\square \Phi(\mu), t\square}_{\delta} d^{\square}[\Phi] \rhd t}
$$

$$
MPRec \quad \frac{(n \Rightarrow P[\text{rec } x. P/x]) \rhd m \xrightarrow{\square \mu, t\square}_{\delta} d \rhd t}{(n \Rightarrow \text{rec } x. P) \rhd m \xrightarrow{\square \mu, t\square}_{\delta} d \rhd t}
$$

For any sequence $w = x_1 x_2 x_3 ... \in \{s, c, r, a\}^+$, $\mathcal{P}_w$ denotes $\mathcal{P}_{x_1} \cap \mathcal{P}_{x_2} \cap \mathcal{P}_{x_3} ...$ and $\mathcal{D}_w$ denotes the set of timed states of processes in $\mathcal{P}_w$.

We show how the three equivalences relate when:

- The language allows process synchronization or only visible actions are allowed.

- The language allows choices at the same time "timed alternative compositions" or also at different times "alternative timed compositions".
- The language allows relabelling functions which preserve the duration of the actions (that is, they rename actions having the same duration) or also rename actions with (possibly) different durations.
- The language allows the description of processes which can perform finitely many actions (though of unbounded number) at a fixed time or also infinitely many.

It turns out that if the language allows (a) only visible actions, (b) only processes which can perform finitely many actions at a fixed time, (c) only choices at the same time and (d) only duration preserving relabelling functions, then eager tests, lazy tests and maximal progress tests have the same discriminating power. In such languages, eager equivalence, lazy equivalence and maximal progress equivalence coincide.

7.1   Process Synchronization

The following propositions show that when process synchronization is allowed eagerness, laziness and maximal progress have different discriminating power.

Proposition 11. *There are processes P and Q such that $P \sim_{AM} Q$ but not $P \sim_{lAM} Q$ and $P \sim_{mpAM} Q$.*

Proof. Consider processes:

$$P = a.nil \quad \text{and} \quad Q = (a.b.nil | \bar{b}.c.nil) \backslash \{b\}$$

They are eager equivalent whereas they are not lazy and maximal progress equivalent. Indeed, eager transition $0 \Rightarrow a.nil \xrightarrow[\Delta(a)]{\langle a,0 \rangle} \Delta(a) \Rightarrow nil$ can be matched by transition $(0 \Rightarrow a.b.nil | 0 \Rightarrow \bar{b}.c.nil) \backslash \{b\} \xrightarrow[\Delta(a)]{\langle a,0 \rangle} (\Delta(a) \Rightarrow b.nil | 0 \Rightarrow \bar{b}.c.nil) \backslash \{b\}$. This latter state cannot perform any further action because the two parallel partners cannot synchronize at the same time (see rule *Synch* in Table 5). Differently, the synchronization is possible according to the lazy and maximal progress operational semantics because the r.h.s. partner can delay its execution to match the synchronization with the l.h.s. partner.

Proposition 12. *There are processes P and Q such that $P \sim_{mpAM} Q$ and $P \sim_{lAM} Q$ but not $P \sim_{AM} Q$.*

Proof. Consider processes:

$$P = a.(b.nil | \bar{b}.c.nil) \backslash \{b\} \quad \text{and} \quad Q = (a.b.nil | \bar{b}.c.nil) \backslash \{b\}$$

They are maximal progress equivalent whereas they are not eager equivalent. Indeed, any maximal progress transition

$$(0 \Rightarrow a.(b.nil | \bar{b}.c.nil)) \backslash \{b\} \triangleright 0 \xrightarrow[\Delta(a)]{\langle a,t \rangle} ((t + \Delta(a)) \Rightarrow b.nil | (t + \Delta(a)) \Rightarrow \bar{b}.c.nil) \backslash \{b\} \triangleright t$$

can be matched by a maximal progress transition

$$(0 \Rightarrow a.b.nil|0 \Rightarrow \bar{b}.c.nil)\backslash\{b\} \triangleright 0 \xrightarrow[\Delta(a)]{\langle a,t \rangle} ((t + \Delta(a)) \Rightarrow b.nil|0 \Rightarrow \bar{b}.c.nil)\backslash\{b\} \triangleright t$$

and these target states are maximal progress equivalent. Both of them can perform a τ action at time $t + \Delta(a)$ reaching states that are syntactically equal. On the other hand the above target states are not eager equivalent because the former one can perform a synchronization at time $t + \Delta(a)$, while the latter cannot. Of course, in the eager case, t would be 0.

The proof that P and Q are lazy equivalent is completely similar.

Proposition 13. *There are processes P and Q such that $P \sim_{mpAM} Q$ but not $P \sim_{lAM} Q$.*

Proof. Consider processes:

$$P = (\text{wait } 3. \, a.b.nil|\text{wait } 1. \, (\text{wait } 1. \, nil + \bar{a}.nil))\backslash\{a\}$$

and

$$Q = \text{wait } 3. \, nil|\text{wait } 1. \, \text{wait } 1. \, nil$$

These are maximal progress equivalent whereas they are not lazy equivalent. In the maximal progress case, indeed, the synchronization on channel a cannot be performed because at time 1 the $\bar{a}$ action in the non deterministic composition of the r.h.s. component of the parallel composition will be disabled.

On the other hand, in the lazy setting, process P can perform lazy transitions

$$(0 \Rightarrow \text{wait } 3. \, a.b.nil|0 \Rightarrow \text{wait } 1. \, (\text{wait } 1. \, nil + \bar{a}.nil))\backslash\{a\} \triangleright 0 \xrightarrow[3]{\langle \tau,t \rangle}$$

$$(t + 3 \Rightarrow a.b.nil|0 \Rightarrow \text{wait } 1. \, (\text{wait } 1. \, nil + \bar{a}.nil))\backslash\{a\} \triangleright t \xrightarrow[1]{\langle \tau,t+2 \rangle}$$

$$(t + 3 \Rightarrow a.b.nil|t + 3 \Rightarrow (\text{wait } 1. \, nil + \bar{a}.nil))\backslash\{a\} \triangleright t + 2.$$

This enables a synchronization on channel a and then the execution of a visible action b. This execution sequence cannot be matched by Q.

The following proposition states a more positive result. It says that lazy equivalence is finer than maximal progress equivalence.

Proposition 14. *Let $P, Q \in \mathcal{P}_{AM}$. Then, $P \sim_{lAM} Q$ implies $P \sim_{mpAM} Q$.*

Proof. We state that relation:

$$\Re = \{(d_1 \triangleright n, d_2 \triangleright n) \mid d_1 \triangleright n \sim_{lAM} d_2 \triangleright n \text{ and } \min_\tau(d_1) = \min_\tau(d_2) \geq n\}$$

where function $\min_\tau(d)$ [9], for a generic state d, provides the minimum time for which a τ action can be performed, is a maximal progress bisimulation.

Remark 4. It is worth of noting that the positive result stated in Proposition 14, does not hold in the general language of timed states. Consider, for instance, $d_1 \triangleright 1 = (0 \Rightarrow \text{wait } 1.nil|1 \Rightarrow a.nil) \triangleright 1$ and $d_2 \triangleright 1 = (1 \Rightarrow \text{wait } 1.nil|1 \Rightarrow a.nil) \triangleright 1$ that are maximal progress equivalent but not lazy equivalent. This is also the reason why bisimulation $\Re$ in Proposition 14 relates states that can perform invisible actions at a time greater or equal than the global clock.

---

[9] There are different ways to define $\min_\tau(d)$. A possible one is to consider the rules in Table 9 by abstracting from the global clock in the description of states.

For the rest of this section, unless stated otherwise, we assume that processes can only perform visible actions. Over such a language, of course, maximal progress equivalence reduces to lazy equivalence.

7.2   Choosing at the Same Time

We distinguish between languages that allow different alternatives to be chosen at different times or only at the same time.

However, processes that allow different alternatives to be chosen at different times are not expressible in the language $\mathcal{P}_{AM}$ because delays are not present in CIPA, while they are key operators in $TCCS$. Then, let us introduce a delay operator also in CIPA: $(t).P$ is the process which will evolve into P after exactly t time units. The operational rules of the new operator in the various interpretations of CIPA basic actions are those given in Table 10. Of course, rule Delay should be added to those in Table 5, rule LDelay should be added to those in Table 7 and rule MPDelay should be added to those in Table 9, respectively.

Table 10. Transition Rule for eager, lazy and maximal progress CIPA delays.

$$Delay \quad \frac{n + m \Rightarrow P \xrightarrow[\delta]{\square\mu, t\square} d}{n \Rightarrow (m).P \xrightarrow[\delta]{\square\mu, t\square} d}$$

$$LDelay \quad \frac{((n + n^{\square}) \Rightarrow P) \rhd m \xrightarrow[\delta]{\square\mu, t\square} d \rhd t}{(n \Rightarrow (n^{\square}).P) \rhd m \xrightarrow[\delta]{\square\mu, t\square} d \rhd t}$$

$$MPDelay \quad \frac{((n + n^{\square}) \Rightarrow P) \rhd m \xrightarrow[\delta]{\square\mu, t\square} d \rhd t}{(n \Rightarrow (n^{\square}).P) \rhd m \xrightarrow[\delta]{\square\mu, t\square} d \rhd t}$$

According to the new delay operator, if P and Q are $\mathcal{P}_{AM}$ processes, "alternative timed compositions" are of the form

$$(t_1).P \; + \; (t_2).Q$$

where t_1 and t_2 are different delays and P, Q do not contain delay operators a the top level[10]. "Timed alternative compositions" are, instead, of the form

$$(t).(P \; + \; Q)$$

These two choice operators are conceptually different. In $(t).(P + Q)$ the choice only involves the functionality of the system (the choice between P and Q),

---

[10] This non deterministic choice operator behaves as the weak non deterministic choice $\oplus$ in $TCCS$ [MT90].

whereas in $(t_1).P + (t_2).Q$ the choice involves timed alternatives (timed functionalities) of the system.

Let $\cong$ be the least congruence which holds the laws in Table 11 and $\mathcal{S} \subseteq \mathcal{P}$ (ranged over by s_1, s_2,...) be the set of closed terms generated by the following grammar (terms without delays operators at the top level)[11]:

$$s ::= nil \mid a.q \mid \sum_{i \in I} s_i \mid \prod_{i \in I} s_i \mid s \backslash B \mid s[\Phi] \mid x \mid rec\ x.s$$

Table 11. Delay Distribution Equations.

$$
\begin{array}{|l|}
\hline
(n+m).p = (n).(m).p \\
(n).(p_1 \mid p_2) = (n).p_1 \mid (n).p_2 \\
(n).(p_1 + p_2) = (n).p_1 + (n).p_2 \\
(n).(p \backslash B) = (n).p \backslash B \\
(n).(p[\Phi]) = (n).p[\Phi] \\
rec\ x.(n)s = (n).(s\{rec\ x.(n).s/x\}) \\
\hline
\end{array}
$$

Then, we say that a choice $\sum_{i \in I} P_i$ is at the same time when either $\sum_{i \in I} P_i \in \mathcal{S}$ or $\sum_{i \in I} P_i \cong (n).\sum_{i \in I} s_i$ for some $n \in \mathbb{N}^+$. $\sum_{i \in I} P_i$ is at different times, otherwise.

The next propositions show that lazy equivalence is strictly finer than eager equivalence. It is worth of noting that this result contrasts with the one in [Cor00] stating that lazy equivalence does not imply eager equivalence when completing times of action execution are observable in place of the initial ones.

Proposition 15. If processes with choices at different times are allowed then there are P and Q in $\mathcal{P}_v$ such that $P \sim_{AM} Q$ does not imply $P \sim_{lAM} Q$.

Proof. Consider the following pair of processes

$$P = (a \mid (k).b) + a.b \quad \text{and} \quad Q = a \mid (k).b$$

where $k \in \mathbb{N}^+$ is such that $k = \Delta(a)$. They are eager equivalent since each transition out of the r.h.s. addend of P can be matched by a corresponding transition out of Q. Moreover, they are not lazy equivalent. Any lazy transition

$$(0 \Rightarrow P) \rhd 0 \xrightarrow[\Delta(a)]{\langle a, t \rangle} (\Delta(a) + t \Rightarrow b) \rhd t,$$

with $t > 0$, cannot be matched by Q.

Proposition 16. Let $P, Q \in \mathcal{P}_v$. Then $P \sim_{lAM} Q$ implies $P \sim_{AM} Q$.

Proof. We state that relation:

$$\Re = \{(d_1, d_2) \mid d_1 \rhd n \sim_{lAM} d_2 \rhd n \text{ for some } n,\ d_1 \xrightarrow[\delta]{\langle \mu, t \rangle},\ d_2 \xrightarrow[\delta']{\langle \gamma, t \rangle}, \text{ and } t \geq n\}$$

is an eager bisimulation.

---

[11] Note that we also extend the syntax to allow unbounded and infinite non deterministic compositions, $I \subseteq \mathbb{N}$.

For the rest of this section besides process synchronization we consider only choices at the same time. Hence we concentrate on $\mathcal{P}_{vc}$ processes.

7.3   Relabelling by Preserving Action Duration

We distinguish between languages with relabelling functions which do not preserve the duration of the actions (e.g., $\Phi(a) = b$ with $\Delta(a) \neq \Delta(b)$ is allowed), and those with duration preserving relabelling functions (i.e., $\Delta(a) = \Delta(\Phi(a))$ for every $a \in Act$).

If non-duration preserving relabelling functions are taken into account then lazy equivalence is strictly finer than eager equivalence. Indeed, lazy equivalence implies eager equivalence by Proposition 16, while the vice versa does not hold by the following statement.

Proposition 17. If processes with non-duration preserving relabelling functions are allowed then there are P and Q in $\mathcal{P}_{vc}$ such that $P \sim_{AM} Q$ does not imply $P \sim_{lAM} Q$.

Proof. Consider a simple variation of the pair of processes given in Proposition 13. Let c be an action of duration 3, d and e be actions of duration 1 and $\Phi(c) = \Phi(d) = \Phi(e) = f$. Then processes

$$P = ((c.a.b.nil | d.(e.nil + \bar{a}.nil)) \backslash \{a\})[\Phi]$$

and

$$Q = (c.nil | d.e.nil)[\Phi]$$

are eager equivalent but not lazy equivalent. The proof follows similar lines than the one in Proposition 13.

Then we also assume that only duration preserving relabelling functions are taken into account.

7.4   Performing Finitely Many Actions at the Same Time

We distinguish between languages with processes which are able to perform infinitely many visible actions at a fixed time and languages with processes which are able to perform only finitely many visible actions at a fixed time (in the rest of the paper we will always omit "visible"). As an example, consider processes

$$P = \prod_{i \in \mathbb{N}} \{p_i = a\} \qquad \text{and} \qquad Q = \sum_{i \in \mathbb{N}} \underbrace{a | \ldots | a}_{i \text{ times}}$$

and note that process P can perform an infinite sequence of a-actions at time 0, whereas process Q can only perform finite sequences of a-actions (although of unbounded length) at the same time.

Processes with infinitely many actions at a given time can be defined in two ways:

(a) *Unguarded Recursion.* That is, a variable x in a rec $x.p$ term can appear outside the scope of an $a.(\_)$ prefix operator. For instance, process rec $x.(x|a.nil)$ uses unguarded recursion to generate infinite concurrent a-actions, by assuming that the execution starts at time 0.

(b) *Infinite Parallel Composition.* That is, processes of the form $\prod_{i\in I} p_i$, where I can be infinite.

We now prove that lazy equivalence is strictly finer than eager equivalence when unguarded recursion or infinite parallel composition are allowed. As in the previous sections lazy equivalence implies eager equivalence by Proposition 16, while the vice versa does not hold. The proof of this latter result is independent from the fact that the infinite actions are generated by unguarded recursion or infinite parallel composition. Thus, we will use p_∞ to denote a generic process which can generate infinitely many actions labelled with a starting at time 0. It can be either process $p_r = $ rec $x.(x\,|\,a.nil)$ (in case of unguarded recursion) or process $p_s = \prod_{i\in I}\{p_i = a\}$ with I infinite set (in the case of infinite parallel composition).

The next proposition shows that eager equivalence does not imply lazy equivalence.

Proposition 18. If processes with infinitely many actions at a given time are allowed then there are P and Q in $\mathcal{P}_{vcr}$ such that $P \sim_{AM} Q$ does not imply $P \sim_{lAM} Q$.

Proof. Processes P and Q defined as

$$P = b.c.nil|d.p_\infty \quad \text{and} \quad Q = b.nil|d.p_\infty$$

where $\Delta(d) < \Delta(b)$, are eager equivalent but not lazy equivalent.

The two processes can perform eager transitions labelled by b and d at time 0 leading to the target states: $d_1 \triangleright 0 = (\Delta(b) \Rightarrow c.nil|\Delta(d) \Rightarrow p_\infty) \triangleright 0$ and $d_2 \triangleright 0 = (\Delta(b) \Rightarrow nil|\Delta(d) \Rightarrow p_\infty) \triangleright 0$. $d_1 \triangleright 0$ and $d_2 \triangleright 0$ are eager equivalent. Indeed, $\Delta(d) < \Delta(b)$ and hence action c can never be performed by the former state. By contrast, $d_1 \triangleright 0$ can always perform action c in the lazy setting while $d_2 \triangleright 0$ cannot. Hence, P and Q are not lazy equivalent.

7.5   A Coincidence Result Between Eagerness and Laziness

The main result of this section states that when the language allows only

- visible actions,
- finitely many actions to be performed at a given time,
- choices at the same time, and
- duration preserving relabelling functions,

then eager equivalence and lazy equivalence coincide. This result says, in other words, that when experimenting over processes we have two "equivalent" ways to proceed: step-by-step (eager experiments) or jumping through time (lazy experiments).

Theorem 3. Let $P, Q \in \mathcal{P}_{vcra}$. Then $P \sim_{lAM} Q$ if and only if $P \sim_{AM} Q$.

Proof. We just prove the *if* implication because the *only if* case follows by Proposition 16. Then it suffices to state that

$$\Re = \{(d' \triangleright t, d'' \triangleright t) | d' \simeq \Pi_{i \in I} (t_i \Rightarrow P_i), d'' \simeq \Pi_{i \in I} (t_i \Rightarrow Q_i), I = \{1, .., n\} \text{ and,}$$
$$\forall i \in I, (t_i \Rightarrow P_i) \sim_{AM} (t_i \Rightarrow Q_i), P_i, Q_i \in \mathcal{S}\}$$

is a $\sim_{lAM}$-bisimulation.

References

[AM93]   Aceto, L., and Murphy, D. (1993), On the ill–timed but well–caused, *in* "Proceedings, CONCUR'93" (E.Best, Ed.), Lecture Notes in Computer Science **715**, pp. 97-111, Springer-Verlag, Berlin.

[AM95]   Aceto, L., and Murphy, D. (1996), Timing and causality in process algebra, *Acta Informatica* **33** (4), pp. 317-350.

[BB91]   Baeten, J., and Bergstra, J. (1991), Real time process algebra, *Formal Aspects of Computing* **3** (2), pp. 142-188.

[BLS2000] Bérard, B. and Labroue, A. and Schnoebelen, Ph. (2000) Verifying performance equivalence for Timed Basic Parallel Processes. In *FOSSACS 2000*, LNCS **1784**, Springer Verlag, 35–47.

[BK89]   Bergstra, J.A., Klop, and J.W. (1989), Process theory based on bisimulation semantics, *in* "Proceedings, Linear Time, Branching Time and Partial Orders in Logic and Models for Concurrency," Lecture Notes in Computer Science **354**.

[CN96]   Cleaveland, R., and Natarajan, V. (1996), An algebraic theory of process efficiency, *in* "Proceedings, LICS'96," pp. 63-72.

[CPS93]   Cleaveland, R., Parrow, J., and Steffen, B. (1993), The concurrency workbench: A semantics-based tool for the verification of concurrent systems, *in* "Proceedings, ACM Transaction on Programming Languages and Systems," **15**.

[CZ91]   Cleaveland, R., and Zwarico, A. (1991), A theory of testing for real-time, *in* "Proceedings, LICS'91," pp. 110-119.

[Cor98]   Corradini, F. (1998), On performance congruences for process algebras, *Information and Computation* **145**, pp. 191-230.

[Cor00]   Corradini, F. (2000), Absolute versus Relative Time in Process Algebras, *Information and Computation* **156**, pp. 122-172.

[CDI99]   Corradini, F., D'Ortenzio, D., and Di Cola, D. (1999), On the relationships among four Timed Process Algebras, *Fundamenta Informaticae* **38**, pp. 377-395.

[CD01]   Corradini, F., and Di Cola, D. (2001) On Testing Urgency through Laziness over Processes with Durational Actions. *Theoretical Computer Science* **258**, pp. 393-407.

[CD03]   Corradini, F., and Di Cola, D. (2003), The expressive power of urgent, lazy and busy-waiting actions in timed processes, *Mathematical Structures in Computer Science* **13**, pp. 619-656.

[CFP01]   Corradini, F., Ferrari G.L., and Pistore, M. (2001), On the semantics of durational actions, *Theoretical Computer Science* **269**, pp. 47-82.

[CP96]   Corradini, F., and Pistore, M. (1996), Specification and verification of
           timed lazy systems, *in* "Proceedings, MFCS'96," Lecture Notes in Com-
           puter Science **1113**, pp. 279-290, Springer-Verlag, Berlin.

[CP01]   Corradini, F., and Pistore, M. (2001), 'Closed Interval Process Algebra'
           versus 'Interval Process Algebra', *Acta Informatica* **37**, pp. 467-509.

[FM95]   Ferrari, G.-L., and Montanari, U. (1995), Dynamic matrices and the cost
           analysis of concurrent programs, *in* "Proceedings, AMAST'95," Lecture
           Notes in Computer Science **936**, pp. 307-321, Springer-Verlag, Berlin.

[GW89]   van Glabbeek, R., and Weijland, W.P. (1989), Branching time and ab-
           straction in bisimulation semantics, *in* "Proceedings, Information Process-
           ing'89," (G.X. Ritter, Ed.), pp.613-618.

[GR93]   Gorrieri, R., and Roccetti, M. (1993), Towards performance evaluation in
           process algebras, *in* "Proceedings, AMAST'93," Workshop in Computing
           Series, pp. 289-296, Springer-Verlag.

[GRS95]   Gorrieri, R., Roccetti, M., and Stancampiano, E. (1995) A theory of pro-
           cesses with durational actions, *Theoretical Computer Science* **140** (1), pp.
           73-94.

[Gro93]   Groote, J.F. (1993), Transition system specification with negative
           premises, *Theoretical Computer Science* **118**, pp.263-299.

[Hoa85]   Hoare, C.A.R. (1989), "Communicating Sequential Processes," Prentice
           Hall.

[HR95]   Hennessy, M., and Regan T. (1995), A temporal process algebras, *Infor-
           mation and Computation* **117**, pp. 221-239.

[KH92]   Arun-Kumar, and S., Hennessy, M. (1992), An Efficiency Preorder for
           Processes, *Acta Informatica* **29**, pp. 737-760.

[Mil89]   Milner, R. (1989), "Communication and concurrency," International series
           on computer science, Prentice Hall International.

[MPW92]   Milner, R., Parrow, J., and Walker, D. (1992), A Calculus of Mobile Pro-
           cesses, part I and II, *Information and Computation* **100**, pp. 1-78.

[MT90]   Moller, F., Tofts, C. (1990), A Temporal Calculus of Communicating Sys-
           tems, *in* "Proceedings, CONCUR'90," Lecture Notes in Computer Science
           459, pp. 401-414, Springer-Verlag, Berlin.

[MT91]   Moller, F., Tofts, C. (1991), Relating Processes with Respect to Speed,
           in "Proceedings, CONCUR'91," Lecture Notes in Computer Science **527**,
           pp. 424-438, Springer-Verlag, Berlin.

[NS91]   Nicollin, X., Sifakis, J. (1991), An Overview and Synthesis on Timed Pro-
           cess Algebras, *in* "Proceedings, Real Time: Theory in Practice," Lecture
           Notes in Computer Science **600**, pp. 526-548, Springer-Verlag, Berlin.

[RR88]   Reed, G.M., Roscoe, A.W.D (1988), A timed model for communicating
           sequential processes, *Theoretical Computer Science* **58**, pp. 249-261.

[UY97]   Ulidowski, I., Yuen, S. (1997), Extending process languages with time, *in*
           "Proceedings, AMAST'97," Lecture Notes in Computer Science **1349**, pp.
           524-538, Springer-Verlag, Berlin.

[Vog95]   Vogler, W. (1995), Timed Testing of Concurrent Systems, *Information and
           Computation* **121** (2), pp. 149-171.

[Yi90]   Yi, W. (1990), Real time behaviour of asynchronous agents, *in* "Proceed-
           ings, CONCUR'90," Lecture Notes in Computer Science **358**, pp. 502-520,
           Springer-Verlag, Berlin.

Real Time and Stochastic Time

Mario Bravetti

Università di Bologna, Dipartimento di Scienze dell'Informazione
Mura Anteo Zamboni 7, 40127 Bologna, Italy
bravetti@cs.unibo.it

Abstract. We present a theory for the design and analysis of concurrent/distributed systems with real-time and stochastic time aspects. We start by presenting the model of Interactive Generalized Semi-Markov Processes (IGSMP): a compositional model for representing the class of stochastic processes known as Generalised Semi-Markov Processes (GSMPs), i.e. probabilistic timed systems where durations of delays are expressed by random variables with a general probability distribution. Technically, IGSMPs extend GSMPs with action transitions representing the ability of a process to interact with another process. Then, we introduce the calculus of Interactive Generalized Semi-Markov Processes, a stochastic process algebra which produces IGSMPs as semantic models of its terms. This is obtained by expressing the concurrent execution of delays through a simple probabilistic extension of Van Glabbeek and Vaandrageer's ST semantics based on dynamic names. We also present observational equivalence over IGSMPs, we observe that it is a congruence for all the operators of the calculus and we produce an axiomatization for this equivalence which is complete over finite-state strongly guarded processes. Finally, we present a case study on queuing systems $G/G/1/q$.

1 Introduction

The development of a software product requires, similarly as the other industrial products, an engineering cycle which is mainly composed of an initial specification stage and of a successive implementation stage. By using formal methods, it is possible to develop non-ambiguous specifications of systems which are analyzable with automated software tools. In particular, it is possible to verify the correctness of such specifications with respect to a certain set of requirements or to carry out a preliminary analysis of system performance, so to detect the design decisions that give the best results.

The importance of considering the behavior of concurrent systems with respect to time during their design process has been widely recognized [3, 28, 23, 21, 2, 4, 22, 18, 10, 5]. In particular two different approaches for expressing and analyzing time properties of systems have been developed which are based on formal description paradigms.

A first approach is devoted to the *evaluation of the performance* of concurrent systems (see e.g. [23, 21, 4, 22, 18, 10, 5]). According to this approach the time

M. Bernardo and F. Corradini (Eds.): SFM-RT 2004, LNCS 3185, pp. 132–180, 2004.

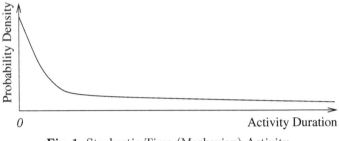

Fig. 1. Stochastic Time (Markovian) Activity.

Fig. 2. Real-Time Activity.

spent by a system in a certain activity is expressed probabilistically through a distribution of duration. Performance measures of systems can then be evaluated via mathematical or simulative techniques. This approach has led to the definition of *stochastic process algebras*, an extension of standard process algebras where a distribution of duration is associated with each action of a process. In most cases, as in [23, 21, 4, 22, 10], the expressiveness of such algebras is limited to exponential distributions of time, because this causes the passage of time to be "memoryless". As a consequence it is possible to completely avoid explicitly representing durations in semantic models. Moreover the limitation to *exponential distributions* allows for a straightforward transformation of the semantic model of a system into a *Continuous Time Markov Chain* (CTMC), a stochastic process which is easily mathematically analyzable for deriving performance measures. For this reason they are called *Markovian process algebras*. It is worth noting that the limitation imposed over durations is very strong because not even deterministic (fixed) durations can be expressed.

A second approach concentrates on the aspect of *real-time*, i.e. the expression of time constraints and the verification of exact time properties (see [3, 28] and the references therein). By this approach the parts of the system that are critical from the viewpoint of time bounds can be validated during the design phase through techniques such as e.g. *model checking* [3]. In this view *timed automata* have been developed by extending standard labeled transition systems with the representation of time by means of *clocks*. The time value assumed by a clock in a timed automata increases as time passes. In timed automata we have transitions representing the setting of a clock with a certain time value and transitions which can be executed provided that clocks satisfy a certain time constraint (see e.g. [3, 28]).

Using stochastic models with generally distributed probabilistic time provides a way for expressing and analyzing both stochastic time and real-time aspects of systems (see [6, 5]). The different aspects of time expressed by the Stochastic Time and Real-Time approaches can be seen as being *orthogonal*.

Fig. 3. Activity with a Fixed Duration.

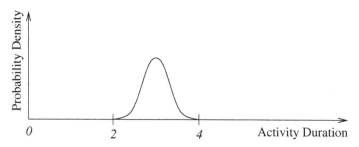

Fig. 4. Generally Distributed Activity.

According to the first approach the possible values for the duration of an activity are quantified through probabilistic (exponential) distributions, but no time constraint is expressible: all duration values are possible with probability greater than zero. In Fig. 1 we depict the probability density for the duration values of an activity with an exponentially distributed duration.

According to the second approach some interval of time is definable for doing something, but the actual time the system spends in-between interval bounds is expressed non-deterministically. For instance, in Fig. 2 we depict an activity whose duration must be between 2 and 4 time units. Note that activities with a deterministic (fixed) duration are expressed when interval bounds coincide. For instance, in Fig. 3 we depict an activity whose duration is certainly 3.

A specification paradigm capable of expressing both aspects of time should be able of expressing both time constraints and a probabilistic quantification for the possible durations which satisfy such constraints. We obtain such an expressive power by considering stochastic models capable of expressing *general probability distributions* for the duration of activities. In this way time constraints are expressible via probability distribution functions that associate probability greater than zero only to time values that are possible according to the constraints. Technically, the set of possible time values for the duration of an activity is given by the *support* of the associated duration distribution. This idea of deriving real-time constraints from distribution supports was introduced in [6]. For instance, in Fig. 4 we depict an activity with a distribution whose support is the interval of Fig. 2. Note that with this approach we can also represent deterministic durations via trivial distribution functions that give all the probability to a single value of time.

Representing the real-time and probabilistic-time in a single specification paradigm allows us to model a concurrent system more precisely by expressing and analyzing the relationships between the two aspects of time. Moreover, the capability of expressing general distributions gives the possibility of producing much more realistic specifications of systems. System activities which have an uncertain duration could be represented probabilistically by more adequate distributions than exponential ones (e.g. Gaussian distributions or experimentally determined distributions).

This paper surveys the contents of [9, 14] and [5] chapters 6 and 7. In particular, we present (in Sect. 2) the model of Interactive Generalized Semi-Markov Processes (IGSMP) [14, 9, 5], a compositional model for representing real-time and stochastic time in concurrent/distributed systems. Conceptually, IGSMPs are an extension of Generalised Semi-Markov Processes (GSMPs), i.e. probabilistic timed systems where durations of delays are expressed by random variables with a general probability distribution, with action transitions representing the ability of a process to interact with another process. The technical machinery for IGSMPs can be seen as a probabilistic extension of that used in the pure real-time context for Timed Automata. In the case an IGSMP specification is complete from both the interaction and performance viewpoints then it is possible to formally derive the underlying GSMP for stochastic analysis purposes. Then, we present (in Sect. 3) the calculus of Interactive Generalized Semi-Markov Processes [14, 5], a stochastic process algebra which produces IGSMPs as semantic models of its terms. Technically, such an algebra is designed by expressing the concurrent execution of delays through a simple probabilistic extension of the dynamic name technique we introduced in [13] for expressing Van Glabbeek and Vaandrageer's ST semantics. We also show that observational equivalence over IGSMPs is a congruence for all the operators of the calculus and we produce an axiomatization for this equivalence which is complete over finite-state strongly guarded processes. Moreover, we present (in Sect. 4) a case study on queuing systems G/G/1/q, i.e. queuing systems with one server and a FIFO queue with q-1 seats, where interarrival time and service time are generally distributed. We also show how to derive the performance model of such queuing systems: a Generalised Semi-Markov Process. Finally, we report (in Sect. 5) some concluding remarks. Proof of theorems can be found in [5].

2   Interactive Generalized Semi-Markov Processes

In this section we introduce the compositional model of Interactive Generalized Semi-Markov Processes (IGSMPs). First of all, let us briefly recall the definition of a Generalized Semi-Markov Processes (GSMPs) [26].

A GSMP is a stochastic process representable by a transition system of the following kind. There is a fixed set of *elements* (an analogue of the clocks in a timed automaton) each with an associated probabilistic duration expressed by a time probability distribution. Each state of the transition system has an associated set of *active* elements taken from the set above. Such elements "decay" at a certain rate (for the sake of simplicity in this paper we will assume that all elements decay at the same rate) and the system sojourns in the state until an active element *dies* (completes its duration). When this happens a probabilistic state change occurs via a transition labeled with the terminated element and the other elements continue their life in the reached state, thus carrying out their residual duration. Whenever a state is entered where a previously dead element re-becomes active then the element *is born* again and executed for another time period determined from its associated probability duration distribution.

The following constraints must be satisfied from a GSMP:

- When the process moves from a state to another, no more than one element can be born or die contemporaneously.
- The active elements that do not die in a state must be again active in every reachable successive state (they keep their residual duration).

Example 1. As we will further comment, Fig. 5 and Fig. 16 represent the following two GSMPs: Fig. 5 a GSMP which executes two elements δ_1 and δ_2 in parallel; Fig. 16 a GSMP which, first executes element i, then it executes, with probability "0.4" element δ_1, with probability "0.6" element δ_2. In the figures states are labeled with the associated set of active elements. Moreover in the bottom of figures we associate a Probability Distribution Function to each element. Note that while the transition labeled by i in Fig. 16 leads to a probabilistic state change, the other transitions of Fig. 5 and Fig. 16 lead to a successive state with probability 1 (hence the probability information and the little bar are omitted).   □

In this section, we start by defining IGSMPs as an extension of GSMPs with action transitions representing the ability of a process to interact with another process in a concurrent/distributed system. From an IGSMP which is complete both from the interaction and performance viewpoints it is possible to derive a GSMP by means of the formal procedure introduced in [5] and sketched in this section.

Then, we observe that, in order to make it possible to define a bisimulation based equivalence over IGSMPs as a simple probabilistic extension of standard weak bisimulation [27], it is essential to adopt a canonical form for names of clocks (elements) used in an IGSMP. As a consequence, we define well-named IGSMPs as IGSMPs which follow a fixed rule for the names of clocks which is based on the dynamic name approach we introduced in [13] in the context of classical ST semantics.

Moreover, we consider the problem of adequately developing a semantics for IGSMPs in terms of (continuously infinite state) probabilistic transition systems with numeric transitions representing time delays. In particular, we introduce Interactive Stochastic Timed Transition Systems (ISTTSs) to be used as semantic models for IGSMPs. As we will see, since IGSMPs introduce the capability of expressing non-deterministic choices in Generalised Semi-Markov Processes (GSMPs), it is important that the definition of such a semantics corresponds to a correct way of executing IGSMPs in the presence of adversaries resolving non-determinism. More precisely, we define the IGSMP semantics in such a way that the probabilistic duration of a clock is not decided all at once when the clock starts as done in [18], but step by step in each system state (in the theory of GSMPs this corresponds to recording spent lifetimes instead of residual lifetimes of delays). In this way an adversary cannot take decisions a priori, based on the knowledge he may get about the future behavior of the system.

This section is structured as follows. In Sect. 2.1 we present the basic concepts on which our approach is based. Then, in Sect. 2.2 we formalise the model of IGSMPs and the model of well-named IGSMPs. Moreover we show that the class of well-named IGSMPs is closed with respect to CSP parallel composition and hiding and we introduce a notion of weak bisimulation over well-named IGSMPs. Then, in Sect. 2.3 we sketch the formal procedure of [5] for deriving a performance model in the form of a *GSMP* from a complete IGSMP system specification. Moreover, in Sect. 2.4 we introduce the model of Interactive Stochastic Timed Transition Systems (ISTTSs), i.e. probabilistic transition systems (where probability is expressed by means of probability spaces over continuously infinite states) with numeric transitions representing time delays. We show that the class of ISTTSs is closed with respect to CSP parallel composition and hiding and we introduce a notion of weak bisimulation over ISTTSs. Finally, in Sect. 2.5 we present the semantics for IGSMPs which maps IGSMPs onto ISTTSs by recording spent lifetimes of delays. We show that weakly bisimilar IGSMPs give rise to weakly bisimilar semantic models and that the semantic mapping is compositional with respect to both CSP parallel composition and hiding.

2.1 Basic Concepts

The Basic Idea. Some previous efforts have been made in order to develop models for general distributions [21, 2, 29]. With respect to such approaches, which somehow face this problem by starting from process algebra semantical viewpoint, in [11] we have introduced the idea that a specification paradigm expressing systems with generally distributed delays should originate from probabilistic models which are well-founded from the viewpoint of probability theory.

The stochastic processes mainly studied in the literature for performance evaluation purposes are in increasing order of expressivity: continuous time Markov chains (CTMCs), semi-Markov processes (SMPs), and generalized semi-Markov processes (GSMPs). The difference among them lies in the set of instants of process life which satisfy the Markov property, i.e. those instants such that the future behavior of the stochastic process depends only on the current state of the process and not on its past behavior. For CTMCs the Markov property holds in every instant of process life, for SMPs it holds only in the instants of state change, and for GSMPs it never holds, but can be retrieved through a different representation of process states (each state is turned into a continuous infinity of states) by the standard technique of [17] of introducing information about spent or residual lifetimes. Since CTMCs can represent only activities with an exponentially distributed duration (only this distribution has the required memoryless property), the only candidates for representing systems with generally distributed durations are SMPs and GSMPs, and we now show that GSMPs are actually needed for our purposes. Consider the example of two delays δ_1 and δ_2 executed in parallel, the former with a deterministic duration 5 and the latter with a Gaussian duration with mean 0.5 and variance 1. This situation can be represented as in Fig. 5. In Fig. 5 each state is labeled with the set of delays which are in execution during the period of time the system sojourns in the

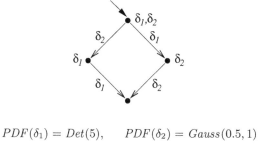

$$PDF(\delta_1) = Det(5), \quad PDF(\delta_2) = Gauss(0.5, 1)$$

Fig. 5. Parallel Execution of Generally Distributed Delays.

state. In the beginning both delays are in contemporaneous execution and the system sojourns in the first state until one delay terminates. When this happens the system performs the transition labeled with the terminated action. Suppose that δ_1 terminates before δ_2 and the system reaches the state labeled with δ_2. In this state the delay δ_2 continues its execution until it terminates. As a consequence the sojourn time of the system in the state labeled with δ_2 (which is given by the residual distribution of delay δ_2) is not determined simply by the fact that the system is in this state, but depends on the time δ_2 has already spent in execution in the first state. In particular since we can no longer rely on the memoryless property (which is enjoyed only by exponential distributions) the residual distribution of δ_2 is different for every value of time spent. Therefore the process is not Markovian even in the instant when this state is entered.

This example shows that even the simple case of two parallel delays with generally distributed durations cannot be represented by an SMP. The process of the example is, instead, a GSMP (δ_1 and δ_2 are its elements and state labels in Fig. 5 denote active elements). This can be seen as follows. If we imagine to give a different representation of the process where we replace the state labeled with δ_2 with infinitely many states each denoting a different spent lifetime for the delay δ_2, we can retrieve the Markov property. The sojourn time in each of the newly derived states would then be determined by the state itself (it would be given by the distribution of delay δ_2 conditioned on a particular value for the spent lifetime) and not by the previous behavior of the process. Another way to retrieve the Markov property would be to consider residual lifetimes instead of spent lifetimes.

Despite of the fact that in GSMPs the Markov property in instants of state change can be retrieved via an infinite state representation, when we consider the initial finite state system description (as that of Fig. 5) we have that the system behavior in a certain state indeed depends on what happened previously. In particular, delays executed in a state cannot be simply be considered as starting in that state as for CTMCs (or SMPs), but the may continue their execution from previous states. In other words a delay can no longer be considered as being executed *atomically* in a single transition, but we have to represent delays that start in a certain state, evolve through several states, and terminate in

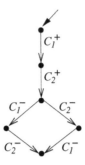

$$PDF(C_1) = Det(5), \quad PDF(C_2) = Gauss(0.5, 1)$$

Fig. 6. Event-Based Representation of Parallel Execution of Delays.

another state (in the previous example both δ_1 and δ_2 start in the first state and may terminate in another state). As a consequence the execution of a generally distributed delay must be characterized in models by the *two events* of *delay start* and *delay termination*.

In [21, 29] the Markovian representation of system behavior via delays "atomically" executed in transitions (which are labeled by the duration distribution of such delays) is adapted to systems with general distributions by adding to such transitions some information uniquely determining (through e.g. a pointer) the state where the delay labeling the transition is actually started. On the contrary, we prefer to stick to the notation of GSMPs, where representing the execution of generally distributed delays is simply done by: uniquely *identifying* each delay with a different *element* (similar to a clock of a timed automata), associating to each *element* the duration distribution of the delay it represents as in Fig. 5, assuming that element execution continues when going from state to state, and making explicit events of element start (or clock reset in timed automata). In this way we have a system representation which can be easily transformed into a GSMP (see Sect. 2.3) or a timed automata (see [5]) for analysis purposes.

In particular we represent temporal delays by clocks and we explicitly represent both basic events of start and termination of a clock C explicitly by means of a clock start transition C^+ and a clock termination transition C^-. On the other hand we do not explicitly indicate the set of clocks which are being executed in a state (the active elements in states of the GSMP represented in Fig. 5 as state labels) since such information can be easily inferred from its outgoing clock termination transitions. The resulting event-based representation of the system of Fig. 5 is depicted in Fig. 6, where delays δ_1 and δ_2 are represented by clocks C_1 and C_2, respectively, and we initially start both clocks by means of two explicit clock start transitions executed in zero time. To be precise, in our model we will consider clock start transitions labeled with pairs $\langle C^+, w \rangle$, where w is a *weight* used for representing probabilistic choices. In this way we reach the same expressivity as GSMPs.

A Model for Timed Concurrent Systems with General Distributions.
By following the "interactive" idea of [22], an IGSMP represents the behavior
of a component by employing both *standard action transitions*, representing the
interactive behavior of the component, and *clock start transitions* and *clock termination transitions*, representing the timed probabilistic behavior of the component. Action transitions are just standard CCS/CSP transitions: when several
action transitions are enabled in an IGSMP state, the choice among them is just
performed non-deterministically and when IGSMPs are composed in parallel
they synchronize following the CSP [24] approach, where the actions belonging
to a given set S are required to synchronize. Clock start transitions are labeled
with a clock name and a weight and represent the event of starting of a temporal delay whose probabilistic duration is given by the distribution associated
with the clock. When several clock start transitions are enabled in an IGSMP
state, the choice between them is performed probabilistically according to the
weights of the transitions. Clock termination transitions are labeled with a clock
name and represent the event of termination of the corresponding temporal delay. A system stays in a state enabling several termination transitions until one
of the temporal delays currently in execution terminates and the corresponding
transition is performed.

Besides IGSMPs, we also define *well-named IGSMPs*, a canonical form for
names of clocks used in an IGSMP which is based on the dynamic name approach presented in [13] in the context of ST semantics. In particular, similarly
as in [13] where the name associated with the two events of action start and
action termination generated by the execution of an action is a pair consisting
of the type a of the action and an index $i \in \mathbb{N}$, in a well-named IGSMP names
n of clocks C_n consist of pairs "f, i", where f is the probability distribution
associated with the clock (f is the "type" of the clock) and i an index. For each
different distribution f, the index to be used when a new clock with distribution f starts is determined by a fixed rule: we choose the minimum index not
currently used by the other clocks with the same distribution f already in execution [13]. The use of a fixed rule makes it possible to define equivalence as a
simple probabilistic extension of standard weak bisimulation without having to
associate clock names in the definition of equivalence.

We will define CSP parallel composition and hiding of well-named IGSMPs.
As we will see, in order to obtain well-named IGSMPs as the result of such
operations we have to suitably rename clocks. This is done by following the
technique introduced in the dynamic name approach of [13].

IGSMPs may include both internal and external non-deterministic choices.
While external non-deterministic choices may be resolved through synchronization with other system components (they are not present in system specifications
which are complete from an interaction viewpoint), internal non-determinism
represents an inherent underspecification of the system performance. Therefore
adversaries (or schedulers) play an important role in the performance analysis
of IGSMPs in that they allow internal non-determinism to be removed from an
IGSMP, thus turning it, essentially, into a GSMP. In [5] a formal procedure is

presented which turns IGSMPs which are complete both from the interaction and performance viewpoints into GSMPs. As we will see, this is done essentially by turning: *IGSMP* clocks into elements of the *GSMP* and *IGSMP* weighted choices into probabilistic choices of a *GSMP*.

Dealing with Non-determinism in Systems with General Distributions. As we already explained, introducing non-determinism in probabilistic systems with general distributions causes new problems to arise with respect to the classical theory of GSMPs. Such problems derive from the interplay of non-deterministic choices and the probabilistic behavior of clocks when IGSMPs are actually executed. In particular, if we follow the classical approach of discrete event simulation (see e.g. [16]), in the instant a clock starts, the clock is set to a temporal value sampled from its duration distribution. As time passes the clock counts down and it terminates when it reaches value zero. From a technical viewpoint this means that, while the GSMP proceeds from state to state, we keep track of the quantity of time that clocks must still spend in execution (the *residual lifetimes* of the clocks). This approach to the execution of an IGSMP, which has been previously applied in [18] to systems including non-determinism and generally distributed time, has the drawback that an adversary can base its decisions (concerning non-deterministic choices) on the knowledge obtained a priori about the future behavior of the system, e.g. the information about the quantity of time that a delay will spend in execution.

In this paper we will consider an alternative approach to the execution of systems including non-determinism and generally distributed time which adequately handles non-deterministic choices. The idea is that we want the probabilistic duration of a generally distributed delay not to be decided all at once when the delay starts, but step by step in each system state. More precisely, this is realized by keeping track of the quantity of time spent by clocks in execution (*spent lifetimes* of clocks), and by evaluating, when a new IGSMP state is entered, the distribution of the residual duration of the clock from (*i*) the duration distribution associated with the clock, and (*ii*) the time it has already spent in execution. Such an approach, which is based on recording spent lifetimes instead of residual lifetimes, is adherent to the classical behavior of Timed Automata [28] where clocks are increased (and not decreased) while time passes. Besides it indeed solves the problem of executing a system with non-deterministic choices because, since the residual duration of clocks is sampled in every state traversed by the IGSMP, the adversary cannot gain a priori knowledge on the system behavior. Finally, considering spent lifetimes instead of residual lifetimes is correct also from a probabilistic viewpoint, because in probability theory the two approaches are both valid alternative ways to interpret a GSMP [17]. It is worth noting that the choice of adopting this alternative approach for representing the execution of an IGSMP is conceptual and not at all related with the technical differences between the formalism considered in [18] and IGSMPs. We could apply the technique used in [18] to IGSMPs as well.

Similarly as in [18], based on our approach to the execution of an IGSMP, we produce a semantics for IGSMPs which maps an IGSMP onto a transition system where: (i) the passage of time is explicitly represented by transitions labeled with numeric time delays and (ii) duration probability distributions are turned into infinitely branching probabilistic choices which lead to states performing numeric time delays with different durations. Differently from [18], we express semantic models of IGSMPs by means of "interactive" probabilistic timed transition systems which can be themselves composed and for which we define a notion of weak bisimulation. This allows us to develop a semantic mapping which is compositional with respect to parallel composition and hiding.

2.2   Definition of Interactive Generalized Semi-Markov Process

In this section we will present the model of Interactive Generalized Semi-Markov Processes (IGSMPs) and of well-named interactive generalized semi-Markov processes: a canonical form for IGSMPs which introduces some constraints on clock names and makes it simple to establish equivalence over IGSMPs.

The IGSMP Model. The model of Interactive Generalized Semi-Markov Processes extends that of Generalized Semi-Markov Processes by expressing in addition to GSMP clocks (or elements) execution, also the execution of standard actions which can synchronize and have a zero duration. As far as probabilistic delays are concerned, they are modeled as in GSMPs by means of clocks C (which are like elements) whose duration is expressed through general probability distributions. In the following we will distinguish different clocks used in an IGSMP through "names", where C_n denotes the clock with name n. In an IGSMP the execution of a clock C_n is represented by means of two events: the event of clock start C_n^+ followed by the relative event of clock termination C_n^-. Therefore in an IGSMP we have three types of transitions: standard action transitions representing action execution, clock start transitions representing events C_n^+ and clock termination transitions representing events C_n^-. When a transition C_n^+ is performed by the IGSMP the clock C_n starts and continues its execution in every state traversed by the IGSMP. Whenever the clock C_n terminates, then the IGSMP executes the corresponding termination transition C_n^-. In particular, since, as in GSMPs, each started clock C_n which has not terminated yet must continue its execution in each state traversed by the IGSMP, all such states must have an outgoing transition C_n^-. Obviously clocks which can be simultaneously under execution in an IGSMP state must have different names (even if they have the same duration distribution), so that the event of termination of a clock C_n^- is always uniquely related to the corresponding event of start of the same clock C_n^+. Similarly as GSMPs, IGSMPs can also express probabilistic choices. This is obtained by associating with each start transition C_n^+ a weight $w \in \mathbb{R}^+$. In this way when a state of the IGSMP enables several clock start transitions $\langle C_n^+, w \rangle$, the choice of the clock to be started is performed probabilistically according to the weights w of the transitions. For instance, a state enabling two transitions labeled with $\langle C_n^+, w \rangle$ and $\langle C_{n'}^+, w' \rangle$ respectively starts clock C_n with probability $w/(w+w')$ and starts clock $C_{n'}$ with probability $w'/(w+w')$. On the other hand, IGSMPs also have, in addition to GSMPs, the capability of expressing non-deterministic choices. This because, as in standard labeled transition systems deriving from CCS/CSP terms, in the states of an IGSMP action transitions are just non-deterministically chosen. Alternative transitions labeled with invisible τ actions represent internal non-deterministic choices, while alternative transitions labeled with visible actions a (which are seen as incomplete potential transitions which wait for a synchronization with other system components) represent external non-deterministic choices which depend on the environment. An IGSMP represents a complete system (at least from the interaction viewpoint) only when it does not include any transition labeled by a visible action. Visible actions are synchronized via a CSP synchronization policy and a hiding operator is used to turn (synchronized) visible actions into complete invisible actions. This approach differs from that of the stochastic automaton model of [18], where two different kinds of semantics have to be defined in order to describe the *actual behavior* of closed systems and the *potential behavior* of open systems. In our approach both the potential and the actual behavior of the system are represented within the same model and complete systems are obtained by hiding all the actions of the model.

More precisely, in an IGSMP we have four different kinds of state:

- *silent states*, enabling invisible action transitions τ and (possibly) visible action transitions a only. In such states the IGSMP just performs a non-deterministic choice among the τ transitions in zero time and may potentially interact with the environment through one of the visible actions (see e.g. Fig. 7.a).
- *probabilistic states*, enabling $\langle C_n^+, w \rangle$ transitions and (possibly) visible action transitions a only. In such states the IGSMP just performs a probabilistic choice among the clock start transitions in zero time and may potentially interact with the environment through one of the visible actions (see e.g. Fig. 7.b).
- *timed states*, enabling C_n^- transitions and (possibly) visible action transitions a only. In such states the IGSMP executes all the clocks labeling the outgoing termination transitions according to their residual duration distribution. The clock that terminates first determines the transition to be performed. Note that since, as in GSMPs, we assume that clocks cannot terminate at the same instant, we always have a unique clock terminating before the other ones (see e.g. Fig. 7.c). While the IGSMP sojourns in the state, it may (at any time) potentially interact with the environment through one of the outgoing visible action transitions.
- *waiting states*, enabling standard visible actions only or no transition at all. In such states the IGSMP sojourns indefinitely. It may, at any time, potentially interact with the environment through one of the outgoing visible action transitions (see e.g. Fig. 7.d).

In the following we present the formal definition of Interactive Generalized Semi-Markovian Transition System (IGSMTS), then we will define Interactive

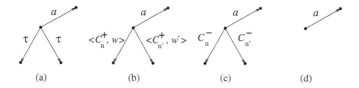

Fig. 7. Some examples of possible states of an IGSMP.

Generalized Semi-Markov Processes as IGSMTSs possessing an initial state. Formally, we denote with *PDF* the set of probability distribution functions over $\mathbb{R}$ ranged over by $f, g, \ldots$ and with PDF^+ the set of probability distribution functions over $\mathbb{R}$ such that $f(x) = 0$ for $x < 0$ (representing duration distributions). Weights, belonging to $\mathbb{R}^+$, are ranged over by $w, w', \ldots$. Moreover, we denote the set of standard action types used in a IGSMTS by *Act*, ranged over by $\alpha, \alpha', \ldots$. As usual *Act* includes the special type τ denoting internal actions. The set $Act - \{\tau\}$ is ranged over by $a, b, \ldots$. The set of clocks of an IGSMTS is denoted by $\mathcal{C} = \{C_n \mid n \in \mathcal{C}Names\}$, where $\mathcal{C}Names$ is a set of clock names. Given a set $\mathcal{C}$, we denote with $\mathcal{C}^+ = \{\langle C_n^+, w \rangle \mid C_n \in \mathcal{C}, w \in \mathbb{R}^+\}$ the set of events denoting the starting of a clock and $\mathcal{C}^- = \{C_n^- \mid C_n \in \mathcal{C}\}$ the set of events denoting the termination of a clock. Let $\mathcal{C}^+ \cup \mathcal{C}^-$ be ranged over by $\theta, \theta', \ldots$. The set of states of an IGSMTS is denoted by Σ, ranged over by $s, s', \ldots$. We assume the following abbreviations that will make the definition of IGSMTSs easier. Let us suppose that $T \subseteq (\Sigma \times Labels \times \Sigma)$ is a transition relation, where *Labels* is a set of transition labels, ranged over by l. We use $s \xrightarrow{\;l\;} s'$ to stand for $(s, l, s') \in T$, $s \xrightarrow{\;l\;}$ to stand for $\exists s' : s \xrightarrow{\;l\;} s'$, and $s \xrightarrow{\;l\;}\!\!\!\!\!/\;\;$ to stand for $\not\exists s' : s \xrightarrow{\;l\;} s'$.

Definition 1. *An Interactive Generalized Semi-Markovian Transition System (IGSMTS) is a tuple $\mathcal{G} = (\Sigma, \mathcal{C}, D, Act, T_+, T_-, T_a)$ with*

- *Σ a set of states,*
- *$\mathcal{C}$ a set of clocks,*
- *$D : \mathcal{C} \longrightarrow PDF^+$ a function that assigns a duration probability distribution function to each clock,*
- *Act a set of standard actions,*
- *$T_+ \subseteq (\Sigma \times \mathcal{C}^+ \times \Sigma)$, $T_- \subseteq (\Sigma \times \mathcal{C}^- \times \Sigma)$, and $T_a \subseteq (\Sigma \times Act \times \Sigma)$ three transition relations representing clock start and termination events and action execution, respectively, such that[1]:*
  1 *$\forall s \in \Sigma.$*
  $$s \xrightarrow{\;\tau\;} \implies \not\exists \theta. s \xrightarrow{\;\theta\;}$$
  2 *$\forall s \in \Sigma.$*
  $$\exists C_n, w. s \xrightarrow{\;\langle C_n^+, w \rangle\;} \implies \not\exists C_{n'}. s \xrightarrow{\;C_{n'}^-\;}$$

---

[1] For the sake of readability here and in the rest of the paper we assume the following operator precedence when writing constraints for transition relations: existential quantifier > "and" operator > implication.

3 $\exists \mathcal{S} : \Sigma \longrightarrow \mathcal{P}(\mathcal{C})$ *the active clock* function, *such that* $\forall s \in \Sigma$.

$a)$

$\quad - s \xrightarrow{\quad \alpha \quad} s' \implies \mathcal{S}(s') = \mathcal{S}(s)$

$\quad - s \xrightarrow{\langle C_n^+, w \rangle} s' \implies \mathcal{S}(s') = \mathcal{S}(s) \cup \{C_n\}$

$\quad - s \xrightarrow{\quad C_n^- \quad} s' \implies C_n \in \mathcal{S}(s) \ \wedge \ \mathcal{S}(s') = \mathcal{S}(s) - \{C_n\}$

$b)$ $\exists C_n, w. \ s \xrightarrow{\langle C_n^+, w \rangle} \implies C_n \notin \mathcal{S}(s)$

$c)$ $C_n \in \mathcal{S}(s) \ \wedge \ s \xrightarrow{\ \tau \ }\!\!\!\!\!\!/ \ \ \wedge \ \not\exists C_{n'}, w. \ s \xrightarrow{\langle C_{n'}^+, w \rangle} \implies s \xrightarrow{\ C_n^- \ }$

4 $\forall s \in \Sigma$.

$s \xrightarrow{\langle C_n^+, w \rangle} s' \implies act(s') \subseteq act(s)$

where the enabled action function $act : \Sigma \longrightarrow \mathcal{P}(Act)$ *is defined by* $act(s) =$ $\{\alpha \mid s \xrightarrow{\ \alpha \ } \}$. $\qquad\qquad\qquad\qquad\qquad\qquad\qquad\qquad\qquad\qquad \square$

Definition 2. *An Interactive Generalized Semi-Markov Process (IGSMP) is a tuple* $\mathcal{G} = (\Sigma, \mathcal{C}, D, Act, T_+, T_-, T_a, s_0)$, *where* $s_0 \in \Sigma$ *is the initial state of the IGSMP and* $(\Sigma, \mathcal{C}, D, Act, T_+, T_-, T_a)$ *is an IGSMTS such that function* $\mathcal{S}$ *in item 3 of Definition 1 also satisfies* $\mathcal{S}(s_0) = \emptyset$. $\qquad\qquad \square$

The constraints over transition relations T_+, T_- and T_a guarantee that each state of the IGSMP belongs to one of the four kind of states above. In particular, the first requirement says that if a state can perform internal τ actions then it cannot perform events of clock starts or clock terminations. Such a property derives from the assumption of *maximal progress*: the possibility of performing internal actions prevents the execution of delays. The second requirement says that if a state can perform clock start events then it cannot perform clock termination events. Such a property derives from the assumption of *urgency of delays*: clock start events cannot be delayed but must be performed immediately, hence they prevent the execution of clock termination transitions. The third requirement checks that clock starting and termination transitions are consistent with the set of clocks that should be in execution in each state of the IGSMP. This is done by defining a function $\mathcal{S}$ which maps each state onto the expected set of clocks in execution, i.e. the set of clocks which have started but not terminated yet. In particular, in the initial state s_0 such a set is empty. The constraint $a)$ defines the construction rule of the active clock set for each state reachable from s_0. In the case of a transition from a state s to a state s' labeled with a standard action, the active clocks of s' stem from the active clocks of s, as no clock can be terminated given that a standard action has been performed. If a transition from s to s' is labeled with a clock start event $\langle C_n^+, w \rangle$, then s' inherits the active clock set of s and adds to this set the started clock C_n. Finally, in the case of a transition from s to s' labeled with a clock termination event C_n^-, s' inherits the active clock set of s without such a terminated clock C_n. Constraints $b)$ and $c)$ concern the legality of the outgoing transitions of a state. In particular, the former says that the name of a clock labeling a starting transition must be fresh (i.e. no clock with such a name must be currently in execution). The latter says that each state without τ and $\langle C_n^+, w \rangle$ outgoing transitions must have a $C_{n'}^-$ outgoing transition for each active clock $C_{n'}$. This definition preserves both the maximal progress and the urgency of delays assumptions and, in each state where it is possible, guarantees the possibility of terminating each delay that is still active. The fourth requirement of Definition 1 implements the following constraint over the structure of IGSMPs which makes their theory simpler. The unique role of clock start transitions in an IGSMP must be to lead to a timed state where the started clocks are actually executed, hence the execution of such transitions cannot cause new behaviors to be performable by the IGSMP. As we will see in Sect. 3, such a constraint is satisfied by the semantic models of terms of the calculus of IGSMPs, hence we consider this constraint not to be really restrictive for our purposes. Formally, we require that the set of action transitions enabled after a clock start transition is a subset of (or equal to) the set of action transitions enabled before such a transition. This guarantees that no new behaviors can be introduced by clock start transitions because: (i) no new behavior beginning with a τ transition can be executable after a clock start transition (states enabling clock start transitions cannot enable τ transitions), and (ii) every potential behavior beginning with a transition a executable after a clock start transition can never be actually executed by hiding a, because before the clock start transition there is a potential behavior beginning with the same action a, which, when hidden, preempts the clock start (see the following subsection about the hiding of IGSMPs).

The Well-Named IGSMP Model. As already explained, the model of well-named IGSMPs introduces a canonical form for names of clocks used in an IGSMP which is based on the dynamic name approach of [13] and makes it simple to develop an equivalence notion over IGSMPs which matches clocks with the same duration distribution.

The constraint on the use of clock names in an IGSMP that we consider concerns the names n which are used for clocks when they start. As we already explained the name used for a starting clock must be fresh, i.e. no clock with such a name must be currently in execution. The requirement that we now add is that the new clock name which is used must depend from the duration distribution f associated with the starting clock and from the names of the clocks (with the same distribution f) already in execution, according to a fixed rule. In particular, we take the set of clock names to be defined by $CNames = (PDF^+ \times \mathbb{N}^+)$, where "$f, i$" is a name for a clock with associated distribution f. The name "f, i" which is used for a starting clock must be such that i is the least $i \in \mathbb{N}^+$ which is not used in the name of any clock with the same distribution f already in execution. Note that, using just duration distributions as clock names is not sufficient because indexes $i \in \mathbb{N}^+$ are needed in order to have different clock names when clocks with the same duration distribution are simultaneously executed.

By applying the dynamic name technique introduced in [13] to clock names, we have that, since the method to compute the index for a starting clock is fixed, clocks of systems that perform equivalent execution traces get the same names. As a consequence, when establishing equivalence of well-named IGSMPs we do not have to associate clock names but we can rely on a simple extension of standard bisimulation.

Since in a well-named IGSMP names for clocks cannot be chosen arbitrarily and the clock names which are considered make it clear by themselves which is the duration distribution associated with a clock, with respect to IGSMTSs (Definition 1), in the definition of well-named IGSMTSs we omit set $\mathcal{C}$ and function D.

Definition 3. *A well-named Interactive Generalized Semi-Markovian Transition System is a tuple $\mathcal{G} = (\Sigma, Act, T_+, T_-, T_a)$ where Σ and Act are defined as in Definition 1, while the definition of the transition relations T_+, T_- and T_a is obtained from that given in Definition 1 by substituting the constraint b) of item 3 with the stronger constraint:*

$$b) \quad \exists C_{f,i}, w \cdot s \xrightarrow{\langle C_{f,i}^+, w \rangle} \implies i = \min\{j \mid j \in \mathbb{N}^+, C_{f,j} \notin \mathcal{S}(s)\} \qquad \square$$

Note that the new version of constraint b) guarantees that the name used for a starting clock is always fresh as required by the old version of constraint b) (see Definition 1).

Definition 4. *A well-named Interactive Generalized Semi-Markov Process is a tuple $\mathcal{G} = (\Sigma, Act, T_+, T_-, T_a, s_0)$, where $s_0 \in \Sigma$ is the initial state of the well-named IGSMP and $(\Sigma, Act, T_+, T_-, T_a)$ is a well-named IGSMTS such that function $\mathcal{S}$ in item 3 of Definition 1 also satisfies $\mathcal{S}(s_0) = \emptyset$.* $\square$

As an important remark, we would like to point out that, since the rule expressed by constraint b) of Definition 4 reuses the indexes i of terminated clocks, each IGSMP with a finite set of states can be transformed into a well-named IGSMP with a finite set of states, by renaming clocks.

Parallel of Well-Named IGSMPs. Now, we address the problem of defining parallel composition à la CSP [24] of well-named IGSMPs, where the standard actions of a given set S are required to synchronize and the synchronization of two actions of type a is again an action of type a.

Intuitively, it should be clear that when composing in parallel two IGSMPs, a suitable renaming of the clocks is necessary in order to obtain an IGSMP, i.e. to preserve the requirements on transition relations of Definition 2. Indeed composing in parallel two IGSMPs could lead to some conflict concerning the identification of the clocks of the composed model through names. More precisely, we have to cope with a name conflict whenever two clocks with the same name "f, i" are simultaneously in execution in both IGSMPs. In such a case the same name identifies two different clocks by compromising the relationship between the start and termination events of the two clocks. When considering well-named IGSMPs instead of just IGSMPs we have in addition the problem of preserving the rule for the name of starting clocks expressed by constraint b) of Definition 4.

The solution that we adopt, which is taken from the dynamic name technique of [13], consists in using l and r (left and right) as references to the two well-named IGSMPs $\mathcal{G}', \mathcal{G}''$ which are composed in parallel by $\mathcal{G}' \|_S \mathcal{G}''$ and relating each clock name locally used in $\mathcal{G}'$ (or $\mathcal{G}''$) to the corresponding well-named IGSMP $\mathcal{G}'$ (or $\mathcal{G}''$) through the reference l (or r). In this way C_{f,l_i} (C_{f,r_i}) denotes the clock $C_{f,i}$ executed by $\mathcal{G}'$ ($\mathcal{G}''$). In order to obtain a well-named IGSMP, when building the composed model, such "extended" names are renamed so that the rule for the name of starting clocks expressed by constraint b) of Definition 4 is satisfied. For instance, let us suppose that both $\mathcal{G}'$ and $\mathcal{G}''$ execute a clock with the same duration distribution f. For both well-named IGSMPs in isolation we represent such an event by activating the clock $C_{f,1}$. Somehow in the composed model we have to distinguish such clocks through names because they can be simultaneously in execution. Let us suppose that in $\mathcal{G}' \|_S \mathcal{G}''$ the first delay with distribution f that starts is the one executed by $\mathcal{G}'$. According to the well-naming rule, in the composed model $\mathcal{G}' \|_S \mathcal{G}''$ such a clock must get name "$f, 1$". Hence we map $C_{f,1}$ to the "extended" name of the clock $C_{f,1}$ executed by $\mathcal{G}'$, thus creating the following mapping:

$$C_{f,1} \longrightarrow C_{f,l_1}$$

denoting that the first clock with distribution f of the composed model $C_{f,1}$ corresponds to the first clock with distribution f of the lefthand well-named IGSMP. Then, if the second clock to be executed is the clock $C_{f,1}$ belonging to the righthand well-named IGSMP, in the composed model we create the fresh name "$f, 2$" (according to the well-naming rule) and have in addition the following mapping:

$$C_{f,2} \longrightarrow C_{f,r_1}$$

In Table 1 we present an example of execution of a composed model $\mathcal{G}' \|_S \mathcal{G}''$ by showing how the mapping function (between the clock names of the composed model $\mathcal{G}' \|_S \mathcal{G}''$ and the corresponding clock names locally used in $\mathcal{G}'$ and $\mathcal{G}''$) for clocks with distribution f evolves.

Table 1. Renaming of the clocks in $\mathcal{G}^{\square} \|_S \mathcal{G}^{\boxplus}$.

Well-named IGSMPs	Composed Model	Mapping Function
$\mathcal{G}^{\square}$ starts $C_{f,1}$	$\mathcal{G}^{\square} \|_S \mathcal{G}^{\boxplus}$ starts $C_{f,1}$	$C_{f,1} \longrightarrow C_{f,l_1}$
$\mathcal{G}^{\boxplus}$ starts $C_{f,1}$	$\mathcal{G}^{\square} \|_S \mathcal{G}^{\boxplus}$ starts $C_{f,2}$	$C_{f,1} \longrightarrow C_{f,l_1}$ $C_{f,2} \longrightarrow C_{f,r_1}$
$\mathcal{G}^{\boxplus}$ starts $C_{f,2}$	$\mathcal{G}^{\square} \|_S \mathcal{G}^{\boxplus}$ starts $C_{f,3}$	$C_{f,1} \longrightarrow C_{f,l_1}$ $C_{f,2} \longrightarrow C_{f,r_1}$ $C_{f,3} \longrightarrow C_{f,r_2}$
$\mathcal{G}^{\boxplus}$ ends $C_{f,1}$	$\mathcal{G}^{\square} \|_S \mathcal{G}^{\boxplus}$ ends $C_{f,2}$	$C_{f,1} \longrightarrow C_{f,l_1}$ $C_{f,3} \longrightarrow C_{f,r_2}$
$\mathcal{G}^{\square}$ starts $C_{f,2}$	$\mathcal{G}^{\square} \|_S \mathcal{G}^{\boxplus}$ starts $C_{f,2}$	$C_{f,1} \longrightarrow C_{f,l_1}$ $C_{f,2} \longrightarrow C_{f,l_2}$ $C_{f,3} \longrightarrow C_{f,r_2}$

By following such a procedure, we build the composed model by dynamically storing all current mappings between the clock names of the composed model and the local clock names of the two well-named IGSMPs by employing a table (mapping function) for each distribution f. In general, when a clock $C_{f,i}$ with distribution f is started by one of the two composed well-named IGSMPs, we do the following: (i) we choose the first index j for the distribution f which is unused in the composed model (by checking the table related to the duration probability distribution f), and we use the name "f,j" for the clock in the composed model; (ii) we add to the table related to distribution f the mapping $C_{f,j} \longrightarrow C_{f,l_i}$ if the clock is executed by the lefthand well-named IGSMP or $C_{f,j} \longrightarrow C_{f,r_i}$ if the clock is executed by the righthand well-named IGSMP. When a clock $C_{f,i}$ with distribution f is terminated by one of the two composed well-named IGSMPs, we do the following: (i) we establish the name "f,j" associated with the terminating clock in the composed model by checking the table related to distribution f (it must include $C_{f,j} \longrightarrow C_{f,l_i}$ if the clock is executed by the lefthand well-named IGSMP or $C_{f,j} \longrightarrow C_{f,r_i}$ if the clock is executed by the righthand well-named IGSMP); (ii) we remove from the table related to the duration probability distribution f the mapping for the name "f,j" of the composed model.

Now we formally define the parallel composition $\mathcal{G}_1 \|_S \mathcal{G}_2$ of two well-named IGSMPs $\mathcal{G}_1$ and $\mathcal{G}_2$, where the synchronization set S is a subset of $Act - \{\tau\}$.

We denote with $Loc = \{l, r\}$, ranged over by loc, the set of locations, where l stands for left and r for right. We denote an *index association*, whose elements are associations (j, loc_i), with *iassoc*, which ranges over the set $IAssoc$ of partial bijections from $\mathbb{N}^+$ to $Loc \times \mathbb{N}^+$. Moreover, a mapping M is a relation from PDF^+ to $\mathbb{N}^+ \times (Loc \times \mathbb{N}^+)$ such that $\forall f \in PDF^+.M_f \in IAssoc$ [2], i.e. M is a mapping including an index association for each different duration distribution. We denote the set of mappings M by $\mathcal{M}$. In the following we use the shorthand $f : (j, loc_i)$ to stand for $(f, (j, loc_i)) \in M$ that represents the clock mapping $C_{f,j} \longrightarrow C_{f,loc_i}$. Finally we make use of the auxiliary function $n : IAssoc \longrightarrow \mathbb{N}^+$ that computes the new index to be used for a clock name according to the well-naming rule, by choosing the minimum index not used by the other clocks with the same distribution already in execution, i.e. $n(iassoc) = min\{k \,|\, k \notin dom(iassoc)\}$.

Definition 5. *The parallel composition $\mathcal{G}_1 \|_S \mathcal{G}_2$ of two well-named IGSMPs $\mathcal{G}_1 = (\Sigma_1, Act, T_{+,1}, T_{-,1}, T_{a,1}, s_{0,1})$ and $\mathcal{G}_2 = (\Sigma_2, Act, T_{+,2}, T_{-,2}, T_{a,2}, s_{0,2})$, with S being the synchronization set, is the tuple $(\Sigma, Act, T_+, T_-, T_a, (s_{0,1}, s_{0,2}, \emptyset))$ with:*

- $\Sigma = \Sigma_1 \times \Sigma_2 \times \mathcal{M}$ *the set of states,*
- $T_+ \subseteq (\Sigma \times \mathcal{C}^+ \times \Sigma)$, $T_- \subseteq (\Sigma \times \mathcal{C}^- \times \Sigma)$, *and* $T_a \subseteq (\Sigma \times Act \times \Sigma)$ *the least transition relations, such that* $\forall (s_1, s_2, M) \in \Sigma$.

$$\mathbf{1_l} \; s_1 \xrightarrow{\alpha} s_1', \; \alpha \notin S \implies (s_1, s_2, M) \xrightarrow{\alpha} (s_1', s_2, M)$$

$$\mathbf{2} \; s_1 \xrightarrow{a} s_1' \wedge s_2 \xrightarrow{a} s_2', \; a \in S \implies (s_1, s_2, M) \xrightarrow{a} (s_1', s_2', M)$$

---

[2] Given a relation M from A to B, we denote with M_a the set $\{b \in B \,|\, (a,b) \in M\}$.

Fig. 8. Example of Well-Named IGSMP.

$$\mathbf{3_1} \quad s_1 \xrightarrow{\langle C^+_{f,i},w\rangle} s'_1 \wedge s_2 \xrightarrow{\tau} \!\!\!\!\not\longrightarrow \quad \Longrightarrow$$

$$(s_1, s_2, M) \xrightarrow{\langle C^+_{f,n(M_f)},w\rangle} (s'_1, s_2, M \cup \{f : (n(M_f), l_i)\})$$

$$\mathbf{4_1} \quad s_1 \xrightarrow{C^-_{f,i}} s'_1 \wedge s_2 \xrightarrow{\tau}\!\!\!\!\not\longrightarrow \wedge \; \not\exists C_{g,h}, w.\, s_2 \xrightarrow{\langle C^+_{g,h},w\rangle} \wedge \, f : (j, l_i) \in M \; \Longrightarrow$$

$$(s_1, s_2, M) \xrightarrow{C^-_{f,j}} (s'_1, s_2, M - \{f : (j, l_i)\})$$

and also the symmetric rules $\mathbf{1_r}, \mathbf{3_r}, \mathbf{4_r}$ referring to the local transitions of $\mathcal{G}_2$, which are obtained from the rules $\mathbf{1_1}, \mathbf{3_1}, \mathbf{4_1}$ by exchanging the roles of states s_1 (s'_1) and s_2 (s'_2) and by replacing l_i with r_i, hold true.

$-$ *$(s_{0,1}, s_{0,2}, \emptyset) \in \Sigma$ the initial state*   □

Each state $s \in \Sigma$ of the composed model is represented by a triple including a pair of states ($s_1 \in \Sigma_1$ and $s_2 \in \Sigma_2$) and an auxiliary memory M containing all the index associations currently active in such a state. Rules **1** (**2**) describe the behavior of the composed model in the case of a standard action α performed by one (or both, via a synchronization) well-named IGSMPs, when $\alpha \notin S$ ($\alpha \in S$). Rules **3** and **4** define the behavior of the composed model in the case of delays locally performed by components. When in $\mathcal{G}_1$ ($\mathcal{G}_2$) occurs a transition labeled with $\langle C^+_{f,i}, w\rangle$, denoting the beginning of a delay with duration distribution f, then the new index $n(M_f)$ is determined for identifying the action at the level of the composed model, and the new mapping $f : (n(M_f), l_i)$ ($f : (n(M_f), r_i)$) is added to M. Conversely, when in $\mathcal{G}_1$ ($\mathcal{G}_2$) occurs a transition labeled with $C^-_{f,i}$, denoting the termination of a clock with duration distribution f, the particular clock with index j associated to l_i (r_i) in M_f terminates at the level of the composed model, and the index j becomes available. Note that the negative clauses in the premises enforce the maximal progress and the urgency of delays assumptions.

Example 2. Called $\mathcal{G}$ the well-named IGSMP of Fig. 8 which repeatedly executes delays with distribution f, we depict in Fig. 9 the well-named IGSMP $\mathcal{G} \parallel_\emptyset \mathcal{G}$. In Fig. 8 and 9 and in the following we consider C^+_n to be a shorthand for $<C^+_n, 1>$.   □

Theorem 1. *Let $\mathcal{G}_1$ and $\mathcal{G}_2$ be two well-named IGSMPs. Then for each $S \subseteq Act - \{\tau\}$, $\mathcal{G}_1 \parallel_S \mathcal{G}_2$ is a well-named IGSMP.*   □

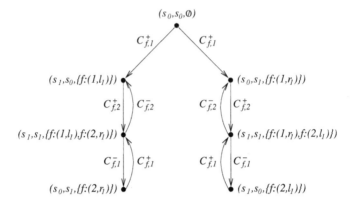

Fig. 9. Example of Parallel Composition of Well-Named IGSMPs.

Hiding of Well-Named IGSMPs. Now, we address the problem of defining hiding of well-named IGSMPs, where the standard actions of a given set L are turned into invisible τ actions.

As we already explained, the capability of hiding actions makes it possible to turn visible "incomplete" actions into invisible "complete" ones, thus giving the possibility of building a complete system from several system components. In particular while a visible action transition (as long as it is enabled) can delay indefinitely before being performed, when such an action is turned into an invisible action it must be executed in zero time.

Now we formally define the hiding $\mathcal{G}/L$ of a well-named IGSMP $\mathcal{G}$, where the set L of the visible actions to be hidden is a subset of $Act - \{\tau\}$.

Definition 6. *The hiding $\mathcal{G}/L$ of a well-named IGSMP $\mathcal{G} = (\Sigma, Act, T_{+,1}, T_{-,1}, T_{a,1}, s_0)$ with L being the set of visible actions to be hidden is the tuple $(\Sigma, Act, T_+, T_-, T_a, s_0)$ where $T_+ \subseteq (\Sigma \times \mathcal{C}^+ \times \Sigma)$, $T_- \subseteq (\Sigma \times \mathcal{C}^- \times \Sigma)$, and $T_a \subseteq (\Sigma \times Act \times \Sigma)$ are the least set of transitions, such that $\forall s \in \Sigma$.* [3]

$$\mathbf{1} \ s \xrightarrow{\alpha}_1 s', \ \alpha \notin L \implies s \xrightarrow{\alpha} s'$$
$$\mathbf{2} \ s \xrightarrow{a}_1 s', \ a \in L \implies s \xrightarrow{\tau} s'$$
$$\mathbf{3} \ s \xrightarrow{\theta}_1 s' \wedge \not\exists a \in L. \, s \xrightarrow{a}_1 \implies s \xrightarrow{\theta} s' \qquad \square$$

Rules **1** and **2** are standard. Rule **3** says that the effect of the hiding operator over states of $\mathcal{G}$ which enable standard actions in L is to preempt all clock related transitions according to the maximal progress assumption.

Theorem 2. *Let $\mathcal{G}$ be a well-named IGSMP. Then for each $L \subseteq Act - \{\tau\}$, $\mathcal{G}/L$ is a well-named IGSMP.* $\qquad \square$

---

[3] In order to distinguish transition of $T_{+,1}$, $T_{\boxempty,1}$ and $T_{a,1}$ from transitions of T_+, $T_{\boxempty}$ and T_a we denote the former with " $\xrightarrow{\quad}_1$" and the latter simply with " $\xrightarrow{\quad}$".

Equivalence of Well-Named IGSMPs. Now we will introduce a notion of weak bisimulation over well-named IGSMPs. In particular such a notion matches start and termination events of clocks with the same duration distribution by using strong bisimulation, deals with probabilistic choices similarly as in [25], and abstracts from standard τ actions similarly as in [27]. In the following Sect. 3 we will see that weak bisimulation is a congruence with respect to both parallel composition and hiding operators.

In our context we express cumulative probabilities by aggregating weights.

Definition 7. *Let* $\mathcal{G} = (\Sigma, Act, T_+, T_-, T_a)$ *be a well-named IGSMTS. The function* $TW : \Sigma \times PDF^+ \times \mathcal{P}(\Sigma) \longrightarrow \mathbb{R}^+ \cup \{0\}$, *which computes the aggregated weight that a state* $s \in \Sigma$ *reaches a set of states* $I \in \mathcal{P}(\Sigma)$ *by starting a delay with duration distribution* $f \in PDF^+$ *is defined as*[4]:

$$TW(s, f, I) = \sum \{\!| w \mid \exists i \in \mathbb{N}^+, s' \in I. \ s \xrightarrow{\langle C^+_{f,i}, w \rangle} s' |\!\}$$

$\square$

We are now in a position to define the notion of weak bisimilarity for well-named IGSMPs (in the style of that of [22]). Let $NPAct = Act \cup \mathcal{C}^-$, the set of non-probabilistic actions, be ranged over by σ. Besides, let $\overset{\sigma}{\Longrightarrow}$ denote $(\xrightarrow{\tau})^* \xrightarrow{\sigma} (\xrightarrow{\tau})^*$, i.e. a sequence of transitions including a single σ transition and any number of τ transitions. Moreover, we define $\overset{\hat{\sigma}}{\Longrightarrow} = \overset{\sigma}{\Longrightarrow}$ if $\sigma \neq \tau$ and $\overset{\hat{\tau}}{\Longrightarrow} = (\xrightarrow{\tau})^*$, i.e. a possibly empty sequence of τ transitions.

Definition 8. *Let* $\mathcal{G} = (\Sigma, Act, T_+, T_-, T_a)$ *be a well-named IGSMTS. An equivalence relation* β *on* Σ *is a weak bisimulation iff* $s_1 \ \beta \ s_2$ *implies*

- *for every* $\sigma \in NPAct$ *and* $s'_1 \in \Sigma$,
$$s_1 \xrightarrow{\sigma} s'_1 \ implies \ s_2 \overset{\hat{\sigma}}{\Longrightarrow} s'_2 \ for \ some \ s'_2 \ with \ s'_1 \ \beta \ s'_2,$$
- $s_2 \overset{\hat{\tau}}{\Longrightarrow} s'_2$ *for some* s'_2 *such that, for every* $f \in PDF^+$ *and equivalence class* I *of* β,
$$TW(s_1, f, I) = TW(s'_2, f, I)$$

$\square$

Example 3. In Fig. 10 we depict the minimal semantic model for the well-named IGSMP of Fig. 9, which is obtained by merging weakly bisimilar states. The weight 2 of the initial transition derives from the aggregation of the weights of the two initial transitions in the model of Fig. 18. However since in the initial state there is no alternative to such a transition, its weight is not relevant for the actual behavior (in isolation) of the IGSMP.

$\square$

---

[4] We use $\{\!|$ and $|\!\}$ to denote multiset parentheses. The summation of an empty multiset is assumed to yield 0. Since the method for computing the new index of a delay f that starts in a state P is fixed, we have that several transitions f^+ leaving P have all the same index i.

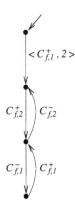

Fig. 10. Minimal Well-Named IGSMP.

2.3   Deriving the Performance Model from an IGSMP

In this section we sketch the formal procedure of [5] for deriving a GSMP from an IGSMP system specification. In particular this transformation is possible only if the specification of the system is *complete* both from the *interaction* and from the *performance* points of view.

An IGSMP specification is complete from the interaction viewpoint if the system specified is not a part of a larger system which may influence its behavior, hence when every standard action appearing in the IGSMP is an *internal* τ action.

An IGSMP specification is complete from the performance viewpoint if all the choices in which the specified system may engage are quantified probabilistically. This means that the IGSMP must not include silent states actually leading to a non-deterministic choice among different future behaviors. In other words a silent state either must have only one outgoing τ transition, or all its outgoing τ transitions must lead to equivalent behaviors. This notion can be formally defined as follows: An IGSMP is complete w.r.t. performance if it can be reduced, by aggregating weakly bisimilar states (see Sect. 2.2), to a model without silent states.

The formal procedure for the derivation of the GSMP is composed of three phases.

The first phase consists in *minimizing* the state space Σ of the Well-Named IGSMP $\mathcal{G}$ by aggregating states that are equivalent according to the notion of weak bisimulation defined in Sect. 2.2. Since we supposed that the $\mathcal{G}$ satisfies the two conditions above, a side effect of this minimization is that all τ actions disappear from $\mathcal{G}$.

The second phase is the transformation of every *probabilistic tree* present in the semantic model into a single probabilistic choice. First of all weights are turned into the corresponding probability values. A probabilistic tree is formed by the possible probabilistic paths that go from a given probabilistic state (the root of the tree) to a timed or waiting state (a leaf of the tree). Note that

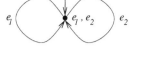

$$ElPDF(e_1) = f, ElPDF(e_2) = f$$

Fig. 11. Derived GSMP.

such trees cannot include loops composed of one or more transitions, because after each clock start the number of clocks in execution strictly increases. To be precise, such trees are directed acyclic graphs (*DAGs*) with root, since a node may have multiple incoming arcs. The probabilistic trees are flattened into a single choice that goes directly from the root to the leaves of the tree.

The final phase is the derivation of the GSMP. The set of elements of the *GSMP* is composed of the clocks $C_{f,i}$ labeling the transitions of $\mathcal{G}$. The states of the *GSMP* are the timed and waiting states of $\mathcal{G}$. A transition leaving a state of the *GSMP* is derived beginning from a clock termination transition leaving the corresponding timed state of $\mathcal{G}$ and, in the case this transition leads to a probabilistic state, a corresponding probabilistic state change occurs in the derived *GSMP*. Each transition of the *GSMP* is labeled by the element $C_{f,i}$ terminating in the corresponding termination transition.

Example 4. In Fig. 11 we show the *GSMP* derived, by applying the translation above, from the Well-Named IGSMP of Fig. 9. In particular the *GSMP* is obtained from the minimal model of Fig. 10, which is the result of the first phase. Since such model does not include standard action transitions the system considered is complete both from the interactive and the performance viewpoints. In the *GSMP* of Fig. 11 the states are labeled by the active elements and the transitions with the terminating elements. Each transition of the *GSMP* lead to a single successive state (the probabilistic state change after consists in trivially selecting that state with probability 1). The elements e_1 and e_2 represent the clocks $C_{f,1}$ and $C_{f,2}$ respectively, and the probability distribution function of both is given by function f. □

2.4   Interactive Stochastic Timed Transition Systems

In this section we introduce Interactive Stochastic Timed Transition Systems (ISTTSs) that will be used in the following to define a semantics for IGSMPs.

The ISTTS Model. In this section we formally define Interactive Stochastic Timed Transition Systems (ISTTS) which include three type of transitions: *standard action transitions*, representing the interactive behavior of a system component, *probabilistic transitions* (expressed by means of probability spaces[5])

---

[5] See, e.g., [5] for a formal definition of probability spaces.

Fig. 12. Some examples of possible states of an ISTTS.

representing (infinitely branching) probabilistic choices and *numeric time transitions* representing a fixed temporal delay.

As far as standard actions are concerned they have exactly the same behavior as in IGSMPs. In ISTTS non-deterministic choices can arise not only from transitions labeled with standard visible actions (like in IGSMPs), but also from transitions representing the passage of time. As usual in the real time literature (see e.g. [28]), several timed transition leaving a state offer the possibility to the observer to choose the amount of time after which he wants to observe the status of the system.

In ISTTS we have two different kinds of state:

- *silent states* which are exactly like in IGSMPs.
- *probabilistic states* enabling probabilistic transitions, expressed by a probability space PS, and (possibly) visible action transitions a only. In such states the ISTTS just chooses a new state in zero time according to the probability space and may potentially interact with the environment through one of its visible actions (see e.g. Fig. 12.a).
- *timed states* enabling numeric timed transitions t and (possibly) visible action transitions a only. In such states the ISTTS just performs a non-deterministic choice among the numeric timed transitions (which cause the amount of time labeling the transition to pass) and may potentially interact with the environment through one of its visible actions (see e.g. Fig. 12.b).

In the following we present the formal definition of Interactive Stochastic Timed Transition System (ISTTS), then we will define Rooted Interactive Stochastic Timed Transition Systems as ISTTSs possessing an initial state. Formally, given a time domain $TD \subseteq \mathbb{R}^+ \cup \{0\}$, we use $t, t', \ldots$, representing time values, to range over TD.

Definition 9. *An Interactive Stochastic Timed Transition System (ISTTS) is a tuple $\mathcal{D} = (\Sigma, TD, Act, P, T_t, T_a)$ with*

- *Σ a possibly infinite set of states,*
- *TD a time domain, i.e. the set of possible values over which the labels of the numeric timed transitions range,*
- *Act a set of standard actions,*
- *$P : \Sigma' \to PS(\Sigma - \Sigma')$, where $\Sigma' \subset \Sigma$ and $PS(\Sigma'')$ denotes the family of probability spaces over sets of states $\Sigma''' \subseteq \Sigma''$, the probabilistic transition relation which associates a probability space with some of the states of the ISTTS; and $T_t \subseteq (\Sigma \times TD \times \Sigma)$ and $T_a \subseteq (\Sigma \times Act \times \Sigma)$ two transition*

relations representing time passage and action execution, respectively. P, T_t and T_a must be such that $\forall s \in \Sigma$.

- $s \xrightarrow{\tau} \implies s \notin dom(P) \land \nexists t.s \xrightarrow{t}$
- $s \in dom(P) \implies \nexists t.s \xrightarrow{t}$
- $s \xrightarrow{\tau} \lor \exists t.s \xrightarrow{t} \lor s \in dom(P)$ ▢

Definition 10. *A Rooted Interactive Stochastic Timed Transition System (RISTTS) is a tuple $\mathcal{D} = (\Sigma, TD, Act, P, T_t, T_a, s_0)$, where $s_0 \in \Sigma$ is the initial state and $(\Sigma, TD, Act, P, T_t, T_a)$ is an ISTTS.* ▢

The meaning of the constraints over transition relations is the following. The first requirement says that (similarly as in IGSMPs) if a state can perform internal τ actions then it can perform neither probabilistic transitions nor timed transitions (*maximal progress* assumption). The second requirement says that (similarly as in IGSMPs) if a state can perform probabilistic transitions then it cannot perform timed transitions (*urgency of choices* assumption). The third requirement says that (similarly as in IGSMPs) we cannot have states where time is not allowed to pass (time deadlocks).

Parallel of Rooted ISTTSs. Now we define, similarly as for IGSMPs, the parallel composition à la CSP of RISTTSs.

In such a parallel composition the numeric timed transitions of the composed RISTTSs are constrained to synchronize, so that the same amount of time passes for both systems, i.e. when time advances for one RISTTS it must also advance for the other RISTTS.

Definition 11. *The parallel composition $\mathcal{D}_1 \parallel_S \mathcal{D}_2$ of two RISTTSs $\mathcal{D}_1 = (\Sigma_1, TD, Act, P_1, T_{t,1}, T_{a,1}, s_{0,1})$ and $\mathcal{D}_2 = (\Sigma_2, TD, Act, P_2, T_{t,2}, T_{a,2}, s_{0,2})$, with $S \subset Act - \{\tau\}$ being the synchronization set, is the tuple $(\Sigma, TD, Act, P, T_t, T_a, (s_{0,1}, s_{0,2}))$ with:*

- $\Sigma = \Sigma_1 \times \Sigma_2$ *the set of states*
- P *the partial function defined over $\Sigma_1 \times \Sigma_2$ obtained from P_1 and P_2 as follows: $\forall s_1 \in \Sigma_1, s_2 \in \Sigma_2$.*

  $P(s_1, s_2) = Id^1_{s_2}(P_1(s_1))$ *if* $s_1 \in dom(P_1) \land s_2 \xrightarrow{t}$

  $P(s_1, s_2) = Id^2_{s_1}(P_2(s_2))$ *if* $s_2 \in dom(P_2) \land s_1 \xrightarrow{t}$

  $P(s_1, s_2) = P(s_1) \cdot P(s_2)$ *if* $s_1 \in dom(P_1) \land s_2 \in dom(P_2)$

  $P(s_1, s_2)$ *is not defined   otherwise*

  with $Id^1_{s_2} : \Sigma_1 \longrightarrow (\Sigma_1 \times \{s_2\})$ defined by $\forall s \in \Sigma_1. Id_{s_2}(s) = (s, s_2)$ and $Id^2_{s_1} : \Sigma_2 \longrightarrow (\{s_1\} \times \Sigma_2)$ defined by $\forall s \in \Sigma_2. Id_{s_1}(s) = (s_1, s)$.
- $T_t \subseteq (\Sigma \times TD \times \Sigma)$ *and* $T_a \subseteq (\Sigma \times Act \times \Sigma)$ *the least transition relations, such that*

  1_l $s_1 \xrightarrow{\alpha} s'_1, \alpha \notin S \implies (s_1, s_2) \xrightarrow{\alpha} (s'_1, s_2)$

  1_r $s_2 \xrightarrow{\alpha} s'_2, \alpha \notin S \implies (s_1, s_2) \xrightarrow{\alpha} (s_1, s'_2)$

$$\mathbf{2}\ s_1 \xrightarrow{\ a\ } s_1' \wedge s_2 \xrightarrow{\ a\ } s_2',\ a \in S \implies (s_1, s_2) \xrightarrow{\ a\ } (s_1', s_2')$$

$$\mathbf{3}\ s_1 \xrightarrow{\ t\ } s_1' \wedge s_2 \xrightarrow{\ t\ } s_2' \implies (s_1, s_2) \xrightarrow{\ t\ } (s_1', s_2')$$

$- (s_{0,1}, s_{0,2}) \in \Sigma$ *the initial state.*   □

The probability space associated by function P to the states of the composed model is determined as follows.

Whenever only a RISTTS, e.g. $\mathcal{D}_1$ in state s_1, engages in a probabilistic choice (and such a choice is not prevented by the maximal progress assumption) we evaluate the probability space in the composed model by considering the probability space $Id_{s_2}^1(P_1(s_1))$ "induced" by applying function $Id_{s_2}^1$ to the states in the domain of the probability space $P_1(s_1)$ (see, e.g., [5] for a formal definition of induced probability spaces). Whenever both RISTTSs engage in probabilistic choices, we produce a single global probability space by computing the "product" of the two probability spaces (see, e.g., [5] for a formal definition of product of probability spaces): a probability space whose domain is the cartesian product of the initial domains and where individual choices are assumed performed independently.

When evaluating action transitions we just make use of standard rules. Finally we require timed transitions to synchronize.

Theorem 3. *Let $\mathcal{D}_1$ and $\mathcal{D}_2$ be two RISTTSs. Then for each $S \subseteq Act - \{\tau\}$, $\mathcal{D}_1 \|_S \mathcal{D}_2$ is a RISTTS.*   □

Hiding of Rooted ISTTSs. Now we define, similarly as for IGSMPs, the hiding of RISTTSs.

Definition 12. *The hiding $\mathcal{D}/L$ of a RISTTS $\mathcal{D}_1 = (\Sigma, TD, Act, P_1, T_{t,1}, T_{a,1}, s_0)$, with $L \subset Act - \{\tau\}$ being the set of visible actions to be hidden, is the tuple $(\Sigma, TD, Act, P, T_t, T_a, s_0)$, with:*

- *P the partial function obtained from P_1 by removing from its domain those states (and the associated probability spaces) which enable at least one transition labeled with an action in L*
- *$T_t \subseteq (\Sigma \times TD \times \Sigma)$ and $T_a \subseteq (\Sigma \times Act \times \Sigma)$ the least transition relations, such that $\forall s \in \Sigma$.* [6]

$$\mathbf{1}\ s \xrightarrow{\ \alpha\ }_1 s',\ \alpha \notin L \implies s \xrightarrow{\ \alpha\ } s'$$

$$\mathbf{2}\ s \xrightarrow{\ a\ }_1 s',\ a \in L \implies s \xrightarrow{\ \tau\ } s'$$

$$\mathbf{3}\ s \xrightarrow{\ t\ }_1 \wedge\ \not\exists a \in L.\ s \xrightarrow{\ a\ }_1 \implies s \xrightarrow{\ t\ }$$ □

Similarly as for IGSMPs, in the definition of the hiding operator in addition to standard rules we make use of rules which enforce the maximal progress assumption.

Theorem 4. *Let $\mathcal{D}$ be a RISTTS. Then for each $L \subseteq Act - \{\tau\}$, $\mathcal{D}/L$ is a RISTTS.*   □

---

[6] In order to distinguish transition of $T_{t,1}$ and $T_{a,1}$ from transitions of T_t and T_a we denote the former with "$\longrightarrow_1$" and the latter simply with "$\longrightarrow$".

Equivalence of Rooted ISTTSs. Now we introduce a notion of weak bisimulation for RISTTSs which constitutes an extension of the approach of [25] to probability spaces and abstracts from standard τ actions similarly as in [27].

Given an equivalence relation β on a set Σ and a set $I \subseteq \Sigma$, we first define the function $EC_{I,\beta} : I \rightarrow \Sigma/\beta$ which maps each state $s \in I$ into the corresponding equivalence class $[s]_\beta$ in Σ.

Definition 13. Let $\mathcal{D} = (\Sigma, TD, Act, P, T_t, T_a)$ be an ISTTS. An equivalence relation β on Σ is a weak bisimulation iff $s_1 \, \beta \, s_2$ implies

- for every $\alpha \in Act$,
$$s_1 \xrightarrow{\alpha} s_1' \text{ implies } s_2 \xRightarrow{\hat{\alpha}} s_2' \text{ for some } s_2' \text{ with } s_1' \, \beta \, s_2',$$
- for every $t \in TD$,
$$s_1 \xrightarrow{t} s_1' \text{ implies } s_2 \xrightarrow{t} s_2' \text{ for some } s_2' \text{ with } s_1' \, \beta \, s_2',$$
- $s_2 \xRightarrow{\hat{\tau}} s_2'$ for some s_2' with $EC_{\Sigma_{P(s_1)},\beta}(P(s_1)) \approx EC_{\Sigma_{P(s_2')},\beta}(P(s_2'))$

where Σ_{PS} denotes the set of states in the domain of the probability space PS and "$\approx$" denotes equivalence between probability spaces, i.e. coincidence of probabilities over the intersection of domains and zero probability for all states not included in such intersection (see [5] for a formal definition).

Two states s_1 and s_2 are weakly bisimilar, denoted by $s_1 \approx s_2$, iff (s_1, s_2) is included in some weak bisimulation. Two RISTTSs $(\mathcal{D}_1, s_{0,1})$ and $(\mathcal{D}_2, s_{0,2})$ are weakly bisimilar, if their initial states $s_{0,1}$ and $s_{0,2}$ are weakly bisimilar in the ISTTS obtained with the disjoint union of $\mathcal{D}_1$ and $\mathcal{D}_2$.   □

In the last item we exploit induced probability spaces to check that states s_1 and s_2' have the same aggregated probability to reach the same equivalence classes.

2.5   A Semantics for Interactive Generalized Semi-Markov Processes

In this section we present a semantics for well-named Interactive Generalized Semi-Markov Processes which maps them onto Interactive Stochastic Timed Transition Systems. Such a semantics explicitly represents the passage of time by means of transitions labeled with numeric time delays and turns probability distributions of durations into infinitely branching probabilistic choices which lead to states performing numeric time delays with a different duration. In particular, differently from [18] where a technique based on *residual lifetimes of clocks* is used, the states of the semantics of an Interactive Generalized Semi-Markov Process encode the *spent lifetimes of clocks*. This means that, in a timed state of the IGSMP where several clocks $C_{n_1} \ldots C_{n_k}$ are in execution, the time delay originated by a clock C_{n_i} is determined according to its residual distribution of duration which is evaluated from (i) its associated duration distribution and (ii) its spent lifetime. Once we have sampled a time value t_i from the residual duration distribution of each clock C_{n_i}, we just take the minimum t_{min} of the sampled values and we consider the clock $C_{n_{min}}$ which sampled such a time value. Such a "winning clock" is the clock that terminates in the timed state of the IGSMP. After this event the other clocks (which are still in execution) carry over their spent lifetimes, which now is given by $t'_i = t_i + t_{\min}$. Since, according to this approach, the residual duration of a clock is re-sampled in each IGSMP state until it terminates, an adversary (or scheduler) which resolves non-deterministic choices in an IGSMP cannot gain information about the future behavior of the system on which to base its decisions.

Example 5. Let us consider the IGSMP depicted in Fig. 13, where three temporal delays are started by activating three clocks C_{n_1}, C_{n_2}, and C_{n_3}. In particular, we concentrate on the case in which C_{n_2} is the first clock to terminate.

In Fig. 14 we show the semantics of the IGSMP of Fig. 13 obtained by following an approach similar to that of [18], which encodes in each state the *residual lifetimes of clocks*. Each state is enriched with the set of active clocks together with their residual lifetimes. In state $\langle s_0, \emptyset \rangle$ (where no clock is active) three numeric time delays t_1, t_2, and t_3 are sampled and associated with the lifetime of the clocks C_{n_1}, C_{n_2}, and C_{n_3}, respectively. Depending on which is the clock $C_{n_{\min}}$ sampling the minimum time value t_{min} in $\langle s_0, \emptyset \rangle$, we move to one of three different classes of states, one for each possible winning clock. Afterwards, a temporal transition labeled with a numeric time value t between 0 and t_{min} is taken, and each residual duration is accordingly modified by subtracting t_{min} from the residual lifetime of each clock. For the sake of readability in Fig. 14 we just depict one trace leading from s_0 to a state s_1 which belongs to the class of states for which C_{n_2} is the winning clock (i.e. t_2 is t_{min}), and then from s_1 to s_2 via the transition labeled with the time value t_2, so that in s_2 the clock C_{n_2} is terminated. In s_2 the residual lifetimes of the remaining active clocks C_{n_1} and C_{n_3} are $t_1 - t_{min}$ and $t_3 - t_{min}$ respectively. By exploiting this information an adversary may already know which clock between C_{n_1} and C_{n_3} will terminate first and consequently guide the nondeterministic choice in s_2.

In Fig. 15 we show the semantics of the IGSMP of Fig. 13 obtained by following the approach that we adopt in this paper, which is based on the *spent lifetimes of clocks*. Each state is enriched with: (i) the set of active clocks together with their spent lifetimes, and (ii) a pair $C_n : t$ containing the time value sampled by the winning clock in a timed state of the IGSMP and the clock name. The latter field is set to "$-$" whenever the IGSMP is not in a timed state. The sampling executed in $\langle s_0, \emptyset, - \rangle$ leads to a state where the three starting clocks are associated with the spent lifetime 0 (because the corresponding transition does not represent a passage of time but simply the result of the sampling), and the winning clock C_n and its sampled value are reported too. As in the case of Fig. 14, in Fig. 15 we just report one trace leading from s_0 to a state s_1 which belongs to the class of states for which C_{n_2} is the winning clock (i.e. C_{n_2} is $C_{n_{\min}}$ and t_2 is its sampled value), and then from s_1 to s_2 via the transition labeled with the value t_2, so that in s_2 the clock C_{n_2} is terminated. In state s_2 the spent lifetimes of the remaining active clocks C_{n_1} and C_{n_3} are both equal to t_2, and their residual durations depend on both such a value and the duration distribution associated with the clocks. Since, according to this approach, the time to termination of clocks C_{n_1} and C_{n_3} is re-sampled, an adversary cannot

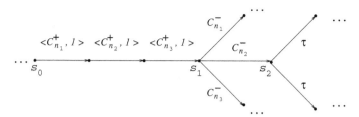

Fig. 13. Example of an IGSMP.

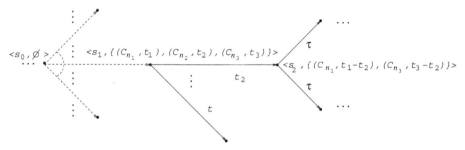

Fig. 14. Example of semantics based on residual lifetimes.

gain in advance any information about the future behavior of the system and he cannot exploit this information when resolving the nondeterministic choice in s_2.

In the following we introduce some preliminary definitions which are needed to define the semantics of IGSMPs.

Definition 14. *Given a duration probability distribution $f \in PDF^+$ and a time value $t \in \mathbb{R}^+$, we denote by $[f \mid t]$ the residual duration distribution of a clock C_n with duration distribution f which, after t time units from when it started, has not terminated yet (t is its spent lifetime). More formally, if T is a random variable with distribution f, i.e. $\forall t' \in \mathbb{R}$. $f(t') = P(T \leq t')$, then $[f \mid t]$ is the probability distribution defined as follows. For all $t' \in \mathbb{R}$ we have that:*

$$[f \mid t](t') = P(T \leq t' + t \mid T > t) \qquad \square$$

Theorem 5. *Given $f \in PDF^+$ and $t \in \mathbb{R}^+$, we have that for all $t' \in \mathbb{R}^+ \cup \{0\}$:*

$$[f \mid t](t') = \frac{f(t + t') - f(t)}{1 - f(t)} \qquad \square$$

Consider a family of probability distribution functions $f_1, \ldots, f_k \in PDF$. We denote by $\mathcal{R}(f_1, \ldots, f_k)$ the corresponding probability space over the domain $\mathbb{R}^k$ containing tuples of real values that can be sampled by $f_1, \ldots, f_k$ (sample space).

Definition 15. *Let the residual duration distribution of the set of clocks C_{n_1}, $\ldots, C_{n_k}$ in execution in an IGSMP state be $f_1, \ldots, f_k$, i.e. the probability that*

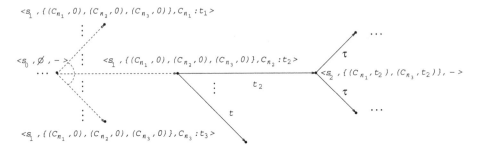

Fig. 15. Example of semantics based on spent lifetimes.

a certain tuple of residual durations $(t_1, \ldots, t_k)$ is sampled from the clocks is described by the probability space $\mathcal{R}(f_1, \ldots, f_k)$. For each $I \subseteq \{1, \ldots, k\}$ such that $|I| \geq 2$, the event $Term(I)$ of contemporaneous termination of the clocks $\{C_{n_i} \mid i \in I\}$ in execution is the following subset of the sample space $\mathbb{R}^k$:

$$Term(I) = \{(t_1, \ldots, t_k) \mid \exists t. \, (\forall i \in I. \, t_i = t) \wedge (\forall i \notin I. \, t_i > t\} \qquad \square$$

Since in an IGSMP clocks in execution in a state cannot terminate at the same time instant we have that each event $Term(I)$ of contemporaneous termination of a subset $\{C_{n_i} \mid i \in I\}$ of the clocks in execution $C_{n_1}, \ldots, C_{n_k}$ occurs with probability 0. We exploit this fact in order to reduce the domain of the probability space for a set of active clocks. In particular instead of considering the entire $\mathcal{R}(f_1, \ldots, f_k)$ we can just restrict to consider $\breve{\mathcal{R}}(f_1, \ldots, f_k)$ whose domain is $\breve{\mathbb{R}}^k = \mathbb{R}^k - \bigcup_{I \subseteq \{1,\ldots,k\}, |I| \geq 2} Term(I)$.

We are now in a position to formally define the semantics of an IGSMP.

Definition 16. The semantics of an IGSMP $\mathcal{G} = (\Sigma, \mathcal{C}, D, Act, T_+, T_-, T_a, s_0)$ is the RISTTS $[\![\mathcal{G}]\!] = (\Sigma', \mathbb{R}^+ \cup \{0\}, Act, P, T_t, T'_a, s'_0)$ where:

- $\Sigma' = (\Sigma \times Spent \times Sample)$ is the set of states of the RISTTS, where Spent, ranged over by v, is the set of partial functions from $\mathcal{C}$ to $\mathbb{R}^+ \cup \{0\}$, expressing the time already spent in execution by the clocks currently in execution in the IGSMP (clocks in the domain of Spent), and Sample, ranged over by sample, is the set $(\mathcal{C} \times (\mathbb{R}^+ \cup \{0\})) \cup \{-\}$, where a pair (C_n, t), also written $C_n : t$, denotes that the IGSMP is currently executing a set of clocks and that clock C_n has sampled the minimum residual time delay with t being the value of such a delay; while "$-$" denotes that started clocks are not under execution (e.g. the IGSMP is in a choice state or in a silent state).
- $\mathbb{R}^+ \cup \{0\}$ is the time domain: we consider continuous time.
- Act is the set of standard actions considered in the IGSMP.
- P, which associates a probability space (expressing next state probability) to some of the states in Σ', is defined to be the least partial function on Σ' satisfying the operational rules in the first part of Table 2.
- T_t is the set of timed transitions which are defined as the least relation over $\Sigma' \times (\mathbb{R}^+ \cup \{0\}) \times \Sigma'$ satisfying the operational rules in the second part of Table 2.

Table 2. Semantic rules for IGSMPs.

$$(\mathbf{P1}) \quad \frac{(\exists C_n.\ s \xrightarrow{C_n^-}) \ \wedge \ \{C_{n_1},\dots,C_{n_k}\} = dom(v)}{P(\langle s,v,-\rangle) = Sample_{s,v}^{\{n_i\}}(\ \check{\mathcal{R}}([D(C_{n_1}) \mid v(C_{n_1})],\dots,[D(C_{n_k}) \mid v(C_{n_k})])\ )}$$

$$(\mathbf{P2}) \quad \frac{(\exists C_n,w.\ s \xrightarrow{<C_n^+,w>}) \ \wedge \ Pr = \{\ (\ <C_n,s^\blacksquare>,\ w/TW(s)\ ) \mid s \xrightarrow{<C_n^+,w>} s^\blacksquare\}}{P(\langle s,v,-\rangle) = \sum_{<C_n,s'>\blacksquare\, dom(Pr)} Pr(<C_n,s^\blacksquare>)\cdot P(\langle s^\blacksquare,v\cup\{(C_n,0)\},-\rangle)}$$

$$(\mathbf{T1}) \quad \langle s,v,C_n:t\rangle \xrightarrow{t'} \langle s,v+t^\blacksquare,-\rangle \quad 0\le t^\blacksquare < t$$

$$(\mathbf{T2}) \quad \frac{s \xrightarrow{C_n^-} s^\blacksquare}{\langle s,v,C_n:t\rangle \xrightarrow{t} \langle s^\blacksquare,(v-C_n)+t,-\rangle}$$

$$(\mathbf{T3}) \quad \frac{(\not\exists\theta.\ s \xrightarrow{\theta}) \ \wedge \ s \not\xrightarrow{\ \tau\ }}{\langle s,\emptyset,-\rangle \xrightarrow{t} \langle s,\emptyset,-\rangle} \quad t\ge 0$$

$$(\mathbf{A1}) \quad \frac{s \xrightarrow{\alpha} s^\blacksquare}{\langle s,v,-\rangle \xrightarrow{\alpha} \langle s^\blacksquare,v,-\rangle} \qquad\qquad (\mathbf{A2}) \quad \frac{s \xrightarrow{a} s^\blacksquare}{\langle s,v,C_n:t\rangle \xrightarrow{a} \langle s^\blacksquare,v,-\rangle}$$

$$TW(s) = \sum\{\!\{\ w \mid \exists C_n.\ s \xrightarrow{<C_n^+,w>}\ \}\!\}$$

$$Sample_{s,v}^{\{n_i\}}(t_1,\dots,t_k) = \langle s,v,C_{n_{min}}:t_{min}\rangle$$

where min is the only index i such that: $\quad t_i = \min_{j\blacksquare\{1,\dots,k\}} t_j$

- T'_a is the set of action transitions which are defined as the least relation over $\Sigma' \times Act \times \Sigma'$ satisfying the operational rules in the third part of Table 2.
- $s'_0 = \langle s_0,\emptyset,-\rangle$ is the initial state of the RISTTS, where the IGSMP is in the initial state and no clock is in execution. □

In Table 2 we make use of the following notation. Given $v \in Spent$, we define $v - C_n$ to be the partial function obtained from v by removing C_n (and the associated value) from its domain. We define $v + t$, with $t \in \mathbb{R}^+ \cup 0$, to be the partial function obtained from v by adding t to the time value associated with each clock in the domain of v. We use the notation $\{\mathbf{n}_i\}$ to stand for $\{\mathbf{n}_i\}_{i=1\dots k}$, representing the sequence of names $n_1,\dots n_k$ (in Table 2 the length k of the sequence is always clarified by the context in which $\{\mathbf{n}_i\}$ is used). Finally in the fourth part of Table 2 we define two auxiliary functions. The function $TW : \Sigma \longrightarrow \mathbb{R}^+ \cup \{0\}$ computes the overall weight of the clock start transitions leaving a state of an IGSMP. Moreover, given a state of the IGSMP $s \in \Sigma$, a partial function mapping active clock into their spent lifetimes $v \in Spent$, and a sequence $\{n_1, \ldots, n_k\}$ of clock indexes, the function $Sample_{s,v}^{\{\mathbf{n}_i\}}$ maps a tuple $(t_1, \ldots, t_k)$ of time values sampled by clocks into the corresponding state $\langle s, v, C_{n_{\min}} : t_{\min} \rangle$ reached in the RISTTS, where min is the index of the clock which sampled the least time value. Note that function $Sample_{s,v}^{\{\mathbf{n}_i\}}$ is used in Table 2 for deriving (via induction) a probability space over the states of the RISTTS from the probability space $\check{\mathcal{R}}([D(C_{n_1}) \mid v(C_{n_1})], \ldots, [D(C_{n_k}) \mid v(C_{n_k})])$ over residual durations sampled by active clocks in a state of the IGSMP. Finally, we assume that, for every distribution f, $[f|0]$ is defined so that it yields the distribution f itself.

The following theorem shows that the semantics of well-named IGSMPs preserves weak bisimulation and is indeed compositional.

Theorem 6. *Let $\mathcal{G}'$, $\mathcal{G}''$ be two well-named IGSMPs. It holds that:*

- *If $\mathcal{G}' \approx \mathcal{G}''$ then $[\![\mathcal{G}']\!] \approx [\![\mathcal{G}'']\!]$;*
- *For each $S \subseteq Act - \{\tau\}$ we have $[\![\mathcal{G}']\!] \,\|_S [\![\mathcal{G}'']\!] \approx [\![\mathcal{G}' \,\|_S \mathcal{G}'']\!]$;*
- *For each $L \subseteq Act - \{\tau\}$ we have $[\![\mathcal{G}']\!]/L \approx [\![\mathcal{G}'/L]\!]$.* $\square$

3   Calculus of Interactive Generalized Semi-Markov Processes

In this section we introduce the calculus of Interactive Generalized Semi-Markov Processes, a stochastic process algebra which can express probabilistic timed delays with general distributions and synchronizable actions with zero duration. The calculus of *IGSMPs* is equipped with a structural operational semantics which generates semantic models in the form of well-named *IGSMPs*, the interactive extension of *GSMPs* presented in the previous Sect. 2. This is obtained by expressing the concurrent execution of delays through a simple probabilistic extension of ST semantics based on dynamic names [13]. We also show that the notion of observational congruence over *IGMSPs*, obtained by modifying weak bisimulation over *IGSMPs* (introduced in the previous Sect. 2) in the standard way [27], is a congruence for all the operators of the calculus over strongly guarded processes and we produce an axiomatization for this equivalence which is complete over finite-state strongly guarded processes.

This section is structured as follows. In Sect. 3.1 we present the basic concepts on which our approach is based. Then, in Sect. 3.2 we present the calculus of Interactive *GSMPs* and its operational semantics. Finally, in Sect. 3.3 we present the notion of observational congruence and in Sect. 3.4 its complete axiomatization.

3.1   Basic Concepts

The Basic Idea. Previous work has been done in order to try to extend the expressiveness of Markovian process algebras to probabilistic time with general distributions (see e.g. [21, 2, 29]). The main point in doing this is to understand how to define the algebra operational semantics and semantic reasoning, e.g. the definition of an adequate notion of bisimulation based equivalence. Once recognized that we have to produce a system representation like that of the IGSMP model presented in Sect. 2 when dealing with general distributions, an important issue is how to develop a calculus suitable for generating IGSMPs, so to have a fully compositional approach. The problem of developing a semantics for a process algebra with generally distributed delays (expressed, e.g., by $f._-$ prefixes, where f is a probability distribution) is essentially the problem of representing the execution of a temporal delay as the combination of a start and a termination event in such a way that pair of events derived from the execution of a delay are somehow related, e.g. by deriving a unique clock name for the delay (see Sect. 2). As we recognized in [12] such problem is not new in the literature, but exactly corresponds to consider classical *ST semantics* [20] for delays. With respect to the definition of ST semantics the "type" of a delay is simply its duration distribution f and what we observe of a system is its ability of performing delays of certain types f. In particular *identification* of delays by means of clock names is obtained if we use a technique for expressing ST semantics based on names (like the static and dynamic name techniques presented in [13]) and not, e.g., on pointers [15]. The use of such a semantics cause clock names to be generated for delays by the semantics, thus obtaining models with clocks like IGSMPs.

Another important issue to address when developing a semantics for a process algebra with generally distributed delays is how to interpret a choice "$_-$ + $_-$" between delays. Our claim (introduced in [11]) is that, while in the "Markovian world" the most natural solution is to adopt a *race policy* where the choice is solved in favor of the delay which terminates first, when we consider general distributions a convenient solution is to adopt a *preselection policy* where, first one of the delays is selected according to a probabilistic choice, and then the selected delay is executed. A justification for this claim can be found in the difference between the structure of GSMPs, where probabilistic choices are explicitly represented, and CTMCs, where probabilistic choices are implicitly expressed by races between exponential delays. For example an intuitive semantics of $f.\underline{0} + g.\underline{0}$, where f and g are generally distributed delays, should generate a GSMP like that of Fig. 16, where "i" is an auxiliary dummy element with zero duration which causes the process to leave immediately the first state[7].

The GSMP of Fig. 16 first performs a probabilistic choice between f and g (e.g. according to probabilities 0.4 and 0.6) and then executes the selected delay. This corresponds to using the *preselection policy* instead of the race policy to solve choices. Obviously we must somehow syntactically express the probability associated with delays in a choice (in the GSMP above 0.4 and 0.6 for f and g, respectively). This can be done by using delay prefixes $<f, w>._-$ in the algebra, so that the weight w determines the probability of selecting the delay. In this way the GSMP would be obtained from, e.g., $<f, 4>.\underline{0} + <g, 6>.\underline{0}$. Notably, such a preselection policy is naturally obtained from ST semantics applied to

---

[7] An equivalent representation of the GSMP of Fig. 16 which allows us to leave out the element i can be obtained by associating directly with the states labeled with δ_1 and δ_2 the probability of being the initial state.

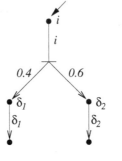

$$PDF(\delta_1) = f, \quad PDF(\delta_2) = g, \quad PDF(i) = Det(0)$$

Fig. 16. Choice of Generally Distributed Delays.

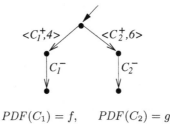

$$PDF(C_1) = f, \quad PDF(C_2) = g$$

Fig. 17. Event-Based Representation of Choice of Delays.

$<f, w>._{\_}$ prefixes by associating the weight w with the transition representing the delay start. For instance in the case of $<f, 4>.\underline{0} + <g, 6>.\underline{0}$ we would obtain the IGSMP of Fig. 17 whose performance model is the GSMP of Fig. 16.

In [21, 2, 29] efforts have been made in order to try to adapt the interleaving semantics of standard process algebras [27, 24] to deal with general distributions (similarly as already done in the simpler context of Markovian process algebras), instead of splitting delays in starting and terminating events as in the ST semantics. When doing this, the basic idea is considering actions as starting in the first state they become enabled. In order for the starting point of actions to be observable the interleaving semantics had to be enriched with additional information: in [21] transitions are enriched with *start references*, in [29] transitions are enriched with information about causality relations among actions, and in [2] actions must be differently identified with indexes before the semantic rules are applied. As a matter of fact these semantics are not actually interleaving since, even if they consider choices to be resolved with race policy, the expansion law $a.\underline{0} \parallel b.\underline{0} = a.b.\underline{0} + b.a.\underline{0}$ is no longer valid, due to the fact that distributions are not memoryless. Hence there is no advantage in trying to keep the semantics in an interleaving atomic form and to preserve the rather tricky race policy for the alternative composition operator "$\_ + \_$".

On the contrary, if we use ST semantics we also obtain an expansion law for generally distributed delays at the level of clock start and clock termination events which allow us to produce a complete axiomatization over finite-state algebraic specifications.

A Semantics for Concurrent Systems with General Distributions. The process algebra that we will consider (called calculus of IGSMPs) is an extension of a standard process algebra [27, 24] with new prefixes "$<f, w>.\_$", representing timed delays with general probability duration distribution f and associated weight w, which produces well-named IGSMPs as semantic models of its terms.

As we already explained, we define the operational semantics of a delay f through a realization of ST semantics based on names. In [13] we have introduced two name based techniques for expressing ST semantics. With the first one ST semantics is expressed by assigning *static names* to delays, i.e. names determined according to their syntactical position in the system, while in the second one we use *dynamic names*, i.e. names computed dynamically while the system evolves. When defining the semantics of the calculus of IGSMPs, we use the dynamic name technique which, with respect to the static name technique, has the advantage of generating semantic models such that ST bisimulation can be simply established via the standard notion of observational congruence [27]. In particular, the use of the dynamic name technique allows us to derive semantic models in the form of well-named IGSMPs presented in Sect. 2, for which equivalence is defined as a simple extension of probabilistic bisimulation [25] (so that existing results and tools can be exploited). On the contrary, using static names for the semantics of generally distributed delays requires a more complex definition of bisimulation which associates the names of the delays of one process with the names of the corresponding delays used by the other one.

A delay is represented in semantic models as a combination of the event of start of the delay f^+ and the event of termination of the delay f^-. Moreover, according to the dynamic name technique, we dynamically assign indexes i to delays so that the execution of a delay is represented by the two events f_i^+ and f_i^- and no confusion arises (in the connection between delay starts and delay terminations) when multiple delays with the same distribution f are concurrently executed. We resolve choices among several delays by means of preselection policy. In a choice a delay is selected with probability proportional to its associated weight. For instance $<f, w>.\underline{0} + <g, w'>.\underline{0}$ represents a system which performs a delay of distribution f with probability $w/(w + w')$ and a delay of distribution g with probability $w'/(w + w')$. Choices are expressed in semantic models by associating weights to transitions f_i^+ representing the start of a delay. With respect to the definition of well-named IGSMPs of Sect. 2, in the rest of the paper we will use "$<f_i^+, w>$" and "f_i^-" as shorthands for "$<C_{f,i}^+, w>$" and "$C_{f,i}^-$", respectively, in transition labels.

The semantics of standard actions a (including internal τ) in *IGSMP* is, instead, just the standard interleaving semantics. This reflects the fact that these actions have zero duration and can be considered as being executed atomically.

In general, the semantics of terms of the calculus of IGSMPs is simply defined via SOS by extending the standard interleaving semantics for action prefixes [27] with ST semantics via dynamic names for delay prefixes "$<f, w>$". This can be done easily with the technique introduced in [13] which is compositional. Moreover, the interrelation among the three kind of derived transitions is captured in the semantics by: (i) applying a notion of priority of delay start transitions over delay termination transitions due to the assumption that probabilistic choices are resolved urgently, and (ii) applying a notion of priority of τ transitions over time related transitions due to the maximal progress assumption. We also show that the notion of observational congruence over terms of the calculus, obtained by modifying weak bisimulation over well-named *IGSMPs* defined in Sect. 2.2 in the standard way [27], is a congruence for all the operators of the calculus over strongly guarded processes and we produce an axiomatization for this equivalence which is complete over finite-state strongly guarded processes.

3.2   The Calculus of Interactive GSMPs

Syntax of Terms and Informal Semantics of Operators. The calculus of interactive *GSMPs* is an extension of a standard process algebra with operators of CCS/CSP [27, 24] which allows us to express priority, probabilistic choices and probabilistic delays with arbitrary distributions. This is done by including into the calculus, in addition to standard actions, a special kind of actions representing delays. Delays are represented as $<f, w>$ and are characterized by a *weight* w and a *duration distribution* f. The weight $w \in \mathbb{R}^+$ determines the probability of choosing the delay in a choice among several delays. The duration distribution $f \in PDF^+$ denotes the probability distribution function of the delay duration. The possibility of expressing priority derives from the interrelation of delays and standard τ actions. In particular we make the maximal progress assumption: the system cannot wait if it has something internal to do. Therefore we assume that, in a choice, τ actions have priority over delays, i.e. $\tau.P + <f, w>.Q$ behaves as $\tau.P$.

Let Act be the set of action types as in Sect. 2.2; $TAct = \{<f, w> \mid f \in PDF^+ \wedge w \in \mathbb{R}^+\}$ be the set of delays[8]; Var be a set of process variables ranged over by X, Y, Z; and $ARFun = \{\varphi : Act \longrightarrow Act \mid \varphi(\tau) = \tau \wedge \varphi(Act - \{\tau\}) \subseteq Act - \{\tau\}\}$ be a set of *action relabeling functions*, ranged over by φ.

Definition 17. *We define the language IGSMP as the set of terms generated by:*
$$P ::= \underline{0} \mid X \mid <f, w>.P \mid \alpha.P \mid P + P \mid P/L \mid P[\varphi] \mid P \|_S P \mid recX.P$$
where $L, S \subseteq Act - \{\tau\}$. An IGSMP process is a closed term of IGSMP. We denote by $IGSMP_g$ the set of strongly guarded terms of IGSMP [9]. $\square$

"$\underline{0}$" denotes a process that cannot move. The operators "." and "+" are the CCS prefix and choice. The choice among delays is carried out through the preselection policy by giving each of them a probability proportional to its weight. Note that alternative delays are not executed concurrently, first one of

---

[8] In the following we consider f to be a shorthand for $<f, 1>$ when this is clear from the context.

[9] We consider the delay $<f, w>$ as being a guard in the definition of strong guardedness.

them is chosen probabilistically and then the selected delay is executed. Moreover τ actions have priority over delays in a choice. "$/L$" is the hiding operator which turns into τ the actions in L, "$[\varphi]$" is the relabeling operator which relabels visible actions according to φ. "$\|_S$" is the CSP parallel operator, where synchronization over actions in S is required. Finally "$recX$" denotes recursion in the usual way.

In this paper we will just consider terms of $IGSMP_g$, i.e. strongly guarded terms of our calculus. Weakly guarded processes can be dealt with by using an approach like that introduced in [5, 7].

Operational Semantics. As explained in Sect. 3.1, we employ the dynamic name technique of [13] for giving semantics to generally distributed delays f.

The problem of preserving the relationship between starts and terminations of delays arises, like in the ST semantics of standard process algebras, when several delays of the same type f are being executed in parallel. When a delay f terminates (event f^-) we need some information for establishing which event of delay start (f^+) it refers to. By using the dynamic name technique introduced in [13] this is obtained by generating a fresh name f_i for each starting delay f, where $i \in \mathbb{N}$ is the minimum index not already used by the other delays with distribution f that have started but not yet terminated, thus obtaining names for clocks in the format required by well-named IGSMPs. In particular, due to the adoption of preselection policy (see Sect. 3.1) starting events generated by delay prefixes $<f, w>$ are represented in semantic models by a transitions labeled by $<f_i^+, w>$, where i is determined as explained above. The termination of a delay prefix $<f, w>$ is simply represented by a transition labeled by f_i^-, where the "identifier" i uniquely determines which delay f is terminating.

Moreover the dynamic name technique introduced in [13] allows us to dynamically assign names to delays, according to the rule formerly described, via SOS semantics (hence in a *compositional way*) through the idea of *levelwise renaming*. In order to obtain structural compositionality it is necessary to determine at each syntactical level of a term, e.g. in the case of the parallel composition operator, the computations of $P \parallel Q$ from the computations of P and Q. This is done, as described in Sect. 2.2 when composing in parallel well-named IGSMPs, by suitably renaming delays occurring in the computations of P and Q. In particular, in the operational semantics the mapping $M \in \mathcal{M}$ recording delay renamings for a certain parallel operator (see Sect. 2.2) is expressed as an additional parameter of that parallel operator in state terms. For every delay f started by $P \parallel_{S,M} Q$, M records the association between the name f_i, generated according to the well-naming rule for identifying f at the level of $P \parallel_{S,M} Q$, and the name f_j (which in general is different from f_i), generated according to the well-naming rule for identifying the same delay f inside P (or Q). In this way when, afterwards, such a delay f terminates in P (or Q) the name f_j can be re-mapped to the correct name f_i at the level of $P \parallel_{S,M} Q$, by exploiting the information included in M. As explained in Sect. 2.2, in M the delay f of $P \parallel_{S,M} Q$ which gets index i is uniquely identified by expressing the unique name j it gets in P or in Q and the "location" of the process that executes it: *left* if P, *right* if Q. Such an association is represented inside M by the triple $f:(i, loc_j)$.

Table 3. Standard Rules.

$$\alpha.P \xrightarrow{\alpha} P$$

$$\frac{P \xrightarrow{\alpha} P^{\scriptscriptstyle\square}}{P + Q \xrightarrow{\alpha} P^{\scriptscriptstyle\square}} \qquad\qquad \frac{Q \xrightarrow{\alpha} Q^{\scriptscriptstyle\square}}{P + Q \xrightarrow{\alpha} Q^{\scriptscriptstyle\square}}$$

$$\frac{P \xrightarrow{\alpha} P^{\scriptscriptstyle\square}}{P \parallel_{S,M} Q \xrightarrow{\alpha} P^{\scriptscriptstyle\square}\parallel_{S,M} Q} \; \alpha \notin S \qquad\qquad \frac{Q \xrightarrow{\alpha} Q^{\scriptscriptstyle\square}}{P \parallel_{S,M} Q \xrightarrow{\alpha} P \parallel_{S,M} Q^{\scriptscriptstyle\square}} \; \alpha \notin S$$

$$\frac{P \xrightarrow{a} P^{\scriptscriptstyle\square} \quad Q \xrightarrow{a} Q^{\scriptscriptstyle\square}}{P \parallel_{S,M} Q \xrightarrow{a} P^{\scriptscriptstyle\square}\parallel_{S,M} Q^{\scriptscriptstyle\square}} \; a \in S$$

$$\frac{P \xrightarrow{a} P^{\scriptscriptstyle\square}}{P/L \xrightarrow{\tau} P^{\scriptscriptstyle\square}/L} \; a \in L \qquad\qquad \frac{P \xrightarrow{\alpha} P^{\scriptscriptstyle\square}}{P/L \xrightarrow{\alpha} P^{\scriptscriptstyle\square}/L} \; a \notin L$$

$$\frac{P \xrightarrow{\alpha} P^{\scriptscriptstyle\square}}{P[\varphi] \xrightarrow{\varphi(\alpha)} P^{\scriptscriptstyle\square}[\varphi]} \qquad\qquad \frac{P\{recX.P/X\} \xrightarrow{\alpha} P^{\scriptscriptstyle\square}}{recX.P \xrightarrow{\alpha} P^{\scriptscriptstyle\square}}$$

In order to define the operational semantics for the processes of *IGSMP*, we need a richer syntax to represent states. Let $TAct^+ = \{<f_i^+, w> \mid f \in PDF^+ \wedge i \in \mathbb{N}^+ \wedge w \in \mathbb{R}^+\}$ be the set of delay starts, where $<f, w>$ represents the beginning of the delay $<f, w>$ identified by i [10]. Besides let $TAct^- = \{f_i^- \mid f \in PDF^+ \wedge i \in \mathbb{N}^+\}$ be the set of delay terminations, where f_i^-, represents the termination of the delay with duration distribution f identified by i. η ranges over $Act \cup TAct \cup TAct^+ \cup TAct^-$.

The set $IGSMP_s$ of state terms of *IGSMP* is generated by:

$$P ::= \underline{0} \mid X \mid \eta.P \mid P + P \mid P/L \mid P[\varphi] \mid P \parallel_{S,M} P \mid recX.P$$

We denote by $IGSMP_{sg}$ the set of strongly guarded terms of $IGSMP_s$. We consider the operators "$\parallel_S$" occurring in a *IGSMP* term P as being "$\parallel_{S,\emptyset}$" when P is regarded as a state.

The semantics of state terms produces a transition system labeled over $Act \cup TAct^+ \cup TAct^-$, ranged over by $\gamma, \gamma', \ldots$. Such a transition system is defined as being the well-named *IGSMTS* [11] $\mathcal{G} = (IGSMP_{sg}, Act, T_+, T_-, T_a)$, where: T_a is the least subset of $IGSMP_{sg} \times Act \times IGSMP_{sg}$ satisfying the standard operational rules of Table 3, T_+ is obtained from the least multiset over $IGSMP_{sg} \times TAct^+ \times IGSMP_{sg}$ satisfying the operational rules of Table 4 (similarly to [23], we consider a transition to have arity m if and only if it can be derived in m possible ways from the operational rules) by summing the weights of the multiple occurrences

---

[10] In the following we consider f_i^+ to be a shorthand for $<f_i^+, 1>$ when this is clear from the context.

[11] We recall that we consider f_i^+ and $f_i^{\scriptscriptstyle\square}$ as being shorthands for $C_{f,i}^+$ and $C_{f,i}^{\scriptscriptstyle\square}$ in the transitions of the IGSMTS.

Table 4. Rules for Start Moves.

$$<f,w>.P \xrightarrow{<f_i^+,w>} f_i^{\square}.P \qquad\qquad <f_i^+,w>.P \xrightarrow{<f_i^+,w>} P$$

$$\frac{P \xrightarrow{<f_i^+,w>} P^{\square} \wedge Q \xrightarrow{\tau}\!\!\!\!/}{P+Q \xrightarrow{<f_i^+,w>} P^{\square}} \qquad\qquad \frac{Q \xrightarrow{<f_i^+,w>} Q^{\square} \wedge P \xrightarrow{\tau}\!\!\!\!/}{P+Q \xrightarrow{<f_i^+,w>} Q^{\square}}$$

$$\frac{P \xrightarrow{<f_i^+,w>} P^{\square} \wedge Q \xrightarrow{\tau}\!\!\!\!/}{P\|_{S,M}Q \xrightarrow{<f_{n(M_f)}^+,w>} P^{\square}\|_{S,M\square\{f:(n(M_f),l_i)\}}Q}$$

$$\frac{Q \xrightarrow{<f_i^+,w>} Q^{\square} \wedge P \xrightarrow{\tau}\!\!\!\!/}{P\|_{S,M}Q \xrightarrow{<f_{n(M_f)}^+,w>} P\|_{S,M\square\{f:(n(M_f),r_i)\}}Q^{\square}}$$

$$\frac{P \xrightarrow{<f_i^+,w>} P^{\square} \wedge \not\exists a \in L.\, P \xrightarrow{a}}{P/L \xrightarrow{<f_i^+,w>} P^{\square}/L} \qquad\qquad \frac{P \xrightarrow{<f_i^+,w>} P^{\square}}{P[\varphi] \xrightarrow{<f_i^+,w>} P^{\square}[\varphi]}$$

$$\frac{P\{recX.P/X\} \xrightarrow{<f_i^+,w>} P^{\square}}{recX.P \xrightarrow{<f_i^+,w>} P^{\square}}$$

of the same transition, and T_- is the least subset of $IGSMP_{sg} \times TAct^- \times IGSMP_{sg}$ satisfying the operational rules of Table 5. In Tables 4 and 5 we use $P \xrightarrow{a}$ to stand for $\exists P' : P \xrightarrow{a} P'$, $P \xrightarrow{\tau}\!\!\!\!/$ to stand for $\not\exists Q : P \xrightarrow{\tau} Q$ and $P \xrightarrow{<f_k^+,w>}\!\!\!\!/$ to stand for $\not\exists f,w,k,Q : P \xrightarrow{<f_k^+,w>} Q$.

The rules of Table 4 define the transitions representing the start of a delay, by taking into account the priority of "τ" actions over delays. In particular the rules for parallel composition and hiding are exactly as those defined in Sect. 2.2.

The rules of Table 5 define the transitions representing the termination of a delay, by taking into account the priority of "τ" actions over delay related transitions and the priority of delay starts over delay terminations. In particular the rules for parallel composition and hiding are exactly as those defined in Sect. 2.2.

Note that even if the operational rules in Tables 4 and 5 include negative premises, this does not cause inconsistencies because when applying such rules for deriving the moves of a term P, the negative premises always refer to the moves of a subterm of P (and not of P itself), hence the operational semantics is stratifiable.

Table 5. Rules for Termination Moves.

$$f_i^\square . P \xrightarrow{f_i^-} P$$

$$\frac{P \xrightarrow{f_i^-} P^\square \wedge Q \xrightarrow{\tau} \not\rightarrow \wedge Q \xrightarrow{<f_k^+,w>} \not\rightarrow}{P + Q \xrightarrow{f_i^-} P^\square} \qquad \frac{Q \xrightarrow{f_i^-} Q^\square \wedge P \xrightarrow{\tau} \not\rightarrow \wedge P \xrightarrow{<f_k^+,w>} \not\rightarrow}{P + Q \xrightarrow{f_i^-} Q^\square}$$

$$\frac{P \xrightarrow{f_i^-} P^\square \wedge Q \xrightarrow{\tau} \not\rightarrow \wedge Q \xrightarrow{<f_k^+,w>} \not\rightarrow}{P \parallel_{S,M} Q \xrightarrow{f_j^-} P^\square \parallel_{S,M_\square \{f:(j,l_i)\}} Q} \quad f:(j,l_i) \in M$$

$$\frac{Q \xrightarrow{f_i^-} Q^\square \wedge P \xrightarrow{\tau} \not\rightarrow \wedge P \xrightarrow{<f_k^+,w>} \not\rightarrow}{P \parallel_{S,M} Q \xrightarrow{f_j^-} P \parallel_{S,M_\square \{f:(j,r_i)\}} Q^\square} \quad f:(j,r_i) \in M$$

$$\frac{P \xrightarrow{f_i^-} P^\square \wedge \not\exists a \in L. P \xrightarrow{a}}{P/L \xrightarrow{f_i^-} P^\square/L} \qquad \frac{P \xrightarrow{f_i^-} P^\square}{P[\varphi] \xrightarrow{f_i^-} P^\square[\varphi]}$$

$$\frac{P\{recX.P/X\} \xrightarrow{f_i^-} P^\square}{recX.P \xrightarrow{f_i^-} P^\square}$$

We are now in a position to define the well-named *IGSMP* obtained as the semantic model of a process of the calculus.

Definition 18. *The semantic model $\mathcal{G}[\![P]\!]$ of $P \in IGSMP_g$ is the well-named IGSMP defined by $\mathcal{G}[\![P]\!] = (S_P, Act, T_{+,P}, T_{-,P}, T_{a,P}, P)$, where:*

- S_P *is the least subset of $IGSMP_{sg}$ such that:*
  - $P \in S_P$
  - *if $P' \in S_P$ and $P' \xrightarrow{\gamma} P''$, then $P'' \in S_P$*
- $T_{+,P}, T_{-,P}$ *and $T_{a,P}$ are the restriction of T_+, T_- and T_a to $S_P \times Act \times S_P$, $S_P \times TAct^+ \times S_P$ and $S_P \times TAct^- \times S_P$.* □

Example 6. In Fig. 18 we depict the semantic model of $recX.f.X \parallel_\emptyset recX.f.X$. As expected, we obtain the same well-named IGSMP as that derived in Sect. 2 via parallel composition of two well-named IGSMPs that repeatedly execute f delays (see Fig. 9). □

In the following theorem, where we consider "P/L", "$P[\varphi]$", and "$P \parallel_S P$" to be *static* operators [27], we show that finite semantic models are obtained for a wide class of recursive systems.

Theorem 7. *Let P be a $IGSMP_g$ process such that for each subterm $recX.Q$ of P, X does not occur free in Q in the context of a static operator. Then P is a finite state process.*

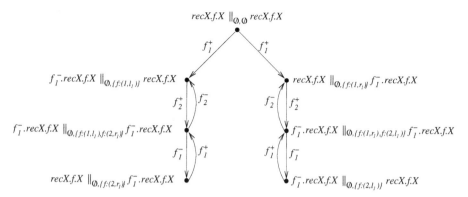

Fig. 18. Example of recursive system.

Note that the class of processes considered in this corollary includes strictly the class of *nets of automata*, i.e. terms where no static operator occurs in the scope of any recursion.

3.3 Observational Congruence for IGSMP

In this section we introduce the notion of observational congruence over $IGSMP_{sg}$ processes, and we will show it to be a congruence with respect to all the operators of our calculus. Such a notion is defined, starting from the notion of weak bisimulation over Well-Named IGSMPs we defined in Sect. 2.2, according to the classical notion of observational congruence [27] and probabilistic bisimulation [25]. In the definition of observational congruence we make use of function TW defined in Sect. 2.2.

Definition 19. *Two closed terms P, Q of $IGSMP_{sg}$ are observational congruent, written $P \simeq Q$, iff:*

- *for every $\sigma \in NPAct$ and $P' \in IGSMP_{sg}$,*
  $P \xrightarrow{\sigma} P'$ *implies* $Q \xRightarrow{\sigma} Q'$ *for some Q' with $P' \approx Q'$,*
- *for every $\sigma \in NPAct$ and $Q' \in IGSMP_{sg}$,*
  $Q \xrightarrow{\sigma} Q'$ *implies* $P \xRightarrow{\sigma} P'$ *for some P' with $P' \approx Q'$,*
- *for every $f \in PDF^+$ and equivalence class I of β,*
  $TW(P, f, I) = TW(Q, f, I)$ □

We consider $\simeq$ as being defined also on the open terms of $IGSMP_{sg}$ by extending observational congruence with the standard approach of [27].

Theorem 8. $\simeq$ *is a congruence w.r.t. all the operators of IGSMP, including recursion.*

3.4 Axiomatization

In this section we present an axiom system which is complete for $\simeq$ on finite state $IGSMP_{sg}$ terms.

$(A1)$	$P + Q = Q + P$	$(A2)$	$(P + Q) + R = P + (Q + R)$
$(A3)$	$\alpha.P + \alpha.P = \alpha.P$	$(A4)$	$P + \underline{0} = P$

$(Tau1)$	$\gamma.\tau.P = \gamma.P$	$(Tau2)\ \ P + \tau.P = \tau.P$
$(Tau3)$	$\alpha.(P + \tau.Q) + \alpha.Q = \alpha.(P + \tau.Q)$	

$(TAct)\quad <f,w>.P = <f_1^+,w>.f_1^{\blacksquare}.P$

$(Prob)\quad <f_i^+,w>.P + <f_i^+,w^{\blacksquare}>.P = <f_i^+,w + w^{\blacksquare}>.P$

$(Pri1)\ \ \tau.P + \theta.Q = \tau.P \qquad (Pri2)\ \ <f_i^+,w>.P + g_j^{\blacksquare}.Q = <f_i^+,w>.P$

$(Hi1)$	$\underline{0}/L = \underline{0}$	$(Hi2)$	$(\gamma.P)/L = \gamma.(P/L)\qquad \gamma \notin L$
$(Hi3)$	$(a.P)/L = \tau.(P/L)\quad a \in L$	$(Hi4)$	$(P + Q)/L = P/L + Q/L$

$(Rel1)$	$\underline{0}[\varphi] = \underline{0}$	$(Rel2)$	$(\alpha.P)[\varphi] = \varphi(\alpha).(P[\varphi])$
$(Rel3)$	$(\theta.P)[\varphi] = \theta.(P[\varphi])$	$(Rel4)$	$(P + Q)[\varphi] = P[\varphi] + Q[\varphi]$

$(Par)\quad P \parallel_{S,M} Q = P \parallel\!\!\!\perp_{S,M} Q + Q \parallel\!\!\!\perp_{S,\overline{M}} P + P \mid_{S,M} Q$

$(LM1)$	$\underline{0} \parallel\!\!\!\perp_{S,M} P = \underline{0}$	
$(LM2)$	$(a.P) \parallel\!\!\!\perp_{S,M} Q = \underline{0}$	$a \in S$
$(LM3)$	$(\alpha.P) \parallel\!\!\!\perp_{S,M} Q = \alpha.(P \parallel_{S,M} Q)$	$\alpha \notin S$
$(LM4)$	$(<f_i^+,w>.P) \parallel\!\!\!\perp_{S,M} Q = <f_{n(M_f)}^+,w>.(P \parallel_{S,M\blacksquare\{f:(n(M_f),l_i)\}} Q)$	
$(LM5)$	$(f_i^{\blacksquare}.P) \parallel\!\!\!\perp_{S,M} Q = f_j^{\blacksquare}.(P \parallel_{S,M\blacksquare\{f:(j,l_i)\}} Q)$	$f:(j,l_i) \in M$
$(LM6)$	$(P + Q) \parallel\!\!\!\perp_{S,M} R = P \parallel\!\!\!\perp_{S,M} R + Q \parallel\!\!\!\perp_{S,M} R$	

$(SM1)$	$P \mid_{S,M} Q = Q \mid_{S,M} P$	
$(SM2)$	$\underline{0} \mid_{S,M} P = \underline{0}$	
$(SM3)$	$(\gamma.P) \mid_{S,M} (\gamma^{\blacksquare}.Q) = \underline{0}$	$(\gamma \notin S \ \vee\ \gamma \neq \gamma^{\blacksquare}) \wedge \tau \notin \{\gamma,\gamma^{\blacksquare}\}$
$(SM4)$	$(\tau.P) \mid_{S,M} Q = P \mid_{S,M} Q$	
$(SM5)$	$(a.P) \mid_{S,M} (a.Q) = a.(P \parallel_{S,M} Q)$	$a \in S$
$(SM6)$	$(P + Q) \mid_{S,M} R = P \mid_{S,M} R + Q \mid_{S,M} R$	

$(Rec1)$	$recX.P = recY.(P\{Y/X\})$ provided that Y is not free in $recX.P$
$(Rec2)$	$recX.P = P\{recX.P/X\}$
$(Rec3)$	$Q = P\{Q/X\} \Rightarrow Q = recX.P$ provided that X is strongly guarded in P

Fig. 19. Axiomatization for IGSMP.

The axiom system $\mathcal{A}_{IGSMP}$ for $\simeq$ on $IGSMP_{sg}$ terms is formed by the axioms presented in Fig. 19. In this figure "$\parallel\!\!\!\perp$" and "$\mid$" denote, respectively, the left merge and synchronization merge operators. Moreover θ ranges over $TAct^+ \cup TAct^-$. We recall from Sect. 3.2 that $\gamma, \gamma', \ldots$ range over $Act \cup TAct^+ \cup TAct^-$.

The axioms $(Pri1)$ and $(Pri2)$ express the two kinds of priorities of $IGSMP$, respectively, priority of τ actions over (semi-)delays and priority of delay starts over delay terminations. The axiom (Par) is the standard one except that when the position of processes P and Q is exchanged we must invert left and right inside M. The inverse $\overline{M}$ of a mapping M is defined by $\overline{M} = \{f : (i, r_j) \mid f : (i, l_j) \in M\} \cup \{f : (i, l_j) \mid f : (i, r_j) \in M\}$. Axioms $(LM4)$ and $(LM5)$ just reflect the operational rules of the parallel operator for a delay move of the left-hand process. The axioms $(Rec1 - 3)$ handle strongly guarded recursion in the standard way [27].

If we consider the obvious operational rules for "$\|_{S,M}$" and "$|_{S,M}$" that derive from those we presented for the parallel operator[12] then the axioms of $\mathcal{A}_{IGSMP}$ are sound.

A sequential state is defined to be one which includes "0", "X" and operators "$.$", "$+$", "$recX$" only; leading to the following theorem.

Theorem 9. *If an IGSMP$_{sg}$ process P is finite state, then $\exists P' : \mathcal{A}_{IGSMP} \vdash P = P'$ with P' sequential state.*

For sequential states the axioms of $\mathcal{A}_{IGSMP}$ involved are just the standard axioms of [27], and the axioms for priority and probabilistic choice. From Theorem 9 we derive the completeness of $\mathcal{A}_{IGSMP}$.

Theorem 10. $\mathcal{A}_{IGSMP}$ *is complete for $\simeq$ over finite state IGSMP$_{sg}$ processes.*

Example 7. Let us consider the system $recX.f.X \|_{\emptyset} recX.f.X$ of the previous Example 6. In the following we show how this process can be turned into a sequential process. In the following we let f_i^+ stand for $<f_i^+, 1>$ and we abbreviate $\mathcal{A}_{IGSMP} \vdash P = Q$ with $P = Q$. Moreover we let $P \equiv recX.f.X$ and $P' \equiv f_1^-.recX.f.X$. We note that $P = f.recX.f.X = f_1^+.f_1^-.recX.f.X$, by applying $(Rec2)$ and $(TAct)$. In a first phase, we start with the initial state $P \|_{\emptyset,\emptyset} P$ and we express each state in terms of states it may reach after a single prefix. We have:

$$P \|_{\emptyset,\emptyset} P = f_1^+.(P' \|_{\emptyset,\{f:(1,l_1)\}} P) + f_1^+.(P' \|_{\emptyset,\{f:(1,l_1)\}} P)$$

by applying (Par), $(LM4)$ and $(SM3)$. From this equation we derive:

$$P \|_{\emptyset,\emptyset} P = <f_1^+, 2>.(P' \|_{\emptyset,\{f:(1,l_1)\}} P)$$

by applying $(Prob)$. Then, we have:

$$P' \|_{\emptyset,\{f:(1,l_1)\}} P = f_2^+.(P' \|_{\emptyset,\{f:(1,l_1),f:(2,r_1)\}} P')$$

by applying (Par), $(LM4)$, $(LM5)$, $(SM3)$ and $(Pri2)$. Then, we have:

$$P' \|_{\emptyset,\{f:(1,l_1),f:(2,r_1)\}} P' = f_1^-.(P \|_{\emptyset,\{f:(2,r_1)\}} P') + f_2^-.(P \|_{\emptyset,\{f:(1,r_1)\}} P')$$

by applying (Par), $(LM5)$ and $(SM3)$. From this equation we derive:

$$P' \|_{\emptyset,\{f:(1,l_1),f:(2,r_1)\}} P' = f_1^-.(P \|_{\emptyset,\{f:(2,r_1)\}} P') + f_2^-.(P' \|_{\emptyset,\{f:(1,l_1)\}} P)$$

by applying (Par), $(A1)$ and $(SM1)$ to $P \|_{\emptyset,\{f:(1,r_1)\}} P'$. Finally we have:

$$P \|_{\emptyset,\{f:(2,r_1)\}} P' = f_1^+.(P' \|_{\emptyset,\{f:(1,l_1),f:(2,r_1)\}} P')$$

by applying (Par), $(LM4)$, $(LM5)$, $(SM3)$ and $(Pri2)$. Now we perform a second phase where we generate recursive processes and we substitute states with equivalent terms. We start with $P \|_{\emptyset,\{f:(2,r_1)\}} P'$. Since the state itself does not occur in its equivalent term we do not have to generate any recursion. Substituting the state with its equivalent term in the other equations generates the new equation:

---

[12] The definition of the operational rule for "$|_{S,M}$" must allow for actions "τ" to be skipped [1], as reflected by axiom $(SM4)$.

$$P' \parallel_{\emptyset, \{f:(1,l_1), f:(2,r_1)\}} P' =$$
$$f_1^- . f_1^+ . (P' \parallel_{\emptyset, \{f:(1,l_1), f:(2,r_1)\}} P') + f_2^- . (P' \parallel_{\emptyset, \{f:(1,l_1)\}} P).$$

Then we consider the state $P' \parallel_{\emptyset, \{f:(1,l_1), f:(2,r_1)\}} P'$. Since the state itself indeed occurs in its equivalent term, we have to change its equation by generating a recursion as follows:

$$P' \parallel_{\emptyset, \{f:(1,l_1), f:(2,r_1)\}} P' = recY.(f_1^- . f_1^+ . Y + f_2^- . (P' \parallel_{\emptyset, \{f:(1,l_1)\}} P)).$$

Substituting the state with its equivalent term in the remaining equations generates the new equation:

$$P' \parallel_{\emptyset, \{f:(1,l_1)\}} P = f_2^+ . recY.(f_1^- . f_1^+ . Y + f_2^- . (P' \parallel_{\emptyset, \{f:(1,l_1)\}} P)).$$

Now we consider the state $P' \parallel_{\emptyset, \{f:(1,l_1)\}} P$. We change its equation by generating a recursion as follows:

$$P' \parallel_{\emptyset, \{f:(1,l_1)\}} P = recX.(f_2^+ . recY(f_1^- . f_1^+ . Y + f_2^- . X)).$$

Substituting the state with its equivalent term in the remaining equations generates the new equation:

$$P \parallel_{\emptyset, \emptyset} P = <f_1^+, 2>.recX.(f_2^+ . recY(f_1^- . f_1^+ . Y + f_2^- . X)).$$

Therefore we have turned our initial system $recX.f.X \parallel_{\emptyset} recX.f.X$ into the recursive sequential process $<f_1^+, 2>.recX.(f_2^+ . recY(f_1^- . f_1^+ . Y + f_2^- . X))$. Note that the operational semantics of this process generates the labeled transition system of Fig. 10 derived in Sect. 2 as the minimal version of the IGSMP in Fig. 18.   □

4   Example: Queuing Systems G/G/1/q

In this section we present an example of specification with *IGSMP*. In particular we concentrate on Queuing Systems (*QSs*) $G/G/1/q$, i.e. *QSs* which have one server and a FIFO queue with q-1 seats and serve a population of unboundedly many customers. In particular the *QS* has an interarrival time which is generally distributed with distribution f and a service time which is generally distributed with distribution g.

Such a system can be modeled with the calculus of *IGSMPs* as follows. Let a be the action representing the fact that a new customer arrives at the queue of the service center, d be the action representing that a customer is delivered by the queue to the server. The process algebra specification is the following one[13]:

- $QS_{G/G/1/q} \overset{\Delta}{=} Arrivals \parallel_{\{a\}} (Queue_0 \parallel_{\{d\}} Server)$

  - $Arrivals \overset{\Delta}{=} f.a.Arrivals$

---

[13] In the specification we use process constants instead of the operator "$recX$", to denote recursion. The reason being that the use of constants is suitable for doing specifications, while the use of operator "$recX$" is preferable when dealing with axiomatizations. The two constructs are shown to be completely equivalent in [27].

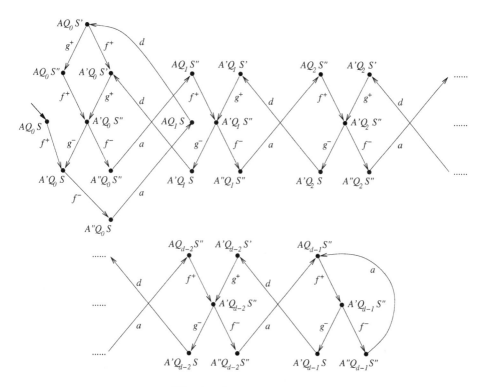

Fig. 20. Semantic Model.

- $Queue_0 \overset{\Delta}{=} a.Queue_1$

  $Queue_h \overset{\Delta}{=} a.Queue_{h+1} + d.Queue_{h-1}$ $\qquad$ $0 < h < q - 1$

  $Queue_{q-1} \overset{\Delta}{=} a.Queue_{q-1} + d.Queue_{q-2}$
- $Server \overset{\Delta}{=} d.g.Server$

We have specified the whole system as the composition of the arrival process, the queue and the server which communicate via action types a and d. Then we have separately modeled the arrival process, the queue, and the server. As a consequence if we want to modify the description by changing the interarrival time distribution f or the service time distribution g, only component *Arrivals* or *Server* needs to be modified while component *Queue* is not affected. Note that the role of actions a and d is defining interactions among the different system components. Such actions have zero duration and they are neglected from the performance viewpoint.

In Fig. 20 we show $\mathcal{G}[\![QS_{G/G/1/q}]\!]$. In this picture A stands for *Arrivals*, A' stands for $f^-.a.Arrivals$, A'' stands for $a.Arrivals$. Similarly, S stands for *Server*, S' stands for $g.Server$, S'' stands for $g^-.Server$. Moreover, Q_h stands for $Queue_h$, for any h. We omit parallel composition operators in terms, so, e.g., AQ_hS stands for $Arrivals \parallel_{\{a\}} (Queue_h \parallel_{\{d\}} Server)$.

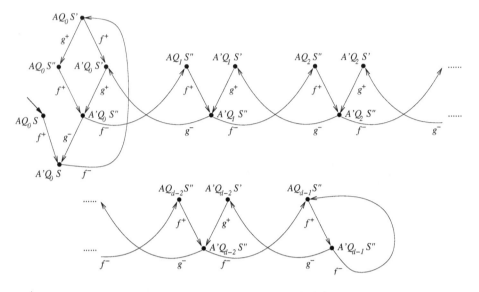

Fig. 21. Minimal Semantic Model.

In order to derive the performance model of the system $QS_{G/G/1/q}$ we have to make sure that it is complete both from the interaction and the performance viewpoints. In Fig. 20 we have visible actions a and d, therefore the behavior of the system can be influenced by interaction with the environment and is not complete. We make it complete by considering $QS_{G/G/1/q}/\{a,d\}$ so that every action in the semantic model of Fig. 20 becomes a τ action. As far as completeness w.r.t. performance is concerned, we present in Fig. 21 the minimal version of $\mathcal{G}[\![QS_{G/G/1/q}/\{a,d\}]\!]$, obtained by aggregating weakly bisimilar states (see Sect. 3.3). Since in the minimal model there are no longer internal τ actions, we have that our system is complete also w.r.t. performance.

By applying the procedure described in Sect. 2.3, hence by solving choice trees in the minimal model of Fig. 21, we finally obtain the *GSMP* of Fig. 22. The elements e_1 and e_2 represent the delays f and g.

5   Conclusion

In this paper we have presented the calculus and the model of Interactive Generalised Semi-Markov Processes. Such a specification language, together with its associated weak bisimulation based theory, constitutes a solid formal basis for specifying and analyzing concurrent/distributed systems with probabilistic generally distributed time, i.e. systems with real-time and stochastic time aspects. As far as system analysis is concerned, we showed that it is possible to derive from complete IGSMP specifications the underlying stochastic process in the form of a GSMP which can be analyzed with standard simulative or analytical techniques. In [6, 5, 8] we also show that from an IGSMP specification it is possi-

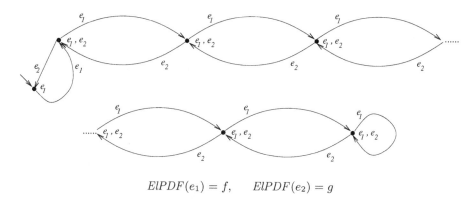

$$ElPDF(e_1) = f, \quad ElPDF(e_2) = g$$

Fig. 22. Derived GSMP.

ble to derive: (i) a pure real-time specification in the form of a timed automata (by considering distribution supports only, thus loosing stochastic quantification over possible time values); and (ii) a pure Markovian specification in the form of a term of a Markovian process algebra (by approximating general distributions with phase-type distributions, thus loosing real-time constraints over time values).

As far as related work is concerned, several algebraic languages which express generally distributed durations like the calculus of *IGSMPs* have been developed. The languages that are closest to *IGSMP*, in that they produce semantic models which represent probabilistic durations via clocks/elements as in *GSMPs* are those of [2, 18]. Conceptually, they somehow correspond to different techniques for dealing with ST semantics. With the language of [2], performance models are derived from terms specifying systems by applying to them a preliminary procedure that gives a different name to each durational action of the term. In this way, each name represents a different clock in the semantic model of the system. In the approach of [2] the events of action starts are not explicitly expressed in the semantic models and choices are resolved via the race policy (alternative actions are executed in parallel and the first action that terminates wins) instead of the preselection policy as in *IGSMP*. The approach of [18], which has been developed concurrently with our work on general distributions (the first papers [19] and [11] on the two approaches appeared at the same workshop), is the most similar to ours. The language presented in [18] is endowed with an abstract semantics which may generate finite intermediate semantic models. With this language clock names must be explicitly expressed in the term that specify the system and the fact that a different name is used for each clock is ensured by alpha-converting clock names while deriving the semantic model similarly as with ST semantics (but no static/dynamic rule is defined for generating clock names). As in *IGSMP* the execution of a clock is represented by the events of clock start and clock termination, but here these two events must be explicitly expressed in the term specifying a system and they are not automatically generated by the operational semantics. Moreover, in the language of [18] choices among clock executions (pairs of start and termination events) are resolved via the race policy instead of the preselection policy as in *IGSMP* and probabilistic choices (which are a basic ingredient of *GSMPs*) cannot be expressed. A drawback of the approaches of [2, 18] w.r.t. the calculus of *IGSMP* is that there is no easy way to express equivalence of systems, hence to produce congruence results and axiomatizations. This is because in order to establish the equivalence of two systems it is necessary to associate in some way the names of the clocks used by one system with the names of the corresponding clocks used by the other one (the same phenomenon that happens when ST semantics is expressed via a static technique). In *IGSMP*, instead, names of clocks are dynamically generated by the operational semantics with a fixed rule. In this way equivalent systems get the same names for clocks and there is no need to associate names of clocks for establishing equivalence. We can, therefore, rely on standard (probabilistic) bisimulation and we have the opportunity to reuse existing results and tools.

References

1. L. Aceto, *"On "Axiomatising Finite Concurrent Processes" "* in SIAM Journal on Computing 23(4):852-863, 1994
2. M. Ajmone Marsan, A. Bianco, L. Ciminiera, R. Sisto, A. Valenzano, *"A LOTOS Extension for the Performance Analysis of Distributed Systems"*, in IEEE/ACM Trans. on Networking 2:151-164, 1994
3. R. Alur, C. Courcoubetis, D. Dill *"Model-Checking in Dense Real-Time"*, in Information and Computation 104:2-34, 1993
4. M. Bernardo, *"Theory and Application of Extended Markovian Process Algebra"*, Ph.D. Thesis, University of Bologna (Italy), 1999
5. M. Bravetti, *"Specification and Analysis of Stochastic Real-Time Systems"*, Ph.D. Thesis, University of Bologna (Italy), 2002.
   Available at http://www.cs.unibo.it/~bravetti
6. M. Bravetti, *"Towards the Integration of Real-Time and Probabilistic-Time Process Algebras"*, in Proc. of the *3rd European Research Seminar on Advances in Distributed Systems (ERSADS '99)*, Madeira Island (Portugal), April 1999
7. M. Bravetti, *"Revisiting Interactive Markov Chains"*, in Proc. of the *3rd Int. Workshop on Models for Time-Critical Systems (MTCS 2002)*, ENTCS 68(5), Brno (Czech Republic), August 2002
8. M. Bravetti, *"An Integrated Approach for the Specification and Analysis of Stochastic Real-Time Systems"*, in Proc. of the *3rd Int. Workshop on Models for Time-Critical Systems (MTCS 2002)*, ENTCS 68(5), Brno (Czech Republic), August 2002
9. M. Bravetti, A. Aldini, *"Non-Determinism in Probabilistic Timed Systems with General Distributions"*, in Proc. of the *2nd Int. Workshop on Models for Time-Critical Systems (MTCS 2001)*, ENTCS 52(3), Aalborg (Denmark), August 2001
10. M. Bravetti, M. Bernardo, *"Compositional Asymmetric Cooperations for Process Algebras with Probabilities, Priorities, and Time"*, in Proc. of the *1st Int. Workshop on Models for Time-Critical Systems (MTCS 2000)*, ENTCS 39(3), State College (PA), 2000

11. M. Bravetti, M. Bernardo, R. Gorrieri, *"From EMPA to GSMPA: Allowing for General Distributions"*, in Proc. of the *5th Int. Workshop on Process Algebras and Performance Modeling (PAPM '97)*, E. Brinksma and A. Nymeyer editors, pp. 17-33, Enschede (The Netherlands), June 1997

12. M. Bravetti, M. Bernardo, R. Gorrieri, *"Towards Performance Evaluation with General Distributions in Process Algebras"*, in Proc. of the *9th Int. Conf. on Concurrency Theory (CONCUR '98)*, D. Sangiorgi and R. de Simone editors, LNCS 1466:405-422, Nice (France), September 1998

13. M. Bravetti, R. Gorrieri, *"Deciding and Axiomatizing Weak ST Bisimulation for a Process Algebra with Recursion and Action Refinement"*, in ACM Transactions on Computational Logic 3(4): 465-520 (2002)

14. M. Bravetti, R. Gorrieri, *"The Theory of Interactive Generalized Semi-Markov Processes"*, in Theoretical Computer Science 282(1): 5-32 (2002)

15. N. Busi, R.J. van Glabbeek, R. Gorrieri, *"Axiomatising ST-Bisimulation Equivalence"*, in Proc. of the *IFIP Working Conf. on Programming Concepts, Methods and Calculi (PROCOMET '94)*, pp. 169-188, S. Miniato (Italy), 1994

16. C.G. Cassandras, *"Discrete Event Systems. Modeling and Performance Analysis"*, Aksen Associates, Irwin, 1993

17. D.R. Cox, *"The Analysis of non-Markovian Stochastic Processes by the Inclusion of Supplementary Variables"*, in Proc. of the Cambridge Philosophical Society 51:433-440, 1955

18. P.R. D'Argenio, *"Algebras and Automata for Timed and Stochastic Systems"*, Ph.D. Thesis, Univ. Twente, 1997

19. P.R. D'Argenio, J.-P. Katoen, E. Brinksma, *"A Stochastic Automata Model and its Algebraic Approach"* in Proc. of the *5th Workshop on Process Algebras and Performance Modelling (PAPM '97)*, pp. 1-16, Enschede (The Netherlands), 1997

20. R.J. van Glabbeek, F.W. Vaandrager, *"Petri Net Models for Algebraic Theories of Concurrency"*, in Proc. of the *Conf. on Parallel Architectures and Languages Europe (PARLE '87)*, LNCS 259:224-242, Eindhoven (The Netherlands), 1987

21. N. Götz, U. Herzog, M. Rettelbach, *"TIPP - A Stochastic Process Algebra"*, in Proc. of the *1st Workshop on Process Algebras and Performance Modelling (PAPM '93)*, pp. 31-36, Edinburgh (UK), 1993

22. H. Hermanns, *"Interactive Markov Chains"*, Ph.D. Thesis, Universität Erlangen-Nürnberg (Germany), 1998

23. J. Hillston, *"A Compositional Approach to Performance Modelling"*, Cambridge University Press, 1996

24. C.A.R. Hoare, *"Communicating Sequential Processes"*, Prentice Hall, 1985

25. K.G. Larsen, A. Skou, *"Bisimulation through Probabilistic Testing"*, in Information and Computation 94:1-28, 1991

26. K. Matthes, *"Zur Theorie der Bedienungsprozesse"*, in Trans. of the *3rd Prague Conf. on Information Theory, Stat. Dec. Fns. and Random Processes*, pp. 513-528, 1962

27. R. Milner, *"Communication and Concurrency"*, Prentice Hall, 1989

28. X. Nicollin, J. Sifakis, S. Yovine, *"Compiling Real-Time Specifications into Extended Automata"*, in IEEE Trans. on Software Engineering, 18(9):794-804, 1992

29. C. Priami, *"Stochastic π-Calculus with General Distributions"*, in Proc. of the *4th Workshop on Process Algebras and Performance Modelling (PAPM '96)*, CLUT, pp. 41-57, Torino (Italy), 1996

On the Semantic Foundations of Standard UML 2.0

Bran V. Selic

IBM Distinguished Engineer
IBM Rational Software Canada
bselic@ca.ibm.com

Abstract. This paper provides an overview of the foundations of the run-time semantics underlying the Unified Modeling Language as defined in revision 2.0 of the official OMG standard. One of the problems with the format used for that standard is that the information relating to semantics is scattered throughout the text making it difficult to obtain a global understanding of how the various fragments fit together. This has led many to incorrectly conclude that UML has little or no semantic content. One of the objectives of this paper is to provide a clear and concise description of the structure and essential content of UML run-time semantics. This can serve as a convenient starting point for researchers who want to work on the problem of UML semantics and, in particular, those who are interested in producing formal models of those semantics.

1 Introduction

An oft-repeated criticism of UML is that it has "no semantics"; that it is primarily a visual notation whose graphical constructs can be interpreted more or less according to whim. One objective of this paper is to dispel such unwarranted criticisms by explaining the structure and content of the semantic foundations that underlie UML based on the most recent revision of the official standard (UML 2.0).

The term "semantics" as used in this paper refers to the run-time interpretations of UML models, that is, the structural entities and behaviors that are represented by the different modeling concepts of UML. For some, the only acceptable definitions of language semantics are ones that are expressed in some well-known *mathematical* formalism, such as Z or CSP. In fact, it is often argued that an accepted mathematical formalism should be the starting point for defining a language, since that greatly increases the likelihood that the semantics will be clean, consistent, and amenable to formal analysis. Computer languages such as Lisp are often cited as successful examples of this approach. However, when it comes to modeling languages such as UML, this may not be the most suitable approach.

This is because UML is intended to model complete systems across a broad spectrum of different application domains. Such models typically go beyond modeling just software and computation. For example, in the analysis and design of real-time and embedded software systems, it may be necessary to model the behavior of some real-world physical entity such as a hardware device or human user. In general, physical things tend to be highly diverse and much more complex than most mathematical formalisms can handle.

An additional consideration related to formal models, is that it is often the case that the same entity may need to be modeled from different viewpoints related to different

M. Bernardo and F. Corradini (Eds.): SFM-RT 2004, LNCS 3185, pp. 181–199, 2004.

sets of concerns. For example, modeling system users from the perspective of performance (e.g., inter-arrival times) is very different than modeling them from the point of view of human-computer interaction.

This suggests that basing UML on any specific concrete mathematical formalism would likely severely hamper one of its primary objectives: to unify a set of broadly applicable modeling mechanisms in a common conceptual framework. This aspect of UML must not be underrated and is one of the key factors behind its widespread adoption. The commonality that it provides makes it possible to use the same tools, techniques, knowledge, and experience in a variety of different domains and situations.

This is not to say that UML is incompatible with formalization. On the contrary – it is crucial that suitable formal representation of its semantics be defined for all the good reasons that such representations provide and in particular because it is one of the keystones of the MDA initiative [4]. In fact, another key objective of this paper is precisely to encourage the development of suitable formalizations of UML by providing a clear specification of what needs to be formalized.

There have already been numerous notable efforts to formally define the run-time semantics of UML (e.g., [2] [3] [12]). However, most of them only cover subsets of UML and are usually only loosely based on the semantics defined in the official UML standard specifications [6] [8] [7].

One problem shared by some of these efforts is that, because they are constructed for a specific purpose or domain, they tend to define a single concrete semantics. This immediately puts them in conflict with the broad scope of UML noted above. In essence, standard UML is the foundation for a "family" of related modeling languages[1]. This means that any formal semantics definition of standard UML should provide the same kind of latitude for different interpretations as the standard itself. In effect, a formalized semantics of standard UML should define a *semantic envelope* of possible concrete semantics.

A major impediment to any kind of formalization of UML semantics is that the standard documents do not cover the semantic aspects in a focused fashion. Instead, due to the idiosyncrasies of the format used for standards, the material is scattered throughout the documents, making it very difficult to develop a consistent global picture[2]. In addition, the standard omits much of the rationale and historical background that is required for a full understanding of these aspects[3]. To rectify these shortcomings, this paper provides a concise synthesized view of the structure, content, and rationale of the run-time semantics defined in the standard.

The following section starts this off with a high-level view of the semantics definitions of standard UML and their relationships. It includes an informal description of the UML view of cause-and-effect relationships that sit at the core of any dynamic semantics specification. The more substantive exploration starts in section 3, which describes the structural semantic foundations. This is followed by a description of the behavioral semantic base in section 4. This base is shared by all the different higher-

---

[1] The term "family of languages" for describing UML was first used by Steve Cook.

[2] To a certain extent, this fragmentation has had a negative impact on the actual definition of the semantics leading to minor inconsistencies and omissions. This issue is discussed further in section 5.

[3] In software, as with most things, it is often useful to know the history of how ideas evolved to fully understand them. Unfortunately, this is often unrecognized in technical cultures.

level behavioral paradigms of UML (e.g., state machines, activities). To assist those interested in a more detailed understanding, section 5 provides a guide that identifies where the various semantic elements described in the paper are located in the actual UML standard document. A brief summary and suggestions for related research are provided at the end of the paper.

2 The Big Picture

The launching of the MDA initiative by the OMG, with its emphasis on using models for more than just documentation or informal design "sketching", generated a strong impetus to expand and clarify the semantics of UML. This was reflected in the definition of the first major revision of UML, UML 2.0, which provides a much more extensive and systematic coverage of semantics relative to earlier versions.

There are two fundamental premises regarding the nature of UML semantics in UML 2.0 that need to be stated up front. The first is the assumption that all behavior in a modeled system is ultimately caused by actions executed by so-called "active" objects (explained below). The second is that UML behavioral semantics only deal with *event-driven*, or discrete, behaviors. This means that continuous behaviors, such as found in many physical systems, are not supported. To be sure, this capability is not precluded, and it is likely that extensions will be defined to provide it. One possible opportunity for this might be the current effort to define a UML for system engineering [5].

2.1 The Semantics Architecture

Fig. 1 identifies the key semantics areas covered by the current UML 2.0 standard. It also shows the dependencies that exist among them.

At the highest level of abstraction, it is possible to distinguish three distinct layers of semantics. The foundational layer is structural. This reflects the premise that is no disembodied behavior in UML – all of it emanates from the actions of structural entities. The next layer is behavioral and provides the foundation for the semantic description of all higher-level behavioral formalisms[4]. This layer (represented by the shaded rectangle in Fig. 1) is called the Behavioral Base and consists of three separate sub-areas arranged into two sub-layers. The bottom sub-layer consists of the *inter-object behavior base,* which deals with how structural entities communicate with each other, and the *intra-object behavior base,* which addresses the behavior occurring within structural entities. The *actions* sub-layer is placed over these two. It defines the semantics of individual actions. Actions are the fundamental units of behavior in UML and are used to define fine-grained behaviors. Their resolution and expressive power are comparable to the executable instructions in traditional programming languages. Actions in this sub-layer are available to any of the higher-level formalisms to be used for describing detailed behaviors. The topmost layer in the semantics hierarchy defines the semantics of the higher-level behavioral formalisms of UML: *activities, state machines,* and *interactions*. These formalisms are dependent on the semantics provided by the lower layers.

---

[4] The term "behavioral formalism" as used throughout this text does not imply formal definition in the mathematical sense, but denotes a distinct behavioral paradigm.

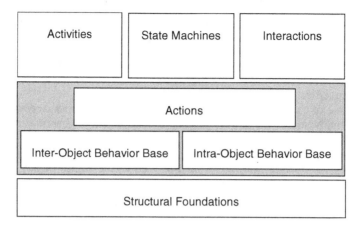

Fig. 1. The UML semantics layers: the Semantics Foundation consists of the bottom two layers – the Structural Foundations and the Behavioral Base (shaded area)

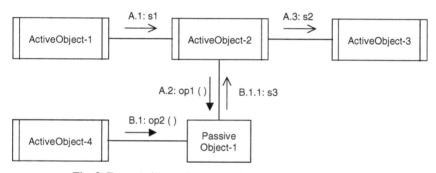

Fig. 2. Example illustrating the basic causality model of UML

This paper deals with the two bottom layers only. These two layers represent the semantic foundations of UML. This is shared substrate that ensures that objects can interact with each other regardless of which specific high-level formalisms are used to describe their behaviors.

2.2   The Basic Causality Model

The "causality model" is a specification how things happen at run time. Instead of a formal treatment, this model is introduced using the example depicted in the collaboration diagram in Fig. 2. The example shows two independent and possibly concurrent threads of causally chained interactions. The first, identified by the thread prefix 'A' consists of a sequence of events that commence with ActiveObject-1 sending signal s1 to ActiveObject-2. In turn, ActiveObject-2 responds by invoking operation op1( ) on PasiveObject-1 after which it sends signal s2 to ActiveObject-3. The second thread, distinguished by the thread prefix 'B', starts with ActiveObject-4 invoking operation op2( ) on PasiveObject-1. The latter responds by executing the method that realizes this operation in which it sends signal s3 to ActiveObject-2.

The causality model is quite straightforward: objects respond to messages that are generated by objects executing communication actions. When these messages arrive, the receiving objects eventually[5] respond by executing the behavior that is matched to that message. The dispatching method by which a particular behavior is associated with a given message depends on the higher-level formalism used and is not defined in the UML specification (i.e., it is a semantic variation point).

In the course of executing its behavior, an object may send messages to other objects, and so on. Note that the term "message" is used here in a generic sense to cover both synchronous and asynchronous communications. In fact, a synchronous communication (call) requires two messages. First is the message from the source to the target identifying the operation to be invoked as well as the values of any arguments. This is followed by a reply message from the target back to the calling object that includes values to be returned to the caller. Because the call is synchronous, the caller is suspended until the reply is received.

2.3   Active Objects: The Sources of Behavior

UML objects are categorized into *active* objects and *passive* objects. The primary difference between them is the manner in which incoming messages are handled by different kinds of objects. Active objects respond only when they execute a receive action. In a sense, active objects control when they interact with their environment. The following definition taken from the UML 2.0 specification describes this crucial characteristic of active objects:

> *[the] point at which an active object responds to communications from other objects is determined solely by the behavior of the active object and not by the invoking object.*

In the context of state machine formalisms, this property of active objects is also known as "run-to-completion". That is, once the active object has accepted a message, no further messages are accepted until the next receive action is executed. For state machines this takes place only after a stable state is reached.

Any messages arriving at an active object between successive receive actions are simply stored in a holding buffer. (Note that this buffer does not necessarily have to be a queue, since stored messages do not have to be processed in the order of arrival. The decision on which of potentially many saved messages to process when the next receive action is executed depends on the scheduling discipline and is a semantic variation point. For instance, priority-based schemes will order messages according to their priority and not according to the arrival order.)

In contrast, passive objects have no say in the matter, they respond when the message arrives, regardless of whether the object is already occupied processing a previous message. This means that concurrency conflicts may occur when accessing passive objects. If this is undesirable, special measures may be needed to ensure mutual exclusion.

No such problems occur for active objects. This freedom from concurrency conflicts without resorting to complex and error-prone conflict management mechanisms

---

[5] An object does not necessarily respond immediately to an arriving message – this depends on the system semantics as well as on the type of behavioral formalism used for the receiver.

is one of the most appealing features of active objects. (Of course, two active objects can still interfere with each other if they share an unprotected passive object.) The price paid for this is the possibility of *priority inversion*, which is a situation where a high-priority message may have to wait until a low-priority message is fully processed.

Following creation, an active object commences execution of its behavior, which it continues to execute until it completes or until the object is terminated by an external agency. In the course of executing its behavior, the active object may execute one or more receive actions.

Note that the semantics of UML active objects are defined independently of any specific implementation technology. Thus, there is no reference to "threads of control" or "processes" in their definition. This means that the concept to be interpreted quite broadly and can be used to model many different kinds of entities, including active entities in the real world.

3 The Structural Foundations

Although not shown in Fig.1, this foundational layer is decomposed into two sub-layers. The *elementary* sub-layer deals with the atoms of structure: objects, links, and the like. At the next level up is the *composites* sub-layer, which describes the semantics of composite structures.

3.1 The Elementary Sub-layer

As noted, all behavior in a system modeled by UML is the result of objects executing actions. However, at this most basic semantics level, an object is not the most fundamental concept. The structural concepts defined at this level are:

- *Pure values.* Pure values are timeless and immutable. They include numbers, strings and character values, Boolean values (true and false), etc. A special kind of pure value is a *reference*, which is a value that uniquely identifies some structural entity[6]. In the UML metamodel, values are specified by instances of the ValueSpecification metaclass. References are represented by the metaclass InstanceValue, which is a subclass of ValueSpecification.

- *Cells.* These are named structural entities capable of storing either pure values or other cells. They are typed, which means that they can only store pure values or structural entities of a particular type. Cells are dynamic entities that can be created and destroyed dynamically. During their existence, their contents may change. Each cell has a unique identity, which distinguishes it from all other cells. The identity of a cell is independent of its contents. A reference is a value that is a concrete representation of the identity of a cell. If a cell contains another cell, the contained cell is destroyed when the containing cell is destroyed. (Note, however, that the contents of the cell are not necessarily destroyed – this is discussed further in section 3.2.) A cell defined in the context of a behavior is called a *variable*.

---

[6] It is interesting to note that value literals, such as "1", can be viewed as references to an abstract entity representing the concept of "one".

- *Objects* are simply cells that are typed by a UML class. This means that they may have associated behaviors and behavioral features. An object may have one or more *slots*, which are simply cells owned[7] by the object. Each slot corresponds to an attribute or part[8] of the class of the object. Active objects will also have cells for buffering messages that have arrived but which have not been processed yet by a receive action.

- *Links* are dynamic structural entities that represent ordered collections (tuples) of object references. Like objects, links are typed, except that the type of a link is an association. UML distinguishes between two kinds of links. *Value links* are immutable entities whose identities are defined by their contents. Consequently, the existence of a value link is dependent on the existence of the objects whose references it contains. *Object links*, on the other hand have an identity that is independent of their contents. Thus, the references contained by an object link can change over time but the link retains its identity. If the type of the object link is an association class, then the link may also have additional slots corresponding to the attributes of the class.

- *Messages* are dynamic passive objects that are created to convey information across links as a result of the execution of communication actions.

UML models may contain representations of structural entities, which serve to capture the state of these entities during some real or imagined instant or time interval. The metamodel for this is shown in Fig. 3. The metaclass InstanceSpecification is a general mechanism for representing instances of various kinds of classifiers, including objects (but also instances of more abstract kinds of classifiers such as collaborations). The structural features of the classifier (attributes, parts, link ends, etc.) are represented by slots and the values contained in the slots by value specifications.

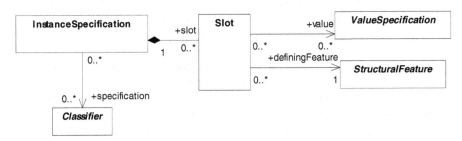

Fig. 3. UML metamodel concepts used for modeling run-time instances and their values

3.2 The Composites Sub-layer

There are several ways in which structural entities combine with each other to produce composites. When considering composites, an important aspect is the way in which the various components of a composite depend on each other:

---

[7] Note that "ownership" is synonymous with containment in this case.

[8] In the UML metamodel, attributes and parts (of structured classes) are modeled slightly differently. However, this is primarily due to technicalities of the way that the metamodel is constructed and does not reflect any fundamental semantic differences.

- *Existence dependencies* are dependencies in which the existence (or non-existence) of one structural entity depends on the existence (or non-existence) of a different entity. In such relationships a dependent entity will be terminated if the structural entity that it depends on is terminated[9]. This is usually an asymmetric relationship since the inverse is generally not the case; that is, an entity may exist independently of its existence dependents.

- *Functional (behavioral) dependencies* are dependencies in which the successful functioning of one structural entity depends on the successful functioning of other functional entities.

Perhaps the most elementary combination of structural elements is the *peer* relationship (Fig. 4). This involves two or more entities communicating with each other over a link[10]. In this case, there may be behavioral dependencies between the communicating entities but there are no structural existence dependencies unless the link is a value link[11].

Fig. 4. The "peer" composite relationship: in this case the existence of the entities at the ends of the link are independent of each other but there are usually functional dependencies between them

A second kind of fundamental structural relationship is *containment* (Fig. 5), which comes in two basic variants:

- *Composition*, in which there is an existence dependency between the containing element and the contained element and

- *Aggregation*, in which the contained element has no existence dependency relative to the container[12].

To understand the difference between the two forms of containment, recall that objects are simply cells that may contain other cells. The distinction between composition and aggregation is whether the object contained in a cell is destroyed along with its containing cell or not. In the case of composition, the object is destroyed when the cell is destroyed, whereas in the case of simple aggregation, the object that was contained in a cell that was destroyed (because its containing cell is destroyed) remains in existence.

---

[9] Note that there are lots of subtleties involved in this seemingly simple notion. For example, do the depending on and dependent entities disappear at the same instant or is there some interval of time involved? Is the dependent entity created at the same time as the entity that it dependents on or not? These are semantic variation points that may be defined differently in different domains or situations.

[10] Not all links are necessarily used for communications. However, the distinction between communication and other types of links is not considered in this paper.

[11] Recall that the existence of value links depends on the existence of their ends. If one of the ends disappears, the link no longer exists.

[12] The two forms of containment are differentiated in the UML notation by the difference between the "full diamond" and the "empty diamond" composition notations.

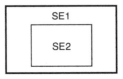

Fig. 5. The composition relationship: the structural entity SE2 is contained within structural entity SE1 and may have an existence dependency on it

The most common use of containment is to encapsulate elements that are part of the hidden implementation structure of the container. (This implies that the container has a functional dependency on the contained element.) However, a container does not necessarily own all of the parts that it uses in its implementation. In case of aggregation, the part is merely "borrowed" from its true owner for the duration of the container. For example, a container might ask a resource manager, such as a buffer pool manager, to "lend" it a set of memory buffers that it needs to do perform its function. Once the task has been completed, the container may return the resource to its owner. The "borrowed" part is also returned automatically to the owner when the container itself is destroyed.

In addition to these two fundamental structural patterns, it has been suggested [11] that a third basic structural pattern exists: *layering*. This is a pattern in which the upper layer has existence and functional dependencies on the lower layer (similar to containment), but the lower layer has no dependencies of any kind on the upper layer. However, at present, there is no direct support for layering in UML, although it can be constructed from a combination of more primitive patterns.

4   The Behavioral Base

In speaking of behavior in UML, care should be taken to distinguish between two subtly different uses of the term. In one case, "behavior" denotes the general intuitive notion of how some system or entity changes state over time. Alternatively, it refers to the specific UML concept shown in the metamodel fragment in Fig. 6[13]. To distinguish these two, the capitalized form of the word will be used when referring specifically to the UML concept (i.e., "Behavior" versus "behavior").

In UML, Behavior is an abstract concept that represents a model element that contains a specification of the behavior of some classifier. At present, UML supports four different concrete specializations of this abstract concept: interactions, activities, and state machines (see Fig. 1). Each of them has its specific semantics as well as its own graphical notation and dedicated diagram type.

The specific semantics of these higher-level behavioral formalisms are outside the scope of this paper. However, it should be noted that, for historical reasons, not all of them fully exploit the available capabilities of the shared base. For instance, the base provides common mechanisms for describing the flow of behavior, including concepts for things such as decision points, iteration, and the like, yet these same types of constructs are also defined in state machines. This is because a large part of the shared behavioral base was introduced at a later stage of UML evolution. Consequently, some work still remains to fully integrate these formalisms on the new shared base.

---

[13] Only the case of class classifiers is considered in this section.

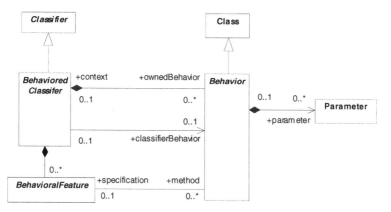

Fig. 6. The relationship between structure and behavior in the UML metamodel

The general Behavior concept captures what is common across all these forms: that they can be attached to a classifier (for a variety of different reasons) and that they may have input and output parameters.

Note that Behavior is a specialization of the Class concept, which means that when behaviors start executing they take on a structural form as kinds of objects. This may seem strange at first, but recall that a behavior may need local variables to keep temporary information that is used to pass information between different actions as well as keeping a record of its execution (e.g., a data and call stack, one or more program counters). The precise form of this execution record is yet another semantic variation point that depends on the specific behavioral form and implementation.

Fig. 6 shows that a classifier can own multiple behavioral specifications. The UML standard does not prescribe what purposes these behaviors serve. For example, a structured class may have behavior specifications that illustrate specific scenarios of interest associated with that class, such as a start-up scenario. However, at most one of those behavior specifications can be used to represent the behavior that starts executing when an object of that class is created and started[14]. This behavior is called the *classifier behavior*. For a passive class, this might be the constructor of the class. For active objects, it is the behavior that initiates the activity of the object and which continues until the object is terminated.

It is important to distinguish the classifier behavior from the overall behavior resulting from the combination of the classifier behavior and the behaviors of its internal part objects.

The model of behaviors in Fig.6 also identifies two other semantically relevant concepts:

- *Behavioral feature* is a *declaration* of a behavior that may be activated by other objects through invocations. Two kinds of behavioral features are defined in UML: *operations* and *receptions*. Operations are invoked through call actions whereas receptions are invoked through asynchronous signal sends (these are discussed in the following section).

---

[14] Note that creation and start of execution are not necessarily coincident. In some systems, a "start" of behavior may require an explicit action, while in others it may be automatic. This is a semantic variation point.

- *Methods* are Behaviors that realize behavioral features. Like classifier behaviors, methods can be specified using any concrete behavioral formalism deemed suitable by the modeler, including a simple action-based specification.

4.1 The Inter-object Behavioral Base

This part of the Behavioral Base deals with communications. UML includes support for both synchronous and asynchronous interactions. Synchronous communications cause the invoking entity to suspend execution of its behavior until a reply is received. An asynchronous communication does not result in a suspension of the invoker who simply continues with execution of its behavior. UML defines several variations on these two basic forms:

- *Synchronous operation call* is an invocation of an operation of the target object. The invoking object is suspended until a reply is received from the target object.
- *Synchronous behavior call* is an invocation of the classifier behavior of the target object. The invoking object is suspended until a reply is received from the target object.
- *Asynchronous operation call* is a call to an operation of the target object. The invoker is not suspended but simply carries on executing its behavior. If there is a reply sent back from the operation, it is ignored.
- *Asynchronous behavior call* is like an asynchronous operation call except that the classifier behavior of the target object is invoked rather than a behavioral feature.
- *Asynchronous signal send* creates a signal with the appropriate parameters, which is then sent to the target object in a message. The target object has to have a corresponding *reception* defined that corresponds to that signal. The invoker is not suspended but simply carries on executing its behavior.
- *Asynchronous signal broadcast* is an asynchronous send with no explicit target objects specified. That is, the message is broadcast into a communications medium, such as a link, where any objects connected to the same medium can pick it up.

Regardless of the precise nature of the call, the underlying transmission mechanism is the same: a message object is created on the sending side that includes information about the invoked behavioral feature or behavior as well as information about the identity of the invoker. The message includes the argument values corresponding to the parameters of the invoked behavior (in case of signals, this information is part of the signal definition). Note that the details of whether the values are copied into the message or whether merely a reference to them is stored in the message are a semantic variation point. This means that both copy and reference semantics can be modeled.

Similarly, any reply information going in the reverse direction is packaged in a message and sent onwards by the invoked object. The semantics and characteristics of the transmission and medium and delivery process (reliability, performance, priorities, etc.) are not defined in standard UML, allowing different specializations according to the domain and circumstances.

UML provides specific actions for each of the above communication types as well as corresponding receive (accept) primitives. This allows modeling of variations of these basic primitives as well as construction of more sophisticated communication models.

In addition to the various modes of communication, the inter-object behavior base defines the following two semantically significant concepts:

- *Events* and *event occurrences*. An event is a specification of a kind of state[15] change. An occurrence of such a state change at run time is an event occurrence. Event occurrences are instantaneous. That is, a state change is assumed to occur at a particular instant rather than taking place over an interval of time. An event can be any kind of state change, such as the start of execution of an action, the sending of a signal, or the writing of a value to a variable. However, four special categories of state changes are particularly distinguished in the UML semantics since they are generally useful:

  - *Call events* represent the reception of a synchronous call by an object.
  - *Signal events* capture the receipt of a specific type of asynchronous signal by an object
  - *Change events* represent the change of value in a Boolean expression
  - *Time events* represent situations where a certain instant of time has arrived

- *Trigger* is a kind of event whose occurrence causes the execution of behavior, such as the trigger of a transition in a state machine. Any of the four kinds of events listed above can act as a trigger. However, not all events are triggers. For example, the sending of a signal does not trigger any behavior execution (although the receipt of that signal by the target does).

4.2 Intra-object Behavioral Base

This part of the Behavioral Base defines the essentials for representing actions and for combining them. The key notion here is that of a basic form of Behavior called an *activity*[16]. In essence, this is a generalization of the concept of procedure found in most common programming languages. Specifically, an activity is a kind of Behavior that may contain a set of *actions* and local variables.

The Actions Model. Actions are used to specify fine-grained behavior in UML, the kind of behavior corresponding to the executable instructions in traditional programming languages. This includes actions used to initiate and receive communications (described in section 4.1), create and destroy objects, read and write cells of various kinds, and so on. Note that, even though actions specify behaviors, they are not Behaviors in the UML sense.

The metamodel fragment shown in Fig. 7 depicts the general model of actions as defined in UML.

In essence, an action is a value transformer that transforms a set of inputs into a set of outputs as illustrated by the conceptual model in Fig. 8. Some actions may affect the state of the system, that is, they may change the values that are stored in the structural elements of the system (variables, object slots, links, etc.). The inputs and outputs of an action are specified by the set of *input pins* and *output pins* respectively.

---

[15] The term "state" here is used in its generic sense to describe some run-time situation existing at a particular instant and does not necessarily imply a formalism based on state machines.

[16] A more elaborate form of this same concept is used for the higher-level activity behavioral formalism.

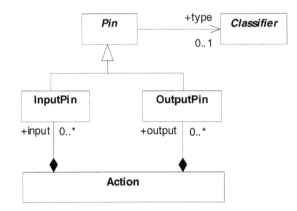

Fig. 7. The UML showing the relationship between actions and pins

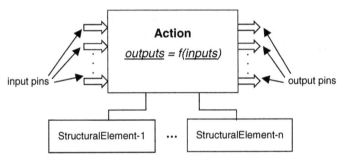

Fig. 8. The conceptual model of actions in UML: in general, an action transforms of a set of inputs to a set of outputs; it may also read and write the values stored in one or more structural elements (variables, attributes, etc.)

Both input and output pins are typed elements, which means that only values of the appropriate type (including compatible subtypes) can appear on them.

An action can only execute if all of its input pins are enabled, that is, if all the values on all of the input pins are available. The point at which an action makes its outputs available is another semantic variation point. For example, in synchronous systems such as Esterel [1], all the outputs become available simultaneously. Other models might allow output values to be generated as soon as they become available and independently of whether the values on other output pins are available.

The run-time effect of an action can be described in terms of the difference in the state of the system from the instant just before the action is executed (pre-condition) to the instant just after execution completes (post-condition).

UML makes no assumptions on the duration of actions. Therefore, semantic models that require zero-time (i.e., instantaneous) execution as well as models that allow for finite execution times for actions are represented.

Flows. An action performs a relatively primitive state transformation and it is usually necessary to combine a number of such transforms to get an overall desired effect. This requires a means of combining actions and their effects to produce more complex transformations. UML defines the concept of *flows* for this purpose. Flows serve to specify the order of execution of combined actions as well as the conditions under which those executions can take place. To provide maximum flexibility, UML supports two different ways of composing actions using either *control flows* and *object (data) flows*. These two correspond to two radically different models of computation. However, regardless of the type of flow used that the relationship between actions and flows can be conveniently modeled by a directed graph, with flows represented by the arcs (edges) of the graph.

Control flows are the most conventional way of combining actions. A control flow between two actions means that the execution of the action at the target end of the flow will start executing after the action at the source end of the control flow has completed its execution.

In some cases, it may be necessary to alter the execution flow in some special way (loops, conditional branches, etc.). This is achieved using special *control nodes*. These include standard control constructs such as forks and joins. In addition control flow can be modified through *guards* (specified by Boolean predicates) on flows which are used for conditional transfer of control. The different control nodes are discussed below.

Data flows, on the other hand, are used for computational models that are based on a fine-grained parallelism. In this case, an action executes as soon as all of its input pin values are available. This means that multiple actions may be executing concurrently, since an action may produce outputs before it has completed its execution and also because a given output can be fed to inputs on multiple different actions. Note that data flows do not connect actions like control flows; instead, they connect input and output pins on actions. Consequently, data-flow dependencies tend to be finergrained than control flows, as some actions have multiple inputs and outputs.

The two types of flows can be combined for sophisticated control over execution. An example of this can be found in the higher-level activities behavioral formalism.

This flow-based model of computation behind actions was inspired by the Petri net formalisms [9] although no specific formal variant of Petri nets was used as its conceptual base. The difference between control and data flows is primarily in the nature of the tokens (control or data) that flow through them.

In the UML metamodel, data and control flows are represented by *activity edges,* which can be either control flow edges (arcs) or object (data) flow edges as shown in Fig. 9.

Nodes. In the UML metamodel, the various types of nodes occurring in activity graphs are represented as special kinds of *activity nodes* (see Fig. 9). *Control nodes* are used to support of control-flow execution (see previous section), *executable nodes* contain behavior that needs to be executed (including actions), and *object nodes* represent values of some kind.

The following are the principal types of control nodes defined in UML:

- *Initial* nodes are used to initiate a flow when an activity starts executing; in effect, they and their outgoing flow identify which executable nodes will be executed first.

- *Flow final* nodes terminate the flows that terminate on them, but not necessarily the containing activity.

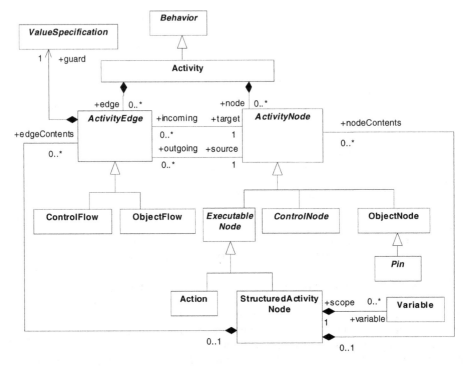

Fig. 9. A simplified version of the UML metamodel that shows the relationships between the key concepts in the Intra-object Behavioral Base: activities, actions, nodes, and flows

- *Final* nodes terminate the activity that contains them and, consequently, all of the active flows in that activity.
- *Decision* nodes are used as the source of a set of alternative flows, each guarded by a separate Boolean expression.
- *Merge* nodes are used to converge multiple incoming flows into a single outgoing flow. No synchronization takes place.
- *Fork* nodes are used to split a flow into multiple concurrent flows.
- *Join* nodes represent synchronization points, where flows come together but do not proceed until all of them arrive[17].

Executable nodes represent nodes that contain actions. A special kind of executable node is a *structured activity node*, which roughly corresponds to the concept of a block in a block-structured programming language. A structured activity node may contain other activity nodes and edges as well as local *variables*. This recursive definition allows the construction of arbitrarily complex hierarchies of nested activity nodes. Specializations of this general concept include node types for explicit modeling alternative and iterative (looping) flows.

---

[17] There are numerous subtleties to the synchronization policies that depend on the nature of the flows, but these are beyond the scope of this paper.

Object nodes are used to specify the values that are transferred through an object (data) flow. Their most obvious use is to model pins (note that Pin is a kind of ObjectNode). That is, the flow of data between individual actions is specified by object flows that connect the output pins of a predecessor action to the input pins of its successor actions.

4.3 Actions

The topmost level of the Behavioral Base is a set of actions that perform different kinds of transformations as well as reading and writing structural entities such as variables and attributes. Actions can be packaged into activities that can then be invoked by any of the higher-level behavioral formalisms. For example, a state machine might use such an activity to describe the fine-grain behavior that occurs in a transition or in an entry action to a state.

The following categories of actions are defined in the Behavioral Base:

- *Communication actions* are actions used for interactions between objects. Their semantics are described in section 4.1 above.
- *Read-Write actions* are actions that access the values of structural entities (read actions) and, in some cases, change these values (write actions). This includes accessing attributes, links, and variables.
- *Structural actions* create and destroy structural elements such as objects, attributes, links, etc. (but not values). In addition, these include actions that dynamically change the classification (type) of structural entities.
- *Computation actions* specify actions that perform standard computations using arithmetic and logical operators, as well as more complex functional transforms.
- *Special actions* include actions for modeling exceptions and for starting the classifier behavior of objects.

In addition to the above action categories, the UML standard defines a set of actions for reading time values. However, the model of time implied in these actions is highly specialized, since it presumes an ideal global clock, such that the value of time is the same in all parts of the system. This makes it unsuitable for modeling many distributed systems or time-sensitive systems, in which the characteristics of individual clocks and phenomena such as time synchronization need to be taken into account. Hence, it is not considered as part of the general semantics foundation.

The details of the semantics of individual actions in these categories are outside the scope of this paper.

Note that some of the higher-level modeling formalisms provide additional actions for describing fine-grained functionality specific to their needs. Such actions are not part of the general semantics framework and are, therefore, not discussed further.

5   Mapping to the UML 2.0 Specification

The UML 2.0 specification is structured according to subject area. Each subject area has a dedicated chapter, which includes the relevant metamodel fragments and a set of concepts defined for that subject area. Within a subject area, there is typically a short informal introduction followed by an alphabetically sorted list of concept descriptions. Each concept description includes a "semantics" section that describes the meaning of that modeling concept. Although this is a convenient organization for reference purposes, it makes it very difficult to deduce how the various semantics fit together.

One of the intentions of this paper was to collect in one place the information from the various dispersed fragments that deal with run-time semantics[18] and to provide the necessary system view. However, this paper is limited to a high-level description and anyone interested in understanding the finer details of these semantics will necessarily have to refer to the specification itself. To assist in this, this section explains where the various semantic elements described in this paper are located in the standard itself.

Note that all references to chapters and section numbers are with respect to the so-called Final Adopted Specification (FAS, for short)[8]. Unfortunately, this means that some of this information will be out of date as the standard and its corresponding specification evolve. (In fact, even as this text is being written, the FAS is being modified as part of the standard OMG standardization process. For instance, there have been some terminology changes related to the notion of events and triggers (these are reflected in the current text).)

Unfortunately, the overall semantics architecture shown in Fig. 1 and most of the terminology used to describe it do not appear anywhere in the specification. They have to be inferred from the semantic dependencies between different metamodel elements. Therefore, the diagram in Fig. 1 represents a synthesis of the relevant information contained in the various text fragments. In this, the author relied extensively on his familiarity with the often undocumented design intent behind many of the UML concepts, since he participated in the actual definition and writing of the standard[19].

The general causality model is described in the introductory part of chapter 13 (CommonBehaviors) and also, in part, in the introduction to chapter 14 (Interactions) and the section on Interaction (14.3.7) and Message (14.3.14).

The structural foundations are mostly covered in two chapters. The elementary level is mostly covered in chapter 7, where the root concepts of UML are specified. In particular, the sections on InstanceSpecifications (section 7.7 of the FAS), Classes and Associations (section 7.11), and Features (section 7.9). The composites level is described primarily in chapter 9 (Composite Structures), with most of the information related to semantics contained in sections 9.3.12 (Property concept) and 9.3.13 (StructuredClassifier). In addition, the introduction to this chapter contains a high-level view of some aspects of composite structures.

The relationship between structure and behavior and the general properties of the Behavior concept, which are at the core of the Behavioral Base are described in CommonBehaviors (in the introduction to chapter 13 and in section 13.3.3 in particular).

---

[18] Not all modeling concepts in UML correspond to run-time concepts, hence, not all semantics descriptions deal with run-time semantics.

[19] In this regard, the UML specification follows the style used in many modern technical standards, which strive for a formality that only permits the inclusion of supposedly objective "facts". Unfortunately, this often leads to the omission of invaluable information related to design rationale.

Inter-object behavior is covered in three separate chapters. The basic semantics of communications actions are described in the introduction to chapter 11 (Actions) and, in more detail, in the sections describing the specific actions (sections 11.3.1, 11.3.2, 11.3.6, 11.3.7, 11.3.8, 11.3.9, 11.3.18, 11.3.37, 11.3.38, 11.3.39). The concepts related to messages are defined in the Interactions chapter (sections 14.3.14 and 14.3.15), while the concepts of events and triggers are defined in the Communications package of CommonBehaviors (chapter 13). Event occurrences are defined in section 14.3.3) of the Interactions chapter.

The basic notion of actions, in the intra-object behavior base, is defined in the introduction to the Activities chapter (chapter 12) and in the section on the Action concept itself (12.3.1). The semantics of flows and nodes mechanisms are also described in the Activities chapter (sections 12.3.2, 12.3.3, 12.3.4, 12.3.6, 12.3.12, 12.3.13, 12.3.15,12.3.17, 12.3.21, 12.3.22, 12.3.23, 12.3.24, 12.3.25, 12.3.27, 12.3.29, 12.3.32, 12.3.34, 12.3.37, 12.3.40).

The various shared actions and their semantics are described in chapter 11.

Finally, the higher-level behavioral formalisms are each described in their own chapters: Activities in chapter 12, Interactions in chapter 14, and State Machines in chapter 15.

One of the consequences of such a dispersed organization of semantics data is that there are bound to be some logical inconsistencies and omissions, given the complexity and informal nature of the specification. Some of these flaws have already been identified and are being fixed as part of the standard finalization process that is currently ongoing. (The FAS is not the final form of the standard; instead, it is published so that implementers and researchers can inspect it and provide feedback.) Undoubtedly, if a formal model of the semantics existed, it would be much easier to detect such flaws. However, as explained earlier, it is the author's opinion that it would not have been appropriate to start with a given mathematical formalism until the broad scope of design intent was described informally. This has now been done with the official UML 2.0 specification and the time may be ripe to fit an appropriate formal model over it.

6   Summary

This paper provides a high-level view of the run-time semantics foundation of standard UML, that is, the semantics that are actually described in the official OMG standard. The purpose is twofold: to dispel persistent and unjustified insinuations that "UML has no semantics" and to provide a convenient starting point for those interested in doing research on the topic of UML semantics.

As noted at the beginning, it is probably inappropriate to define a single concrete formalization of the semantics of UML, since it was intended to be used in a variety of different ways and for a variety of different domains. However, at this point, with the scope of UML defined by the UML 2.0 standard, it seems both feasible and highly desirable to define a general formal semantics of UML. Such a model would serve to more precisely define the *envelope* of possible concrete formalizations. This could then be used as a basis for specializations of that formal model for specific domains and purposes. Also, it could be used to validate alternative formalizations.

References

1. Berry, G.: The Foundations of Esterel, In: G. Plotkin, C. Stirling and M. Tofte (eds.) Proof, Language and Interaction: Essays in Honour of Robin Milner, MIT Press, Cambridge MA (1998)
2. Kleppe, A., Warmer, J.: Unification of Static and Dynamic Semantics of UML: A Study in redefining the Semantics of the UML using pUML Meta Modelling Approach, Klasse Objecten, http://www.cs.york.ac.uk/puml/mmf/KleppeWarmer.pdf, Soest, Netherlands (2003)
3. Ober, I.: Harmonizing Design Languages with Object-Oriented Extensions and an Executable Semantics, Ph.D Thesis at Institut National Polytechnique de Toulouse, Toulouse, France (2004)
4. Object Management Group: MDA Guide (version 1.0.1), OMG document ad/03-06-01, http://www.omg.org/cgi-bin/doc?mda-guide (2003)
5. Object Management Group: UML for Systems Engineering – Request for Proposal, OMG document ad/03-03-41, http://www.omg.org/docs/ad/03-03-41.pdf (2003)
6. Object Management Group: UML 2.0 Infrastructure – Final Adopted Specification, OMG document ad/03-09-15, http://www.omg.org/docs/ad/03-09-15.pdf (2003)
7. Object Management Group: UML 2.0 OCL – Final Adopted Specification, OMG document ad/03-10-14, http://www.omg.org/docs/ad/03-10-14.pdf (2003)
8. Object Management Group: UML 2.0 Superstructure – Final Adopted Specification, OMG document ad/03-08-02, http://www.omg.org/docs/ad/03-08-02.pdf (2003)
9. Peterson, J.: Petri Nets, ACM Computing Surveys, Vol. 9, Issue 3, ACM Press, New York, (1977) 223-252
10. Rumbaugh, J., Jacobson, I., Booch, G.: The Unified Modeling Language Reference Manual (2nd ed.), Addison-Wesley, Boston (2004)
11. Selic, B., Gullekson, G., Ward, P.: Real-Time Object-Oriented Modeling, John Wiley & Sons, New York (1994).
12. Sourrouille, J.L., Caplat, G.: Constraint Checking in UML Modeling, in Proceedings International Conference SEKE'02, ACM-SIGSOFT, (2002) 217-224

A Tutorial on UPPAAL

Gerd Behrmann, Alexandre David, and Kim G. Larsen

Department of Computer Science, Aalborg University, Denmark
{behrmann,adavid,kgl}@cs.auc.dk

Abstract. This is a tutorial paper on the tool UPPAAL. Its goal is to be a short introduction on the flavor of timed automata implemented in the tool, to present its interface, and to explain how to use the tool. The contribution of the paper is to provide reference examples and modeling patterns.

1 Introduction

UPPAAL is a toolbox for verification of real-time systems jointly developed by Uppsala University and Aalborg University. It has been applied successfully in case studies ranging from communication protocols to multimedia applications [30, 48, 22, 21, 29, 37, 47, 38, 27]. The tool is designed to verify systems that can be modelled as networks of timed automata extended with integer variables, structured data types, and channel synchronisation.

The first version of UPPAAL was released in 1995 [45]. Since then it has been in constant development [19, 5, 11, 10, 24, 25]. Experiments and improvements include data structures [46], partial order reduction [18], symmetry reduction [31], a distributed version of UPPAAL [15, 9], guided and minimal cost reachability [13, 44, 14], work on UML Statecharts [26], acceleration techniques [32], and new data structures and memory reductions [16, 12]. UPPAAL has also generated related Ph.D. theses [43, 50, 39, 49, 17, 23, 28, 8]. The tool is now mature with its current version 3.4.6. It features a Java user interface and a verification engine written in C++ . It is freely available at http://www.uppaal.com/.

This tutorial covers networks of timed automata and the flavor of timed automata used in UPPAAL in section 2. The tool itself is described in section 3, and two extensive examples are covered in sections 4 and 5. Finally section 6 introduces 7 common modelling patterns often used with UPPAAL.

2 Timed Automata in UPPAAL

The model-checker UPPAAL is based on the theory of timed automata [4, 36] and its modelling language offers additional features such as bounded integer variables and urgency. The query language of UPPAAL, used to specify properties to be checked, is a subset of CTL (computation tree logic) [33, 3]. In this section we present the modelling and the query languages of UPPAAL and we give an intuitive explanation of time in timed automata.

M. Bernardo and F. Corradini (Eds.): SFM-RT 2004, LNCS 3185, pp. 200–236, 2004.

2.1   The Modelling Language

Networks of Timed Automata. A timed automaton is a finite-state machine extended with clock variables. It uses a dense-time model where a clock variable evaluates to a real number. All the clocks progress synchronously. In UPPAAL, a system is modelled as a network of several such timed automata in parallel. The model is further extended with bounded discrete variables that are part of the state. These variables are used as in programming languages: they are read, written, and are subject to common arithmetic operations. A state of the system is defined by the locations of all automata, the clock constraints, and the values of the discrete variables. Every automaton may fire an edge (sometimes misleadingly called a transition) separately or synchronise with another automaton, which leads to a new state.

Figure 1(a) shows a timed automaton modelling a simple lamp. The lamp has three locations: off, low, and bright. If the user presses a button, i.e., synchronises with press?, then the lamp is turned on. If the user presses the button again, the lamp is turned off. However, if the user is fast and rapidly presses the button twice, the lamp is turned on and becomes bright. The user model is shown in Fig. 1(b). The user can press the button randomly at any time or even not press the button at all. The clock y of the lamp is used to detect if the user was fast ($y < 5$) or slow ($y >= 5$).

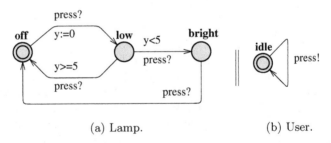

(a) Lamp.   (b) User.

Fig. 1. The simple lamp example.

We give the basic definitions of the syntax and semantics for timed automata. We use the following notations: C is a set of clocks and $B(C)$ is the set of conjunctions over simple conditions of the form $x \bowtie c$ or $x - y \bowtie c$, where $x, y \in C$, $c \in \mathbb{N}$ and $\bowtie \in \{<, \leq, =, \geq, >\}$. A timed automaton is a finite directed graph annotated with conditions over and resets of non-negative real valued clocks.

Definition 1 (Timed Automaton (TA)). *A timed automaton is a tuple* (L, l_0, C, A, E, I), *where L is a set of locations, $l_0 \in L$ is the initial location, C is the set of clocks, A is a set of actions, co-actions and the internal τ-action, $E \subseteq L \times A \times B(C) \times 2^C \times L$ is a set of edges between locations with an action,* *a guard and a set of clocks to be reset, and $I : L \to B(C)$ assigns invariants to locations.*   □

We now define the semantics of a timed automaton. A clock valuation is a function $u : C \to \mathbb{R}_{\geq 0}$ from the set of clocks to the non-negative reals. Let $\mathbb{R}^C$ be the set of all clock valuations. Let $u_0(x) = 0$ for all $x \in C$. We will abuse the notation by considering guards and invariants as sets of clock valuations, writing $u \in I(l)$ to mean that u satisfies $I(l)$.

Definition 2 (Semantics of TA). *Let (L, l_0, C, A, E, I) be a timed automaton. The semantics is defined as a labelled transition system $\langle S, s_0, \to \rangle$, where $S \subseteq L \times \mathbb{R}^C$ is the set of states, $s_0 = (l_0, u_0)$ is the initial state, and $\to \subseteq S \times \{\mathbb{R}_{\geq 0} \cup A\} \times S$ is the transition relation such that:*

- $(l, u) \xrightarrow{d} (l, u + d)$ *if* $\forall d' : 0 \leq d' \leq d \implies u + d' \in I(l)$, *and*
- $(l, u) \xrightarrow{a} (l', u')$ *if there exists* $e = (l, a, g, r, l') \in E$ *s.t.* $u \in g$, $u' = [r \mapsto 0]u$, *and* $u' \in I(l)$,

where for $d \in \mathbb{R}_{\geq 0}$, $u + d$ maps each clock x in C to the value $u(x) + d$, and $[r \mapsto 0]u$ denotes the clock valuation which maps each clock in r to 0 and agrees with u over $C \setminus r$.   □

Timed automata are often composed into a *network of timed automata* over a common set of clocks and actions, consisting of n timed automata $\mathcal{A}_i = (L_i, l_i^0, C, A, E_i, I_i)$, $1 \leq i \leq n$. A location vector is a vector $\bar{l} = (l_1, \ldots, l_n)$. We compose the invariant functions into a common function over location vectors $I(\bar{l}) = \wedge_i I_i(l_i)$. We write $\bar{l}[l_i'/l_i]$ to denote the vector where the ith element l_i of $\bar{l}$ is replaced by l_i'. In the following we define the semantics of a network of timed automata.

Definition 3 (Semantics of a network of Timed Automata). *Let $\mathcal{A}_i = (L_i, l_i^0, C, A, E_i, I_i)$ be a network of n timed automata. Let $\bar{l}_0 = (l_1^0, \ldots, l_n^0)$ be the initial location vector. The semantics is defined as a transition system $\langle S, s_0, \to \rangle$, where $S = (L_1 \times \cdots \times L_n) \times \mathbb{R}^C$ is the set of states, $s_0 = (\bar{l}_0, u_0)$ is the initial state, and $\to \subseteq S \times S$ is the transition relation defined by:*

- $(\bar{l}, u) \to (\bar{l}, u + d)$ *if* $\forall d' : 0 \leq d' \leq d \implies u + d' \in I(\bar{l})$.
- $(\bar{l}, u) \to (\bar{l}[l_i'/l_i], u')$ *if there exists* $l_i \xrightarrow{\tau g r} l_i'$ *s.t.* $u \in g$, $u' = [r \mapsto 0]u$ *and* $u' \in I(\bar{l})$.
- $(\bar{l}, u) \to (\bar{l}[l_j'/l_j, l_i'/l_i], u')$ *if there exist* $l_i \xrightarrow{c?g_i r_i} l_i'$ *and* $l_j \xrightarrow{c!g_j r_j} l_j'$ *s.t.* $u \in (g_i \wedge g_j)$, $u' = [r_i \cup r_j \mapsto 0]u$ *and* $u' \in I(\bar{l})$.   □

As an example of the semantics, the lamp in Fig. 1 may have the following states (we skip the user): $(\texttt{Lamp.off}, y = 0) \to (\texttt{Lamp.off}, y = 3) \to (\texttt{Lamp.low}, y = 0) \to (\texttt{Lamp.low}, y = 0.5) \to (\texttt{Lamp.bright}, y = 0.5) \to (\texttt{Lamp.bright}, y = 1000) \ldots$

Timed Automata in UPPAAL. The UPPAAL modelling language extends timed automata with the following additional features:

Templates automata are defined with a set of parameters that can be of any type (e.g., `int`, `chan`). These parameters are substituted for a given argument in the process declaration.

Constants are declared as `const name value`. Constants by definition cannot be modified and must have an integer value.

Bounded integer variables are declared as `int[min,max] name`, where `min` and `max` are the lower and upper bound, respectively. Guards, invariants, and assignments may contain expressions ranging over bounded integer variables. The bounds are checked upon verification and violating a bound leads to an invalid state that is discarded (at run-time). If the bounds are omitted, the default range of -32768 to 32768 is used.

Binary synchronisation channels are declared as `chan c`. An edge labelled with `c!` synchronises with another labelled `c?`. A synchronisation pair is chosen non-deterministically if several combinations are enabled.

Broadcast channels are declared as `broadcast chan c`. In a broadcast synchronisation one sender `c!` can synchronise with an arbitrary number of receivers `c?`. Any receiver than can synchronise in the current state must do so. If there are no receivers, then the sender can still execute the `c!` action, i.e. broadcast sending is never blocking.

Urgent synchronisation channels are decalred by prefixing the channel declaration with the keyword `urgent`. Delays must not occur if a synchronisation transition on an urgent channel is enabled. Edges using urgent channels for synchronisation cannot have time constraints, i.e., no clock guards.

Urgent locations are semantically equivalent to adding an extra clock x, that is reset on all incomming edges, and having an invariant `x<=0` on the location. Hence, time is not allowed to pass when the system is in an urgent location.

Committed locations are even more restrictive on the execution than urgent locations. A state is committed if any of the locations in the state is committed. A committed state cannot delay and the next transition must involve an outgoing edge of at least one of the committed locations.

Arrays are allowed for clocks, channels, constants and integer variables. They are defined by appending a size to the variable name, e.g. `chan c[4]; clock a[2]; int[3,5] u[7];`.

Initialisers are used to initialise integer variables and arrays of integer variables. For instance, `int i := 2;` or `int i[3] := {1, 2, 3};`.

Expressions in UPPAAL. Expressions in UPPAAL range over clocks and integer variables. The BNF is given in Fig. 2. Expressions are used with the following labels:

Guard. A guard is a particular expression satisfying the following conditions: it is side-effect free; it evaluates to a boolean; only clocks, integer variables, and constants are referenced (or arrays of these types); clocks and clock differences are only compared to integer expressions; guards over clocks are essentially conjunctions (disjunctions are allowed over integer conditions).

Synchronisation. A synchronisation label is either on the form *Expression*!
or *Expression*? or is an empty label. The expression must be side-effect free,
evaluate to a channel, and only refer to integers, constants and channels.

Assignment. An assignment label is a comma separated list of expressions
with a side-effect; expressions must only refer to clocks, integer variables,
and constants and only assign integer values to clocks.

Invariant. An invariant is an expression that satisfies the following conditions:
it is side-effect free; only clock, integer variables, and constants are referenced; it is a conjunction of conditions of the form x<e or x<=e where x is a
clock reference and e evaluates to an integer.

$$
\begin{aligned}
\textit{Expression} \rightarrow\ & \text{ID} \mid \text{NAT} \\
\mid\ & \textit{Expression } \text{'['} \textit{ Expression } \text{']'} \\
\mid\ & \text{'('} \textit{ Expression } \text{')'} \\
\mid\ & \textit{Expression } \text{'++'} \mid \text{'++'} \textit{ Expression} \\
\mid\ & \textit{Expression } \text{'--'} \mid \text{'--'} \textit{ Expression} \\
\mid\ & \textit{Expression AssignOp Expression} \\
\mid\ & \textit{UnaryOp Expression} \\
\mid\ & \textit{Expression BinaryOp Expression} \\
\mid\ & \textit{Expression } \text{'?'} \textit{ Expression } \text{':'} \textit{ Expression} \\
\mid\ & \textit{Expression } \text{'.'} \text{ ID} \\
\textit{UnaryOp } \rightarrow\ & \text{'-'} \mid \text{'!'} \mid \text{'not'} \\
\textit{BinaryOp } \rightarrow\ & \text{'<'} \mid \text{'<='} \mid \text{'=='} \mid \text{'!='} \mid \text{'>='} \mid \text{'>'} \\
\mid\ & \text{'+'} \mid \text{'-'} \mid \text{'*'} \mid \text{'/'} \mid \text{'\%'} \mid \text{'\&'} \\
\mid\ & \text{'|'} \mid \text{'\^{}'} \mid \text{'<<'} \mid \text{'>>'} \mid \text{'\&\&'} \mid \text{'||'} \\
\mid\ & \text{'<?'} \mid \text{'>?'} \mid \text{'and'} \mid \text{'or'} \mid \text{'imply'} \\
\textit{AssignOp } \rightarrow\ & \text{':='} \mid \text{'+='} \mid \text{'-='} \mid \text{'*='} \mid \text{'/='} \mid \text{'\%='} \\
\mid\ & \text{'|='} \mid \text{'\&='} \mid \text{'\^{}='} \mid \text{'<<='} \mid \text{'>>='}
\end{aligned}
$$

Fig. 2. Syntax of expressions in BNF.

2.2   The Query Language

The main purpose of a model checker is verify the model w.r.t. a requirement
specification. Like the model, the requirement specification must be expressed
in a formally well-defined and machine readable language. Several such logics
exist in the scientific literature, and UPPAAL uses a simplified version of CTL.
Like in CTL, the query language consists of path formulae and state formulae[1].
State formulae describe individual states, whereas path formulae quantify over
paths or traces of the model. Path formulae can be classified into *reachability*,
safety and *liveness*. Figure 3 illustrates the different path formulae supported by
UPPAAL. Each type is described below.

State Formulae. A state formula is an expression (see Fig. 2) that can be
evaluated for a state without looking at the behaviour of the model. For instance,

---

[1] In contrast to CTL, UPPAAL does not allow nesting of path formulae.

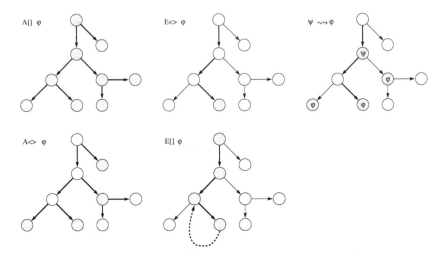

Fig. 3. Path formulae supported in UPPAAL. The filled states are those for which a given state formulae ϕ holds. Bold edges are used to show the paths the formulae evaluate on.

this could be a simple expression, like i == 7, that is true in a state whenever i equals 7. The syntax of state formulae is a superset of that of guards, i.e., a state formula is a side-effect free expression, but in contrast to guards, the use of disjunctions is not restricted. It is also possible to test whether a particular process is in a given location using an expression on the form P.l, where P is a process and l is a location.

In UPPAAL, deadlock is expressed using a special state formula (although this is not strictly a state formula). The formula simply consists of the keyword deadlock and is satisfied for all deadlock states. A state is a deadlock state if there are no outgoing action transitions neither from the state itself or any of its delay successors. Due to current limitations in UPPAAL, the deadlock state formula can only be used with reachability and invariantly path formulae (see below).

Reachability Properties. Reachability properties are the simplest form of properties. They ask whether a given state formula, φ, *possibly* can be satisfied by any reachable state. Another way of stating this is: Does there exist a path starting at the initial state, such that φ is eventually satisfied along that path.

Reachability properties are often used while designing a model to perform sanity checks. For instance, when creating a model of a communication protocol involving a sender and a receiver, it makes sense to ask whether it is possible for the sender to send a message at all or whether a message can possibly be received. These properties do not by themselves guarantee the correctness of the protocol (i.e. that any message is eventually delivered), but they validate the basic behaviour of the model.

We express that some state satisfying φ should be reachable using the path formula $E\diamond \varphi$. In UPPAAL, we write this property using the syntax E<> φ.

Safety Properties. Safety properties are on the form: "something bad will never happen". For instance, in a model of a nuclear power plant, a safety property might be, that the operating temperature is always (invariantly) under a certain threshold, or that a meltdown never occurs. A variation of this property is that "something will possibly never happen". For instance when playing a game, a safe state is one in which we can still win the game, hence we will possibly not loose.

In UPPAAL these properties are formulated positively, e.g., something good is invariantly true. Let φ be a state formulae. We express that φ should be true in all reachable states with the path formulae $A\square\,\varphi$ [2], whereas $E\square\,\varphi$ says that there should exist a maximal path such that φ is always true[3]. In UPPAAL we write A[] φ and E[] φ, respectively.

Liveness Properties. Liveness properties are of the form: something will eventually happen, e.g. when pressing the *on* button of the remote control of the television, then eventually the television should turn on. Or in a model of a communication protocol, any message that has been sent should eventually be received.

In its simple form, liveness is expressed with the path formula $A\diamond\,\varphi$, meaning φ is eventually satisfied[4]. The more useful form is the *leads to* or *response* property, written $\varphi \rightsquigarrow \psi$ which is read as whenever φ is satisfied, then eventually ψ will be satisfied, e.g. whenever a message is sent, then eventually it will be received[5]. In UPPAAL these properties are written as A<> φ and φ --> ψ, respectively.

2.3 Understanding Time

Invariants and Guards. UPPAAL uses a continuous time model. We illustrate the concept of time with a simple example that makes use of an *observer*. Normally an observer is an add-on automaton in charge of detecting events without changing the observed system. In our case the clock reset (x:=0) is delegated to the observer for illustration purposes.

Figure 4 shows the first model with its observer. We have two automata in parallel. The first automaton has a self-loop guarded by x>=2, x being a clock, that synchronises on the channel **reset** with the second automaton. The second automaton, the observer, detects when the self loop edge is taken with the location **taken** and then has an edge going back to **idle** that resets the clock x. We moved the reset of x from the self loop to the observer only to test what happens on the transition before the reset. Notice that the location **taken** is committed (marked **c**) to avoid delay in that location.

---

[2] Notice that $A\square\,\varphi = \neg E\diamond\,\neg\varphi$.

[3] A maximal path is a path that is either infinite or where the last state has no outgoing transitions.

[4] Notice that $A\diamond\,\varphi = \neg E\square\,\neg\varphi$.

[5] Experts in CTL will recognise that $\varphi \rightsquigarrow \psi$ is equivalent to $A\square\,(\varphi \implies A\diamond\,\psi)$.

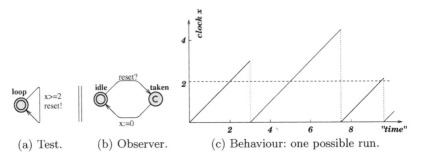

(a) Test.   (b) Observer.   (c) Behaviour: one possible run.

Fig. 4. First example with an observer.

The following properties can be verified in Uppaal (see section 3 for an overview of the interface). Assuming we name the observer automaton Obs, we have:

- A[] Obs.taken imply x>=2 : all resets off x will happen when x is above 2. This query means that for all reachable states, being in the location Obs.taken implies that x>=2.
- E<> Obs.idle and x>3 : this property requires, that it is possible to reacha state where Obs is in the location idle and x is bigger than 3. Essentially we check that we delay at least 3 time units between resets. The result would have been the same for larger values like 30000, since there are no invariants in this model.

We update the first model and add an *invariant* to the location loop, as shown in Fig. 5. The invariant is a progress condition: the system is not allowed to stay in the state more than 3 time units, so that the transition has to be taken and the clock reset in our example. Now the clock x has 3 as an upper bound. The following properties hold:

- A[] Obs.taken imply (x>=2 and x<=3) shows that the transition is taken when x is between 2 and 3, i.e., after a delay between 2 and 3.
- E<> Obs.idle and x>2 : it is possible to take the transition when x is between 2 and 3. The upper bound 3 is checked with the next property.
- A[] Obs.idle imply x<=3 : to show that the upper bound is respected.

The former property E<> Obs.idle and x>3 no longer holds.

Now, if we remove the invariant and change the guard to x>=2 and x<=3, you may think that it is the same as before, but it is not! The system has no progress condition, just a new condition on the guard. Figure 6 shows what happens: the system may take the same transitions as before, but deadlock may also occur. The system may be stuck if it does not take the transition after 3 time units. In fact, the system fails the property A[] not deadlock. The property A[] Obs.idle imply x<=3 does not hold any longer and the deadlock can also be illustrated by the property A[] x>3 imply not Obs.taken, i.e., after 3 time units, the transition is not taken any more.

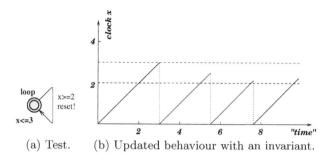

(a) Test.   (b) Updated behaviour with an invariant.

Fig. 5. Updated example with an invariant. The observer is the same as in Fig. 4 and is not shown here.

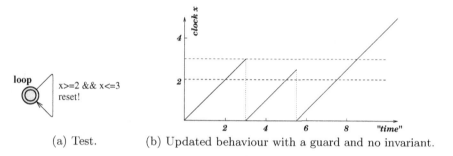

(a) Test.   (b) Updated behaviour with a guard and no invariant.

Fig. 6. Updated example with a guard and no invariant.

Committed and Urgent Locations. There are three different types of locations in UPPAAL: normal locations with or without invariants (e.g., x<=3 in the previous example), urgent locations, and committed locations. Figure 7 shows 3 automata to illustrate the difference. The location marked u is urgent and the one marked c is committed. The clocks are local to the automata, i.e., x in P0 is different from x in P1.

To understand the difference between normal locations and urgent locations, we can observe that the following properties hold:

- E<> P0.S1 and P0.x>0 : it is possible to wait in S1 of P0.
- A[] P1.S1 imply P1.x==0 : it is not possible to wait in S1 of P1.

An urgent location is equivalent to a location with incoming edges resetting a designated clock y and labelled with the invariant y<=0. Time may not progress in an urgent state, but interleavings with normal states are allowed.

A committed location is more restrictive: in all the states where P2.S1 is active (in our example), the only possible transition is the one that fires the edge outgoing from P2.S1. A *state* having a committed location active is said to be committed: delay is not allowed and the committed location must be left in the successor state (or one of the committed locations if there are several ones).

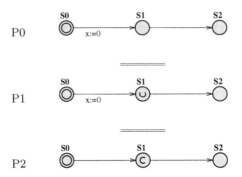

Fig. 7. Automata in parallel with normal, urgent and commit states. The clocks are local, i.e., P0.x and P1.x are two different clocks.

3 Overview of the Uppaal Toolkit

Uppaal uses a client-server architecture, splitting the tool into a graphical user interface and a model checking engine. The user interface, or client, is implemented in Java and the engine, or server, is compiled for different platforms (Linux, Windows, Solaris)[6]. As the names suggest, these two components may be run on different machines as they communicate with each other via TCP/IP. There is also a stand-alone version of the engine that can be used on the command line.

3.1 The Java Client

The idea behind the tool is to model a system with timed automata using a graphical editor, simulate it to validate that it behaves as intended, and finally to verify that it is correct with respect to a set of properties. The graphical interface (GUI) of the Java client reflects this idea and is divided into three main parts: the editor, the simulator, and the verifier, accessible via three "tabs".

The Editor. A system is defined as a network of timed automata, called processes in the tool, put in parallel. A process is instantiated from a parameterized template. The editor is divided into two parts: a tree pane to access the different templates and declarations and a drawing canvas/text editor. Figure 8 shows the editor with the train gate example of section 4. Locations are labeled with names and invariants and edges are labeled with guard conditions (e.g., e==id), synchronizations (e.g., go?), and assignments (e.g., x:=0).

The tree on the left hand side gives access to different parts of the system description:

Global declaration. Contains global integer variables, clocks, synchronization channels, and constants.

---

[6] A version for Mac OS X is in preparation.

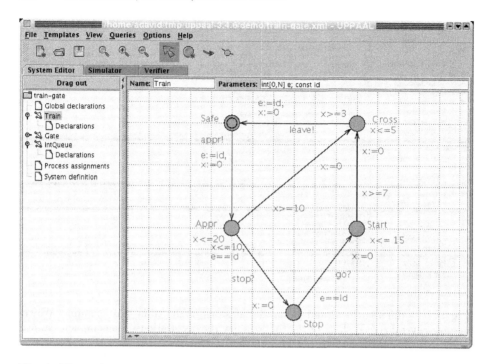

Fig. 8. The train automaton of the train gate example. The *select* button is activated in the tool-bar. In this mode the user can move locations and edges or edit labels. The other modes are for adding locations, edges, and vertexes on edges (called nails). A new location has no name by default. Two text fields allow the user to define the template name and its parameters. Useful trick: The middle mouse button is a shortcut for adding new elements, i.e. pressing it on the the canvas, a location, or edge adds a new location, edge, or nail, respectively.

Templates. `Train`, `Gate`, and `IntQueue` are different parameterized timed automata. A template may have local declarations of variables, channels, and constants.

Process assignments. Templates are instantiated into processes. The process assignment section contains declarations for these instances.

System definition. The list of processes in the system.

The syntax used in the labels and the declarations is described in the help system of the tool. The local and global declarations are shown in Fig. 9. The graphical syntax is directly inspired from the description of timed automata in section 2.

The Simulator. The simulator can be used in three ways: the user can run the system manually and choose which transitions to take, the random mode can be toggled to let the system run on its own, or the user can go through a trace (saved or imported from the verifier) to see how certain states are reachable. Figure 10 shows the simulator. It is divided into four parts:

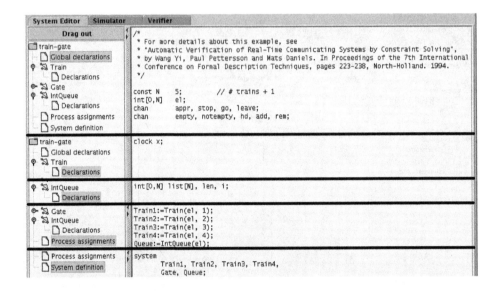

Fig. 9. The different local and global declarations of the train gate example. We superpose several screen-shots of the tool to show the declarations in a compact manner.

The control part is used to choose and fire enabled transitions, go through a trace, and toggle the random simulation.

The variable view shows the values of the integer variables and the clock constraints. UPPAAL does not show concrete states with actual values for the clocks. Since there are infinitely many of such states, UPPAAL instead shows sets of concrete states known as symbolic states. All concrete states in a symbolic state share the same location vector and the same values for discrete variables. The possible values of the clocks is described by a set of constraints. The clock validation in the symbolic state are exactly those that satisfy all constraints.

The system view shows all instantiated automata and active locations of the current state.

The message sequence chart shows the synchronizations between the different processes as well as the active locations at every step.

The Verifier. The verifier "tab" is shown in Fig. 11. Properties are selectable in the *Overview* list. The user may model-check one or several properties[7], insert or remove properties, and toggle the view to see the properties or the comments in the list. When a property is selected, it is possible to edit its definition (e.g., `E<> Train1.Cross and Train2.Stop ...`) or comments to document what the property means informally. The *Status* panel at the bottom shows the communication with the server.

When trace generation is enabled and the model-checker finds a trace, the user is asked if she wants to import it into the simulator. Satisfied properties are

---

[7] Several properties only if no trace is to be generated.

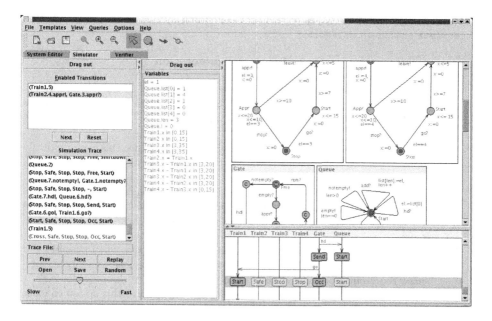

Fig. 10. View of the simulator tab for the train gate example. The interpretation of the constraint system in the variable panel depends on whether a transition in the transition panel is selected or not. If no transition is selected, then the constrain system shows all possible clock valuations that can be reached along the path. If a transition is selected, then only those clock valuations from which the transition can be taken are shown. Keyboard bindings for navigating the simulator without the mouse can be found in the integrated help system.

marked green and violated ones red. In case either an over approximation or an under approximation has been selected in the options menu, then it may happen that the verification is inconclusive with the approximation used. In that case the properties are marked yellow.

3.2   The Stand-Alone Verifier

When running large verification tasks, it is often cumbersome to execute these from inside the GUI. For such situations, the stand-alone command line verifier called `verifyta` is more appropriate. It also makes it easy to run the verification on a remote UNIX machine with memory to spare. It accepts command line arguments for all options available in the GUI, see Table 1.

4   Example 1: The Train Gate

4.1   Description

The train gate example is distributed with UPPAAL. It is a railway control system which controls access to a bridge for several trains. The bridge is a critical shared

Table 1. Options of `verifyta` and the corresponding options in the GUI. Defaults of `verifyta` are shown in boldface.

State Space Representation

-C DBM
   Use DBMs rather than a minimal constrain graph [46] in the state representation used to store reachable states. This increases the memory usage (more so in models with many clocks), but is often faster.

-A Over approximation
   Use convex hull over-approximation [7]. For timed systems, this can drastically increase verification speed. For untimed systems, this has no effect.

-Z Under approximation
   Use bit-state hashing under-approximation. This reduces memory consumption to a more of less fixed amount. The precision of the approximation is controlled by changing the hash table size. Known as *super-trace* in [34, 35].

-T Reuse
   Speed up verification by reusing the generated state-space when possible. For some combinations of properties this option can *possibly* lead to a larger state-space representation, thus nullifying the speedup.

-U When representing states with minimal constraint graphs, this option changes how states are compared. It reduces the memory consumption at the expense of a more time consuming comparison operator. The reduced memory usage might cancel out the overhead. In the GUI, this is always on.

-H Change the size of hash tables used during verification. Can give a speedup for large systems.

State Space Reduction

-S0 None
   Store all reachable states. Uses most memory, but avoids that any state is explored more than once.

-S1 Conservative
   Store all non-committed states. Less memory when committed locations are used, and for most models states are only explored once.

-S2 Aggressive
   Try hard to reduce the number of states stored. Uses much less memory, but might take much more time. Do not combine this option with depth first search, as the running time increases drastically.

Search Order

-b Breadth First
   Search the state space using a breadth first strategy.

-d Depth First
   Search the state space using a depth first strategy.

Trace Options

-t0 Some Trace
   Generate some diagnostic trace.

-t1 Shortest Trace
   Generate the shortest (in number of steps) trace.

-t2 Fastest Trace
   Generate the fastest (smallest time delay) trace.

-f Write traces to XTR trace files (which can be read by the GUI).

-y By default concrete traces (showing both delay and control transitions) are produced. This option produces symbolic traces like those shown in the GUI.

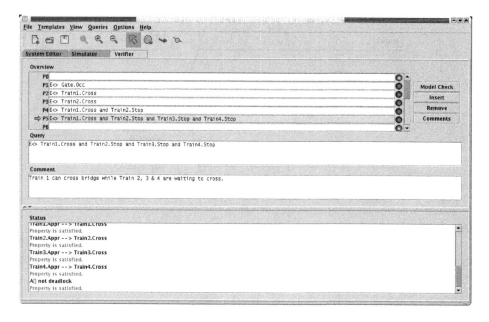

Fig. 11. View of the verification tab for the train gate example.

resource that may be accessed only by one train at a time. The system is defined as a number of trains (assume 4 for this example) and a controller. A train can not be stopped instantly and restarting also takes time. Therefor, there are timing constraints on the trains before entering the bridge. When approaching, a train sends a appr! signal. Thereafter, it has 10 time units to receive a stop signal. This allows it to stop safely before the bridge. After these 10 time units, it takes further 10 time units to reach the bridge if the train is not stopped. If a train is stopped, it resumes its course when the controller sends a go! signal to it after a previous train has left the bridge and sent a leave! signal. Figures 12 and 13 show two situations.

4.2   Modelling in UPPAAL

The model of the train gate has three templates:

Train is the model of a train, shown in Fig. 8.
Gate is the model of the gate controller, shown in Fig. 14.
IntQueue is the model of the queue of the controller, shown in Fig. 15. It is simpler to separate the queue from the controller, which makes it easier to get the model right.

The Template of the Train. The template in Fig. 8 has five locations: Safe, Appr, Stop, Start, and Cross. The initial location is Safe, which corresponds

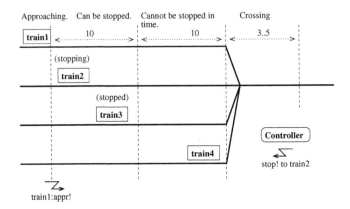

Fig. 12. Train gate example: train4 is about to cross the bridge, train3 is stopped, train2 was ordered to stop and is stopping. Train1 is approaching and sends an appr! signal to the controller that sends back a stop! signal. The different sections have timing constraints (10, 10, between 3 and 5).

to a train not approaching yet. The location has no invariant, which means that a train may stay in this location an unlimited amount of time. When a train is approaching, it synchronises with the controller. This is done by the channel synchronisation appr! on the transition to Appr. The controller has a corresponding appr?. The clock x is reset and the parameterised variable e is set to the identity of this train. This variable is used by the queue and the controller to know which train is allowed to continue or which trains must be stopped and later restarted.

The location Appr has the invariant $x \leq 20$, which has the effect that the location must be left within 20 time units. The two outgoing transitions are guarded by the constraints $x \leq 10$ and $x \geq 10$, which corresponds to the two sections before the bridge: can be stopped and can not be stopped. At exactly 10, both transitions are enabled, which allows us to take into account any race conditions if there is one. If the train can be stopped ($x \leq 10$) then the transition to the location Stop is taken, otherwise the train goes to location Cross. The transition to Stop is also guarded by the condition $e == id$ and is synchronised with stop?. When the controller decides to stop a train, it decides which one (sets e) and synchronises with stop!.

The location Stop has no invariant: a train may be stopped for an unlimited amount of time. It waits for the synchronisation go?. The guard $e == id$ ensures that the right train is restarted. The model is simplified here compared to the version described in [51], namely the slowdown phase is not modelled explicitly. We can assume that a train may receive a go? synchronisation even when it is not stopped completely, which will give a non-deterministic restarting time.

The location Start has the invariant $x \leq 15$ and its outgoing transition has the constraint $x \geq 7$. This means that a train is restarted and reaches the crossing section between 7 and 15 time units non-deterministically.

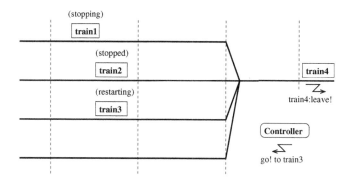

Fig. 13. Now train4 has crossed the bridge and sends a leave! signal. The controller can now let train3 cross the bridge with a go! signal. Train2 is now waiting and train1 is stopping.

The location **Cross** is similar to **Start** in the sense that it is left between 3 and 5 time units after entering it.

The Template of the Gate. The gate controller in Fig. 14 synchronises with the queue and the trains. Some of its locations do not have names. Typically, they are committed locations (marked with a **c**).

The controller starts in the **Free** location (i.e., the bridge is free), where it tests the queue to see if it is empty or not. If the queue is empty then the controller waits for approaching trains (next location) with the **appr?** synchronisation. When a train is approaching, it is added to the queue with the **add!** synchronisation. If the queue is not empty, then the first train on the queue (read by **hd!**) is restarted with the **go!** synchronisation.

In the **Occ** location, the controller essentially waits for the running train to leave the bridge (**leave?**). If other trains are approaching (**appr?**), they are stopped (**stop!**) and added to the queue (**add!**). When a train leaves the bridge, the controller removes it from the queue with the **rem?** synchronisation.

The Template of the Queue. The queue in Fig. 15 has essentially one location **Start** where it is waiting for commands from the controller. The **Shiftdown** location is used to compute a shift of the queue (necessary when the front element is removed). This template uses an array of integers and handles it as a FIFO queue.

4.3 Verification

We check simple reachability, safety, and liveness properties, and for absence of deadlock. The simple reachability properties check if a given location is reachable:

- **E<> Gate.Occ**: the gate can receive and store messages from approaching trains in the queue.

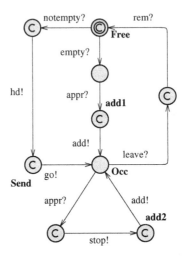

Fig. 14. Gate automaton of the train gate.

- E<> Train1.Cross: train 1 can cross the bridge. We check similar properties
  for the other trains.
- E<> Train1.Cross and Train2.Stop: train 1 can be crossing the bridge
  while train 2 is waiting to cross. We check for similar properties for the
  other trains.
- E<> Train1.Cross && Train2.Stop && Train3.Stop && Train4.Stop is
  similar to the previous property, with all the other trains waiting to cross
  the bridge. We have similar properties for the other trains.

The following safety properties must hold for all reachable states:

- A[] Train1.Cross+Train2.Cross+Train3.Cross+Train4.Cross<=1. There is
  not more than one train crossing the bridge at any time. This expression
  uses the fact that Train1.Cross evaluates to true or false, i.e., 1 or 0.
- A[] Queue.list[N-1] == 0: there can never be N elements in the queue,
  i.e., the array will never overflow. Actually, the model defines N as the number of trains + 1 to check for this property. It is possible to use a queue
  length matching the number of trains and check for this property instead:
  A[] (Gate.add1 or Gate.add2) imply Queue.len < N-1 where the locations add1 and add2 are the only locations in the model from which add! is
  possible.

The liveness properties are of the form Train1.Appr --> Train1.Cross:
whenever train 1 approaches the bridge, it will eventually cross, and similarly
for the other trains. Finally, to check that the system is deadlock-free, we verify
the property A[] not deadlock.

Suppose that we made a mistake in the queue, namely we wrote e:=list[1]
in the template IntQueue instead of e:=list[0] when reading the head on the

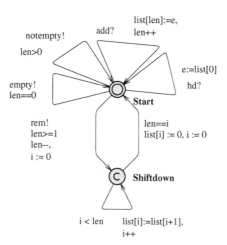

Fig. 15. Queue automaton of the train gate. The template is parameterised with
int[0,n] e.

transition synchronised with hd?. We could have been confused when thinking
in terms of indexes. It is interesting to note that the properties still hold, except
the liveness ones. The verification gives a counter-example showing what may
happen: a train may cross the bridge but the next trains will have to stop. When
the queue is shifted the train that starts again is never the first one, thus the
train at the head of the queue is stuck and can never cross the bridge.

5   Example 2: Fischer's Protocol

5.1   Description

Fischer's protocol is a well-known mutual exclusion protocol designed for n processes. It is a timed protocol where the concurrent processes check for both a
delay and their turn to enter the critical section using a shared variable id.

5.2   Modelling in Uppaal

The automaton of the protocol is given in Fig. 16. Starting from the initial
location (marked with a double circle), processes go to a request location, req,
if id==0, which checks that it is the turn for no process to enter the critical
section. Processes stay non-deterministically between 0 and k time units in req,
and then go to the wait location and set id to their process ID (pid). There it
must wait at least k time units, x>k, k being a constant (2 here), before entering
the critical section CS if it is its turn, id==pid. The protocol is based on the fact
that after (strict) k time units with id different from 0, all the processes that
want to enter the critical section are waiting to enter the critical section as well,
but only one has the right ID. Upon exiting the critical section, processes reset
id to allow other processes to enter CS. When processes are waiting, they may
retry when another process exits CS by returning to req.

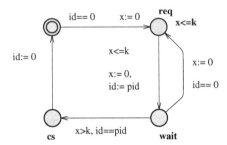

Fig. 16. Template of Fischer's protocol. The parameter of the template is `const pid`. The template has the local declarations `clock x; const k 2;`.

5.3 Verification

The safety property of the protocol is to check for mutual exclusion of the location CS: `A[] P1.cs + P2.cs + P3.cs + P4.cs <= 1`. This property uses the trick that these tests evaluate to true or false, i.e., 0 or 1. We check that the system is deadlock-free with the property `A[] not deadlock`.

The liveness properties are of the form `P1.req --> P1.wait` and similarly for the other processes. They check that whenever a process tries to enter the critical section, it will always eventually enter the waiting location. Intuitively, the reader would also expect the property `P1.req --> P1.cs` that similarly states that the critical section is eventually reachable. However, this property is violated. The interpretation is that the process is allowed to stay in `wait` for ever, thus there is a way to avoid the critical section.

Now, if we try to fix the model and add the invariant `x <= 2*k` to the wait location, the property `P1.req --> P1.cs` still does not hold because it is possible to reach a deadlock state where `P1.wait` is active, thus there is a path that does not lead to the critical section. The deadlock is as follows: `P1.wait` with $0 \leq x \leq 2$ and `P4.wait` with $2 \leq x \leq 4$. Delay is forbidden in this state, due to the invariant on `P4.wait` and `P4.wait` can not be left because $id == 1$.

6 Modelling Patterns

In this section we present a number of useful modelling patterns for UPPAAL. A modelling pattern is a form of designing a model with a clearly stated intent, motivation and structure. We observe that most of our UPPAAL models use one or more of the following patterns and we propose that these patterns are imitated when designing new models.

6.1 Variable Reduction

Intent

To reduce the size of the state space by explicitly resetting variables when they are not used, thus speeding up the verification.

Motivation

Although variables are persistent, it is sometimes clear from the way a model behaves, that the value of a variable does not matter in certain states, i.e., it is clear that two states that only differ in the values of such variables are in fact bisimilar. Resetting these variables to a known value will make these two states identical, thus reducing the state space.

Structure

The pattern is most easily applied to local variables. Basically, a variable v is called inactive in a location l, if along all paths starting from l, v will be reset before it will be used. If a variable v is inactive in location v, one should reset v to the initial value on all incoming edges of l.

The exception to this rule is when v is inactive in all source locations of the incoming edges to l. In this case, v has already been reset, and there is no need to reset it again. The pattern is also applicable to shared variables, although it can be harder to recognise the locations in which the variable will be inactive.

For clocks, UPPAAL automatically performs the analysis described above. This process is called active clock reduction. In some situations this analysis may fail, since UPPAAL does not take the values of non-clock variables into account when analysing the activeness. In those situations, it *might* speed up the verification, if the clocks are reset to zero when it becomes inactive. A similar problem arises if you use arrays of clocks and use integer variables to index into those arrays. Then UPPAAL will only be able to make a coarse approximation of when clocks in the array will be tested and reset, often causing the complete array to be marked active at all times. Manually resetting the clocks *might* speed up verification.

Sample

The queue of the train gate example presented earlier in this tutorial uses the active variable pattern twice, see Fig. 17: When an element is removed, all the remaining elements of the list are shifted by one position. At the end of the loop in the Shiftdown location, the counter variable i is reset to 0, since its value is no longer of importance. Also the freed up element list[i] in the list is reset to zero, since its value will never be used again. For this example, the speedup in verification gained by using this pattern is approximately a factor of 5.

Known Uses

The pattern is used in most models of some complexity.

6.2   Synchronous Value Passing

Intent

To synchronously pass data between processes.

Motivation

Consider a model of a wireless network, where nodes in the network are modelled as processes. Neighbouring nodes must communicate to exchange, e.g., routing

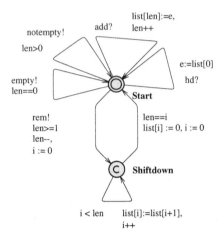

Fig. 17. The model of the queue in the train gate example uses active variable reduction twice. Both cases are on the edge from **Shiftdown** to **Start**: The freed element in the queue is reset to the initial value and so is the counter variable **i**.

information. Assuming that the communication delay is insignificant, the handshake can be modelled as synchronisation via channels, but any data exchange must be modelled by other means.

The general idea is that a sender and a receiver synchronise over shared binary channels and exchange data via shared variables. Since UPPAAL evaluates the assignment of the sending synchronisation first, the sender can assign a value to the shared variable which the receiver can then access directly.

Structure

There are four variations of the value passing pattern, see Fig. 18. They differ in whether data is passed *one-way* or *two-way* and whether the synchronisation is *unconditional* or *conditional*. In one-way value passing a value is transfered from one process to another, whereas two-way value passing transfers a value in each direction. In unconditional value passing, the receiver does not block the communication, whereas conditional value passing allows the receiver to reject the synchronisation based on the data that was passed.

In all four cases, the data is passed via the globally declared shared variable **var** and synchronisation is achieved via the global channels **c** and **d**. Each process has local variables **in** and **out**. Although communication via channels is always synchronous, we refer to a **c!** as a send-action and **c?** as a receive-action. Notice that the *variable reduction* pattern is used to reset the shared variable when it is no longer needed.

In one-way value passing only a single channel **c** and a shared variable **var** is required. The sender writes the data to the shared variable and performs a send-action. The receiver performs the co-action, thereby synchronising with the sender. Since the update on the edge with send-action is always evaluated before

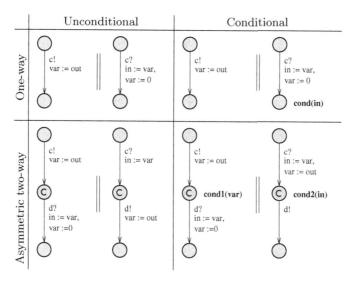

Fig. 18. The are essentially four combinations of conditional, uncoditional, one-way and two-way synchronous value passing.

the update of the edge with the receive-action, the receiver can access the data written by the sender in the same transition. In the conditional case, the receiver can block the synchronisation according to some predicate `cond(in)` involving the value passed by the sender. The intuitive placement of this predicate is on the guard of the receiving edge. Unfortunately, this will not work as expected, since the guards of the edges are evaluated before the updates are executed, i.e., before the receiver has access to the value. The solution is to place the predicate on the invariant of the target location.

Two-way value passing can be modelled with two one-way value passing pattern with intermediate committed locations. The committed locations enforce that the synchronisation is atomic. Notice the use of two channels: Although not strictly necessary in the two-process case, the two channel encoding scales to the case with many processes that non-deterministically choose to synchronise. In the conditional case each process has a predicate involving the value passed by the other process. The predicates are placed on the invariants of the committed locations and therefore assignment to the shared variable in the second process must be moved to the first edge. It might be tempting to encoding conditional two-way value passing directly with two one-way conditional value passing pattern, i.e., to place the predicate of the first process on the third location. Unfortunately, this will introduce spurious deadlocks into the model.

If the above asymmetric encoding of two-way value passing is undesirable, the symmetric encoding in Fig. 19 can be used instead. Basically, a process can non-deterministically choose to act as either the sender or the receiver. Like before, committed locations guarantee atomicity. If the synchronisation is conditional, the predicates are placed on the committed locations to avoid deadlocks. Notice

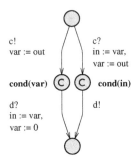

Fig. 19. In contast to the two-way encoding shown in Fig 18, this encoding is symmetric in the sense that both automata use the exact same encoding. The symmetry comes at the cost of a slightly larger state space.

that the symmetric encoding is more expensive: Even though the two paths lead to the same result, two extra successors will be generated.

Sample
The train gate example of this tutorial uses synchronous one-way unconditional value passing between the trains and the gate, and between the gate and the queue. In fact, the value passing actually happens between the trains and the queue and the gate only act as a mediator to decouple the trains from the queue.

Known Uses
Lamport's Distributed Leader Election Protocol. Nodes in this leader election protocol broadcast topology information to surrounding nodes. The communication is not instantaneous, so an intermediate process is used to model the message. The nodes and the message exchange data via synchronous one-way unconditional value passing.

Lynch's Distributed Clock Synchronisation Protocol. This distributed protocol synchronises drifting clocks of nodes in a network. There is a fair amount of non-determinism on when exactly the clocks are synchronised, since the protocol only required this to happen within some time window. When two nodes synchronise non-deterministically, both need to know the other nodes identity. As an extra constraint, the synchronisation should only happen if it has not happened before in the current cycle. Here the asymmetric two-way conditional value passing pattern is used. The asymmetric pattern suffices since each node has been split into two processes, one of them being dedicated to synchronising with the neighbours.

6.3   Atomicity

Intent
To reduce the size of the state space by reducing interleaving using committed locations, thus speeding up the verification.

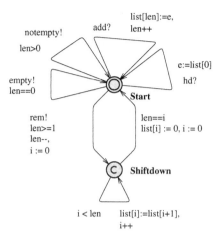

Fig. 20. When removing the front element from the queue, all other elements must be shifted down. This is done in the loop in the **Shiftdown** location. To avoid unnecessary interleavings, the location is marked committed. Notice that the edge entering **Shiftdown** synchronises over the **rem** channel. It is important that target locations of edges synchronising over **rem** in other processes are not marked committed.

Motivation
UPPAAL uses an asynchronous execution model, i.e., edges from different automata can interleave, and UPPAAL will explore all possible interleavings. Partial order reduction is an automatic technique for eliminating unnecessary interleavings, but UPPAAL does not support partial order reduction. In many situations, unnecessary interleavings can be identified and eliminated by making part of the model execute in atomic steps.

Structure
Committed locations are the key to achieving atomicity. When any of the processes is in a committed location, then time cannot pass and at least one of these processes must take part in the next transition. Notice that this does not rule out interleaving when several processes are in a committed location. On the other hand, if only one process is in a committed location, then that process must take part in the next transition. Therefore, several edges can be executed atomically by marking intermediate locations as committed and avoiding synchronisations with other processes in the part that must be executed atomically, thus guaranteeing that the process is the only one in a committed location.

Sample
The pattern is used in the Queue process of the train gate example, see Fig. 20.

Known Uses
Encoding of control structure A very common use is when encoding control structures (like the encoding of a for-loop used in the **IntQueue** process of the train-gate example): In these cases the interleaving semantics is often undesirable.

Multi-casting Another common use is for complex synchronisation patterns. The standard synchronisation mechanism in UPPAAL only supports binary or broadcast synchronisation, but by using committed locations it is possible to atomically synchronise with several processes. One example of this is in the train-gate example: Here the `Gate` process acts as a mediator between the trains and the queue, first synchronising with one and then the other – using an intermediate committed location to ensure atomicity.

6.4   Urgent Edges

Intent
To guarantee that an edge is taken without delay as soon as it becomes enabled.

Motivation
UPPAAL provides urgent locations as a means of saying that a location must be left without delay. UPPAAL provides urgent channels as a means of saying that a synchronisation must be executed as soon as the guards of the edges involved are enabled. There is no way of directly expressing that an edge without synchronisation should be taken without delay. This pattern provides a way of encoding this behaviour.

Structure
The encoding of urgent edges introduces an extra process with a single location and a self loop (see Fig. 21 left). The self loop synchronises on the *urgent* channel `go`. An edge can now be made urgent by performing the complimentary action (see Fig. 21 right). The edge can have discrete guards and arbitrary updates, but no guards over clocks.

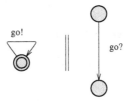

Fig. 21. Encoding of urgent edges. The `go` channel is declared urgent.

Sample
This pattern is used in a model of a box sorting plant (see `http://www.cs.auc.dk/~behrmann/esv03/exercises/index.html#sorter`): Boxes are moved on a belt, registered at a sensor station and then sorted by a sorting station (a piston that can kick some of the boxes of the belt). Since it takes some time to move the boxes from the sensor station to the sorting station, a timer process is used to delay the sorting action. Figure 22 shows the timer (this is obviously not the only encoding of a timer – this particular encoding happens to match the one

used in the control program of the plant). The timer is activated by setting a shared variable `active` to true. The timer should then move urgently from the `passive` location to the `wait` location. This is achieved by synchronising over the urgent channel `go`.

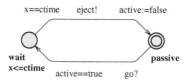

Fig. 22. Sample of a timer using an urgent edge during activation.

6.5   Timers

Intent
To emulate a timer where, in principle, time decreases until it reaches zero, at which point the timer is said to time-out.

Motivation
Although clocks are powerful enough to model timing mechanisms, some systems are more naturally modelled using timers, in particular event based models. In such models, a timer is started, may be restarted, and counts down until a time-out event is generated.

Structure
The pattern gives an equivalent of a timer object mapped on a process in UP-PAAL. We define the following operations for a timer object t:

- `void set(TO)`: this function starts or restarts the timer with a time-out value of TO. The timer will count down for TO time units. TO is an integer.
- `bool expired()`: this function returns *true* if the timer has expired, *false* otherwise. When the timer has not been started yet, it is said to have expired. This function may be called at any time to test the timer.

We map the above defined timer as a process in UPPAAL. When a timer t is to be used in the model, its functions are mapped as follows:

- `t.set(v)` where v is an integer variable is mapped to the synchronisation `set!` and the assignment `value := v`, where the channel `set` and the integer `value` are the parameters of the timer template.
- `t.expired()` is mapped to the guard `value == 0`, where `value` is a parameter of the timer template.

As a variant of this basic timer model, it is possible to generate a time-out synchronisation, urgent or not depending on the needs, by using the pattern to encode urgent edges shown in Fig. 21. If the time-out value is a constant, we can optimise the coding to:

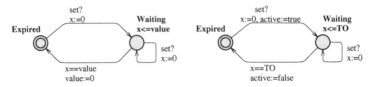

(a) Timer with variable time-out. (b) Timer with constant time-out.

Fig. 23. Template of the timer pattern. Template (a) has `int value; chan set` as parameters and template (b) has `bool active; chan set; const TO` as parameters. Both templates have the local declaration `clock x`.

- `t.set()` (no argument since the time-out is a constant) is mapped to `set!`.
- `t.expired()` is mapped to `active == false` where `active` is a parameter of the template.

The templates are shown in Fig. 23. The two states correspond to the timer having expired (timer inactive) and waiting to time-out (timer active). The template (a) makes use of a feature of UPPAAL to mix integers and clocks in clock constraints. The constraint is dynamic and depends on the value of the integer. When returning to the state `Expired`, the timer resets its `value`, which has the effect to (1) use variable reduction (see pattern 6.1) and (2) to provide a simple way to test for a time-out. The template (b) is simpler in the sense that a constant is used in the clock constraints. Testing for the time-out is equivalent to test on the boolean variable `active`.

Known Uses
A variation of the timer pattern is used in the box sorting machine of the previous pattern (for educational purposes reconstructed in Lego): A timer is activated when a colored brick passes a light sensor. When the timer times out a piston kicks the brick from the transport belt.

6.6   Bounded Liveness Checking

Intent
To check bounded liveness properties, i.e., properties that are guaranteed not only to hold eventually but within some specified upper time-bound. Time-bounded liveness properties are essentially safety properties and hence often computationally easier to verify. Thus moving from (unconditional) liveness properties to a time-bounded versions will not only provide additional information – i.e., if one can provide a valid bound – but will also lead to more efficient verification.

Motivation
For real-time systems general liveness properties are often not sufficiently expressive to ensure correctness: the fact that a particular property is guaranteed

to hold *eventually* is inadequate in case hard real-time deadlines must be observed. What is really needed is to establish that the property in question will hold within a certain upper time-limit.

Structure

We consider two variations of the pattern for a *time-bounded leads-to* operator $\varphi \leadsto_{\leq t} \psi$ expressing that whenever the state property φ holds then the state property ψ must hold within at most t time-units thereafter.

In the first version of the pattern we use a simple reduction for unbounded leadsto. First the model under investigation is extended with an additional clock z which is reset whenever φ starts to hold. The time-bounded leads-to property $\varphi \leadsto_{\leq t} \psi$ is now simply obtained by verifying $\varphi \leadsto (\psi \wedge z \leq t)$.

In the second – and more efficient version – of the pattern we use the method proposed in [47] in which time-bounded leads-to properties are reduced to simple safety properties. First the model under investigation is extended with a boolean variable b and an additional clock z. The boolean variable b must be initialised to *false*. Whenever φ starts to hold b is set to *true* and the clock z is reset. When ψ commences to hold b is set to *false*. Thus the truth-value of b indicates whether there is an obligation of ψ to hold in the future and z measures the accumulated time since this unfulfilled obligation started. The time-bounded leads-to property $\varphi \leadsto_{\leq t} \psi$ is simply obtained by verifying the safety property $A\square(b \implies z \leq t)$.

A third method not reported is based on augmenting the model under investigation with a so-called test-automata, see [2, 1].

We have deliberately been somewhat vague about the exact nature of the required augmentation of the model. The most simple case is when the (state) properties φ and ψ are simple locations l and l' of component automata. In this simple case the settings of z and b are to be added as assignments of the edges entering l and l'.

Sample

In the train gate example presented earlier in this tutorial a natural requirement is that a train is granted access to the crossing within a certain upper time-bound (say 100) after having signalled that it is approaching. In fact, not only is the gate responsible for avoiding collisions on the crossing but also for ensuring a fair and timely handling of requests. In Fig. 24 the `Train` template has been augmented with a local boolean b and a local clock z. b (to be initialised to 0) is set to 1 on the transition to location `Appr` and set to 0 on the two transitions to `Cross`. The clock z is reset on the transition to `Appr`. On the augmented model we now check the safety property `A[](Train1.b==1 imply Train1.z<=100)` which establishes that the bounded liveness property holds for `Train1`. In fact – due to obvious symmetries in the model – it suffices to establish the property for one train, `Train1` say. In this case it would have been advantageous for `Train1` to be singleton template in order to avoid augmenting *all* trains. In particular, the state-space will be substantially smaller in this way.

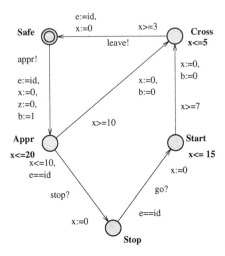

Fig. 24. The Train-Gate augmented to enable time-bounded liveness checking.

Known Uses
Almost any real-time system will have a number of liveness properties where information as to the time-bounds is vital for the correctness of the systems. The Gearbox Controller of [47] offers an excellent example where a long list of time-bounded liveness properties are directly obtained from requirements specified by the company Mecel AB.

6.7   Abstraction and Simulation

Intent
The goal of abstraction is to replace the problem of verifying a very large, infeasible concrete system with a smaller, and hopefully feasible abstract system. In particular, the method could be applied in a *compositional* manner to subsystems, i.e., various concrete subsystems are replaced by suitable abstractions, and the verification effort is conducted on the composition of these abstract subsystems.

Motivation
Despite enormous improvement in the verification capabilities of UPPAAL over the past years – and undoubtedly also for the years to come – state-space explosion is an ever existing problem that will be solved by algorithmic advances[8]. However, in verifying specific properties of a systems it is often only part of the behaviour of the various components which is relevant. Often the designer will have a good intuition about what these relevant parts are, in which case (s)he is able to provide abstractions for the various components, which are still concrete

---
[8] Unless we succeed in showing P=PSPACE.

enough that the given property holds, yet are abstract (and small) enough that the verification effort becomes feasible. To give a sound methodology two requirements should be satisfied. Firstly, the notion of abstraction applied should preserve the properties of interest, i.e., once a property has been shown to hold for the abstraction it should be guaranteed to also hold for the concrete system. Secondly, the abstraction relation should be preserved under composition of systems. In [40, 39] we have put forward the notion of (ready) timed simulation preserving safety properties while being a pre-congruence w.r.t. composition. Moreover, for (suggested) abstractions being deterministic and with no internal transitions, timed simulation may be established using simple reachability checking (and hence by using UPPAAL).

Structure

Let A be a timed automaton suggested as an abstraction for some (sub)system S (possibly a network of timed automata). We assume that A is deterministic (i.e., no location with outgoing edges having overlapping guards) and without any internal transitions. For simplicity we shall assume all channels to be non-urgent and no shared variables exist between S and the remaining system. The extension of the technique to allow for urgency and shared variables can be found in [40]. To show that A is indeed an abstraction of S in the sense that A (ready) timed simulates S a test-automata T_A is constructed in the following manner: T_A has A as a skeleton but with the direction of actions (input/output) reversed. A distinguished new location bad is added and from all locations l and all actions a an a-labelled edge from l to bad is inserted with guard $\neg(g_1 \vee \ldots \vee g_n)$ where $g_1 \ldots g_n$ is the full set of guards of a-labelled edges out of l in the skeleton. Now S is (ready) timed simulated by A – and hence A is a valid abstraction of S – precisely if the location bad is unreachable in the composite system $S\|T_A$. Essentially, T_A observes that all behaviour of S is matchable by A.

Sample

Consider the UPPAAL model in Fig. 25 consisting of a `Sender` a `Receiver` and four pipelining processes `Pi`. Each pipeline process `Pi` has the obligation of reacting to a stimulus from its predecessor on channel `ai` and pass it on to its successor on channel `ai+1`. A local clock is used to model that each pipeline process adds a minimum delay of 2. After having completed the passing on, the pipeline process engages in some internal computation (the small cycle `S2`, `S3`, `S4`). Now assume that we want to verify that the `Receiver` will have received its stimulus no sooner than after 8 time-units, or in general $2n$ in a system with n pipeline processes. Obviously, the system we are looking at is subject to an enormous state-space explosion when we increase the number of pipeline elements. However, for establishing the property in question we need only little information about the various subsystems. For `P1`$\|$`P2` we essentially only need to know that the time from reacting to the initial stimulus from the `Sender` to passing this stimulus on to `P3` is at least 4. We do not need to worry about the internal computation nor the precise moment in time when the stimulus was passed from `P1` to `P2`. In particular we should be able to replace `P1`$\|$`P2` with the

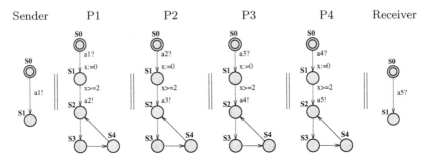

Fig. 25. A small pipelining system.

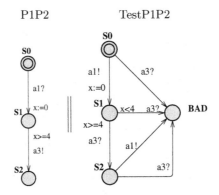

Fig. 26. A suggested abstraction and its test automaton.

much simpler automaton P1P2. To show that this is a valid substitution we simply show that the BAD location is unreachable for the system P1‖P2‖TestP1P2, where TestP1P2 is the test automaton for P1P2. A similar abstraction P3P4 may obviously be given for the subsystem P3‖P4 and the desired property may now be established for the "much" simpler system P1P2‖P3P4, rather than the original system.

Known Uses
The described technique can be found in full details in the Ph.D. thesis of Jensen [39]. In [40] the technique has been successfully applied to the verification of a protocol for controlling the switching between power on/off states in audio/video components described in [42].

7   Conclusion

UPPAAL is a research tool available for free at http://www.uppaal.com/ that features an intuitive graphical interface. It has been ported to different platforms and it is in constant development. There are different development branches and tools that make use of UPPAAL:

Cost–UPPAAL supports cost annotations of the model and can do minimal cost reachability analysis [44]. This version also has features for guiding the search. This version can be downloaded from `http://www.cs.auc.dk/~behrmann/_guiding/`.

Distributed–UPPAAL runs on multi-processors and clusters using the combined memory and CPU capacity of the system [15, 9].

T–UPPAAL test case generator for black-box conformance testing, see `http://www.cs.auc.dk/~marius/tuppaal/`.

Times is a tool set for modelling, schedulability analysis, and synthesis of (optimal) schedules and executable code. The verification uses UPPAAL [6].

On-going work on the model-checker includes support for hierarchical timed automata, symmetry reduction, UCode (UPPAAL code, large subset of C), improved memory management, etc. The tool has been successfully applied to case studies ranging from communication protocols to multimedia applications:

Bang & Olufsen audio/video protocol. An error trace with more than 2000 transition steps was found [30].

TDMA Protocol Start-Up Mechanism was verified in [48].

Bounded retransmission protocol over a lossy channels was verified in [22].

Lip synchronization algorithm was verified in [21].

Power-down controller in an audio/video component was designed and verified in collaboration with Bang & Olufsen in [29].

Guided synthesis of control programs for a steel production plant was done in [37]. The final control programs were compiled to run on a lego model of the real plant.

Gearbox controller was formally designed and analysed in [47].

Lego Mindstorm programs written in "Not Quite C" have been verified in [38].

Field bus protocol was modelled and analysed in [27].

UPPAAL is also used in a number of courses on real-time systems and formal verification:

- `http://user.it.uu.se/~paupet/#teaching`
  Real-time and formal method courses at Uppsala University.
- `http://csd.informatik.uni-oldenburg.de/teaching/fp_realzeitsys_ws0001/result/eindex.html`
  Practical course "Real-Time Systems" at the University of Oldenburg.
- `http://fmt.cs.utwente.nl/courses/systemvalidation/`
  System Validation (using Model Checking) at the University of Twente.
- `http://www.cs.auc.dk/~behrmann/esv03/`
  Embedded Systems Validation at Aalborg University.
- `http://www.cs.auc.dk/~kgl/TOV04/Plan.html`
  Test and Verification at Aalborg University.
- `http://www.seas.upenn.edu/~pappasg/EE601/F03/`
  Hybrid Systems at the University of Pennsylvania.

- http://www.it.uu.se/edu/course/homepage/proalgebra
  Process Algebra at Uppsala University.
- http://www.cs.auc.dk/~luca/SV/
  Semantics and Verification.
- http://www.cs.depaul.edu/programs/courses.asp?subject=SE&courseid=533
  Software Validation and Verification at DePaul University.
- http://www.cs.bham.ac.uk/~mzk/courses/SafetyCrit/
  Safety Critical Systems and Software Reliability at the University of Birmingham.
- http://fmt.cs.utwente.nl/courses/sysontomg/
  Systeem-ontwikkelomgevingen at the University of Twente.

Finally the following books have parts devoted to UPPAAL:

- *Concepts, Algorithms and Tools for Model-Checking* [41]: Lecture notes in its current form. It treats both Spin and UPPAAL.
- *Systems and Software Verification: Model-checking Techniques and Tools* [20]: This book identifies 6 important tools and has a chapter on UPPAAL.

References

1. Luca Aceto, Patricia Bouyer, Augusto Burgueño, and Kim Guldstrand Larsen. The power of reachability testing for timed automata. *Theoretical Computer Science*, 1–3(300):411–475, 2003.
2. Luca Aceto, Augusto Burgueño, and Kim G. Larsen. Model checking via reachability testing for timed automata. In Bernhard Steffen, editor, *Tools and Algorithms for Construction and Analysis of Systems, 4th International Conference, TACAS '98*, volume 1384 of *Lecture Notes in Computer Science*, pages 263–280. Springer–Verlag, April 1998.
3. Rajeev Alur, Costas Courcoubetis, and David L. Dill. Model-checking for real-time systems. In *5th Symposium on Logic in Computer Science (LICS'90)*, pages 414–425, 1990.
4. Rajeev Alur and David L. Dill. Automata for modeling real-time systems. In *Proc. of Int. Colloquium on Algorithms, Languages, and Programming*, volume 443 of *LNCS*, pages 322–335, 1990.
5. Tobias Amnell, Gerd Behrmann, Johan Bengtsson, Pedro R. D'Argenio, Alexandre David, Ansgar Fehnker, Thomas Hune, Bertrand Jeannet, Kim G. Larsen, M. Oliver Möller, Paul Pettersson, Carsten Weise, and Wang Yi. UPPAAL - Now, Next, and Future. In F. Cassez, C. Jard, B. Rozoy, and M. Ryan, editors, *Modelling and Verification of Parallel Processes*, number 2067 in Lecture Notes in Computer Science Tutorial, pages 100–125. Springer–Verlag, 2001.
6. Tobias Amnell, Elena Fersman, Leonid Mokrushin, Paul Pettersson, and Wang Yi. Times – a tool for modelling and implementation of embedded systems. In *TACAS 2002*, volume 2280 of *Lecture Notes in Computer Science*, pages 460–464. Springer–Verlag, April 2002.
7. Felice Balarin. Approximate reachability analysis of timed automata. In *17th IEEE Real-Time Systems Symposium*. IEEE Computer Society Press, 1996.
8. Gerd Behrmann. *Data Structures and Algorithms for the Analysis of Real Time Systems*. PhD thesis, Aalborg University, 2003.

9. Gerd Behrmann. Distributed reachability analysis in timed automata. *Software Tool For Technology Transfer (STTT)*, 2004. Currently available in the Online First edition of STTT.

10. Gerd Behrmann, Johan Bengtsson, Alexandre David, Kim G. Larsen, Paul Pettersson, and Wang Yi. UPPAAL implementation secrets. In *Proc. of 7th International Symposium on Formal Techniques in Real-Time and Fault Tolerant Systems*, 2002.

11. Gerd Behrmann, Alexandre David, Kim G. Larsen, M. Oliver Möller, Paul Pettersson, and Wang Yi. UPPAAL - present and future. In *Proc. of 40th IEEE Conference on Decision and Control*. IEEE Computer Society Press, 2001.

12. Gerd Behrmann, Alexandre David, Kim G. Larsen, and Wang Yi. Unification & sharing in timed automata verification. In *SPIN Workshop 03*, volume 2648 of *LNCS*, pages 225–229, 2003.

13. Gerd Behrmann, Ansgar Fehnker, Thomas Hune, Kim G. Larsen, Paul Pettersson, and Judi Romijn. Efficient guiding towards cost-optimality in UPPAAL. In T. Margaria and W. Yi, editors, *Proceedings of the 7th International Conference on Tools and Algorithms for the Construction and Analysis of Systems*, number 2031 in Lecture Notes in Computer Science, pages 174–188. Springer–Verlag, 2001.

14. Gerd Behrmann, Ansgar Fehnker, Thomas Hune, Kim G. Larsen, Paul Pettersson, Judi Romijn, and Frits Vaandrager. Minimum-cost reachability for priced timed automata. In Maria Domenica Di Benedetto and Alberto Sangiovanni-Vincentelli, editors, *Proceedings of the 4th International Workshop on Hybrid Systems: Computation and Control*, number 2034 in Lecture Notes in Computer Sciences, pages 147–161. Springer–Verlag, 2001.

15. Gerd Behrmann, Thomas Hune, and Frits Vaandrager. Distributed timed model checking - How the search order matters. In *Proc. of 12th International Conference on Computer Aided Verification*, Lecture Notes in Computer Science, Chicago, Juli 2000. Springer–Verlag.

16. Gerd Behrmann, Kim G. Larsen, Justin Pearson, Carsten Weise, and Wang Yi. Efficient timed reachability analysis using clock difference diagrams. In *Proceedings of the 12th Int. Conf. on Computer Aided Verification*, volume 1633 of *Lecture Notes in Computer Science*. Springer–Verlag, 1999.

17. Johan Bengtsson. *Clocks, DBMs and States in Timed Systems*. PhD thesis, Uppsala University, 2002.

18. Johan Bengtsson, Bengt Jonsson, Johan Lilius, and Wang Yi. Partial order reductions for timed systems. In *Proceedings of the 9th International Conference on Concurrency Theory*, September 1998.

19. Johan Bengtsson, Kim G. Larsen, Fredrik Larsson, Paul Pettersson, Yi Wang, and Carsten Weise. New generation of UPPAAL. In *Int. Workshop on Software Tools for Technology Transfer*, June 1998.

20. Beatrice Berard, Michel Bidoit, Alain Finkel, Francois Laroussinie, Antoine Petit, Laure Petrucci, Philippe Schnoebelen, and Pierre McKenzie. *Systems and Software Verification: Model-Checking Techniques and Tools*. Springer–Verlag, 2001.

21. Howard Bowman, Giorgio P. Faconti, Joost-Pieter Katoen, Diego Latella, and Mieke Massink. Automatic verification of a lip synchronisation algorithm using UPPAAL. In Bas Luttik Jan Friso Groote and Jos van Wamel, editors, *In Proceedings of the 3rd International Workshop on Formal Methods for Industrial Critical Systems. Amsterdam , The Netherlands*, 1998.

22. Pedro .R. D'Argenio, Joost-Pieter. Katoen, Theo C. Ruys, and Jan Tretmans. The bounded retransmission protocol must be on time! In *In Proceedings of the 3rd International Workshop on Tools and Algorithms for the Construction and Analysis of Systems*, volume 1217 of *LNCS*, pages 416–431. Springer–Verlag, April 1997.

23. Alexandre David. *Hierarchical Modeling and Analysis of Timed Systems*. PhD thesis, Uppsala University, November 2003.

24. Alexandre David, Gerd Behrmann, Kim G. Larsen, and Wang Yi. New UPPAAL architecture. In Paul Pettersson and Wang Yi, editors, *Workshop on Real-Time Tools*, Uppsala University Technical Report Series, 2002.

25. Alexandre David, Gerd Behrmann, Kim G. Larsen, and Wang Yi. A tool architecture for the next generation of UPPAAL. In *10th Anniversary Colloquium. Formal Methods at the Cross Roads: From Panacea to Foundational Support*, LNCS, 2003.

26. Alexandre David, M. Oliver Möller, and Wang Yi. Formal verification of UML statecharts with real-time extensions. In Ralf-Detlef Kutsche and Herbert Weber, editors, *Fundamental Approaches to Software Engineering, 5th International Conference, FASE 2002*, volume 2306 of *LNCS*, pages 218–232. Springer–Verlag, 2002.

27. Alexandre David and Wang Yi. Modelling and analysis of a commercial field bus protocol. In *Proceedings of the 12th Euromicro Conference on Real Time Systems*, pages 165–172. IEEE Computer Society, 2000.

28. Elena Fersman. *A Generic Approach to Schedulability Analysis of Real-Time Systems*. PhD thesis, Uppsala University, November 2003.

29. Klaus Havelund, Kim G. Larsen, and Arne Skou. Formal verification of a power controller using the real-time model checker UPPAAL. 5th International AMAST Workshop on Real-Time and Probabilistic Systems, available at `http://www.uppaal.com`, 1999.

30. Klaus Havelund, Arne Skou, Kim G. Larsen, and Kristian Lund. Formal modelling and analysis of an audio/video protocol: An industrial case study using UPPAAL. In *Proceedings of the 18th IEEE Real-Time Systems Symposium*, pages 2–13, December 1997.

31. M. Hendriks, G. Behrmann, K.G. Larsen, P. Niebert, and F.W. Vaandrager. Adding symmetry reduction to uppaal. In *Proceedings First International Workshop on Formal Modeling and Analysis of Timed Systems (FORMATS 2003)*, volume 2791 of *Lecture Notes in Computer Science*, 2003.

32. Martijn Hendriks and Kim G. Larsen. Exact acceleration of real-time model checking. In E. Asarin, O. Maler, and S. Yovine, editors, *Electronic Notes in Theoretical Computer Science*, volume 65. Elsevier Science Publishers, April 2002.

33. Thomas A. Henzinger. Symbolic model checking for real-time systems. *Information and Computation*, 111:193–244, 1994.

34. Gerard J. Holzmann. *Design and Validation of Computer Protocols*. Prentice-Hall, 1991.

35. Gerard J. Holzmann. An analysis of bitstate hashing. *Formal Methods in System Design*, 13:289–307, 1998.

36. John E. Hopcroft and Jeffrey D. Ullman. *Introduction of Automata Theory, Languages, and Computation*. Addison Wesley, 2001.

37. Thomas Hune, Kim G. Larsen, and Paul Pettersson. Guided synthesis of control programs using UPPAAL. In Ten H. Lai, editor, *Proc. of the IEEE ICDCS International Workshop on Distributed Systems Verification and Validation*, pages E15–E22. IEEE Computer Society Press, April 2000.

38. Torsten K. Iversen, Kåre J. Kristoffersen, Kim G. Larsen, Morten Laursen, Rune G. Madsen, Steffen K. Mortensen, Paul Pettersson, and Chris B. Thomasen. Model-checking real-time control programs – Verifying LEGO mindstorms systems using UPPAAL. In *Proc. of 12th Euromicro Conference on Real-Time Systems*, pages 147–155. IEEE Computer Society Press, June 2000.

39. Henrik Ejersbo Jensen. *Abstraction-Based Verification of Distributed Systems*. PhD thesis, Aalborg University, June 1999.

40. Henrik Ejersbo Jensen, Kim Guldstrand Larsen, and Arne Skou. Scaling up uppaal automatic verification of real-time systems using compositionality and abstraction. In Mathai Joseph, editor, *Formal Techniques in Real-Time and Fault-Tolerant Systems, 6th International Symposium, FTRTFT 2000*, volume 1926 of *Lecture Notes in Computer Science*, pages 19–20. Springer–Verlag, 2000.

41. Joost-Pieter Katoen. *Concepts, Algorithms, and Tools for Model Checking*. http://www.it-c.dk/people/hra/mcpa/katoen.ps, 1999.

42. Arne Skou Klaus Havelund, Kim Guldstrand Larsen. Formal verification of a power controller using the real-time model checker UPPAAL. In *5th Int. AMAST Workshop on Real-Time and Probabilistic Systems*, volume 1601 of *Lecture Notes in Computer Science*, pages 277–298. Springer–Verlag, 1999.

43. Kåre J. Kristoffersen. *Compositional Verification of Concurrent Systems*. PhD thesis, Aalborg University, August 1998. http://www.itu.dk/people/kjk/publications.html.

44. Kim G. Larsen, Gerd Behrmann, Ed Brinksma, Ansgar Fehnker, Thomas Hune, Paul Pettersson, and Judi Romijn. As cheap as possible: Efficient cost-optimal reachability for priced timed automata. In G. Berry, H. Comon, and A. Finkel, editors, *Proceedings of CAV 2001*, number 2102 in Lecture Notes in Computer Science, pages 493–505. Springer–Verlag, 2001.

45. Kim G. Larsen, Paul Pettersson, and Wang Yi. UPPAAL in a nutshell. *Int. Journal on Software Tools for Technology Transfer*, 1(1–2):134–152, October 1997.

46. Fredrik Larsson, Kim G. Larsen, Paul Pettersson, and Wang Yi. Efficient verification of real-time systems: Compact data structures and state-space reduction. In *Proc. of the 18th IEEE Real-Time Systems Symposium*, pages 14–24. IEEE Computer Society Press, December 1997.

47. Magnus Lindahl, Paul Pettersson, and Wang Yi. Formal design and analysis of a gearbox controller. *Springer International Journal of Software Tools for Technology Transfer (STTT)*, 3(3):353–368, 2001.

48. Henrik Lönn and Paul Pettersson. Formal verification of a TDMA protocol startup mechanism. In *Proc. of the Pacific Rim Int. Symp. on Fault-Tolerant Systems*, pages 235–242, December 1997.

49. Brian Nielsen. *Specification and Test of Real-Time Systems*. PhD thesis, Aalborg University, 2000.

50. Paul Pettersson. *Modelling and Verification of Real-time Systems Using Timed Automata: Theory and Practice*. PhD thesis, Uppsala University, 1999.

51. Wang Yi, Paul Petterson, and Mats Daniels. Automatic verification of real-time communicating systems by constraint-solving. In *Seventh International Conference on Formal Description Techniques*, pages 223–238, 1994.

The IF Toolset*

Marius Bozga, Susanne Graf, Ileana Ober, Iulian Ober, and Joseph Sifakis

VERIMAG, 2 avenue de Vignate, F-38610 Gières

Abstract. This paper presents an overview on the IF toolset which is an environment for modelling and validation of heterogeneous real-time systems. The toolset is built upon a rich formalism, the IF notation, allowing structured automata-based system representations. Moreover, the IF notation is expressive enough to support real-time primitives and extensions of high-level modelling languages such as SDL and UML by means of structure preserving mappings.

The core part of the IF toolset consists of a syntactic transformation component and an open exploration platform. The syntactic transformation component provides language level access to IF descriptions and has been used to implement static analysis and optimisation techniques. The exploration platform gives access to the graph of possible executions. It has been connected to different state-of-the-art model-checking and test-case generation tools.

A methodology for the use of the toolset is presented at hand of a case study concerning the Ariane-5 Flight Program for which both an SDL and a UML model have been validated.

1 Introduction

Modelling plays a central role in systems engineering. The use of models can profitably replace experimentation on actual systems with incomparable advantages such as:

- ease of construction by integration of heterogeneous components,
- generality by using genericity, abstraction, behavioural non determinism
- enhanced observability and controllability, especially avoidance of probe effect and of disturbances due to experimentation
- finally, possibility of analysis and predictability by application of formal methods.

Building models which faithfully represent complex systems is a non trivial problem and a prerequisite to the application of formal analysis techniques. Usually, modelling techniques are applied at early phases of system development and at high abstraction level. Nevertheless, the need of a unified view of the various life-cycle activities and of their interdependencies, motivated recently,

* This work was supported in part by the European Commission through the projects IST-1999-29082 ADVANCE, IST-1999-20218 AGEDIS and IST-2001-33522 OMEGA.

the so called model-based development [OMG03a,Sif01,STY03] which heavily relies on the use of modelling methods and tools to provide support and guidance for system design and validation.

Currently, validation of real-time systems is done by experimentation and measurement on specific platforms in order to adjust design parameters and hopefully achieve conformity to QoS requirements. Model based development intends to replace experimentation on real prototypes by validation on virtual prototypes (models). Furthermore, a key idea is the use of successive model transformations in design methodologies to derive from some initial high level description low level descriptions close to implementations. Achieving such ambitious goals raises hard and not yet completely resolved problems discussed in this section.

Heterogeneity. A real-time system is a layered system consisting of an application software implemented as a set of interacting tasks, and of the underlying execution platform. It continuously interacts with an external environment to provide a service satisfying QoS requirements characterising the dynamics of the interaction. Models of real-time systems should represent faithfully interactive behaviour taking into account implementation choices related to resource management and scheduling as well as execution speed of the underlying hardware

The models of real-time systems involve heterogeneous components with different execution speeds and interaction modes. There exist two main sources of heterogeneity: interaction and execution.

Heterogeneity of interaction results from the combination of different kinds of interaction.

Interactions can be *atomic* or *non atomic*. The result of atomic interactions cannot be altered through interference with other interactions. Process algebras and synchronous languages assume atomic interactions. Asynchronous communication (SDL, UML) or method call are generally non atomic interactions. Their initiation and their completion can be separated by other events.

Interactions can involve *strict* or *non strict* synchronisation. For instance, rendez-vous and method calls require strict interactions. On the contrary, broadcast of synchronous languages and asynchronous communication do not need strict synchronisation. A process (sender) can initiate an interaction independently of the possibility of completion by its environment.

Heterogeneity of execution results from the combination of two execution paradigms.

Synchronous execution is typically adopted in hardware, in synchronous languages, and in time triggered architectures and protocols. It considers that a system execution is a sequence of steps. It assumes synchrony, meaning that the system's environment does not change during a step, or equivalently "that the system is infinitely faster than its environment". The synchronous paradigm has a built-in strong assumption of fairness: in a step all the system components execute a quantum computation defined by using either quantitative or logical time.

The *asynchronous* paradigm does not adopt any notion of global execution step. It is used in languages for the description of distributed systems such as SDL and UML, and programming languages such as Ada and Java. The lack of built-in mechanisms for sharing resources between components can be compensated through scheduling. This paradigm is also common to all execution platforms supporting multiple threads, tasks, etc.

Modelling time. Models for real-time systems should allow modelling progress of time in order to express various kinds of timing information e.g., execution times of actions, arrival times of events, deadlines, latency.

Timed models can be defined as extensions of untimed models by adding time variables used to measure the time elapsed since their initialisation. They can be represented as machines that can perform two kinds of state changes: actions and time steps. Actions are timeless state changes of the untimed system; their execution may depend on and modify time variables. In a time step, all time variables increase uniformly. There exists a variety of timed formalisms extensions of Petri nets [Sif77], process algebras [NS91] and timed automata [AD94]. Any executable untimed description e.g., application software, can be extended into a timed one by adding explicitly time variables or other timing constraints.

Timed models use a notion of logical time. Contrary to physical time, logical time progress can block, especially as a result of inconsistency of timing constraints. The behaviour of a timed model is characterised by the set of its runs, that is the set of maximal sequences of consecutive states reached by performing transitions or time steps. The time elapsed between two states of a run is computed by summing up the durations of all the time steps between them. For a timed model to represent a system, it is necessary that it is *well-timed* in the sense that in all its runs time diverges.

As a rule, in timed models there may exist states from which time cannot progress. If time can progress from any state of a timed model, then it is always possible to wait and postpone the execution of actions which means that it is not possible to model action *urgency*. Action urgency at a state is modelled by disallowing time progress. This possibility of stopping time progress goes against our intuition about physical time and constitutes a basic difference between the notions of physical and logical time. It has deep consequences on timed systems modelling by composition of timed components.

Often timed extensions of untimed systems are built in an ad hoc manner at the risk of producing over-constrained or incomplete descriptions. It is essential to develop a methodology for adding compositionally timing information to untimed models to get a corresponding timed model.

The IF toolset is an environment for modelling and validation of heterogeneous real-time systems. It is characterised by the following features:

- Support for high level modelling with formalisms such as SDL, UML used by users in some CASE tool. This is essential to ease usability by practitioners and to allow the use of state-of-the-art modelling technology. Furthermore, the use of high level formalisms allows validating realistic models which can be simplified if necessary by using automated tools. This avoids starting with simplified models constructed in an ad hoc manner as it is the case for other tools using low level description languages e.g., automata.

– Translation of high level models into an intermediate representation, the IF notation, that serves as a semantic model. This representation is rich and expressive enough to describe the main concepts and constructs of source languages. It combines composition of extended timed automata and dynamic priorities to encompass heterogeneous interaction. Priorities play an important role for the description of scheduling policies as well as the restriction of asynchronous behaviour to model run-to-completion execution. We consider a class of timed automata which are by construction well-timed. The developed translation methods for SDL and UML preserve the overall structure of the source model and the size of the generated IF description increases linearly with the size of the source model. IF is used as a basis for model simplification by means of static analysis techniques and the application of light structural analysis techniques e.g., checking sufficient conditions for deadlock-freedom of processes. It is also used for the generation of lower level models e.g., labelled transitions systems used for verification purposes.

– Combined use of various validation techniques including model-checking, static analysis on the intermediate representation and simulation. A methodology has been studied at Verimag for complex real-time applications.

– Expression of requirements to be validated on models by using *observers*. These can be considered as a special class of models equipped with primitives for monitoring and checking for divergence from some nominal behaviour. Our choice for monitors rather than declarative formalisms such as temporal logic or Live Sequence charts [DH99] is motivated by our concern to be close to industrial practice and to avoid as much as possible inconsistency in requirements.

The paper is organised as follows. Section 2 presents the overall architecture of the IF toolset. Section 3 is the main section of the paper. It starts with a presentation of IF including its main concepts and constructs and their semantics. Then the overall architecture of the toolset and its features for simulation, analysis and validation are described. Finally the translation principle from UML to IF is explained by showing how the main UML concepts and constructs can be mapped into IF.

Section 4 presents an example illustrating the application of the toolset to the modelling and validation of the Ariane-5 Flight Program. For this non trivial case study, we provide a validation methodology and results. Section 5 presents concluding remarks about the toolset and the underlying modelling and validation methodology.

2   Setting the Context – The Overall Architecture

Figure 1 describes the overall architecture of the toolset, the most important components as well as their inter-connections. We distinguish three different description levels: the *specification level* (UML, SDL), the *intermediate description level (IF)*, and the Labelled Transition Systems (LTS) level.

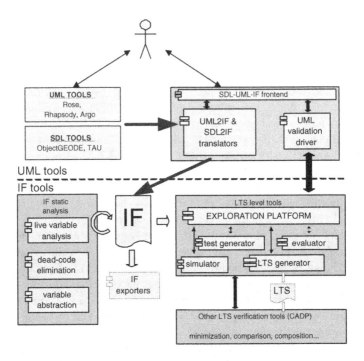

Fig. 1. IF toolset architecture.

Specification level. This corresponds to the description provided by the user in some existing specification language. To be processed, descriptions are automatically translated into their IF descriptions. Currently, the main input specification formalisms are UML and SDL.

Regarding UML, any UML tool can be used as long as it can export the model in XMI [OMG01], the standard XML format. The IF toolset includes a translator from UML which produces IF descriptions. The translator accepts specifications produced by RATIONAL ROSE [IBM], RHAPSODY [Ilo] or ARGO UML [RVR+].

Intermediate description level (IF). IF descriptions are generated from specifications. IF is an intermediate representation based on timed automata extended with discrete data variables, communication primitives, dynamic process creation and destruction. This representation is expressive enough to describe the basic concepts of modelling and programming languages for distributed real-time systems.

The abstract syntax tree of an IF description can be accessed through an API. Since all the data (variables, clocks) and the communication structure are still explicit, high-level transformations based on static analysis [Muc97] or program slicing [Wei84,Tip94] can be applied. All these techniques can be used to transform the initial IF description into a "simpler" one while preserving safety properties. Moreover, this API is well-suited to implement exporters from IF to other specification formalisms.

LTS level. The LTS are transition graphs describing the executions of IF descriptions. An *exploration API* allows to represent and store states as well as to compute on demand the successors of a given state. This API can be linked with "generic" exploration programs performing any kind of *on-the-fly* analysis.

Using the exploration API, several validation tools have been developed and connected to work on IF descriptions. They cover a broad range of features: interactive/random/guide simulation, on-the-fly model checking using observers, on-the-fly temporal logic model checking, exhaustive state space generation, scheduling analysis, test case generation. Moreover, through this API are connected the CADP toolbox [FGK+96] for the validation of finite models as well as TGV [FJJV96,JM99] for test case generation using on-the-fly techniques.

3   Description of the Formalism/Technique/System/Tool

3.1   The IF Notation

IF is a notation for systems of components (called *processes*), running in parallel and interacting either through shared variables or asynchronous signals. Processes describe sequential behaviours including data transformations, communications and process creation. Furthermore, the behaviour of a process may be subject to timing constraints. The number of processes may change over time: they may be created and deleted dynamically.

The semantics of a system is the LTS obtained by interleaving the behaviour of its processes. To enforce scheduling policies, the set of runs of the LTS can be further restricted using dynamic priorities.

Processes. The behaviour of a *process* is described as a timed automaton, extended with data. A process has a unique process identifier (*pid*) and local memory consisting of variables (including clocks), control states and a queue of pending messages (received and not yet consumed).

A process can move from one control state to another by executing some *transition.* As for state charts [Har87,HP98], control states can be hierarchically structured to factorize common behaviour. Control states can be *stable* or *unstable.* A sequence of transitions between two stable states defines a *step.* The execution of a step is *atomic,* meaning that it corresponds to a single transition in the LTS representing the semantics. Notice that several transitions may be enabled at the same time, in which case the choice is made non-deterministically.

Transitions can be either *triggered* by signals in the input queue or be *spontaneous.* Transitions can also be *guarded* by predicates on variables, where a guard is the conjunction of a data guard and a time guard. A transition is enabled in a state if its trigger signal is present and its guard evaluates to true. Signals in the input queue are a priori consumed in a fifo fashion, but one can specify in transitions which signals should be *"saved"* in the queue for later use.

Transition *bodies* are *sequential programs* consisting of elementary actions (variable or clock assignments, message sending, process creation/destruction, resource requirement/release, etc) and structured using elementary control-flow statements (like if-then-else, while-do, etc). In addition, transition bodies can use external functions/procedures, written in an external programming language (C/C++).

Signals and Signalroutes. *Signals* are typed and can have data parameters. Signals can be addressed directly to a process (using its *pid*) and/or to a signal route which will deliver it to one or more processes. The destination process stores received signals in a fifo buffer.

Signalroutes represent specialised communication media transporting signals between processes. The behaviour of a signalroute is defined by its delivery policy (FIFO or multi-set), its connection policy (peer to peer, unicast or multicast), its delaying policy ("zero delay", "delay" or "rate") and finally its reliability ("reliable" or "lossy"). More complex communication media can be specified explicitly as IF processes.

In particular, signalroutes can be connected at one end with an implicitly defined "environment process" **env**. In transitions triggered by signals from the environment, the trigger signal is considered as present whenever the transition guard evaluates to true.

Data. The IF notation provides the *predefined basic types* bool, integer, real, pid and clock, where *clock* is used for variables measuring time progress. Structured data types are built using the *type constructors* enumeration, range, array, record and abstract. Abstract data types can be used for manipulating external types and code.

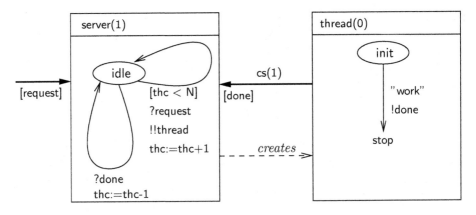

Fig. 2. Illustration of the multi-threaded server example.

Example 1. The IF description below describes a system consisting of a **server** process creating up to N **thread** processes for handling **request** signals. A graphical representation of the system is given in Figure 2.

```
system Server;
signal request();                // signals with parameter types
signal done(pid);

signalroute entry(1)             // signalroutes and their signals
   from env to server
   with request;

signalroute cs(1) #delay[1,2]
   from thread to server
   with done;
                                 // definition of process types
process thread(0);               // and initial number of instances
   fpar parent pid, route pid;   // formal parameters received at creation

   state init #start ;           // 1 state + 1 outgoing transition
      informal "work";           // informal action labelled "work"
      output done()              // sending of the done signal
       via route to parent;      // received by parent
      stop;                      // terminate process, destroy instance
   endstate;
endprocess;

process server(1);
   var thc integer;              // local variables
   state idle #start ;           // 1 state + 2 outgoing transitions
      provided thc < N;          // first transition: guard
      input request();           // trigger
         fork thread(self, {cs}0); // create thread process and passing
                                 // own pid and signalroute cs as params
         task thc := thc + 1;
         nextstate -;            // end of transition - back to idle

      input done();              // second transition
         task thc := thc - 1;
         nextstate -;
   endstate;
endprocess;
endsystem;
```

Composition (System). The semantics associates with a system a global LTS. At any point of time, its state is defined as the tuple of the states of its living components: the states of a process are the possible evaluations of its attributes (control state, variables and signal queue content). The states of a signalroute are lists of signals *"in transit"*. The transitions of the global LTS representing a system are steps of processes and signal deliveries from signalroutes to signal queues where in any global state there is an outgoing transition for all enabled transitions of all components (interleaving semantics). The formal definition of the semantics can be found in [BL02b].

System models may be highly nondeterministic, due to the nondeterminism of the environment which is considered as open and to the concurrency between their processes. For the validation of functional properties, leaving this second type of nondeterminism non resolved is important in order to verify correctness independently of any particular execution order. Nevertheless, going towards an implementation means resolving a part of this non determinism and choosing an execution order satisfying time related and other nonfunctional constraints.

In IF, such additional restrictions can be enforced by dynamic priorities defined by rules specifying that whenever for two process instances some condition (state predicate) holds, then one has less priority than the other. An example is

$$p1 \prec p2 \text{ if } p1.group = p2.group \text{ and } p2.counter < p1.counter$$

which for any process instances which are part of some *"group"*, gives priority to those with the smallest values of the variable *counter* (e.g., the less frequently served).

Time. The time model of IF is that of *timed automata with urgency* [BST98], [BS00] where the execution of a transition is an *event* defining an *instant* of state change, whereas time is progressing in states. Urgency is expressed by means of an *urgency* attribute of transitions. This attribute can take the values *eager*, *lazy* or *delayable*. *Eager* transitions are executed at the point of time at which they become enabled - if they are not disabled by another transition. *Delayable* transitions cannot be disabled by time progress. *Lazy* transitions may be disabled by time progress.

Like in timed automata, time distances between events are measured by variables of type "clock". Clocks can be created, set to some value or reset (deleted) in any transition. They can be used in time guards to restrict the time points at which transitions can be taken.

Local clocks allow the specification of timing constraints, such as durations of tasks (modelled by time passing in a state associated with this task, see example below), deadlines for events in the same process. Global time constraints, such as end-to-end delays, can be expressed by means of global clocks or by observers (explained in the next section).

Example 2. A timed version of the **thread** process of the example 1 is given. An extra state **work** introduced for distinguishing the instant at which work starts and the instant at which it ends and and to constrain the duration between them. The intention is to model an execution time of *"work"* of 2 to 4 time units.

The *thread* process goes immediately to the **work** state - the start transition is **eager** - and sets the clock *wait* is set to 0 in order to start measuring time progress. The transition exiting the **work** state is **delayable** with a time guard expressing the constraint that the time since the clock **wait** has been set should be at least 2 but not more than 4.

```
process thread(0);                    state work ;
  fpar parent pid, route pid;           urgency delayable;
  var wait clock;                       when wait >= 2 and wait <= 4;
  state init #start ;                     output done()
    urgency eager;                          via route to parent;
    informal "work";                     stop;
    set wait := 0;                      endstate;
      nextstate work;                 endprocess;
  endstate;
```

Resources. In order to express mutual exclusion it is possible to declare shared *resources*. These resources can be used through particular actions of the form "**require some-resource**" and "**release some-resource**".

Observers. Observers express in an operational way safety properties of a system by characterising its acceptable execution sequences. They also provide a simple and flexible mechanism for controlling model generation. They can be used to select parts of the model to explore and to cut off execution paths that are irrelevant with respect to given criteria. In particular, observers can be used to restrict the environment of the system.

Observers are described in the same way as IF processes i.e., as extended timed automata. They differ from IF processes in that they can react *synchronously* to events and conditions occurring in the observed system. Observers are classified into:

- *pure* observers - which express requirements to be checked on the system.
- *cut* observers - which in addition to monitoring, guide simulation by selecting execution paths. For example, they are used to restrict the behaviour of the environment.
- *intrusive* observers - which may also alter the system's behaviour by sending signals and changing variables.

Observation and intrusion mechanisms. For monitoring the system *state*, observers can use primitives for retrieving values of *variables*, the *current state* of the processes, the contents of *queues*, etc.

For monitoring *actions* performed by a system, observers use constructs for retrieving events together with data associated with them. Events are generated whenever the system executes one of the following actions: signal output, signal delivery, signal input, process creation and destruction and informal statements.

Observers can also monitor time progress, by using their own clocks or by monitoring the clocks of the system.

Expression of properties. In order to express properties, observer states can be marked as *ordinary*, *error* or *success*. *Error* and *success* are both terminating states. Reaching a success state (an error state) means satisfaction (non satisfaction). *Cut* observers use a *cut* action which stops exploration.

Example 3. The following example illustrates the use of observers to express a simple safety property of a protocol with one transmitter and one receiver, such as the alternating bit protocol. The property is: *Whenever a **put(m)** message is received by the **transmitter** process, the **transmitter** does not return to state **idle** before a **get(m)** with the same m is issued by the **receiver** process.*

```
pure observer safety1;                    nextstate err;
  var m data;                         match output get(n);
  var n data;                           nextstate decision;
  var t pid;                         endstate;
  state idle #start ;                state decision #unstable ;
    match input put(m) by t;          provided n = m;
      nextstate wait;                   nextstate idle;
  endstate;                           provided n <> m;
  state wait;                           nextstate wait;
    provided ({transmitter}t)         endstate;
      instate idle;                   state err #error ;
      nextstate err;                  endstate;
    match output put(n)             endobserver;
```

3.2   Simulation, Analysis and Validation

Core Components of the IF Toolset. The core components of the IF toolset are shown in Figure 3.

Syntactic Transformations Component. This component deals with syntactic transformations including the construction of an abstract syntax tree (AST) from an IF description. The tree is a collection of C++ objects representing all the syntactic elements present in IF descriptions. The AST reflects precisely the syntactic structure of IF descriptions: a system includes processes, signalroutes, types; a process includes states and variables; states include their outgoing transitions and so on.

This component has an interface giving access to the abstract syntax tree. Primitives are available to traverse the tree and to consult or to modify its elements. There are primitives allowing to write the tree back as an IF textual description. The syntactic transformation component has been used to build several applications. The most important ones are code generators (either simulation code or application code), static analysis transformations (operating at syntactic level), translations to other languages (including a translation to the Promela language of SPIN [Hol91]) and pretty printers.

Exploration Platform. This component has an API providing access to the LTS corresponding to IF descriptions. The interface offers primitives for representing and accessing states and labels as well as basic primitives for traversing LTS: an *init* function which gives the initial state, and a *successor* function which computes the set of enabled transitions and successor states from a given state.

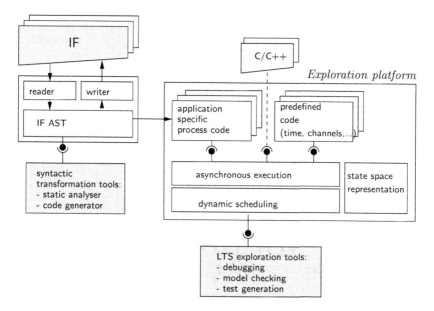

Fig. 3. Functional view of the IF Core Components.

These are the key primitives for implementing any on-the-fly forward enumerative exploration or validation algorithm.

Figure 3 shows the structure of the exploration platform. The main features of the platform are simulation of the process execution, non-determinism resolution, management of time and representation of the state space.

The exploration platform can be seen as an operating system where process instances are plugged-in and jointly executed. Process instances are either application specific (coming from IF descriptions) or generic (such as time or channel handling processes).

Simulation time is handled by a specialised process managing clock allocation/deallocation, computing time progress conditions and firing timed transitions. There are two implementations available, one for discrete time and one for dense time. For discrete time, clock values are explicitly represented by integers. Time progress is computed with respect to the next enabled deadline. For dense time, clock valuations are represented using variable-size Difference Bound Matrices (DBMs) as in tools dedicated to timed automata such as KRONOS [Yov97] and UPPAAL [LPY98].

The exploration platform composes all active processes and computes global states and the corresponding system behaviour. The exploration platform consists of two layers sharing a common state representation:

– *Asynchronous execution layer.* This layer implements the general interleaving execution of processes. The platform asks successively each process to execute its enabled steps. During a process execution, the platform manages all inter-process operations: message delivery, time constraints checking, dynamic creation and destruction, tracking of events. After a completion of a step by a process, the platform takes a snapshot of the performed step, stores it and delivers it to the second layer.

- *Dynamic scheduling layer.* This layer collects all the enabled steps. It uses a set of dynamic priority rules to filter them. The remaining ones, which are maximal with respect to the priorities, are delivered to the user application via the exploration API.

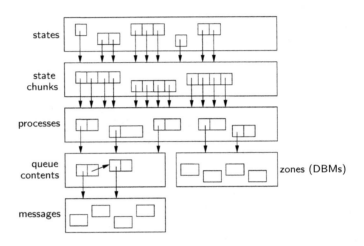

Fig. 4. Internal state representation.

- *State representation.* Global states are implicitly stored by the platform. The internal state representation is shown in figure 4. It preserves the structural information and seeks for maximal sharing. The layered representation involves a unique table of messages. Queues are lists of messages, represented by suffix sharing. On top of them, there is a table of process states, all of them sharing queues in the table of queues. Processes are then grouped into fixed size state chunks, and finally, global states are variable-size lists of chunks. Tables can be represented either by using hash tables with collision or by binary trees. This scheme allows to explicitly represent several millions of structured states.

The exploration platform and its interface has been used as back-ends of debugging tools (interactive or random simulation), model checking (including exhaustive model generation, on the fly μ-calculus evaluation, model checking with observers), test case generation, and optimisation (shortest path computation).

This architecture provides features for validating heterogeneous systems. Exploration is not limited to IF descriptions: all kinds of components with an adequate interface can be executed in parallel on the exploration platform. It is indeed possible to use C/C++ code (either directly, or instrumented accordingly) of already implemented components.

Another advantage of the architecture is that it can be extended by adding new interaction primitives and exploration strategies. Presently, the exploration platform supports asynchronous (interleaved) execution and asynchronous point-to-point communication between processes. Different execution modes, like synchronous or run-to-completion, or additional interaction mechanisms, such as broadcast or rendez-vous, are obtained by using dynamic priorities [AGS00].

Concerning the exploration strategies, reduction heuristics such as partial-order reduction or some form of symmetry reduction are already incorporated in the exploration platform. More specific heuristics may be added depending on a particular application domain.

Static Analysis. Practical experience with IF has shown that simplification by means of static analysis is crucial for dealing successfully with complex specifications. Even simple analysis such as live variables analysis or dead-code elimination can significantly reduce the size of the state space of the model. The available static analysis techniques are:

Live variables analysis This technique transforms an IF description into an equivalent smaller one by removing globally dead variables and signal parameters and by *resetting* locally dead variables [Muc97]. Initially, all the local variables of the processes and signal parameters are considered to be dead, unless otherwise specified by the user. Shared variables are considered to be always live. The analysis alternates local (standard) live variables computation on each process and inter-process liveness attributes propagation through input/output signal parameters until a global fixpoint is reached.

Dead-code elimination. This technique transforms an IF description by removing unreachable control states and transitions under some user-given assumptions about the environment. It solves a simple static reachability problem by computing, for each process separately, the set of control states and transitions which can be statically reached starting from the initial control state. The analysis computes an upper approximation of the set of processes that can be effectively created.

Variable abstraction. This technique allows to compute abstractions by eliminating variables and their dependencies which are not relevant to the user. The computation proceeds as for live variables analysis: processes are analysed separately, and the results obtained are propagated between them by using the input/output dependencies. Contrary to the previous techniques which are exact, simplification by variable abstraction may introduce additional behaviours. Nevertheless, it always reduces the size of the state representation.

By using variable abstraction it is possible to extract automatically system descriptions for symbolic verification tools accepting only specific types of data e.g., TREX [ABS01] which accepts only counters, clocks and queues. Moreover, this technique allows to compute finite-state abstractions for model checking.

Validation Components

Model-checking using EVALUATOR The EVALUATOR tool implements an on-the-fly model checking algorithm for the alternation free μ-calculus [Koz83]. This is a branching time logic, based upon propositional calculus with fixpoint operators. The syntax is described by the following grammar:

$$\varphi ::= T \mid X \mid \neg\varphi \mid \varphi \wedge \varphi \mid <a> \varphi \mid \mu X.\varphi$$

For a given LTS representing a specification, the semantics of a formula is defined as the set of states satisfying it, as follows:

- T (true) holds in any state
- $\neg$ and $\wedge$ are the usual boolean operators
- $<a> \varphi$ is true in a state if there exists a transition labelled by a leading to a state which satisfies φ
- $\mu X.\varphi$ denotes the usual least fix point operator (where X is a free variable of φ representing a set of states)

This logic can be used to define macros expressing usual requirements such as: "there is no deadlock", "any action a is eventually followed by an action b", "it is not possible to perform an action a followed by an action b, without performing an action c in between", etc.

Comparison or minimisation with ALDEBARAN. ALDEBARAN [BFKM97] is a tool for the comparison of LTS modulo behavioural preorder or equivalence relations. Usually, one LTS represents the system behaviour, and the other its requirements. Moreover, ALDEBARAN can also be used to reduce a given LTS modulo a behavioural equivalence, possibly by taking into account an observation criterion.

The preorders and equivalences available in ALDEBARAN include usual simulation and bisimulation relations such as strong bisimulation [Par81], observational bisimulation [Mil80], branching bisimulation [vGW89], safety bisimulation [BFG+91], etc. The choice of the relation depends on the class of properties to be preserved.

Test case generation using TGV. TGV [FJJV96,JM99] is a tool for test generation developed by IRISA and VERIMAG. It is used to automatically generate test cases for conformance testing of distributed reactive systems. It generates test cases from a formal specification of the system and a test purpose.

3.3 Translating UML to IF

The toolset supports generation of IF descriptions from both SDL [BFG+99] and UML [OGO04]. We describe the principles of the translation from UML to IF.

UML Modelling. We consider a subset of UML including its object-oriented features and which is expressive enough for the specification of real-time systems. The elements of models are classes with structural features and relationships (associations, inheritance) and behaviour descriptions through state machines and operations.

The translation tool adopts a particular semantics for concurrency based on the UML distinction between active and passive objects. Informally, a set of passive objects form together with an active object an *activity group*. Activity groups are executed in run-to-completion fashion, which means that there is no concurrency between the objects of the same activity group. Requests (asynchronous signals or method calls) coming from outside an activity group are queued and treated one by one. More details on this semantics can be found in [DJPV02,HvdZ03].

The tool resolves some choices left open by UML, such as the concrete syntax of the action language used in state machines and operations.

Additionally, we use a specialisation of the standard UML profile for Scheduling, Performance and Time [OMG03b]. Our profile, formally described in [GOO03], provides two kinds of mechanisms for timing: imperative mechanisms including timers, clocks and timed transition guards, and declarative mechanisms including linear constraints on time distances between events.

To provide connectivity with existing CASE tools such as RATIONAL ROSE [IBM], RHAPSODY [Ilo] or ARGO UML [RVR+], the toolset reads models using the standard XML representation for UML (XMI [OMG01]).

The Principles of the Mapping from UML to IF. Runtime UML entities (objects, call stacks, pending messages, etc.) are identifiable as a part of the system state in IF. This allows tracing back to UML specifications from simulation and verification.

Objects and concurrency model. Every UML class X is mapped to a process P_X with a local variable for each attribute or association of X. As inheritance is flattened, all inherited attributes and associations are replicated in the processes corresponding to each subclass. The class state machine is translated into the process behaviour.

Each activity group is managed at runtime by a special IF process, of type *group manager*, which is responsible of sequentialising requests coming from objects outside the activity group, and of forwarding them to the objects inside when the group is stable. Run-to-completion is implemented by using the dynamic priority rule

$$y \prec x \text{ if } x.leader = y$$

which means that *all objects of a group have higher priorities than their group manager*. For every object x, $x.leader$ points to the manager process of the object's activity group. Thus, as long as at least one object inside an activity group can execute, its group manager will not initiate a new run-to-completion step. Notice that adopting a different execution mode can be done easily by just eliminating or adding new priority rules.

Operations and polymorphism. The adopted semantics distinguishes between *primitive operations* - described by a method with an associated action - and *triggered operations* - described directly in the state machine of their owner class. Triggered operations are mapped to actions embedded directly in the state machine of the class.

Each primitive operation is mapped to a handler process whose run-time instances represent the activations and the stack frames corresponding to calls.

An operation call (either primitive or triggered) is expressed in IF by using three signals: a *call* signal carrying the call parameters, a *return* signal carrying the return value, and a *completion* signal indicating completion of computation of the operation, which may be different from *return*. Therefore, the action of invoking an operation is represented in IF by sending a *call* signal. If the caller is in the same activity group, then the *call* is directed to the target object and is handled immediately. Alternatively, if the caller is in a different group, the *call* is directed to the object's *group manager* and is handled in a subsequent run-to-completion step.

The handling of incoming primitive calls by an object is modelled as follows: in every state of the callee object (process), upon reception of a call signal, the callee creates a new instance of the operation's handler. The callee then waits until completion, before re-entering the same stable state in which it received the call.

Mapping operation activations into separate processes has several advantages:

- It provides a simple solution for handling *polymorphic* (dynamically bound) calls in an inheritance hierarchy. The receiver object knows its own identity, and can answer any *call* signal by creating the appropriate version of the operation handler from the hierarchy.
- It allows for extensions to other types of calls than the ones currently supported by the semantics (e.g. non-blocking calls). It also preserves modularity and readability of the generated model.
- It allows to distinguish the relevent instants in the context of timing analysis.

Mapping of UML observers. In order to specify and verify dynamic properties of UML models, we define a notion of *UML observer* [OGO04] which is similar to IF observers (see section 3.1).

Observers are described by classes stereotyped with ≪*observer*≫. They can own attributes and methods, and can be created dynamically. We defined in [OGO04] event types such as operation invocation, operation return, object creation, etc.

Several examples of observers are provided in section 4.3.

Mapping of real-time concepts. The mapping of UML timers and clocks to IF is straightforward. Declarative constraints on duration between events are expressed by means of clocks and time guards or observers [OGO04].

4   An Example: The Ariane-5 Flight Program[1]

We present a real-world case study on the modelling and validation of the Flight Program of Ariane-5 by using the IF toolset.

This work has been initiated by EADS Launch Vehicles in order to evaluate the maturity and applicability of formal validation techniques. This evaluation consisted in formally specifying some parts of an existing software, on a re-engineering basis, and verifying some critical requirements on this specification. The Ariane-5 Flight Program is the embedded software which autonomously controls the Ariane-5 launcher during its flight, from the ground, through the atmosphere, and up to the final orbit.

The specification and validation have been studied in two different contexts:

- A first study carried out on a re-engineered SDL model has been conducted in 2001. The SDL model was translated automatically to IF, simplified by static analysis, simulated and verified using μ-calculus properties as well as behavioural model minimisation and comparison.
- A second study carried out on a re-engineered UML model, has been conducted more recently in the framework of the IST OMEGA project [Con03]. The goal was to evaluate both the appropriateness of extensions of UML to model this type of real-time system, and the usability of IF validation tools. In this study, the UML model has been translated automatically to IF, simplified by static analysis, simulated and verified against properties expressed as *observers*.

We summarise the relevant results of both experiments, and we give principles of a *verification methodology* that can be used in connection with the IF toolset. For such large examples, push-button verification is not sufficient and some iterative combination of analysis and validation is necessary to cope with complexity.

4.1   Overview of the Ariane-5 Flight Program

The Ariane-5 example has a relatively large UML model: 23 classes, each one with operations and a state machine. Its translation into IF has 7000 lines of code.

The Launcher Flight. An Ariane-5 launch begins with ignition of the main stage engine (EPC - *Etage Principal Cryotechnique*). Upon confirmation that it is operating properly, the two solid booster stages (EAP - *Etage Accélérateur à Poudre*) are ignited to achieve lift-off.

After burn-out, the two solid boosters (EAP) are jettisoned and Ariane-5 continues its flight through the upper atmosphere propelled only by the cryogenic main stage (EPC). The fairing is jettisoned too, as soon as the atmosphere is thin

---

[1] Ariane-5 is an European Space Agency Project delegated to CNES (Centre National d'Etudes Spatiales).

enough for the satellites not to need protection. The main stage is rendered inert immediately upon shut-down. The launch trajectory is designed to ensure that the stages fall back safely into the ocean.

The storable propellant stage (EPS - *Etage à Propergol Stockable*) takes over to place the geostationary satellites in orbit. Payload separation and attitudinal positioning begin as soon as the launcher's upper section reaches the corresponding orbit. Ariane-5's missions ends 40 minutes after the first ignition command.

A final task remains to be performed - that of passivation. This essentially involves emptying the tanks completely to prevent an explosion that would break the propellant stage into pieces.

The Flight Program. The Flight Program entirely controls the launcher, without any human interaction, beginning 6 minutes 30 seconds before lift-off, and ending 40 minutes later, when the launcher terminates its mission.

The main functions of the Flight Program are the following ones:

- *flight control*, involves navigation, guidance and control algorithms,
- *flight regulation*, involves observation and control of various components of the propulsion stages (engines ignition and extinction, boosters ignition, etc),
- *flight configuration*, involves management of launcher components (stage separation, payload separation, etc).

We focused on *regulation* and *configuration* functions. The *flight control* is a relatively independent synchronous reactive control system.

The Environment. In order to obtain a realistic functional model of the Flight Program restricted to regulation and configuration functionalities, we need to take into account its environment. This has been modelled by two external components abstracting the actual behaviour of the flight control part and the ground:

- the *flight control* includes several processes describing a nominal behaviour. They send, with some controlled degree of uncertainty, the right flight commands, with the right parameters at the right moments in time.
- the *ground* part abstracts the nominal behaviour of the launch protocol on the ground side. It passes progressively the control of the launcher to the on board flight program, by providing the launch date and all the confirmations needed for launching. Furthermore, it remains ready to take back the control, if some malfunctioning is detected during the launch procedure.

Requirements. With the help of EADS engineers, we identified a set of about twenty functional safety requirements ensuring the right service of the Flight Program. The requirements have been classified into three classes:

- *general requirements*, not necessarily specific to the Flight Program but common to all critical real-time systems. They include basic untimed properties such as the absence of deadlocks, livelocks or signal loss, and basic timed properties such as the absence of timelocks, Zeno behaviours or deadlines missed;

- *overall system requirements*, specific to the Flight Program and concerning its global behaviour. For example, the global sequence of the flight phases is respected: ground, vulcain ignition, booster ignition, ...;
- *local component requirements*, specific to the Flight Program and regarding the functionality of some of its parts. This category includes for example checking the occurrence of some actions in some component (e.g. payload separation occurs eventually during an attitudinal positioning phase, or the stop sequence no. 3 can occur only after lift-off, or the state of engine valves conforms to the flight phase, etc.).

4.2   UML Model

The Ariane-5 Flight Program is modelled in UML as a collection of objects communicating mostly through asynchronous signals, and whose behaviour is described by state machines. Operations (with an abstract body) are used to model the guidance, navigation and control tasks. For the modelling of timed behaviour and timing properties, we are using the OMEGA real-time UML profile [GOO03], which provides basic primitives such as timers and clocks. The model shown in figure 5 is composed of:

- a global controller class responsible for flight configuration (*Acyclic*);
- a model of the regulation components (e.g. *EAP*, *EPC* corresponding to the launcher's stages);
- a model of the regulated equipment (e.g. *Valves*, *Pyros*);
- an abstract model of the cyclic GNC tasks (*Cyclics*, *Thrust_monitor*, etc.);
- an abstract model of the environment (classes *Ground* for the external events and *Bus* for modelling the communication with synchronous GNC tasks).

The behaviour of the flight regulation components (EAP, EPC) involves mainly the execution of the firing/extinction sequence for the corresponding stage of the launcher (see for example a fragment of the EPC stage controller's state machine in figure 6). The sequence is time-driven, with the possibility of safe abortion in case of anomaly.

The flight configuration part implements several tasks: EAP separation, EPC separation, payload separation, etc. In their case too, the separation dates are provided by the control part, depending on the current flight evolution.

4.3   Validation Using the IF Toolset

Validation is a complex activity, involving the iterated application of verification and analysis phases as depicted in figure 7.

Translation to IF and Basic Static Analysis. provides a first sanity check of the model. In this step, the user can find simple compile-time errors in the model (name errors, type errors, etc.) but also more elaborate information (uninitialised or unused variables, unused signals, dead code).

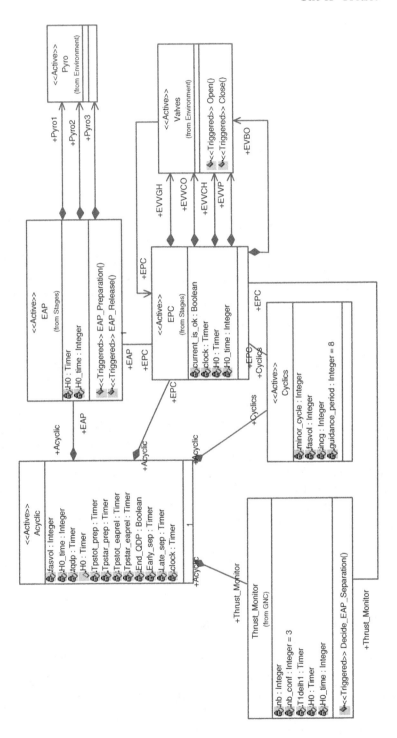

Fig. 5. Structure of the UML specification (part).

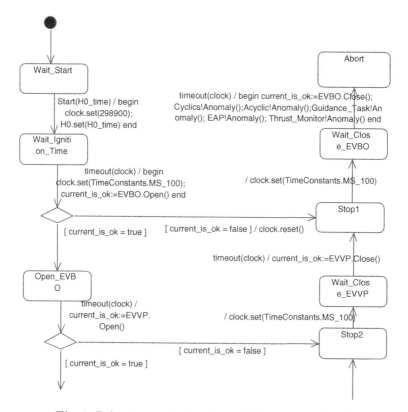

Fig. 6. Behaviour of the EPC regulation process (part).

Model Exploration. The validation process continues with a debugging phase. Without being exhaustive, the user begins to explore the model in a guided or random manner. Simulation states do not need to be stored as the complete model is not explicitly constructed at this moment.

The aim of this phase is to inspect and validate known nominal scenarios of the specification. Moreover, the user can *test* simple safety properties, which must hold on all execution paths. Such properties are generic ones, such as absence of deadlocks and signal loss, or more specific ones such as local assertions.

Advanced Static Analysis. The aim is to simplify the IF description. We use the following static analysis techniques to reduce both the state vector and the state space, while completely preserving its behaviour:

- A specific analysis technique is the elimination of redundant clocks [DY96]. Two clocks are *dependent* in a control state if their difference is constant and can be statically computed at that state.

  The initial SDL version of the Flight Program used no less than 130 timers. Using our static analysis tool we were able to reduce them to only 55 timers, functionally independent ones. Afterwards, the whole specification has been rewritten taking into account the redundancy discovered by the analyser.

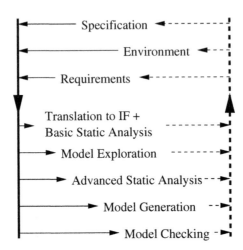

Fig. 7. Validation methodology in IF.

- A second optimisation identifies live equivalent states by introducing systematic resets for dead variables in certain states of the specification.
  For this case study, the live reduction has not been particularly effective due to the reduced number of variables (others than clocks) used in the specification. Our initial attempts to generate the model without live reduction failed. Finally, using live reduction we were able to build the model but still, it was of unmanageable size, about $2 \cdot 10^6$ states and $18 \cdot 10^6$ transitions.
- The last optimisation is dead-code elimination. We used this technique to automatically eliminate some components which do not perform any relevant action.

LTS Generation. The LTS generation phase aims to build the state graph of the specification by exhaustive simulation. In order to cope with the complexity, the user can choose an adequate state representation e.g., discrete or dense representation of time as well as an exploration strategy e.g., traversal order, use of partial order reductions, scheduling policies, etc.

The use of partial order reduction has been necessary to construct tractable models. We applied a simple *static* partial order reduction which eliminates spurious interleaving between internal steps occurring in different processes at the same time. Internal steps are those which do not perform visible communication actions, neither signal emission or access to shared variables. This partial order reduction imposes a fixed exploration order between internal steps and preserves *all* the properties expressed in terms of visible actions.

Example 4. By using partial order reduction on internal steps, we reduced the size of the model by 3 orders of magnitude i.e, from $2 \cdot 10^6$ states and $18 \cdot 10^6$ transitions to $1.6 \cdot 10^3$ states and $1.65 \cdot 10^3$ transitions, which can be easily handled by the model checker.

We considered two different models of the environment. A *time-deterministic* one, where actions take place at precise moments in time and a *time- nondeterministic* one where actions take place within predefined time intervals. Table 1 presents in each case the sizes of the models obtained depending on the generation strategy used.

Table 1. Verification Results. The model minimisation and model checking experiments are performed on the smallest available models i.e, obtained with both live and partial order reduction.

		time deterministic	time non-deterministic
model generation	− live reduction − partial order	state explosion	state explosion
	+ live reduction − partial order	2201760 st. 18706871 tr.	state explosion
	+ live reduction + partial order	1604 st. 1642 tr.	195718 st. 278263 tr.
model verification	model minimisation	~ 1 sec.	~ 20 sec.
	model checking	~ 15 sec.	~ 120 sec.

Model Checking. Once the model has been generated, three model checking techniques have been applied to verify requirements on the specification:

1. Model checking of μ-calculus formulae using EVALUATOR.

Example 5. The requirement expressing that *"the stop sequence no. 3 occurs only during the flight phase, and never on the ground phase"* can be expressed by the following μ-calculus formula, verified with EVALUATOR:

$$\neg\, \mu X. < EPC!Stop\_3 > T\ \lor\ < \overline{EAP!Fire} > X$$

This formula means that the system cannot execute the *stop sequence no. 3* without executing the firing of the EAP first.

2. Construction of reduced models using ALDEBARAN. A second approach, usually much more intuitive for a non expert end-user, consists in computing an abstract model (with respect to given observation criteria) of the overall behaviour of the specification. Possible incorrect behaviours can be detected by visualising such a model.

Example 6. All safety properties involving the firing actions of the two principal stages, EAP and EPC, and the detection of anomalies are preserved on the

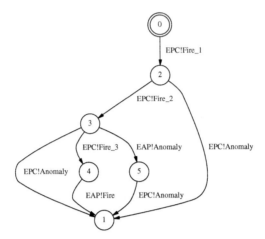

Fig. 8. Minimal model.

LTS in figure 8 generated by ALDEBARAN. It is the quotient model with respect to safety equivalence [BFG+91] while keeping observable only the actions above. For instance it is easy to check on this abstract model that, whenever an anomaly occurs *before* action *EPC!Fire_3* (ignition of the Vulcain engine), then nor this action nor *EAP!Fire* action are executed and therefore the entire launch procedure is aborted.

Table 1 gives the average time required for verifying each kind of property by temporal logic model checking and model minimisation respectively.

3. Model checking with observers. We also used *UML observers* to express and check requirements. Observers allow us to express in a much simpler manner most safety requirements of the Ariane-5 specification. Additionally, they allow to express *quantitative* timing properties, something which is difficult to express with μ-calculus formulas.

Example 7. Figures 9 to 11 show some of the properties that were checked on the UML model:

Figure 9: between any two commands sent by the flight program to the valves there should elapse at least 50ms.

Figure 10: if some instance of class *Valve* fails to open (i.e. enters the state *Failed_Open*) then
- No instance of the *Pyro* class reaches the state *Ignition_done*.
- All instances of class *Valve* shall reach one of the states *Failed_Close* or *Close* after at most 2 seconds since the initial valve failure.
- The events *EAP_Preparation* and *EAP_Release* are never emitted.

Figure 11: if the *Pyro1* object (of class *Pyro*) enters the state *Ignition_done*, then the *Pyro2* object shall enter the state *Ignition_done* at a system time between $TimeConstants.MN\_5*2 + Tpstot\_prep$ and $TimeConstants.MN\_5*2 + Tpstar\_prep$.

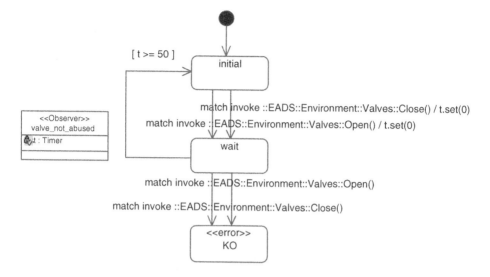

Fig. 9. A timed safety property of the Ariane-5 model.

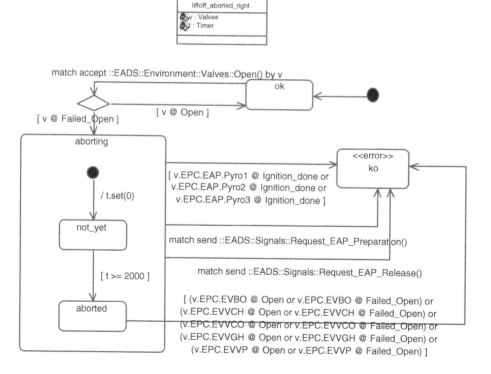

Fig. 10. A timed safety property of the Ariane-5 model.

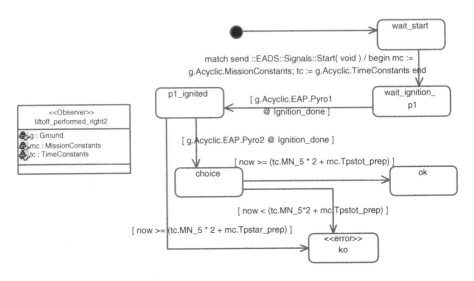

Fig. 11. A timed safety property of the Ariane-5 model.

5   Conclusion

The IF toolset is the result of a long term research effort for theory, methods and tools for model-based development. It offers a unique combination of features for modelling and validation including support for high level modelling, static analysis, model-checking and simulation. Its has been designed with special care for openness to modelling languages and validation tools thanks to the definition of appropriate API's. For instance, it has been connected to explicit model checking tools such as SPIN [Hol91] and CADP [FGK+96], to symbolic and regular model checker tools such as TREX [ABS01], LASH [BL02a], the PVS-based abstraction tool INVEST [BLO98] and to the automatic test generation and execution tools TGV [FJJV96], AGATHA [LRG01] and SPIDER [HN04].

The IF notation is expressive and rich enough to map in a structural manner most of UML concepts and constructs such as classes, state machines with actions, activity groups with run-to-completion semantics. The mapping flattens the description only for inheritance and synchronous calls and this is necessary for validation purposes. It preserves all relevant information about the structure of the model. This provides a basis for compositional analysis and validation techniques that should be further investigated.

The IF notation relies on a framework for modelling real-time systems based on the use of priorities and of types of urgency studied at Verimag [BST98], [BS00], [AGS02]. The combined use of behaviour and priorities naturally leads to layered models and allows compositional modelling of real-time systems, in particular of aspects related to resource sharing and scheduling. Scheduling policies can be modelled as sets of dynamic priority rules. The framework supports composition of scheduling policies and provides composability results for deadlock freedom of the scheduled system. Priorities are also an elegant mechanism for restricting non determinism and controlling execution. Run-to-completion execution and mutual exclusion can be modelled in a straightforward manner. Finally, priorities prove to be a powerful tool for modelling both heterogeneous interaction and heterogeneous execution as advocated in [GS03]. The IF toolset fully supports this framework. It embodies principles for structuring and enriching descriptions with timing information as well as expertise gained through its use in several large projects such as the IST projects OMEGA [Con03,GH04], AGEDIS [Con02] and ADVANCE [Con01].

The combination of different validation techniques enlarges the scope of application of the IF toolset. Approaches can differ according to the characteristics of the model. For data intensive models, static analysis techniques can be used to simplify the model before verification, while for control intensive models partial order techniques and observers are very useful to cope with state explosion. In any case, the combined use of static analysis and model checking by skilled users proves to be a powerful means to break complexity. Clearly, the use of high level modelling languages involves some additional cost in complexity with respect to low level modelling languages e.g., languages based on automata. Nevertheless, this is a price to pay for validation of real life systems whose faithful modelling requires dynamically changing models with infinite state space. In our methodology, abstraction and simplification can be carried out automatically by static analysis.

The use of observers for requirements proves to be very convenient and easy to use compared to logic-based formalisms. They allow a natural description, especially of real-time properties relating timed occurrences of several events. The "operational" description style is much more easy to master and understand by practitioners. The limitation to safety properties is not a serious one for well-timed systems. In fact, IF descriptions are by construction well-timed - time can always progress due to the use of urgency types. Liveness properties become bounded response, that is safety properties.

The IF toolset is unique in that it supports rigorous high level modelling of real-time systems and their properties as well as a complete validation methodology. Compared to commercially available modelling tools, it offers more powerful validation features. For graphical editing and version management, it needs a front end that generates either XMI or SDL. We are currently using RATIONAL ROSE and OBJECTGEODE. We have also connections from RHAPSODY and ARGO UML.

Compared to other validation tools, the IF toolset presents many similarities with SPIN. Both tools offer features such as a high level input language, integration of external code, use of enumerative model checking techniques as well as static optimisations. In addition, IF allows the modelling of real-time concepts and the toolset has an open architecture which eases the connection with other tools.

References

[ABS01]   A. Annichini, A. Bouajjani, and M. Sighireanu. TReX: A Tool for Reachability Analysis of Complex Systems. In *Proceedings of CAV'01, (Paris, France)*, volume 2102 of *LNCS*. Springer, 2001.

[AD94]   R. Alur and D.L. Dill. A Theory of Timed Automata. *Theoretical Computer Science*, 126:183–235, 1994.

[AGS00]   K. Altisen, G. Gössler, and J. Sifakis. A Methodology for the Construction of Scheduled Systems. In M. Joseph, editor, *proc. FTRTFT 2000*, volume 1926 of *LNCS*, pages 106–120. Springer-Verlag, 2000.

[AGS02]   K. Altisen, G. Gössler, and J. Sifakis. Scheduler Modeling Based on the Controller Snthesis Paradigm. *Journal of Real-Time Systems, special issue on "control-theoretical approaches to real-time computing"*, 23(1/2):55–84, 2002.

[BFG+91]   A. Bouajjani, J.Cl. Fernandez, S. Graf, C. Rodriguez, and J. Sifakis. Safety for Branching Time Semantics. In *Proceedings of ICALP'91*, volume 510 of *LNCS*. Springer, July 1991.

[BFG+99]   M. Bozga, J.Cl. Fernandez, L. Ghirvu, S. Graf, J.P. Krimm, L. Mounier, and J. Sifakis. IF: An Intermediate Representation for SDL and its Applications. In R. Dssouli, G. Bochmann, and Y. Lahav, editors, *Proceedings of SDL FORUM'99 (Montreal, Canada)*, pages 423–440. Elsevier, June 1999.

[BFKM97]   M. Bozga, J.Cl. Fernandez, A. Kerbrat, and L. Mounier. Protocol Verification with the Aldebaran Toolset. *Software Tools for Technology Transfer*, 1(1+2):166–183, December 1997.

[BL02a]   B. Boigelot and L. Latour. The Liege Automata-based Symbolic Handler LASH. http://www.montefiore.ulg.ac.be/ boigelot/research/lash, 2002.

[BL02b]   M. Bozga and Y. Lakhnech. IF-2.0: Common Language Operational Semantics. Technical report, Verimag, 2002.

[BLO98]   S. Bensalem, Y. Lakhnech, and S. Owre. Computing Abstractions of Infinite State Systems Compositionally and Automatically. In A. Hu and M. Vardi, editors, *Proceedings of CAV'98 (Vancouver, Canada)*, volume 1427 of *LNCS*, pages 319–331. Springer, June 1998.

[BS00]   S. Bornot and J. Sifakis. An Algebraic Framework for Urgency. *Information and Computation*, 163:172–202, 2000.

[BST98]   S. Bornot, J. Sifakis, and S. Tripakis. Modeling Urgency in Timed Systems. In *International Symposium: Compositionality - The Significant Difference*, volume 1536 of *LNCS*. Springer-Verlag, 1998.

[Con01]   ADVANCE Consortium. http://www.liafa.jussieu.fr/ advance - website of the IST ADVANCE project, 2001.

[Con02]   AGEDIS Consortium. http://www.agedis.de - website of the IST AGEDIS project, 2002.

[Con03]   OMEGA Consortium. http://www-omega.imag.fr - website of the IST OMEGA project., 2003.

[DH99]   W. Damm and D. Harel. LSCs: Breathing Life into Message Sequence Charts. In P. Ciancarini, A. Fantechi, and R. Gorrieri, editors, *FMOODS'99 IFIP TC6/WG6.1 Third International Conference on Formal Methods for Open Object-Based Distributed Systems*. Kluwer Academic Publishers, 1999. Journal Version to appear in Journal on Formal Methods in System Design, July 2001.

[DJPV02]   W. Damm, B. Josko, A. Pnueli, and A. Votintseva. Understanding UML: A
           Formal Semantics of Concurrency and Communication in Real-Time UML.
           In *Proceedings of FMCO'02*, LNCS. Springer Verlag, November 2002.
[DY96]   C. Daws and S. Yovine. Reducing the Number of Clock Variables of Timed
           Automata. In *Proceedings of RTSS'96 (Washington, DC, USA)*, pages 73–
           82. IEEE Computer Society Press, December 1996.
[FGK+96]   J.Cl. Fernandez, H. Garavel, A. Kerbrat, R. Mateescu, L. Mounier, and
           M. Sighireanu. CADP: A Protocol Validation and Verification Toolbox.
           In R. Alur and T.A. Henzinger, editors, *Proceedings of CAV'96 (New
           Brunswick, USA)*, volume 1102 of *LNCS*, pages 437–440. Springer, Au-
           gust 1996.
[FJJV96]   J.C. Fernandez, C. Jard, T. Jéron, and C. Viho. Using On-the-fly Veri-
           fication Techniques for the Generation of Test Suites. In *Proceedings of
           CAV'96*, number 1102 in LNCS. Springer, 1996.
[GH04]   S. Graf and J. Hooman. Correct development of embedded systems. In
           *European Workshop on Software Architecture: Languages, Styles, Models,
           Tools, and Applications (EWSA 2004), co-located with ICSE 2004, St An-
           drews, Scotland*, LNCS, May 2004.
[GOO03]   S. Graf, I. Ober, and I. Ober. Timed Annotations in UML. In *Work-
           shop SVERTS on Specification and Validation of UML models for Real
           Time and Embedded Systems, a satellite event of UML 2003, San Fran-
           cisco, October 2003*, Verimag technical report 2003/10/22 or http://www-
           verimag.imag.fr/EVENTS/2003/SVERTS/, October 2003.
[GS03]   G. Gössler and J. Sifakis. Composition for Component-Based Modeling.
           In *proc. FMCO'02*, volume 2852 of *LNCS*. Springer-Verlag, 2003.
[Har87]   D. Harel. Statecharts: A Visual Formalism for Complex Systems. *Sci. Com-
           put. Programming 8, 231-274*, 1987.
[HN04]   A. Hartman and K. Nagin. The AGEDIS Tools for Model Based Testing.
           In *Proceedings of ISSTA'2004*, 2004.
[Hol91]   Gerard J. Holzmann. *Design and Validation of Computer Protocols*. Pren-
           tice Hall Software Series, 1991.
[HP98]   D. Harel and M. Politi. *Modeling Reactive Systems with Statecharts: The
           STATEMATE Approach*. McGraw-Hill, 1998.
[HvdZ03]   J. Hooman and M.B. van der Zwaag. A Semantics of Communicating Re-
           active Objects with Timing. In *Proceedings of SVERTS'03 (Specification
           and Validation of UML models for Real Time and Embedded Systems)*, San
           Francisco, October 2003.
[IBM]   IBM. Rational ROSE Development Environment.
[Ilo]   Ilogix. Rhapsody Development Environment.
[JM99]   T. Jéron and P. Morel. Test Generation Derived from Model Checking.
           In N. Halbwachs and D. Peled, editors, *Proceedings of CAV'99 (Trento,
           Italy)*, volume 1633 of *LNCS*, pages 108–122. Springer, July 1999.
[Koz83]   D. Kozen. Results on the Propositional μ-Calculus. *Theoretical Computer
           Science*, 1983.
[LPY98]   K.G. Larsen, P. Pettersson, and W. Yi. UPPAAL in a Nutshell. *Journal
           on Software Tools for Technology Transfer*, 1:134–152, 1998.
[LRG01]   D. Lugato, N. Rapin, and J.P. Gallois. Verification and tests generation
           for SDL industrial specifications with the AGATHA toolset. In *Real-Time
           Tools Workshop affiliated to CONCUR 2001, Aalborg, Denmark*, 2001.
[Mil80]   R. Milner. *A Calculus of Communication Systems*, volume 92 of *LNCS*.
           Springer, 1980.

[Muc97]   S. Muchnick. *Advanced Compiler Design Implementation*. Morgan Kaufmann Publishers, 1997.

[NS91]   X. Nicollin and J. Sifakis. An Overview and Synthesis on Timed Process Algebras. In *Proc. CAV'91*, volume 575 of *LNCS*. Springer-Verlag, July 1991.

[OGO04]   I. Ober, S. Graf, and I. Ober. Model Checking of UML Models via a Mapping to Communicating Extended Timed Automata. In *11th International SPIN Workshop on Model Checking of Software, 2004*, volume LNCS 2989, pages 127–145, 2004.

[OMG01]   OMG. Unified Modeling Language Specification (Action Semantics). OMG Adopted Specification, December 2001.

[OMG03a]   OMG. Model Driven Architecture. http://www.omg.org/mda, 2003.

[OMG03b]   OMG. Standard UML Profile for Schedulability, Performance and Time, v. 1.0. OMG document formal/2003-09-01, September 2003.

[Par81]   D. Park. Concurrency and Automata on Infinite Sequences. *Theoretical Computer Science*, 104:167–183, March 1981.

[RVR+]   A. Ramirez, Ph. Vanpeperstraete, A. Rueckert, K. Odutola, J. Bennett, and L. Tolke. ArgoUML Environment.

[Sif77]   J. Sifakis. Use of Petri Nets for Performance Evaluation. In *Proc. 3rd Intl. Symposium on Modeling and Evaluation*, pages 75–93. IFIP, North Holland, 1977.

[Sif01]   J. Sifakis. Modeling Real-Time Systems — Challenges and Work Directions. In T.A. Henzinger and C. M. Kirsch, editors, *Proc. EMSOFT'01*, volume 2211 of *LNCS*. Springer-Verlag, 2001.

[STY03]   J. Sifakis, S. Tripakis, and S. Yovine. Building Models of Real-Time Systems from Application Software. *Proc. IEEE*, 91(1):100–111, 2003.

[Tip94]   F. Tip. A Survey of Program Slicing Techniques. Technical Report CS-R9438, CWI, Amsterdam, The Netherlands, 1994.

[vGW89]   R.J. van Glabbeek and W.P. Weijland. Branching-Time and Abstraction in Bisimulation Semantics. Technical Report CS-R8911, CWI, Amsterdam, The Netherlands, 1989.

[Wei84]   M. Weiser. Program Slicing. *IEEE Transactions on Software Engineering*, SE-10(4):352–357, 1984.

[Yov97]   S. Yovine. KRONOS: A Verification Tool for Real-Time Systems. *Software Tools for Technology Transfer*, 1(1+2):123–133, December 1997.

Embedded Software Analysis with MOTOR

Joost-Pieter Katoen[1], Henrik Bohnenkamp[1],
Ric Klaren[1], and Holger Hermanns[1,2]

[1] Faculty of Electrical Engineering, Mathematics and Computer Science,
University of Twente, The Netherlands
[2] Saarland University, D-66123 Saarbrücken, Germany

Abstract. This paper surveys the language MODEST, a Modelling and
Description language for Stochastic and Timed systems, and its accompanying tool-environment MOTOR. The language and tool are aimed to
support the modular description and analysis of reactive systems while
covering both functional and non-functional system aspects such as hard
and soft real-time, and quality-of-service aspects. As an illustrative example, the modeling and analysis of a device-absence detecting protocol
in plug-and-play networks is described and is shown to exhibit some
undesired behaviour.

1 Introduction

Background and motivation. The prevailing paradigm in computer science to
abstract from physical aspects is gradually being recognized to be too limited
and too restricted. Instead, classical abstractions of software that leave out "non-
functional" aspects such as cost, efficiency, and robustness need to be adapted
to current needs. In particular this applies to the rapidly emerging field of *"embedded"* software [14,32].

Embedded software controls the core functionality of many systems. It is
omnipresent: it controls telephone switches and satellites, drives the climate
control in our offices, runs pacemakers, is at the heart of our power plants, and
makes our cars and TVs work. Whereas traditional software has a rather trans-
formational nature mapping input data onto output data, embedded software
is different in many respects. Most importantly, embedded software is subject
to complex and permanent interactions with their – mostly physical – environment via sensors and actuators. Typically software in embedded systems does
not terminate and interaction usually takes place with multiple concurrent processes at the same time. Reactions to the stimuli provided by the environment
should be prompt (timeliness or responsiveness), i.e., the software has to "keep
up" with the speed of the processes with which it interacts. As it executes on
devices where several other activities go on, non-functional properties such as
efficient usage of resources (e.g., power consumption) and robustness are important. High requirements are put on performance and dependability, since the
embedded nature complicates tuning and maintenance.

Embedded software is an important motivation for the development of modeling techniques that on the one hand provide an easy migration path for design

M. Bernardo and F. Corradini (Eds.): SFM-RT 2004, LNCS 3185, pp. 268–293, 2004.

engineers and, on the other hand, support the description of quantitative system aspects. This has resulted in various extensions of light-weight formal notations such as SDL (System Description Language) and the UML (Unified Modeling Language), and in the development of a whole range of more rigorous formalisms based on e.g., stochastic process algebras, or appropriate extensions of automata such as timed automata [1], and probabilistic automata [41]. Light-weight notations are typically closer to engineering techniques, but lack a formal semantics; rigorous formalisms do have such formal semantics, but their learning curve is typically too steep from a practitioner's perspective and they mostly have a restricted expressiveness.

The modeling formalism MODEST. This paper surveys MODEST, a description language that has a rigid formal basis (i.e., semantics) and incorporates several ingredients from light-weight notations such as exception handling[1], modularization, atomic assignments, iteration, and simple data types, and illustrates the accompanying tool support MOTOR by modeling and analyzing a device-absence detecting protocol in plug-and-play embedded networks.

MODEST is based on classical process algebra like CSP and CCS, and counts therefore as a *compositional* specification formalism: the description of complex behaviour is obtained by combining the descriptions of more simple components. Inherent to process algebra is the elegant way of specifying concurrent computations. MODEST is enhanced with convenient language ingredients like simple data-structures and a notion of exception handling. It is capable to express a rich class of non-homogeneous stochastic processes and is therefore most suitable to capture non-functional system aspects. MODEST may be viewed as an overarching notation for a wide spectrum of prominent models in computer science, ranging from labeled transition systems, to timed automata [1, 13] (and probabilistic variants thereof [31] and stochastic processes such as Markov chains and (continuous-time and generalised) Markov decision processes [22, 24, 35, 41].

Approach. With MODEST, we take a *single-formalism, multi-solution* approach. Our view is to have a single system specification that addresses various aspects of the system under consideration. Analysis thus refers to the same system specification rather than to different (and potentially inconsistent) specifications of system perspectives like in the UML. Analysis takes place by extracting simpler models from MODEST specifications that are tailored to the specific property of interest. For instance, for checking reachability properties, a possible strategy is to "distill" an automaton from the MODEST specification and feed it into an existing model checker such as SPIN [28] of CADP [19]. On the other hand, for carrying out an evaluation of the stochastic process underlying a MODEST specification, one may resort to discrete-event simulation, as, for instance, offered by the MÖBIUS tool environment.

---

[1] Exception handling in specification languages has received scant attention. Notable exceptions are Enhanced-LOTOS [21] and Esterel [6].

The tool-environment MOTOR. In order to facilitate the analysis of MODEST specifications, the tool MOTOR [11] has been developed. Due to the enormous expressiveness of MODEST, ranging from labeled transition systems to Markov decision processes and timed automata, there is no generic analysis method at our disposal that is able to cover all possible models. Instead, MOTOR aims at supporting a variety of analysis methods tailored to a variety of tractable sub-models. Our philosophy is to connect MOTOR to existing tools rather than implementing successful analysis techniques anew. Currently, connections to the CADP toolbox [19] and the multi/formalism - multi/solution MÖBIUS tool environment [18] have been established. The former is aimed at assessing qualitative properties, whereas the latter is a performance evaluation tool supporting numerical methods and discrete-event simulation techniques. The case study described in this paper exploits the simulation facilities of MÖBIUS.

Organization of this survey. Section 2 introduces the main syntactical constructs of MODEST by means of modeling some example mutual exclusion protocols and presents its semantics by means of some examples. Section 3 briefly describes the MOTOR tool environment. Section 4 presents the modeling and analysis of a protocol in highly dynamic networked embedded systems and shows how this analysis reveals an undesired phenomenon. Section 5 finally concludes and gives some directions for future work. This paper is intended as a tutorial and does neither provide details of the syntax and semantics of MODEST, nor the implementation details of MOTOR and the full details of the case study. Pointers to relevant papers where such details can be found are given in the various sections.

2   The Modeling Language MoDeST

2.1   Syntax

This section introduces the main syntactical constructs of MODEST by means of modeling some example mutual exclusion protocols. The first one is a typical mutual exclusion algorithm where global variables are used to regulate the access to the critical section. The second algorithm uses timing to synchronize this access, whereas the latter is a randomized algorithm and does only guarantee mutual exclusion with a certain probability (that differs from one). A more detailed description of the MODEST language can be found in [16].

Pnueli's mutual exclusion algorithm. The first example is a mutual exclusion protocol for two processes, called P and Q, due to Pnueli [38]. There is a single shared variable s which is either 0 or 1, and initially 1. Besides, each process has a local Boolean variable y that initially equals 0 and that may be inspected by the other process. The MODEST specification of this algorithm is given below. Actions and assignments are the most elementary syntactical constructs in MODEST. The global declaration part (cf. the first two lines) contains action, variable and constant (if any) declarations. In this paper, we adopt the convention that action names consist of two parts connected by an underscore. The model consists of the parallel composition of two processes as specified by the par-construct in the last four lines. Although in this example there is no communication between the processes via actions, the principle of par is that processes execute actions in common synchronously, and other actions autonomously. Such communication mechanism is rather common in process algebras such as CSP [27] and is a convenient mechanism for compositional modeling. A process description consists of an optional declaration part (absent in this example) of local actions and variables and a behaviour description, in this example consisting of a simple do-iteration for both P and Q. The statement s = false, y0 = true is a multiple assignment in which variable y0 is set to true and s to false in a single, atomic step. The when-statement may be read as "wait until". The other statements have the obvious meaning.

The intuition behind this protocol is as follows. The variables y0 and y1 are used by each process to signal the other process of active interest in entering the critical section. On leaving the non-critical section, a process sets its own local variable y to 1. In a similar way this variable is reset to 0 once the critical section is left. The global variable s is used to resolve a tie situation between the processes. It serves as a logbook in which each process that sets its y variable to 1 signs at the same time. The test at the third line says that process P may enter its critical section if either y1 equals 0 – implying that its competitor is not interested in entering its critical section – or if s differs from 0 – implying that its competitor performed its assignment to y1 after P assigned 1 to y.

```
action enter_cs1, enter_cs2;
bool s = true, y0 = 0, y1 = 0;

process P() {
  do {
  :: {= s = false, y0 = true =};
     when (!y1 || s)
        enter_cs1;    // CS
     y0 = false       // leave CS
  }
}

process Q() {
  do {
  :: {= s = true, y1 = true =};
     when (!y0 || !s)
        enter_cs2;    // CS
     y1 = false
  }
}

par {
:: P()
:: Q()
}
```

Fischer's timed mutual exclusion algorithm. As a second example we treat the mutual exclusion algorithm by Fischer [40] where time in combination with a shared variable is used to avoid processes to be in their critical section simultaneously. This algorithm is probably the most well-known benchmark example for real-time model checkers. Apart from the standard types bool, int and float for data, variables of the type clock can be used to measure the elapse of time. Clocks are set to 0 and advance implicitly, as opposed to ordinary data variables that need to be changed by means of explicit assignments. In the sequel we will use x and y to range over clock variables. All clocks run at the same pace. Clocks are a kind of alarm clocks that expire once they meet a value of type float. Such values can be of the usual form or can be samples from probability distributions (as we will see in the next example). Each process in Fischer's protocol has a single local clock x that is compared with the constant threshold values d and k to grab a ticket and check whether it is still the ticket's owner, respectively. The MODEST specification of the protocol is as follows.

```
int v;                          // ticket
action enter_cs, ...            // action declarations

process P (int id) {            // behaviour of a single thread
  clock x;                      // P's private timer
  const float k = 2.0, d = 1.0;
  do {
  :: when (v == 0) x = 0;       // once ticket is free, start timer
    do {
    :: when (x <= d)            // wait for exactly k time units
       take_ticket {= v = id, x = 0 =};  // grab the ticket
      alt {
      :: when (v != id) x = 0;   // no longer own ticket
      :: when (v == id && x >= k) // ticket is still yours
           enter_cs;
         break {= v = 0 =}       // release ticket
      }
    }
  }
}

par {
:: relabel { take_ticket, enter_cs } by {take_ticket1,enter_cs1 } in P(1)
:: relabel { take_ticket, enter_cs } by {take_ticket2,enter_cs2 } in P(2)
}
```

A few remarks are in order. The when-statement that may guard an action (or assignment) may refer to data variables (like v) and clocks (e.g., x). In the latter case, the guarded action becomes enabled as soon as the condition in the when-clause becomes valid (and no other action becomes enabled at an earlier time instant). Note that the evaluation of the guards in a when-statement, the execution of the action and, if any, the mulitple assignments, is performed as a single atomic step, i.e., without interference of other parallel threads. This is similar to the well-known test-and-set principle [5][pp. 43] where the value of a shared variable is tested (i.e., a guard) and set (i.e., the assignment associated with an action) in a single step.

Remark 1. In this survey, we assume a maximal progress semantics that conforms to the semantics as taken by the discrete-event simulator of MOTOR-MÖBIUS. In case such maximal progress assumption is not adopted, an urgent clause may be used to force actions to happen at some time. This is similar to location invariants in timed automata [1, 13] and allows for the specification of non-deterministic timing. For instance, the following MODEST fragment:

```
clock x = 0;
urgent (x >= 75)
  when (x >= 20)
    enter_cs;
```

specifies that action enter_cs is enabled from 20 time units since resetting clock x, and that it should ultimately happen when x equals 75, as indicated by the urgent-clause.   □

In Fischer's protocol, process P, for instance, waits until the global variable v – modeling a ticket that is needed to enter the critical section – equals zero and then sets the timer x. Subsequently, it waits exactly two time units before assigning P's id to v and is allowed to enter its critical section only when v still equals its id. In case it does not own the ticket, it has to wait again. The choice between v == 0 and v == id is syntactically represented by the alt-construct that also allows for modeling non-deterministic choices. Recall that in case none of these conditions is met, the process waits. On leaving the critical section, the ticket is released and the entire procedure starts again. Note that the entire system is composed of two processes that are obtained from the blueprint P by instantiating it with the ids one and two and relabeling the actions in an appropriate way in order to avoid unintended synchronizations. By means of relabeling, actions are renamed in the behaviour expression, e.g., rename a by b in P will result in a process that behaves like P except that any syntactic occurrence of a in P is renamed into a.

Randomized Fischer's mutual exclusion algorithm. The last example is a randomized variant of Fischer's algorithm due to Gafni and Mitzenmacher [20]. The main difference is that the main activities in the protocol, such as inspecting the global variable v, and entering the critical section, are governed by exponential (or gamma) distributions. A MODEST specification of the case with gamma distributions is as follows.

```
int v = 0;     // ticket

process P (int id) {
clock x;
float k;
do {
:: when (v == 0) {= k = GAMMA(...), x = 0 =};
   do {
   :: when ( (x == k) && (v == 0) )
      take_ticket; {= v = id, k = GAMMA(...), x = 0 =};
      alt {
      :: when ( (v != id) ) break
      :: when ( (x == k) && (v == id) )
         enter_cs {= k = GAMMA(...) =};
         when (x == k) break {= v = 0 =}
      }
   }
}
}
```

```
par {
:: relabel { take_ticket, enter_cs } by {take_ticket1, enter_cs1} in P(1)
:: relabel { take_ticket, enter_cs } by {take_ticket2, enter_cs2} in P(2)
}
```

Other randomizedmutual exclusion protocols in [20] can be obtained in a similar way. Note that the value of variable k is determined by sampling a gamma-distribution. By requiring x == k in the when-clauses, it is enforced that the amount of time that has elapsed is indeed governed by a gamma-distribution.

Other syntactical constructs. It remains to explain the palt-construct that is used to model probabilistic choice. A palt-statement is in fact an action that has several alternative (multiple) assignments that can take place with accompanying successive statements. The likelihood of these alternatives is determined by weights. For instance,

```
take_ticket palt {
              :1: {= v = id, x = 0 =} P(v)
              :3: {= v = 0, x = 0 =} P(v)
              }
```

specifies that on the occurrence of action take_ticket, v will be set to id with probability $\frac{1}{1+3} = \frac{1}{4}$ and to zero with probability $\frac{3}{4}$. In both cases, x is reset. Note that the occurrence of the action, the resolution of the probabilistic choice, and the multiple assignments are executed atomically. In fact, an ordinary action occurrence with some multiple assignments can be viewed as syntactic sugar for a palt-statement with a single alternative.

As the case study furtheron does not use exception handling, we refrain from introducing this operator here.

Remark 2. The syntax of the control and data structures in MODEST is very similar to that of PROMELA, the protocol modeling language that is used as input language to the model checker SPIN [28]. For instance, similar constructs to do, alt, when, multiple assignments and process exist in PROMELA. There are, however, some differences. As PROMELA is aimed at describing protocols, communication channels and primitives to send and receive messages along them are first-class citizens in the language. In MODEST such communication buffers need to be modeled explicitly as separate processes. PROMELA incorporates an atomic-statement in which a sequence of statements can be executed atomically, i.e., without interference of other parallel processes; MODEST only supports multiple assignments. The main add-ons in MODEST are: the possibility of specifying discrete probabilistic branching (using palt) [2], real-time, and randomizedtime delays. Besides, the formal semantics of MODEST (see below) provides an unambiguous interpretation.   □

---

[2] A similar construct has recently been suggested in a probabilistic variant of PROMELA [3].

2.2 Semantics

Stochastic timed automata. The MODEST semantics is defined in terms of an extension of timed automata. The extension is needed to accommodate for the palt-construct and the random delays. Whereas timed automata are aimed to finitely represent infinite-state real-time systems, our variant – baptized stochastic timed automata – focuses on finitely representing stochastic timed systems. (As for timed automata, the underlying interpretation of such models is indeed an infinite-state, infinitely branching structure.) In case a MODEST specification does not cover any probabilistic choice, the semantics obtains the symbolic automata one intuitively expects (cf. Fig. 1). In these automata, transitions are

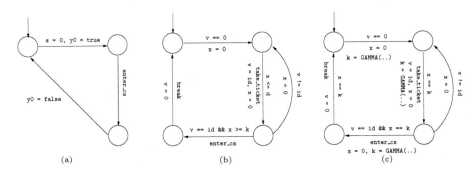

Fig. 1. Automata for a single thread in (a) Pnueli's, (b) Fischer's and (c) randomized Fischer's mutex algorithm.

equipped with an action (that may be subject to interaction with other parallel processes), a guard and a multiple assignment. All these attributes are optional with the condition that either an action or an assignment is present. An action is absent for statements like x = 0;, a guard is absent (i.e., true) in absence of a when-statement, and a (multiple) assignment is absent for actions without accompanying assignments. If actions synchronize, the resulting transition is decorated with the common action, the joined multiple assignments (provided they do not assign to the same variables), and the conjunction of guards.

To treat discrete probabilistic branching, the concept of transition is refined cf. Fig. 2. A transition is a one-to-many edge labeled with an action and a guard (as before), but where different multiple assignments are possible, and where each alternative has an associated weight to determine the likelihood. The intuitive interpretation of the simple stochastic timed automaton in Fig. 2, for instance, is as follows. Once the conditions v != id and x == k hold (and the environment is able to participate, if needed, in action take_ticket), both outgoing transitions of state s are enabled, and one of them is non-deterministically chosen. On selecting the rightmost transition, action take_ticket is performed, and there are two possible successor states. With probability $\frac{1}{4}$ the assignments v = id and x = 0 are performed (atomically) and the automaton moves to state u, while with the remaining probability $\frac{3}{4}$, x and v are both reset to zero, and the next state equals t. When the leftmost transition is chosen, there is a single alternative (i.e., a probabilistic choice with one alternative that occurs with probability one).

Fig. 2. A simple stochastic timed automaton.

Operational semantics. The mapping from MODEST onto stochastic timed automata is defined by means of structured operational semantics [34]. This semantics is a simple adaptation of the usual operational semantics of programming languages and process calculi. The slight adaptation is needed to accommodate probabilistic choices. Let us consider some examples. The standard inference rule for actions

$$a \xrightarrow{a,tt} \sqrt{}$$

states that action a can perform execute a at any time (i.e., guard is true), and evolves into the successfully terminated behaviour $\sqrt{}$. Note that $\sqrt{}$ is not a syntactical entity, but is just used to define the semantics. For MODEST, this rule is written as:

$$a \xrightarrow{a,tt} \mathcal{P}$$

where $\mathcal{P}$ is a trivial distribution such that $\mathcal{P}(\varnothing, \sqrt{}) = 1$, i.e., the probability of performing no assignments and evolving into $\sqrt{}$ equals one. The inference rule for MODEST actions is thus a simple generalization of the standard inference rules for actions. The target of a transition for MODEST is no longer an expression (like $\sqrt{}$) but a *probability space* with accompanying probability measure (e.g., a trivial distribution). The same applies to the other operators. For instance, for alternative composition, the standard inference rule

$$\frac{P_i \xrightarrow{a,g} P_i' \quad (1 \leqslant i \leqslant k)}{\mathsf{alt}\{:: P_1 \ \ldots \ :: P_k\} \xrightarrow{a,g} P_i'}$$

stating that whenever the alternative P_i can make an a, g-move, then the alternative composition can do so as well, is generalized yielding:

$$\frac{P_i \xrightarrow{a,g} \mathcal{P}_i \quad (1 \leqslant i \leqslant k)}{\mathsf{alt}\{:: P_1 \ \ldots \ :: P_k\} \xrightarrow{a,g} \mathcal{P}_i}$$

Note, again, that the target of an expression is a probability space, viz. $\mathcal{P}_i$.

The semantics of the new operators is defined as follows. For probabilistic choice the inference rule is

$$a \text{ palt } \{:w_i\colon A_i \ ; \ P_i\}_{i \in I} \xrightarrow{a, tt} \mathcal{P} \text{ with } \mathbf{P}(A_i, P_i) = \frac{w_i}{\sum_{j \in I} w_j}$$

where, for simplicity, it is assumed here that all P_i's are distinct and where $\mathbf{P}$ is the probability measure of probability space $\mathcal{P}$. It is, in fact, an alternative composition in which one of the alternatives (i.e., P_i) and the associated multiple assignments (i.e., A_i) is chosen with a certain probability that is determined by the weights. Here, it is assumed that all weights (i.e., w_i) are strictly positive. Weights can either be constant, like in our examples, but may also be an expression[3]. Guards as specified by when-statements can be handled easily:

$$\frac{P \xrightarrow{a,g} \mathcal{P}}{\text{when}(b) \ P \xrightarrow{a, b \wedge g} \mathcal{P}}$$

where b is a boolean expression. Thus, if P can perform action a with guard g, when(b) P can perform a with guard $b \wedge g$. The semantics of do-statements, relabeling, breaks, and process instantiation are standard and omitted here. We conclude with parallel composition. First, note that:

$$\text{par}\{:: P_1 \ \ldots \ :: P_k\} \stackrel{\text{def}}{=} (\ldots ((P_1 \|_{B_1} P_2) \ldots)) \|_{B_{k-1}} P_k$$

where $\|_B$ is CSP-like parallel composition [27] and

$$B_j = \left(\bigcup_{i=1}^{j} \alpha(P_i) \right) \cap \alpha(P_{j+1})$$

where $\alpha(P)$ denotes the set of actions that P can be involved in. This observation allows us to define the semantics of the **par**-construct in terms of $\|_B$ where B is the common alphabet of all processes put in parallel. The inference rule for standard CSP parallel composition for executing autonomous actions, i.e., actions that are not subject to any interaction with other parallel processes, is defined as follows:

$$\frac{P \xrightarrow{a,g} P' \text{ and } P' \neq \sqrt{}}{P \|_B Q \xrightarrow{a,g} P' \|_B Q} \text{ and } \frac{P \xrightarrow{a,g} \sqrt{}}{P \|_B Q \xrightarrow{a,g} Q \backslash B}$$

where $Q \backslash B$ equals behaviour Q except that actions in the set B are prohibited. This conforms to the idea that Q should synchronize on such actions with P, where P is impossible to do so. For MODEST, these rules are generalized towards:

$$\frac{P \xrightarrow{a,g} \mathcal{P} \qquad a \notin B}{P \|_B Q \xrightarrow{a,g} \mathcal{R}} \text{ with } \begin{array}{l} \mathbf{R}(A, P' \|_B Q) = \mathbf{P}(A, P') \\ \mathbf{R}(A, Q \backslash B) \quad = \mathbf{P}(A, \sqrt{}) \end{array}$$

---

[3] The semantics of the latter case is more involved and omitted here.

For synchronizations, the inference rule is readily obtained from the inference rules for CSP-synchronization:

$$\frac{P \xrightarrow{a,g} \mathcal{P} \quad Q \xrightarrow{a,g'} \mathcal{Q} \quad a \in B}{P \,\|_B\, Q \xrightarrow{a,g \wedge g'} \mathcal{R}}$$

where the probability space $\mathcal{R}$ is the product of $\mathcal{P}$ and $\mathcal{Q}$ defined by

$$\mathbf{R}(A \cup A', P' \,\|_B\, Q') \;=\; \mathbf{P}(A, P') \cdot \mathbf{Q}(A', Q')$$

in case both P and Q do not successfully terminate and A and A' do not assign values/expressions to the same variables. If one of these processes successfully terminates, a slight modification of this equation applies, cf. [16]. In case P and Q perform (possibly inconsistent) assignments, an exception is raised.

Interpretation of stochastic automata. The interpretation of timed automata is typically defined in terms of infinite-state timed transition systems. For stochastic timed automata this is done in a similar way. A configuration in such transition system records the current state of the stochastic timed automaton and the valuation of all (data and clock) variables. If $s \xrightarrow{a,g} \mathcal{P}$ and the current valuation satisfies guard g, then with probability $\mathbf{P}(A, s')$, where $\mathbf{P}$ is the probability measure of $\mathcal{P}$, the valuation is changed according to the sequence of assignments A, and the next state is s'. Under the maximal progress assumption, time is advanced with some positive amount $d > 0$ if in the current state no other outgoing transition is enabled at some time instant $d' < d$. The advance of time with d means that all values of clock variables are increased by d while letting all other variables unchanged. Note that this interpretation yields a continuous space model with infinitely many states and infinite branching. For a more detailed description of this semantics we refer to [9].

3   The Tool Environment MOTOR

The case study assessed in this paper has been analyzed by means of the MODEST tool environment MOTOR and the performance evaluation environment MÖBIUS. In this section, we will briefly discuss these two tools.

MÖBIUS. This is a performance evaluation tool environment developed at the University of Illinois at Urbana-Champaign, USA [18]. MÖBIUS supports multiple input formalisms and several evaluation approaches for these models. Fig. 3 (a) shows an overview over the MÖBIUS architecture. Atomic models are specified in one of the available input formalisms. Atomic models can be composed by means of state-variable sharing, yielding so called composed models. Notably, atomic models specified in different formalisms can be composed in this way. This allows to specify different aspects of a system under evaluation in the most suitable formalism. Along with an atomic or composed model, the user specifies a reward model, which defines a reward structure on the overall model.

On top of a reward model, the tool provides support to define experiment series, called *Studies*, in which the user defines the set of input parameters for which the composed model should be evaluated. Each combination of input parameters defines a so-called *experiment*. Before analyzing the model experiments, a solution method has to be selected: MÖBIUS offers a powerful (distributed) discrete-event simulator, and, for Markovian models, explicit state-space generators and numerical solution algorithms. It is possible to analyze transient and steady-state reward models. The solver solves each experiment as specified in the *Study*. Results can be administered by means of a database.

The different components constituting a solvable model are specified by means of a series of editors written in Java. Transparent to the user, models are translated into C++ code, compiled and linked together with the necessary supporting libraries, building an executable. The control over build and run of the solver is again done from a Java component. MÖBIUS currently sup-

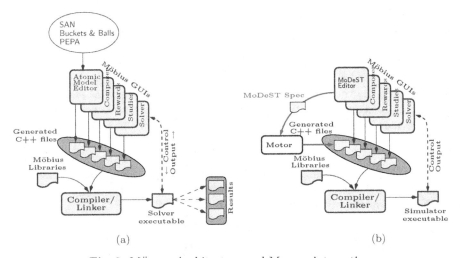

Fig. 3. MÖBIUS Architecture and MOTOR integration.

ports four input formalisms: Bucket and Balls (an input formalism for Markov Chains), SAN (Stochastic Activity Networks) [33, 39], and PEPA (a Markovian Stochastic process algebra) [26]. Recently, the MODEST modeling language has been integrated into the MÖBIUS framework.

MOTOR. In order to facilitate the analysis of MODEST models, we have developed the prototype tool MOTOR [11]. MODEST is a very expressive language, covering a wide range of timed, probabilistic, nondeterministic, and stochastic models. The spectrum of covered models includes ordinary labeled transition systems, discrete and continuous time Markov chains and decision processes, generalized semi-Markov processes, and timed and probabilistic timed automata. These submodels play a crucial role in the context of MOTOR. The enormous expressiveness of MODEST implies that no generic analysis algorithm is at hand. Instead, MOTOR aims at supporting a variety of analysis algorithms tailored to the variety of analyzable submodels. The philosophy behind MOTOR is to connect MODEST to existing tools, rather than re-implementing existing analysis algorithms anew. The advantages of this approach are *(i)* that excellent work of leading research groups is made available for the analysis of MODEST models, and *(ii)* that this is achieved with only moderate implementation effort. This requires a well-designed interfacing structure of MOTOR, which is described in [11].

The first tool MODEST was connected to was the CADP toolbox [19]. The latter is a widespread tool set for the functional design and verification of complex systems.To complement the qualitative analysis of MODEST specifications using CADP we started joint efforts with the MÖBIUS developers [8] to link to the powerful solution techniques of MÖBIUS for quantitative assessment. The main objective was to simulate MODEST models by means of the MÖBIUS distributed discrete-event simulator, because a stochastic simulator can cope with one of the largest class of models expressible in MODEST.

MOTOR *and* MÖBIUS. The integration of MODEST into MÖBIUS is done by means of MOTOR. For this integration, MOTOR has been augmented with a MODEST-to-C++ compiler. From a user-perspective, the MÖBIUS atomic model interface to design MODEST specifications is an ordinary text editor. Whenever a new version of the MODEST specification is saved to disk the MOTOR tool is called automatically in order to regenerate all C++ files (cf. Fig. 3 (b)). Additionally, a supporting C++ library has been written for MÖBIUS, which contains two components: first, a virtual machine responsible for the execution of the MODEST model, and second, an interface to the simulator of MODEST.

As with all other types of atomic models of MÖBIUS is it possible to define reward models and studies on top of MODEST models. The state variables which are accessible for reward specification are the *global variables* of the MODEST specification. Additionally, it is possible to declare constants in the MODEST specification as *extern*, meaning that these constants are actually input parameters of the model, pre-set according to the specified study.

Due to the possibility to specify non-Markov and non-homogeneous stochastic processes, only simulation is currently supported as a suitable evaluation approach for MODEST models within MÖBIUS. While it is in principle possible to identify sublanguages of MODEST corresponding to Markov chain models, this has not been implemented in MOTOR yet.

4   Case Study: Distributed Device-Absence Checking

As an illustrative example application of our framework and tool, we consider the modeling and subsequent analysis of a protocol that is aimed to maintain (and to some extent disseminate) up-to-date information about the presence (or absence) of nodes in a dynamically changing distributed environment. That is to say, the protocol allows for the monitoring of the availability of a node by other nodes. Normally, when a node goes off-line, it informs other nodes by sending a bye-message, but if it suddenly becomes unavailable, no such indication is sent, and the studied protocol comes into play. Important requirements on the protocol are that it should be able to detect the absence of nodes fast (i.e., within about a second) while avoiding to overload devices. Related protocols to this absence-checking protocol [7], nicknamed "ping protocol" in the sequel, are failure detection and monitoring protocols. Failure detection protocols [36, 37] aim to identify whether in a group of nodes, one or more nodes stop executing correctly. In the ping protocol there are two types of nodes, however, only the failure of a single type of node is relevant. Monitoring protocols involve the aggregation of various sorts of data (such as availability information) that are distributed among nodes in the network [30]. The considered protocol is intended as an enhancement to node (or service) discovery protocols that are common in "plug-and-play" distributed systems to find nodes. It is self-organizing in the sense that it continues to operate properly without manual intervention under the – according to different patterns – joining and (un)intentional leaves of nodes.

4.1 The Ping Protocol

Here, we summarize the behaviour of the ping protocol [7]. The protocol originally has been developed as an extension of the service discovery protocol in the UPnP standard (Universal Plug and Play), but may also be used as extension of similar protocols such as SLP, Rendezvous and Jini.

Two types of nodes are distinguished: simple nodes (*devices*) and somewhat more intelligent ones, called *control points* (CPs). The basic protocol mechanism is that a CP continuously probes (i.e., pings) a device that replies to the CP whenever it is (still) present. The essence of the protocol is to automatically adapt the probing frequency in case a device tends to get over- or underloaded. This self-adaptive mechanism is governed by a couple of parameters that are described in more detail furtheron. The CPs are dynamically organized in an overlay network by letting the device, on each probe, return the ids of the last two processes that probed it as well. On the detection of the absence of a device, this overlay network is used to rapidly inform CPs about the leave of the device. For the sake of simplicity, the latter information dissemination phase of the protocol is not considered here.

Device behaviour. A device maintains a probe-counter pc that keeps track of the number of times the device has been probed so far. On the receipt of a probe, this counter is increment by the natural Δ, which typically equals one, and a reply is sent to the probing CP with as parameters the (just updated) value of pc, and the ids of the last two distinct CPs that probed the device. The latter information is needed to maintain the overlay network of CPs[4], whereas

---

[4] By returning two distinct CP ids, the overlay network forms a tree with depth $\log_2 N$ where N is the number of CPs, with a high probability.

the returned value of pc is used by CPs to estimate the load of the device. As Δ is device-dependent, and typically only known by the device itself, a CP cannot distill the actual probing frequency of a device, but only its own perceived probing frequency. Note that Δ can be used by a device to control its load, e.g., for a larger Δ, CPs consider the device to be more (or even over-) loaded sooner, and will adjust (i.e., lower) their probing frequency accordingly resulting in a lower deviceload. Although in principle the value of Δ can be changed during the lifetime of a device, in the sequel we assume it to be constant.

CP behaviour. The behaviour of a CP is more intricate. The basic mechanism for communicating with a device is a bounded retransmission protocol (à la [17]): a CP sends a probe ("are you still there?"), and waits for a reply. In absence of a reply, it retransmits the probe. Otherwise, the CP considers the reply as a notification of the (still) presence of the device, and continues its normal operation. Probes are retransmitted maximally three times. If on none of the four probes a reply is received, the CP considers the device to have left the network, and starts to disseminate this information to other CPs using the overlay network. The protocol allows to distinguish between the timeout value TOF after the first probe and the timeout value after the other (maximally three) probes TOS. Typically, TOS < TOF.

Let us now consider the mechanism for a CP to determine the probing frequency of a device. Let δ be the delay between two consecutive, i.e., not retransmitted, probes. For given constants δ_{min} and δ_{max} with $\delta_{max} \gg \delta_{min}$, the CP has to obey

$$\delta_{min} \leqslant \delta \leqslant \delta_{max}.$$

The value of δ is adapted after each successful probe in the following way. Assume the CP sends a probe to the given device at (its local) time t and receives a reply on that with probe-count pc. (In case of a failed probe, the time at which the retransmitted probe has been sent is taken.) The next probe is sent at time $t' > t$, and let pc' be its returned probe-count. $t'-t$, thus, is the time delay between two successive successful probes. The probeload of the device, as perceived by the CP, is now given as

$$\gamma = \frac{pc' - pc}{t' - t}.$$

The actual probeload of the device equals γ/Δ. For given maximal and minimal probeloads γ_{max} and γ_{min} for the CP, and constant factors $\alpha_{inc}, \alpha_{dec} > 1$, the delay δ is adapted according to the following scheme, where δ' and δ refer to the new and previous value of δ, respectively:

$$\delta' = \begin{cases} \min\left(\alpha_{inc} \cdot \delta, \delta_{max}\right) & \text{if } \gamma > \gamma_{max} \\ \max\left(\frac{1}{\alpha_{dec}} \cdot \delta, \delta_{min}\right) & \text{if } \gamma < \gamma_{min} \\ \delta & \text{otherwise} \end{cases}$$

This adaptive scheme is justified as follows[5]. In case the just perceived probeload γ exceeds the maximal load γ_{max}, the delay is extended (by a factor $\alpha_{inc} > 1$) with the aim to reduce the load. As δ should not exceed the maximal delay δ_{max}, we obtain the first clause of the above formula. This rule thus readjusts the probing frequency of a CP in case the number of CPs (probing the device) suddenly increases. If γ is too low, the delay is shortened in a similar way while obeying $\delta_{min} \leqslant \delta$. The second rule thus readjusts the probing frequency of a CP in case the number of CPs (probing the device) suddenly decreases. In all other cases, the load is between the maximal and minimal load, and there is no need to adjust the delay. Note that the maximal frequency at which a CP may probe a device – given that the protocol is in a stabilized situation – is given by $\max(\frac{1}{\delta_{min}}, \gamma_{max})$. The maximal actual probing frequency of a device is Δ^{-1} times this quantity.

4.2   Modeling in MoDeST

The ping protocol can be modeled in MODEST in a rather straightforward manner. The entire specification consists of the parallel composition of a number of CPs, a number of devices and a network process. By making a precise description of the ping protocol in MoDeST, some small unclarities in the original protocol specification [7] were revealed, such as, e.g., the way in which the ids of the last two (distinct) probing CPs were managed.

As the main aim of our simulation study is an assessment of the self-adaptive mechanism to control the device's probe frequency, the devices are supposed to be present during the entire execution of the simulation (i.e., they are static), whereas the CPs join and leave the network frequently (i.e., they are highly dynamic). In order to govern the leave- and join-pattern of CPs, a separate process is put in parallel to the CPs that synchronizes on `join` and `leave` actions while timing these actions according to some profile as specified in the simulation scenario at hand (see below). For simplicity we omit these actions from the model of the CP as presented below.

The network is modeled as a simple one-place buffer. A shared variable `m` contains the current message in transit (if any) and has fields that contain the various parameters, e.g., `m.src` indicates the address of the source of `m`, `m.lck` indicates whether the structure contains a message, and `m.pc` is the probe counter of a reply message. As the only messages (in our model) from devices to CPs are replies, and from CPs to devices are probes, there is no need to distinguish message types.

To give an impression of the MODEST specification of the ping protocol, we present the (basic, i.e., somewhat simplified) models of a device and CP. The ids of CPs in reply-messages and the bookkeeping of these ids by the device are omitted here, as the dissemination phase is not further considered. The basic behaviour of a device is modeled as follows:

---

[5] To avoid clustering of CPs, in fact, a CP adds a small value to δ' that is randomly determined. For the sake of simplicity, this is not described any further here.

```
process Device (int id) {
  action handle_probe, send_reply ;      // action declarations
  const int Delta = 1.0;                 // probe increase
  clock x;                               // timer for reply time
  int pc = 0,                            // probe counter
      cp;
  float rpldel;                          // reply delay

  do {                                   // actual behaviour
  :: when ( (m.lck) && (m.dst == id) )
       handle_probe {=
         pc += Delta, cp = m.src, m.lck = 0,
         rpldel = min + (max - min)*EXP(...), x = 0 =};
     when ( x >= rpldel )                // rpldel time-units elapsed
       send_reply {= m.src = id, m.dst = cp, m.pc = pc =}
  }
}
```

Here it is assumed that the processing time of the device, i.e., the time between the receipt of a probe and transmitting its reply, is governed by an exponential distribution (see also below), but this could, of course, be any other reasonable distribution. Note that on simulating this model, the maximal progress assumption is adopted, i.e., on the expiration of the delay `rpldel` in the device, a reply is sent immediately. No further delay takes place. The basic behaviour of a CP is modeled as follows:

```
process CP (int id, ) {
  action send_probe, ....                // action declaration
  clock x;                               // timer for timeouts and delays
  int pc = 0,                            // probe counter of last reply
      i = 0;                             // probe counter
  float d = d_max,                       // delay until next probe (=delta)
        to,                              // timeout value
        pl;                              // pingload (= gamma)

  do {
  :: send_probe {= i++, m.src = id, m.dst = dev_id, x = 0, to = TOF =};
     do {                                // wait for reply or timeout
     :: alt {
        :: // timeout and more probe retransmissions allowed
           when ( (x >= to) && (i < 4) )
             send_probe
                 {= i++, m.src = id, m.dst = dev_id, x = 0, to = TOS =};
        :: // reply received in time
           when ( (x < to) && (m.lck) && (m.dst == id) )
             handle_reply {= m.lck = 0, pl = (m.pc - pc)/d, pc = m.pc =};
             alt {                       // adapt delay-to-ping
           :: when (pl > gamma_max)
                 alt { :: when (d * a_inc <= d_max)
                         {= d = d * a_inc =}
```

```
                    :: when (d * a_inc > d_max)
                          {= d = d_max =}
          :: when (pl < gamma_min)
               alt { :: when (d * 1/a_dec > d_min)
                          {= d = d * 1/a_dec =}
                     :: when (d * 1/a_dec <= d_min)
                          {= d = d_min =} }
          :: when ((pl >= gamma_min) && (pl <= gamma_max)) tau  // nop
          };
          x = 0;                   // reset timer
          when ( x >= d )
            i = 0;
            break                            // restart probing
       :: // timeout and no retransmissions further allowed
          when ( (x >= to) && (i == 4) )
            dev_abs {= i = 0, pc = 0 =};   // signal device absence
            break                            // restart probing
       }
    }
}
```

On each outermost iteration, a CP starts by sending an initial probe to the device. As the first waiting time until a reply equals TOF, the variable to is set to that value, and clock x is reset. In the innermost iteration, there are three possibilities. In case the timer expires, signaling that the reply did not come in time, and the number of probe-transmissions did not exceed the maximum, the probe is retransmitted. Note that in this case to is set to TOS. If the timer expires, and the probe has been sent a maximal number of times, the device is assumed to have left the network and the dissemination phase is started. This is modeled in an abstract way using action dev_abs, and an immediate restart of the probing. In case a reply is received in time, the probeload is determined, the time until the next probe is determined, and probing is restarted after this delay d.

The last component of the MODEST specification is the model of the network. As stated before, the network is modeled as a one-place buffer for simplicity. Its model is as follows:

```
process Network () {
  action get_msg, ...     // action declarations
  clock x;                // timer for message delay
  const int ploss = 1;    // message loss probability
  float del;              // random message delay

  do {
  :: when (m.lck != 0)
     get_msg {= m.lck = 0, x = 0, del = min + (max - min)*EXP(...) =};
     tau palt {
         :ploss: lose_msg
         :(10000 - ploss): alt {
                     :: when (x >= del) put_msg {= m.lck = 1 =}
```

```
                          :: when (m.lck != 0) lose_msg  // m overwritten
                          }
              }
       }
}
```

4.3   Analysis with MOTOR

To get insight into the behaviour of the probe protocol, in particular, into the self-adaptive mechanism to control the probe frequency of a device, the MoD-eST model has been analyzed by means of discrete-event simulation using the MOTOR-Möbius interface. The main aim of the analysis was to obtain indications for reasonable values of the parameters of the protocol, in particular of α_{inc}, α_{dec} and TOF and TOS. The original protocol description [7] indicates that $\alpha_{inc} = 2$ and $\alpha_{dec} = \frac{3}{2}$ are appropriate choices, but leaves the other parameters unspecified.

A simulation scenario. To enable a simulation, a description of the configuration of the network (i.e., the number of CPs and devices) and their join- and leave-behaviour need to be given. We consider a configuration consisting of a single device and eight CPs. As our aim is to study the self-adaptive mechanism to control the probe frequency of a device, the device is assumed to be present during the entire simulation whereas the CPs have a more dynamic nature. Two CPs are continuously present, and six CPs join in a bursty fashion, one shortly after the other, are present for a short while, and then four suddenly leave altogether. The four then repeatedly all join and leave, until at some point in time all six CPs leave.

Stochastic assumptions. Various stochastic phenomena of the ping protocol have been modeled such as the transit delay of a message through the network and the connection time of a CP. To give an impression of the assumptions that have been made, we consider a few examples. The device response time, i.e., the delay that is exhibited by a device between receiving a probe and sending its reply is determined by

$$t_{min} + (t_{max} - t_{min}) \cdot p$$

where t_{min} and t_{max} equal 0.06 and 20 msec, respectively, and p is governed by a negative exponential distribution (with rate $\lambda = 3$). The one-way message delay for a fixed network (i.e., Ethernet-like) is determined in a similar way using $t_{max} = 1$, $t_{min} = 0.25$ and $\lambda = 3$, whereas a constant loss probability of 10^{-5} is assumed[6]. The connection times of CPs is chosen to be deterministic, but different for the various CPs.

---

[6] These probability distributions are not intended to reflect the actual delays or loss probabilities, but are merely used as indications. More precise indications are manufacturer specific (and not publicly available).

Simulation parameters. The following parameters exemplify the kind of information that is obtained from a simulation of the MODEST model of the ping protocol:

- N_{msg}, the average number of probes and replies exchanged per second
- P_{false}, the probability that a present device is considered to be absent
- P_{late}, the probability that the time until the next probe is exceeding some predefined maximum (e.g., 0.7 seconds), and
- T_{abs}, the average time until a CP detects the absence of a device.

In order to obtain these measures, the MODEST specification may be equipped with additional variables with the sole purpose of information gathering. For instance, in order to estimate P_{false}, the CP-model is extended with a counter that is incremented when a device is considered to be absent, cf. action dev_abs in the earlier presented model. In a similar way, the model of the device is enriched with a clock that measures the amount of time a probe is arriving too late, i.e., after the deadline of 0.7 seconds.

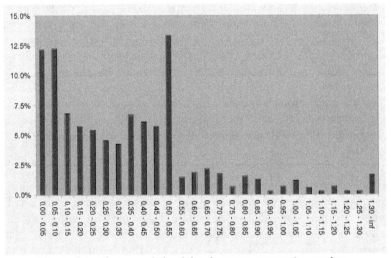

Fig. 4. Distribution of the delay between successive probes.

Some analysis results. To give an impression of the kind of results that can be obtained using the MOTOR tool we present three curves. The first plot (cf. Fig. 4) indicates the probability distribution of the probe delay as perceived at a device. P_{late} equals 0.048 and B equals 5.535 mps (messages per second); the average time-to-ping is about 0.32 seconds. The protocol was run using the values for α_{inc}, γ_{max}, TOF and so on, as indicated in [7] and as summarized in the first row of Table 1.

In our simulation study we concentrated on determining the effect of the values of α, γ and the timeout values TOF and TOS. Fig. 5, for instance, depicts the

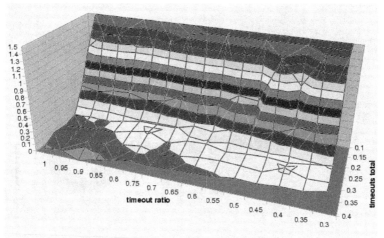

Fig. 5. N_{late} for various timeout values.

effect of the ratio TOS / TOF (x-axis) on the average number of times a present device is wrongly considered to be absent N_{false} (left y-axis) while keeping the sum TOF+TOS (right y-axis) constant. Note that the sum of the timeouts gives an indication about the time a CP needs to determine that a device is absent, as this equals TOF+3·TOS. From the plot we infer that for a fixed ratio of the timeout values, N_{false} rapidly grows when the sums of the timeouts exceeds 0.3 seconds. This effect is not surprising since on shorter timeout periods, a CP will sooner decide that a present device is absent. For a fixed sum of the timeouts, N_{false} slowly decreases on increasing the timeout ratio as the number of (short) timeout periods in which the absence can be wrongly concluded is decreasing. Fig. 6 indicates the bandwidth usage and shows that for a fixed ratio, B grows in this case up to a factor of about 25%. A similar effect can be observed for a fixed total timeout value when the ratio is increased: in case the first timeout period is much longer than the other ones (i.e., TOS/TOF is small), the probability to get a reply on the first probe is relatively large, and there is no need to carry out any retransmissions. If these periods get shorter, this probability is lower, leading to more probes. Using the simulations, the parameters that seem to be adequate for the ping protocol were determined as indicated in the second row of Table 1. Note that in particular, the factors α_{inc} and α_{dec} have changed substantially, as well as the length of the timeout periods. Furthers experiments indicate that with these new parameter values B is basically unchanged, whereas P_{late} is improved significantly, e.g., from 1.772% to 0.718% for the scenario described earlier. More analysis results can be found in [23].

Individual starvation of CPs. The self-adaptive mechanism to control the probe frequency of a device aims at speeding up CPs (i.e., increasing their probing frequency) when other CPs leave the network and at slowing them down when other CPs join. The implicit assumption of this mechanism to work is that all CPs

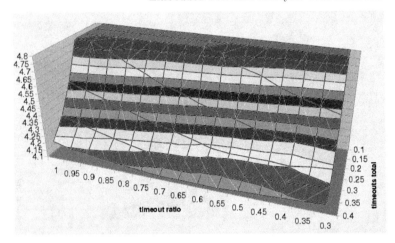

Fig. 6. B for various timeout values.

Table 1. Parameter values prior and after simulations.

	Δ	γ_{max}	γ_{min}	δ_{max}	δ_{min}	α_{inc}	α_{dec}	TOF	TOS
Prior to analyis	4	24	12	30	0.5	$\frac{2}{3}$	2	40	24
After analysis	4	22	14	30	0.5	$\frac{1}{3}$	$\frac{3}{2}$	96	68

are probing at a more or less equal frequency. To obtain an equal spreading of the probing frequency of a device among the probing CPs, slower CPs (that, e.g., just joined) should be able to speed up such that they can match the probing frequency of other CPs. The plot in Fig. 7 shows the spreading of the CPs' probing frequencies in terms of bandwidth usage for a scenario in which four CPs are continuously present, while the other four CPs join at intervals of 50 seconds and leave one by one. The protocol runs according to the parameter values determined in the previous experiment (see above). The individual bandwidth usage of each CP is indicated by a colored curves that are put on top of each other in order to avoid blurring the plots. The lower four curves indicate the bandwidth usage of the static CPs, whereas the upper four curves refer to the CPs that dynamically join and leave the system.

A few remarks are in order. The regular pattern of the CPs joining at regular intervals is clearly recognizable: at each 50 sec there is traffic peak. More importantly, though, is the discrepancy in probing frequencies among the four static CPs: from $t = 250$ on the frequencies of two of these CPs goes towards zero. The protocol mechanism to adapt the probing frequencies also seems not to be able to recover from this problem. The occurrence of the starvation phenomenon can be explained as follows. Suppose several CPs suddenly leave the network in the situation that a slow CP probes at a much lower frequency than another CP. The fast CP detects the absence of the CPs and increases its probing frequency. The slow CP detects this absence much later and the decrease in probeload it

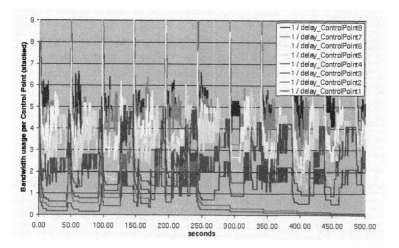

Fig. 7. Bandwidth usage of several CPs.

detects is insufficient to drastically increase its own probing frequency. In the meanwhile the fast CP has speeded up such that the probing frequency of the device is at an appropriate level, and the slow CP does not have any opportunity to increase. In fact, it slows down further. The main cause is that a CP cannot distinguish between the situation in which various other CPs probe a device at a relatively low frequency, and a few (e.g, one) CPs that probe the device at a high frequency.

The starvation problem that was discovered during our analysis was unknown to the designers of the ping protocol, and has caused a major re-design of the protocol. An extended and more detailed description of our experiences on the modeling and analysis of the ping protocol (and its improvements to circumvent the starvation problem) is currently under development [10].

5   Conclusion and Future Perspectives

In this paper, we surveyed the language MODEST that allows for the compositional modeling of complex systems and its accompanying tool-support MOTOR. Our framework is particularly suited for analyzing and describing real-time and probabilistic system aspects. This has been exemplified in this paper by modeling and analyzing the ping protocol, a protocol for checking the absence of nodes by various other nodes in a dynamic distributed system [7]. The key aspect of this protocol is an adaptive mechanism to control the probe load of a node. Our analysis has revealed an undesired side-effect of this adaptive mechanism and has provided useful indications on reasonable parameter values. On the basis of our analysis, a significant re-design of the protocol has been made that is described in a forthcoming paper [10].

Recently, some case studies of a rather different nature have been treated with MODEST and MOTOR. [12] studies the effect of resource failures in a hard real-time scheduling problem for lacquer production. It assesses the quality of schedules (that are synthesized using a real-time model checker) in terms of timeliness ("what is the probability that the hard deadline is missed?") and resource utilization and studies – as for the ping protocol – the sensitivity wrt. different reliability parameters. [29] presents the modeling and analysis of (part of) the recent European standard for train signaling systems ETCS that is based on mobile communication between the various components. Critical issues such as "what is the probability that a wireless connection can be established within 5 seconds?" are assessed with MOTOR.

Issues for future work are, among others, applying MODEST to more practical case studies and extending MOTOR with capabilities to analyze timed automata using the real-time model checker UPPAAL [2] and Markov chains using the probabilistic model checker ETMCC [25]. We are currently linking MOTOR to the in-house conformance test-tool ToRX [4] to enable the on-the-fly automated test generation for real-time (and untimed) systems, and have plans to apply this to the testing of wafer-stepper machines for chip production.

The MOTOR tool is publicly available from the web-site

```
fmt.cs.utwente.nl/tools/motor
```

Acknowledgments

The authors thank Jarno Guidi and Lex Heerink from Philips Research Laboratories for pointing out the ping protocol and discussing its details with us. We thank Pedro D'Argenio for his contributions to the MODEST semantics and Ed Brinksma for inspiring discussions concerning the language design. The model and results for the ping protocol in this paper are based on the work by Johan Gorter who modeled and analyzed the protocol as part of his master's thesis [23].

References

1. R. Alur and D.L. Dill. A theory of timed automata. *Th. Comp. Sc.*, **126**(2):183–235, 1994.
2. T. Amnell, G. Behrmann, J. Bengtsson, P.R. D'Argenio, A. David, A. Fehnker, T. Hune, B. Jeannet, K.G. Larsen, M.O. Möller, P. Pettersson, C. Weise, W. Yi. UPPAAL – Now, next, and future. In: *Modeling and Verification of Parallel Processes*, LNCS 2067:99-124, 2000.
3. C. Baier, F. Ciezinski and M. Groesser. PROBMELA: a modeling language for communicating probabilistic processes. In: *Int. Conf. on Formal Methods and Models for Codesign*, ACM Press, 2004.
4. A. Belinfante, J. Feenstra, R.G. de Vries, J. Tretmans, N. Goga, L. Feijs, S. Mauw and L. Heerink. Formal test automation: a simple experiment. In: *Int. Workshop on Testing of Communicating Systems XII*, pp. 179 - 196, Kluwer, 1999.
5. M. Ben-Ari. *Principles of Concurrent and Distributed Programming*. Prentice Hall, 1990.

6. G. Berry. Preemption and concurrency. In: R.K. Shyamasundar, ed, *Found. of Software Techn. and Th. Comp. Sc.*, LNCS 761: 72–93, 1993.

7. M. Bodlaender, J. Guidi and L. Heerink. Enhancing discovery with liveness. In: *IEEE Consumer Comm. and Networking Conf.*, IEEE CS Press, 2004.

8. H. Bohnenkamp, T. Courtney, D. Daly, S. Derisavi, H. Hermanns, J.-P. Katoen, V. Lam and W.H. Sanders. On integrating the Möbius and MoDeST modeling tools. *Dependable Systems and Networks*, pp. 671–672, 2003, IEEE CS Press.

9. H. Bohnenkamp, P.R. D'Argenio, H. Hermanns, J.-P. Katoen and J. Klaren. MODEST: A compositional modeling formalism for real-time and stochastic systems. 2004 (in preparation).

10. H. Bohnenkamp, J. Gorter, J. Guidi and J.-P. Katoen. A simple and fair protocol to detect node absence in dynamic distributed systems. 2004 (in preparation).

11. H. Bohnenkamp, H. Hermanns, J.-P. Katoen and J. Klaren. The MODEST modelling tool and its implementation. In: *Modelling Techniques and Tools for Comp. Perf. Ev.*, LNCS 2794, 2003.

12. H. Bohnenkamp, H. Hermanns, J. Klaren, A. Mader and Y.S. Usenko. Synthesis and stochastic assessment of schedules for lacquer production. In: *Quantitative Evaluation of Systems*, IEEE CS Press, 2004 (to appear).

13. S. Bornot and J. Sifakis. An algebraic framework for urgency. *Inf. and Comp.*, **163**:172–202, 2001.

14. Special issue on embedded systems. *IEEE Computer*, **33**(9), 2000.

15. M. Bravetti and Gorrieri. The theory of interactive generalized semi-Markov processes. *Th. Comp. Sc.*, **282**(1): 5–32, 2002.

16. P.R. D'Argenio, H. Hermanns, J.-P. Katoen and J. Klaren. MODEST: A modelling language for stochastic timed systems. In: *Proc. Alg. and Prob. Methods*, LNCS 2165: 87–104, 2001.

17. P.R. D'Argenio, J.-P. Katoen, T.C. Ruys and G. Tretmans. The bounded retransmission protocol must be on time! In *Tools and Algorithms for the Construction and Analysis of Systems*, LNCS 1217: 416–431, 1997.

18. D. Deavours, G. Clark, T. Courtney, D. Daly, S. Derasavi, J. Doyle, W.H. Sanders and P. Webster. The MÖBIUS framework and its implementation. *IEEE Tr. on Softw. Eng.*, **28**(10):956–970, 2002.

19. J.-C. Fernandez, H. Garavel, L. Mounier, A. Rasse, C. Rodriguez, and J. Sifakis. A tool box for the verification of LOTOS programs. In *14th IEEE Int. Conf. on Softw. Eng.*, 1992.

20. E. Gafni and M. Mitzenmacher. Analysis of timing-based mutual exclusion with random times. *SIAM J. Comput.*, **31**(3): 816–837, 2001.

21. H. Garavel and M. Sighireanu. On the introduction of exceptions in E-LOTOS. In: *Formal Description Techniques IX*, pp. 469–484. Kluwer, 1996.

22. P.W. Glynn. A GSMP formalism for discrete event systems. *Proc. of the IEEE*, **77**(1):14–23, 1989.

23. J. Gorter. Modeling and analysis of the liveness UPnP extension. Master's thesis, Univ. of Twente, 2004.

24. H. Hermanns. *Interactive Markov Chains – the Quest for Quantified Quality.* LNCS 2428, 2002.

25. H. Hermanns, J.-P. Katoen, J. Meyer-Kayser and M. Siegle. A tool for model checking Markov chains. *J. on Software Tools for Technology Transfer*, **4**(2):153–172, 2003.

26. J. Hillston. *A Compositional Approach to Performance Modelling.* Cambr. Univ. Press, 1996.

27. C. Hoare. *Communicating Sequential Processes.* Prentice-Hall, 1985.
28. G.J. Holzmann. *The* SPIN *Model Checker.* Addison-Wesley, 2002.
29. D.N. Jansen, H. Hermanns and Y.S. Usenko. From StoCharts to MODEST: a comparative reliability analysis of train radio communications. 2004 (submitted).
30. M. Jelasity, W. Kowalczyk and M. van Steen. Newscast computing. Tech. Rep. IR-CS-006, Vrije Univ. Amsterdam, 2003.
31. M. Kwiatkowska, G. Norman, R. Segala, and J. Sproston. Automatic verification of real-time systems with discrete probability distributions. *Th. Comp. Sc.*, **282**:101–150, 2002.
32. E.A. Lee. Embedded software. In: M. Zelkowitz, editor, *Advances in Computers*, vol. **56**, Academic Press, 2002.
33. J.F. Meyer, A. Movaghar and W.H. Sanders. Stochastic activity networks: structure, behavior and application. In: *Int. Workshop on Timed Petri Nets*, pp. 106–115, 1985.
34. G.D. Plotkin. A structural approach to operational semantics. DAIMI FN-19, Aarhus University, 1981.
35. M.L. Puterman. *Markov Decision Processes: Discrete Stochastic Dynamic Programming.* John Wiley & Sons, 1994.
36. M. Raynal and F. Tronel. Group membership failure detection: a simple protocol and its probabilistic analysis. *Distrib. Syst. Engng*, **6**: 95–102, 1999.
37. R. van Renesse, Y. Minsky and M. Hayden. A gossip-style failure detection service In: *IFIP Conf. on Distributed Systems, Platforms, and Open Distributed Processing*, pp. 55–70, 1998.
38. W.-P. de Roever, F.S. de Boer, U. Hannemann, J. Hooman, Y. Lakhnech, M. Poel, and J. Zwiers. *Concurrency Verification: Introduction to Compositional and Noncompositional Methods.* Cambridge Univ. Press, 2001.
39. W.H. Sanders and J.F. Meyer. Stochastic activity networks: formal definitions and concepts. In: *Formal Methods for Performance Evaluation*, LNCS 2090: 315–344, 2001.
40. F.B. Schneider, B. Bloom and K. Marzullo. Putting time into proof outlines. In: *REX Workshop on Real-Time:Theory in Practice*, LNCS 600: 618-639, 1991.
41. R. Segala and N.A. Lynch. Probabilistic simulations for probabilistic processes. *Nordic J. of Computing*, **2**(2): 250–273, 1995.

Author Index